VIOLENCE AND POLITICS

MORE NEW POLITICAL SCIENCE READERS

After The Fall
1989 and the Future of Freedom
Edited by George N. Katsiaficas

Explorations in African Political Philosophy
Identity, Community, Ethics
Edited by Teodros Kiros
With a Preface by K. Anthony Appiah

Latino Social Movements
Edited by Rodolfo D. Torres and George N. Katsiaficas

Liberation, Imagination, and the Black Panther Party
A New Look at the Panthers and Their Legacy
Edited by Kathleen Cleaver and George N. Katsiaficas

The Politics of Cyberspace
Edited by Chris Toulouse and Timothy W. Luke

The Promise of Multiculturalism
Education and Autonomy in the 21st Century
Edited by George N. Katsiaficas and Teodros Kiros

Violence and Politics

Globalization's Paradox

**Edited by
Kenton Worcester,
Sally Avery Bermanzohn,
and Mark Ungar**

A New Political Science Reader

ROUTLEDGE
NEW YORK AND LONDON

Published in 2002 by
Routledge
29 West 35th Street
New York, NY 10001

Published in Great Britain by
Routledge
11 New Fetter Lane
London EC4P 4EE

Routledge is an imprint of the Taylor & Francis Group.

10 9 8 7 6 5 4 3 2 1

Library of Congress Cataloging-in-Publication Data

Violence and politics : globalization's paradox / edited by Kenton Worcester, Sally Avery Bermanzohn, and Mark Ungar.
p. cm.
"A new political science reader."
Includes bibliographical references and index.
ISBN 0-415-93110-X — ISBN 0-415-93111-8 (pbk.)
1. Political violence. I. Worcester, Kenton. II. Bermanzohn, Sally Avery. III. Ungar, Mark.
JC328.6 .V55 2001
303.6'2—dc21   2001034791

Contents

INTRODUCTION

Violence and Politics

Mark Ungar, Sally Avery Bermanzohn, and Kenton Worcester

As the new century opens, violence has been growing within many countries around the world. In both developed and developing states, violence remains a manifestation of political and economic disputes, a persistent expression of differences in identity, and a tool of those opposing the rights of women and minorities. Fragile governments in Africa, Asia, and Europe are being weakened by civil wars, while stable governments everywhere ignore brutality against groups identified by race, religion, poverty, ethnicity, or sexuality. In every region, moreover, rapid economic change and reform has been associated with rising levels of violence.

The scope and complexity of internal violence is a paradox, because it is occurring in an era of unprecedented democratization and economic growth. Policy makers once anticipated that the growth of democratic regimes and economic prosperity would lead to civil peace. President Clinton predicted in 1994 that democratization will neutralize armed conflict and economic activity will foster stability.[1] But reality turned out to be more complex. In emphasizing a link between growing democratic demands and violence, Jack Snyder points out, in *From Voting to Violence*, that "as more people begin to play a larger role in politics, ethnic conflict within a country becomes more likely."[2] In an era of growing democracy, why do both states and societal groups turn to violence? In an era of growing economic activity, why does disparity of wealth grow and feed violence? Given the wide breadth and innumerable causes of violence, is there any way to understand its dynamics?

This book takes a step toward answering such questions by analyzing patterns of violence in a variety of social, cultural, and regional contexts. Brutality not only devastates those who are directly touched by it, but it also tears the social fabric, undermining the level of trust essential for societies to function. Some social scientists might object that violence is simply too unbounded a concept to be reliably subjected to scientific scrutiny. But the same can be said of such perennial graduate school colloquia themes as "political participation" and "power." Like violence, such issues do not lend themselves to any single, universal, all-purpose theory. Instead, this book asserts that understanding violence requires marshaling and connecting existing intellectual resources in order to extend and deepen our analyses of particular cases and issues. In order to build stronger democratic societies, we need to grapple with the implications of civil war, civil strife, genocide, terrorism, hate crime, and human rights abuse.

Political science has only intermittently taken up issues of political violence *within* countries. Analysis of war *between* countries, which this book does not address, has long been the major focus of study. In *Reflections on Violence*, the political philosopher John Keane criticizes the "paucity of reflection" on "the causes, effects and ethico-political implications of violence."[3] The work of Hannah Arendt, of course, stands out as the major exception. Distinguishing between power and violence in *On Violence*, she defines power as the ability of a population to act on behalf of its beliefs, and violence as the physical instruments of force used to destroy power. "Power and violence are opposites: where the one rules absolutely, the other is absent," she wrote.[4] Violence can subvert power, such as through co-optation and propaganda, and ultimately defeat it, as in Stalin's Russia, unless the instruments of violence are held in check, as in Gandhi's India. We argue, however, that the relationship between violence and power must be reevaluated in a postindustrial, "postideological," and highly integrated world. As both violence and power change and grow more complex, so does the relationship between them. The advent of formal democracy around the world, the changing nature of economic production, and evolving forms of social mobilization all require a new understanding of the link between power, politics, and violence.

Together, the chapters of this volume develop a broad framework to analyze internal violence in the contemporary world. Specifically, six themes run through the book:

1. The key to the politics of violence in specific countries is the exercise of state power and governmental policy to handle violence within society and by the state;
2. Political regime change, including recent transitions to democracy, commonly inflames violence among groups;
3. Persistent patterns of violence, along with state rights abuses, exist in advanced and stable democracies, particularly the United States;
4. In many countries, large-scale economic changes, including programs for economic reform, are associated with rising levels of violence, particularly among distinct groups and classes;
5. Violent scapegoating of racial, religious, ethnic, and sexual minorities persists in many countries, from neighborhood vigilantism to ethnic cleansing; and
6. Violence remains a component of many groups' responses to the state, from spontaneous protests to armed rebellions.

The first theme, the exercise of state power, runs throughout the book. The modern state, as Max Weber asserted, has an exclusive claim to the legitimate use of force. But this commitment is compromised in innumerable ways, such as when state institutions do not protect certain social groups, where patterns of abuse of power by individual state actors go unpunished, or when criminal justice systems fail to punish individuals or groups that perpetrate violent activities. Contemporary states are frequently overwhelmed with the new sets of policy choices constantly confronting them, including the authority of internal security forces, the strength of oversight by independent bodies, and the formation of criminal policy to combat unprecedented levels of violent crime. States may lose control over the institutions created to carry out policy. They may also implement policies that foster violence, such as incarceration of high percentages of the population, the suppression of claims by the poor and powerless groups that are the primary victims of violence, or the manipulation of laws to encourage violence that boosts state agencies' institutional norms. The organization of state authority illustrates the impact of state power. In highly centralized Chile, for example, the central government has the power to determine levels of police violence, while in decentralized Argentina and Brazil the power of the provinces has led to extreme variations in police violence within the country. Under the United States' federalist system, the division of power between state and national levels allowed local officials to deny blacks constitutionally guaranteed civil rights for a century following the Civil War. In assessing the politics of violence, we must consider not only those formal rules that regulate state behavior, but the actual practices and powers of state officials and institutions. The chapters by Bermanzohn, Sharlach, and Ungar underscore this point.

The second theme focuses on violence in the context of regime transition, in which a country's regime has collapsed but a new one has not yet consolidated. In the many countries currently undergoing a transition of regimes, violence is part of that process. Over the past twenty years, every world region has been reshaped by democratization. Latin America, long dominated by military regimes, is now almost entirely comprised of formally democratic ones. In Asia and the former Soviet bloc, rapid economic and political changes have brought democracy to an unprecedented number of countries. Even in Africa and the Middle East, one-party regimes remain the norm but the momentum has shifted toward freer multiparty elections, wider citizen participation, and greater accountability. But while countries have clearly moved toward democratic regimes, they are far from consolidating them. Even with constitutions, competitive elections, and the other hallmarks of formal democracy, most countries are threatened by corruption, political pacts, economic strains, the continuing power of the armed forces, and a range of other weaknesses. Many scholars, in fact, have come to recognize that most current regimes are stuck between a transition from authoritarianism and an actual consolidation of democracy.

Violence is one of the major obstacles to consolidation of democracy. While armed revolutions and ideological divisions have decreased, violence between groups has increased. But while scholars and officials include violence in general as one of the obstacles to consolidation, they have yet to fully explore it as a separate theoretical and empirical concern. They have placed violence within the problematic of democratization, but have not fully grasped that the uses and severity of violence may divert a transition away from democracy toward a new form of authoritarianism. Violence endangers democratic regimes around the world, in every stage of regime transition. And it does so in many different ways, including violence between ethnic groups, violent protest against government policies, violence by police forces, and organized criminal violence. Along with these different causes and forms of violence, the unpredictable processes of democratization constantly alter and confuse states' response to the problem. Studies of violence, this volume demonstrates, should thus be linked to changes in the rules and patterns of state-society relations that comprise a regime. The chapters by Ghadbian and MacGinty examine how changes in political order raise undercurrents of ethnic antagonism to the surface, for example, while Mason looks at how greater organizing and recognition of women's rights spur a backlash against them.

The third theme of this volume is that violence persists also in countries with advanced economies and consolidated democratic regimes. Such violence highlights general trends of internal violence as well as particular national histories. Virulent racism and excessive gun violence in the United States, for example, demonstrate how a strong state and economy do not automatically translate into civic peace. We are skeptical of the distinction drawn by Max Singer and Aaron Wildavsky between a "zone of turmoil" that envelops the developing world and a "zone of peace" that neatly enfolds the postindustrial West.[5] As John Keane has observed, "the world is not so neatly subdivided into peaceful and violent zones."[6] There are many developing countries, such as Costa Rica and Botswana, that have low levels of internal violence. And the converse is true as well. The United States has one of the highest incarceration rates in the world, with a long and continuing record of rights abuses against minorities, immigrants, and other groups. Amnesty International, an organization that investigates violations of international human rights standards, concluded in a 1998 report that there "is a persistent and widespread pattern of human rights violations in the U.S.A. Across the country thousands of people are subjected to sustained and deliberate brutality at the hands of police officers. Cruel, degrading and sometimes life-threatening methods of restraint continue to be a feature of the U.S. criminal justice system."[7] The chapters by Mason and Bermanzohn, by analyzing the use of violence by groups in the United States who oppose abortion rights and civil rights, underscore the persistence and depth of violent acts.

The fourth theme is the relationship between economics and violence. In an era of massive restructuring and global interdependence, economics is intrinsically connected with violence. Just as the transition from feudalism to industrialization entailed widespread violence, so too do current changes to a highly interdependent, postindustrial world economy. Violence has become embedded in the class and market relations among social groups and in the societal effects on global economic trends.

When accompanied by political transformation, economic change can expose long-simmering tensions within a society among groups divided by race, ethnicity, religion, or other kinds of identity. Unequal access to services, favoritism in spending, controls over key assets, and policies creating dependency of one group on another long have aggravated tensions among different groups. When disturbed by political change, such tensions often deteriorate into forms of violence that cannot be easily negotiated away. Such economic relations help fuel civil wars, as in Northern Ireland and the former Yugoslavia, violent rebel movements, as in Peru and Burma, or violent street protests, as in Guyana and Fiji.

In many countries, economic policies also trigger violence among classes. Privatization, cuts in state services, and austerity measures may be necessary to reform inefficient national economies, but they invariably generate violent protest by large sectors of society. Spontaneous urban riots in Egypt, Jordan, South Korea, Peru, and Venezuela against price raises and labor legislation are only a few of many examples of this reaction. Such violence generally subsides if the benefits of economic reform are felt in society. In the majority of cases where new policies do not work or where their benefits are not shared, however, short-term protest evolves into more protracted and uncontrollable forms of violence. As inequalities within countries widen, as middle classes shrink, as cities become sites of extreme wealth and poverty, as the rich increasingly turn to private security forces, as citizens gain wider exposure to images of material goods without the means to acquire them, these forms of violence are inevitable. The chapter by López Maya, Lander, and Ungar helps explain why.

Violence between state and society in general, as well as among groups and classes in particular, is further aggravated by global economic trends. The rapid spread of capital and the standardization of international financial regulations clashes with continuing disparities in labor rights and standards, for one, causing violence against governments and corporations by groups or regions not receiving the benefits or the promise of foreign investment. Increasing environmental and population pressures, meanwhile, will continue to set off scrambles for dwindling resources. When acquiring high prices on the international market, such resources fuel particularly intransigent forms of violence. Despite international attention and peacekeeping efforts, such trends persist in Angola, Sierra Leone, and Congo and threaten violence in areas such as Central Asia, Indonesia, and Brazil.

The book's fifth theme deals with the role of society and societal groups in fomenting violence. On the one hand, violence has become an intrinsic characteristic of intrasocietal relations. Such violence may be caused by state power and policy, or as a reaction to it, but often takes on its own momentum. The civil wars in Algeria disintegrated into a bloodletting that had little to do with the disputed elections that first triggered it, while the civil war in Colombia appears immune to both societal and state efforts to stem it. In many areas of the world, uncontrollable levels of violent crime have generated new forms of vigilante violence. While such violence results in part from societal distrust of state law enforcement agencies, it has often grown beyond any kind of legal reforms or policing efforts. The chapters by Murer and Shannon explore the causes and conceptions behind these developments.

The final theme looks at how social groups use violence in their interactions with the state. Citizens agitating for change inevitably confront state institutions in one form or another. This confrontation may be in the form of spontaneous street protests against policies or long-term armed revolutionary movements against the state itself. Theories of violence, therefore, hold important implications for contemporary democratic politics. The issue is not only whether demands can be met within existing institutional frameworks or whether these demands require comprehensive change. It is also one of efficacy: to determine the best strategy for advancing and realizing broader democratic ambitions. For this reason, we question the saliency of two contending perspectives on violence and politics. On the one hand is a romantic conception that sees violence as a central means by which oppressed peoples liberate themselves from tyranny, and on the other, a pacifism that rejects violence in all forms and contexts. Rather than viewing violence as something to be encouraged or abolished, the most appropriate stance may be one that seeks to limit violence while recognizing that not all forms of violence are equivalent, and that under certain conditions (e.g., self-defense and some revolutionary situations) violence may be justified and even appropriate. What is required is an analysis of the relationship of politics and violence that can inform strategies for building equitable, pacific, and participatory democracies.

The contributions to this volume span a range of topics—from pro-life violence to strategies of militant nonviolence, from hate crimes to state repression, from political Islam to private armies, from fear to economics. This diversity underscores the near-universality of questions of violence. They also call attention to the diverse ways in which violence can reach the political stage—as a statement about the legitimacy of the liberal capitalist state, as an expression of official hostility toward disadvantaged social groups, as potential strategy for social movements, as a tool of physical conflict and male domination, as a legal matter for court adjudication, and as a means by which social forces acquire control over political resources. As the contributions attest, the insertion of violence in political life does not necessarily assume a predictable or stable form, nor are the political implications of violence always clear.

The book opens with Charles Tilly's discussion of the typologies of public violence, ranging from spontaneous street fighting to the conscious mobilization of large-scale force. Drawing on the empirical findings of Ted Gurr and others, Tilly approaches collective violence in a way that places "specific struggles in comparative perspective in hopes of noticing similar causes, effects, and possible interventions."

Ulric Shannon's chapter looks at an increasingly significant phenomenon: the growing threat posed by private armies to public order and state legitimacy in different areas of the world. Drawing on the cases of Sierra Leone and Colombia, Shannon shows how civil war and weak state integration may promote the use of private armies, and how once sturdy distinctions between civilian, soldier, and state may be breaking down with potentially disastrous consequences for human security.

Mark Ungar addresses repression of sexual minorities in Latin America, sub-Saharan Africa, and other parts of the globe. He emphasizes the discrepancy between the recent turn toward democratic rule and the persistence of violence against gays, lesbians, bisexuals, and transgender people. With or without antihomosexual laws, state institutions often carry out antigay policies in such areas as employment and health, while extrajudicial attacks against gays in society are also common. Such violence highlights the need for, and the problems faced by, the lgbt movement.

Bridget Welsh examines the prevalence of violence in East Asia as the product of changes in state power. Her chapter highlights three particular cases: vigilantism in Indonesia, the death penalty in China, and ethnic conflict in the southern Philippines. "Each of these cases," she argues, "decisively shows that 'weak states' contribute to violence and that globalization has played a prominent role in increasing violence in these countries."

Najib Ghadbian analyzes the role of political Islam in the various violent conflicts taking place in the Middle East today. He argues that political, social, and economic conditions—not simply religion—are determining factors. Those who use violence as well as those who reject it can find support for their arguments in Islamic texts. Ghadbian highlights the repression of Muslim populations in countries that do not allow Islamists to contest for power via traditional, nonviolent means.

Lisa Sharlach uses case studies of rape under wartime conditions in Pakistan, Rwanda, and the former Yugoslavia to examine the use of rape as an instrument of war, internal conflict, and ethnic fighting. Sharlach argues that rape is a form of genocide, and that crimes against humanity based on gender should be added to the canons of international law by way of the Geneva Convention on Genocide.

Carol Mason investigates the ongoing transformation of political ideology and strategy within the pro-life movement. Although pro-life bombers, snipers, and assassins are usually described in psychological terms with their deeds portrayed as acts of passion, compulsion, or lunacy, pro-life violence, argues Mason, validates and advances a broader legal and political strategy, one that relies not on isolated actions but on a larger mobilization of terror.

Sally Avery Bermanzohn explores the development of competing political strategies in the U.S. Civil Rights movement and considers the success of Martin Luther King Jr.'s strategy of nonviolence in relation to the turbulent context of the times. King developed a strategy of militant nonviolent resistance at a time when many blacks in the rural South secured weapons to defend themselves against supremacist violence. While many activists contested the strategy of nonviolence, King won the debate in part because his strategy proved effective for mass protest movements operating in the Cold War era and in the new media context of television.

Roger MacGinty interrogates the concept of "hate crime"—violence motivated by prejudice and committed by individuals—in the context of ethno-national conflict and democratization. Drawing on the examples of deeply divided societies, including Northern Ireland and South Africa among others, he explores a twofold paradox. Structural factors, including residential segregation and the existence of armed militia groups, seem to have restrained hate crimes during periods of intense ethno-national conflicts in those countries. On the other hand, transitions toward democracy may bring increases in hate crime against both traditional targets and new ones.

Turning to the economic dimension of internal violence, Margarita López Maya, Luis E. Lander, and Mark Ungar address the link between internal violence and economic policy. Neoliberal measures being adopted by most countries undermine the already precarious existence of the majority of their citizens who live on or below the poverty line. Opposition to such policies, deepened by government corruption and waste, usually explodes into protests that often outlive individual governments and policies. Focusing on Venezuela, whose national riots in 1989 were among the most violent of such protests, the authors address a dimension of violence and politics destined to become increasingly common in an increasingly unequal world.

In a theoretical examination of violence and identity, Jeffrey Murer explains how the formation of identity can stimulate violence. Rejecting the argument that modern violence stems from ancient hatreds, he argues that it comes from the efforts of groups to define themselves in times of uncertainty by casting other groups as enemies. In order to cope when threatening events challenge their collective identity, he argues, groups reshape and stabilize their identity by contrasting themselves against others. A group creates boundaries and rejects undesirable traits by creating an opposition to them, which is likely to generate violence in the process.

In the concluding chapter, John Keane observes that the topic of fear (which is closely bound up with questions of violence and personal security) has been largely neglected by political philosophers and social scientists. Contemporary democracies often boast that they have marginalized (or, as Keane suggests, "privatized") fear, to the point where fear "becomes at most a personal matter to be handled by individuals in their daily lives." Yet Keane maintains that this claim "only hints at the dynamic processes through which actually existing democracies do indeed tend—but not altogether successfully—to reduce the role played by fear in the overall structures of power." His subtle argument points the way forward to an understanding of politics and violence that acknowledges the power of subjective emotional states to frame social and political relations in an unfamiliar light.

NOTES

1. 1994 State of the Union address ("Transcript of Clinton's Address," *New York Times*, January 26, 1994).
2. Jack Snyder, *From Voting to Violence: Democratization and Nationalist Conflict* (New York: Norton, 2000), p. 27.
3. John Keane, *Reflections on Violence* (New York: Verso, 1996), p. 6.
4. Hannah Arendt, *On Violence* (New York: Harcourt Brace, 1970), p. 56.
5. Max Singer and Aaron Wildavsky, *The Real World Order: Zones of Peace/Zones of Turmoil* (New York: Chatham House, 1996).
6. Keane, *Reflections on Violence*, p. 4.
7. *USA: Rights for All* (New York: Amnesty International, 1998), p. 149.

PART ONE

States,
Social Groups,
and Contentious Politics

CHAPTER ONE

Violent and Nonviolent Trajectories in Contentious Politics

Charles Tilly

Perhaps prehistoric people were actually as violent as cartoons of club-wielding cave dwellers suggest. Perhaps not. Over the entire period since the written record of human brutality toward other humans begins around five thousand years ago, the twentieth century certainly sets the world record for sheer numbers of visibly violent deaths from political conflict. Despite the abandon with which Chinese and Mesopotamian kings of 3000 B.C.E. slaughtered their enemies (and sometimes their hapless followers), twentieth-century political violence probably tops those early historical eras in per capita terms as well.

During the first half of the twentieth century, massive interstate wars produced most of the world's political deaths, although deliberate efforts of state authorities to eliminate, displace, or control subordinate populations also accounted for significant numbers of fatalities.[1] During the century's second half, civil war, guerrilla, separatist struggles, domestic political repression, and conflicts between ethnically or religiously divided populations increasingly dominated the landscape of bloodletting.[2] As the century waned, however, some mixed signs of leveling off in the scale of human-to-human political violence appeared. As inhabitants of the twenty-first century, we face the challenge of reversing the long trend—not of eliminating conflict, but of substituting nonlethal for lethal ways of pursuing politics. Russians and Americans simply face different versions of the same fundamental challenge, with a wider range of violent ethnic conflict in and around today's Russia, but acute manifestations of small-scale violence in today's United States.

Ted Robert Gurr's catalogs of violence involving ethnically defined minorities between 1945 and 1999 provide a baseline for thinking about the twenty-first century.[3] Gurr's earlier study followed 233 "nonstate communal groups that were politically salient" from 1945 to 1989. His second study expanded the range to 275 such groups for the period 1986–1998. The list included Turks in Germany, Afro-Brazilians, Chinese in Malaysia, Kurds in Iran, Iraq, Syria, and Turkey, Egyptian

Copts, indigenous Bolivians and Ecuadorians, Hutu and Tutsi in Burundi and Rwanda, Tibetans under Chinese hegemony, and India's Muslims. It also featured self-identified Russians in Ukraine and Estonia, the Gagauz of Moldova, Roma in East Central Europe, Kazakhs in China, Germans in Kazakhstan, Chechens in Russia, and many other majority-minority combinations in the zones dominated by state socialism before 1989.

Gurr's method mixes violence inflicted by governmental agents and allies with that delivered by dissident groups. In fact, state-backed armies, police forces, militias, vigilantes, and other specialists in coercion inflicted a substantial but unknown share of all the damage summed up in Gurr's scores for violent protest and open rebellion.[4] Over the entire set, Gurr's catalogs show substantial increases in nonviolent protest, violent protest, and open rebellion as well for almost every five-year period from 1945 through 1989; by Gurr's rough measures, the frequency of violent conflicts tripled from start to finish. After 1989, the increase from 233 to 275 groups occurred mainly because of rising ethnopolitical conflict in Eastern Europe and the former Soviet Union. Over the world as a whole, according to Gurr's measures, the frequency of open rebellion declined from the mid-1980s, while protest activities up to the level of strikes and riots reached their world peak during the early 1990s, but declined slightly after then.

The Central Intelligence Agency's count of international terrorist incidents from 1968 through 1998 bears a broad resemblance to Gurr's catalog. The *international* terrorist incidents in the count include only those in which a group based outside a given country attacked targets within that country. They therefore exclude relatively contained civil wars such as that of Sri Lanka, but emphatically include Arab and Israeli attacks on each other as well as the work of such groups as the Red Army Faction, the Red Brigade, and the Japanese Red Army. Year to year variation in the frequency of such events depended especially on fluctuations in bombing. Minor spurts occurred during the 1970s, which included the Munich Olympic Village attack of 1972. But the high point came in the five years from 1984 through 1988. After then, terrorist attacks fell off irregularly but substantially. Bombing, armed attacks, and hostage taking all became more common during the peak years. Then all, especially bombing, declined. National liberation movements played an increasingly prominent part in terrorism as the overall frequency of incidents decreased.

For the period of their overlap, Gurr's worldwide catalogs correspond well with Mark Beissinger's counts of "protest events" in the Soviet Union and its successor states from 1987 to 1992.[5] Taking sheer number of events rather than number of participants, Beissinger's evidence shows a dramatic increase in nonviolent protest demonstrations from 1987 through 1990, leveling off in 1991, and decline in 1992. Mass violent events, in contrast, generally remained infrequent from 1987 through 1990 except for a minor peak in mid-1989, but then rose dramatically through 1991 and 1992. Nonviolent demonstrations emphasized nationalist and ethnic issues—generally demands for rights based on nationality or ethnicity. Violent events, however, centered on claims concerning the borders of republics.

During the six-year period, then, a broad shift occurred from peaceful demands for recognition to violent struggles over the fruits of recognition, the territories to be dominated by one titular nationality or another. Extended past 1992, Beissinger's series would most likely show a decline in the sheer number of nationalist and ethnic claims as republics both inside and outside the Russian federation worked out settlements with each other. In such regions as Georgia, Tajikistan, Chechnya, and Northern Ossetia, however, we would witness an intensification of the remaining conflicts. Broadly speaking, the experience of the former Soviet Union matches that of Ted Gurr's international array.

Looking at recent worldwide trends, Gurr draws these judicious conclusions about prospects for attenuation of ethnopolitical conflicts:

- The political assertion of ethnic and other communal identities that spawned new episodes of ethnic warfare during the 1980s and early 1990s will continue, for two reasons. The politics of identity are based most fundamentally on persistent grievances about inequalities and past wrongs, conditions that are part of the heritage of most minorities in most countries. Moreover, movements based on identity have succeeded often enough in recent years to justify emulation and repetition.
- The ethnic conflict management strategies favored by Western states and international organizations are not uniformly effective. Democratic institutions and elections in weak, heterogeneous states often provide incentives and opportunities that increase the chances of ethnopolitical conflict rather than channeling it into conventional politics. Internationally brokered settlements and the atmospherics of cease-fires, amnesties, and signing ceremonies are sometimes a facade behind which protagonists jockey for political advantage and resources that fuel the next round of fighting.
- The states and international and regional organizations that promote democratic and negotiated management of ethnic tensions often walk away after multiparty elections and settlements. Failure of outside parties to provide sustained political and material resources in postconflict situations all but guarantees the eventual renewal of conflict.[6]

We cannot move easily from Gurr's general descriptions or analyses to explanations of particular struggles, much less to detailed scripts for the nonviolent resolution of particular violent conflicts. Yet Gurr's findings set a series of challenges for anyone who wants to improve available descriptions, explanations, and prescriptions: to place specific struggles in comparative perspective in hopes of noticing similar causes, effects, and possible interventions; to sort out prevailing explanations of violent conflicts into more and less plausible; to consider the implications of the more plausible explanations for nonviolent resolution of serious conflicts; to identify processes that reduce the level of violence in political struggle; to specify more precisely how and why certain conflicts shift from violent to nonviolent means. My contribution to our discussion does not meet these deep challenges. It merely sketches a way of thinking about collective violence that clarifies the issues, then spells out implications for more or less violent trajectories of political conflict.

Visibly violent social processes simultaneously attract and repel analysts of human behavior. War, rape, genocide, assassination, assault, football, looting, official execution, collective suicide, mutual flagellation, automobile collisions, airline crashes, gang fights, and struggles pitting police against demonstrators all qualify by some definitions as public violence. Most of them regularly attract headlines when they occur—the more extensive, public, and grisly their consequences the bigger the headlines. Violence makes the news.

In these circumstances, reporters and readers commonly turn to very simple explanations: some humans are violent in nature, others peaceable, so violent events occur when violent people congregate and enjoy free rein. Unfortunately for that sort of explanation, the boundary between violent and peaceable people actually blurs badly. Even individuals who participate energetically in violent events generally spend most of their time and energy on nonviolent activities. Meanwhile persons who live mostly peaceful lives occasionally get involved in organizing or perpetrating violent activities, for example by doing military service, serving on juries, or engaging in contact sports. Other people who flee violent interactions in their daily routines nevertheless support one variety of public violence or another in the proper circumstances, for example by voting for candidates who favor the death penalty, by cheering one group of nationalists in their competition with rivals, or by cooperating in what they call a just war. Indeed, most citizens of most states distinguish sharply between coercive acts committed lawfully by duly constituted agents of their own states (legitimate force) and similar acts committed by other people (illegitimate violence). Nonviolence is a beguiling principle, but one honored more in the breach than in the observance.

In general discussions of the subject, three competing views of violence prevail: as propensity-driven behavior, as instrumental interaction, and as cultural form. Treatments of violence as propensity-driven behavior locate its causes within the actor, calling attention to genetic, emotional, or cognitive peculiarities that incline a given individual, group, or category of persons to damaging behavior more than others. Portrayals of violence as instrumental interaction characterize everything from petty assaults to all-out warfare as means (however inefficient and self-defeating) to power, wealth, prestige, or other ends. To call violence a cultural form—as in the claim that because of the frontier, slavery, or capitalist competition the United States has an exceptionally violent culture—argues that the ready availability of certain ideas, practices, models, and beliefs itself promotes violent action.

The three views suggest very different approaches to inhibiting or promoting violence. Propensity-driven violence calls for the alteration or inhibition of motives, instrumental violence for shifts of incentives and outcomes, cultural violence for teaching new ideas, practices, models, and beliefs. Alas, none of these three broad approaches to violence has yet yielded systematic explanations of the genesis, trajectory, outcome, or sheer variety of public violence as a whole. Perhaps we await the social scientific Newton who will detect underlying regularities in all the diverse phenomena people call violent. More likely, the notion of violence resembles such other widespread but diffuse terms as disorder and goodness: morally powerful categories that do not refer to any causally coherent domain.

In any case, the word "violence" almost always arrives with baggage of disapproval. The distinction of violent from nonviolent social interactions usually depends on a moral boundary, or at least activates one. Precisely because of that moral charge, advocates of one cause or another frequently extend the term "violence" to varieties of harm far outside the range of direct, short-term infliction of physical damage on one person by another. They label hate speech, pornography, poverty, unemployment, malnutrition, and other ills as forms of violence. To call a phenomenon virtual violence is to condemn it, to claim that it damages something valuable even if it produces no physical destruction in the short run. As a consequence, every social scientific attempt to delimit, describe, classify, and explain public violence generates controversy.

We can nevertheless discipline the inquiry by adopting a restrictive definition of the phenomenon under analysis. Collective violence, for present purposes, refers to episodic social interaction that a) immediately inflicts physical damage on persons and/or objects ("damage" includes forcible seizure over restraint or resistance) and b) results at least in part from coordination among persons who perform the damaging acts. At one edge, such a definition excludes strictly individual, private, impulsive, and/or accidental damage to persons or objects. At the other, it excludes long-term, incremental damage such as communication of infectious disease, cumulative wear and tear, exposure to toxic substances, and death hastened by neglect or social pressure. Nevertheless, it includes an immense range of social interactions, from minor scuffles among rival groups of voters to wholesale civil war. Despite a century or more of effort, social scientists have not so far assembled any reliable, important, and systematic body of knowledge that applies to the whole range thus defined.

We therefore have no choice but to differentiate, reviewing analyses of narrower phenomena that bear some family resemblance to each other, probably share some causal processes, and have attracted sustained scholarly attention. Assuming episodic interaction, at least a little communication among actors, and some minimum of damage to persons or objects, let us conjure up a two-dimensional space combining the extent of coordination among damage-doers and the salience of damage in the overall pattern of interaction to produce a crude typology of public violence. In figure 1, "low" coordination means individualized action with little collective planning and signaling, while "high" coordination means activation of differentiated and bounded organizational structure with extensive planning and signaling. "Low" salience of violence means that most of the social interaction involved produces no short-term physical damage, while "high" salience means interaction strongly concentrated on damage.

Other distinctions come immediately to mind. Separation of symmetrical from asymmetrical interaction, for example, usefully distinguishes relatively even contests from situations in which a gang or an oppressor visits violence on a victim having no means of retaliation. Whether agents of a constituted government participate in public violence, as we shall see, significantly affects its character; thus we might also classify public violence by the presence or absence of governmental agents. Again, public violence probably incorporates scale effects, so that damaging interaction involving just two or three people differs qualitatively from otherwise similar interaction involving thousands of people at a time. The present classification gives priority to coordination and salience on the hunch that those two dimensions capture a significant part of the systematic variation about which social scientists have produced useful ideas and findings.

Within the coordination-salience space we can conveniently distinguish seven locations:

- *organizational outcomes*: various forms of collective action generate resistance or rivalry to which one or more parties respond by actions that damage persons and/or objects; examples include demonstrations, protection rackets, gov-

FIGURE 1. A TYPOLOGY OF INTERPERSONAL VIOLENCE

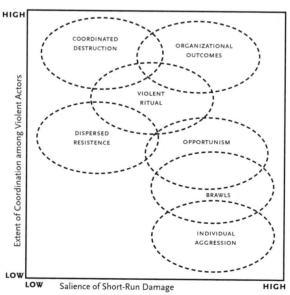

ernmental repression, and military coups, all of which frequently occur with no more than threats of violence, but sometimes produce physical damage

- *coordinated destruction*: persons or organizations specialized in the deployment of coercive means undertake a program of damage to persons and/or objects; examples include war, genocide, collective self-immolation, and some kinds of terrorism
- *opportunism*: as a consequence of shielding from routine surveillance and repression, individuals or clusters of individuals use immediately damaging means to pursue generally forbidden ends; examples include looting, gang rape, revenge killing, and some sorts of military pillage
- *dispersed resistance*: in the course of widespread small-scale and generally non-violent interaction, a number of participants respond to obstacles, challenges, or restraints by means of damaging acts; examples include sabotage, clandestine attacks on symbolic objects or places, assaults of governmental agents, and the more immediately damaging forms of what James Scott has called "weapons of the weak"
- *violent ritual*: two or more relatively well defined and coordinated groups follow a known interaction script entailing the infliction of damage on others as they compete for priority within a recognized arena; examples include gang rivalries, contact sports, some election battles, and some struggles among supporters of teams or stars
- *brawls:* within a previously nonviolent gathering, two or more persons begin attacking each other or each other's property; examples include barroom free-for-alls, small-scale battles at sporting events, and many street fights
- *individual aggression:* a single actor (or several unconnected actors) engage(s) in immediately and predominantly destructive interaction with another actor; examples include single-author rapes, assaults, robberies, and vandalism

Of course these crude types overlap, for example in the activities of the South Asian thugs who sometimes act as enforcers for landlords in disputes with squatters (organizational outcomes) but at other times follow their patrons in large-scale raids on their caste, religious, or political enemies (coordinated destruction). Similarly, the various actions known as terrorism show up in all four corners of the diagram—as clandestine resistance, as a by-product of peaceful claim-making in highly repressive regimes, as part of genocide, and as opportunistic elimination of old enemies. It is nevertheless useful to retain the seven-part division, because within each area thus delineated social scientists have accumulated at least a modicum of systematic knowledge. Let us therefore review them one by one. The following discussion gives extensive attention to organizational outcomes and coordinated destruction, then uses analogies and comparisons with the first two as it treats opportunism, dispersed resistance, violent ritual, brawls, and individual aggression much more summarily.

Organizational Outcomes

A significant share of public violence occurs in the course of organized social processes that are not in themselves intrinsically violent. That is notably the case in collective political struggle. Political regimes differ dramatically in the scope they allow for nonviolent collective making of claims, for example by petitioning, shaming, marching, voting, boycotting, striking, forming special-interest associations, and issuing public messages. On the whole, democratic regimes tolerate such claim making more readily than do their undemocratic neighbors; that is one way we recognize a regime as democratic. Even in democratic regimes, nevertheless, such forms of collective claim making occasionally generate open violence. That occurs for three main reasons.

First, every regime empowers agents—police, troops, headmen, posses, sheriffs, and others—to monitor, contain, and on occasion repress collective claim making. Those agents always have some means of collective coercion at their disposal, and always enjoy some discretion in the use of those means. In one common sequence, claimants challenge repressive agents, occupy forbidden premises, attack symbolically significant objects, or seize property, then agents reply with force. Because variants on that sequence frequently occur, when repressive agents are at hand they actually perform the great bulk of the killing and wounding that occurs in public violence.

Second, collective claim making often concerns issues that sharply divide claimants from regimes, from powerful groups allied with regimes, or from rival groups; examples are campaigns to stop current wars, outlaw abortion, or expel immigrants. In these circumstances, offended parties often respond with counterclaims backed by force, whether governmental or nongovernmental.

Third, in relatively democratic regimes an important share of collective action centers not on specific programs but on identity claims: the public assertion that a group or a constituency it represents is worthy, united, numerous, and committed (WUNC). Assertions of WUNC include marches, demonstrations, mass meetings, occupations of plants or public buildings, vigils, and hunger strikes. Even when the means they adopt are currently legal, all such assertions entail implicit threats to direct WUNC energy toward disruptive action, implicit claims to recognition as valid political actors, and implicit devaluation of other political actors within the same issue area. These features sometimes stimulate counteraction by rivals, objects of claims, or authorities, with public violence the outcome.

Organizational outcomes also include some encounters that do not begin with concerted collective making of claims. Border guards, tax collectors, military recruiters, census takers, and other governmental agents, for example, sometimes generate intense resistance on the part of whole communities as they attempt to impose an unpopular measure. Similarly, audiences at theatrical performances, public ceremonies, or executions occasionally respond collectively to actions of the central figures by attacking those figures, unpopular persons who happen to be present, or symbolically charged objects. By and large, organizational outcomes connect with issues over which groups are also currently contending in nonviolent ways.

One subclass of organizational outcome, however, displays a rather different pattern. Some organizations specialize in controlling coercive means, threatening to use those means if necessary, but seeking compliance without violence if possible. Examples include not only established agents of repression but also mafiosi, racketeers, extortionists, paramilitary forces, and perpetrators of military coups. When such specialists in coercive means encounter or anticipate resistance, they commonly mount ostentatious but selective displays of violence. Their strategy resembles that of many Old Regime European rulers, who lacked the capacity for continuous surveillance and control of their subject populations, but often responded to popular rebellion with exemplary punishment—rounding up a few supposed ringleaders, subjecting them to hideous public executions, and thus warning other potential rebels of what might befall them. The strategy is most successful, ironically, when specialists in coercion never actually have to deploy their violent means.

Coordinated Destruction

Coordinated destruction differs in precisely that regard. It refers to those cases where persons or organizations specialized in the deployment of coercive means undertake a program of actions that damage persons and/or objects. Coordinated destruction overlaps with organizational outcomes because specialists in coercion participate in both and because threats of force sometimes escalate into struggles between coercive organizations. Here, however, the organizations' strategies center, however temporarily, on the production of damage. Examples include war, genocide, collective self-destruction, public penance, and government-backed terror. The major distinctions separate a) lethal contests, b) campaigns of annihilation, and c) ritual harm.

Lethal contests

In lethal contests at least two organized groups of specialists in coercion confront each other, each one using harm to reduce or contain the others' capacity to inflict harm. War is the most general label for this class of coordinated destruction, but different variants go by the names civil war, guerrilla, low-intensity conflict, and conquest. Although lethal contests of various sorts stretch back as far as humanity's historical record runs, the standard image of two or more disciplined national armies engaged in destroying each other within generally accepted rules of combat only applies to a very small historical segment: roughly 1650 to 1950 for Europe, a few much earlier periods for China, and even rarer intervals elsewhere in the world. Outside of those exceptional moments, autonomous raiding parties, temporary feudal levies, mercenary assemblages, bandits, pirates, nomads doubling as cavalry, mobilized villages, and similar conglomerate or part-time forces have fought most historical wars.

Campaigns of annihilation

Lethal contests shade over into campaigns of annihilation when one contestant wields overwhelming force or the object of attack is not an organization specialized in the deployment of coercive means. In recent decades, analysts have employed the term "genocide" for those campaigns in which attackers define their victims in terms of shared heritage and "politicide" for those in which victims belong to a common political category; so far no commonly accepted term has emerged for similar campaigns aimed at members of religious or regional categories. The usual stakes in campaigns of annihilation are collective survival, on one side, and recognition as the sole party with the right to territorial control, on the other. Because of those stakes, such struggles tend to generate vast mobilizations of support extending far beyond the specialists in coercion who initiate them.

Ritual harm

Ritual harm plays a much smaller part in contemporary public violence than do lethal contests and campaigns of annihilation. At times, however, it has assumed considerable importance, for example in the potlatch (aggressive, competitive destruction of the performer's own symbolically charged property) that once marked struggles for precedence along America's northwest coast. Other well known instances include the processions of flagellants once organized regularly by Renaissance Italy's penitent confraternities. Today self-immolation, collective suicide, and hunger strikes occasionally occur as gestures of protest, serving chiefly to dramatize the positions of groups that lack other political resources.

Within the broad category of coordinated destruction, as Ted Gurr's data suggest, a remarkable change occurred during the half century following World War II. Where interstate wars among well identified national armies had predominated for a century or more, shifts toward a much wider variety of coercive forces and toward campaigns of annihilation elevated civil war, broadly defined, to the chief setting of coordinated destruction. Decolonization, expansion of world trade in arms and drugs, reappearance of mercenary forces, and the weakening of central state capacity in many world regions all contributed to that change. As war shifted from interstate competition to internal struggle, paradoxically, external parties—both other states and international organizations—became more heavily involved as suppliers of military means, allies, aid givers, profiteers, and mediators.

Opportunism

Opportunism combines low levels of coordination with high salience of violence within the total interaction. Opportunism benefits from some of the same processes that have favored recent moves away from interstate war toward violent struggle within state boundaries. Looting, gang rape, revenge killing, and some sorts of military pillage all occur more frequently in interstices, peripheries, and lapses of central state control. In fact, opportunistic public violence often occurs as an outgrowth of coordinated destruction. Disbanded but still armed troops, for example, frequently use their arms to prey upon civilians. The destruction wrought by mercenaries during truces, marches, and aftermaths of wars made them the bane of European civilian life during the sixteenth- and seventeenth-century heyday of mercenary armies. Similarly, when major protests or disasters divert the attention of repressive forces, looters and killers often take advantage of relaxed control to pursue their own ends.

Dispersed Resistance

Dispersed resistance involves segmented or weakly coordinated damage to persons or objects in the course of interactions that are not predominantly violent. When governmental agents, landlords, employers, religious authorities, or other powerful people impose innovations, exactions, or constraints on subject populations, members of those populations often resist indirectly and on the small scale. They engage in sabotage, ambushes, clandestine attacks on symbolic objects or places, and temporary acts of resistance, which either inflict damage on authorities or incite violent reprisals from authorities. Fragmented resistance differs from organizational outcomes chiefly in the balance of forces among parties and the scale of organization among the weaker parties. Otherwise, the same regularities that apply to organizational outcomes apply to fragmented resistance.

Violent Ritual

In its most stylized forms, such as the medieval tournament, coordinated destruction comes to resemble violent games. Likewise, such violent games as ritual fights between youths of neighboring villages edge over into coordinated destruction. Still, we can usefully distinguish a class of public violence in which two or more relatively well defined and coordinated groups follow a known interaction script entailing infliction of damage on others as they compete for priority within a recognized arena. Age grades of local youths, organized gangs, sports teams, supporters of powerful or popular figures, electoral factions, and fraternal orders inducting new members all sometimes engage in violent games. Frequently the outcome of the contest produces confirmation or alteration of a rank order that in turn entitles winners and their followers to prestige or privilege. In that sense, violent games stand somewhere between a) WUNC performances (whether violent or not) and b) the public displays of wealth, power, and patronage by which war-lords, crime bosses, political magnates, heads of influential families, caciques, and entertainment stars maintain their credibility.

Brawls

Brawls sometimes take on political significance because members of different well-bounded categories regularly attack each other in the course of routine non-violent interactions: market encounters, barroom gatherings, or public assemblies. Most of the time they dissipate as the participants tire, losers flee, or bystanders separate the antagonists. But now and then brawls escalate into larger confrontations when members of each category join the fray in support of their fellow members. At that point what might have ended with cuts, bruises, and damaged egos becomes a struggle over race, religion, ethnicity, nationality, or political affiliation. Mutual signaling in the presence of a categorical boundary can, in short, both step up coordination among violent actors and increase the salience of short-run damage, thus moving brawls into the zones of violent ritual or coordinated destruction.

Individual Aggression

Individual aggression does not, by definition, count as collective violence. I include it in the typology to mark its presence as a limiting case, to point out that the line between collective brawls and individual aggression remains blurred, yet to insist that most collective violence does not consist of individual aggression writ large. Like a brawl, however, individual aggression sometimes mutates into coordinated destruction by multiple actors. The presence of a previously existing and politically charged boundary between aggressor and victim as well as observers to whom that boundary matters is likely to promote that transformation of individual aggression into collective violence.

In all its forms, public violence interacts closely with nonviolent politics. Violence as organizational outcome or coordinated destruction clearly entails struggles for power and takes shape from the character of power struggles spanning violent and nonviolent action. Violence as opportunism and dispersed resistance often occurs as a by-product of grand political processes: state formation, revolution, war, military conscription, taxation, patron-client realignment. Violent rituals follow their own rules, but frequently intersect with or mutate into other forms of public violence. At first glance, violence may seem the antithesis of orderly public politics. At second glance, most public violence connects closely with politics in general.

That observation certainly applies to the sorts of violence Ted Gurr calls "eth-nopolitical." Although Gurr's own catalogs exclude the less-coordinated forms of collective violence we have reviewed, in general violent ethnic conflicts cover our full range from individual aggression to coordinated destruction. No single explanation of violence can possibly hold over that entire range. As Rogers Brubaker and David Laitin sensibly urge:

> The temptation to adopt currently fashionable terms of practice as terms of analysis is endemic to sociology and kindred disciplines. But it ought to be resisted. The notion of "ethnic violence" is a case in point—a category of practice, produced and reproduced by social actors such as journalists, politicians, foundations officers, and NGO representatives, that should not be (but often is) taken over uncritically as a category of analysis by social scientists. Despite sage counsel urging disaggregation, too much social scientific work in this domain (as in others) involves highly aggregated explananda, as if ethnic violence were a homogeneous substance varying only in magnitude. To build a research program around an aggregated notion of ethnic violence is to let public coding—often highly questionable, as when the Somali and Tadjikistani civil wars are coded as ethnic—drive sociological analysis.[7]

Indeed (as Brubaker and Laitin do not quite say), both the internal and the external labeling of social divisions as ethnic rather than as based on class, faction, locality, clan, or some other organizing principle deserves explanation as a social process in its own right. Yet, pace Brubaker and Laitin, Ted Gurr renders us a crucial service in assembling irresistible evidence of something to explain: dramatic change and variation in the frequency with which collective violence clusters around divisions that participants and observers interpret as ethnic or national.

These heterogeneous forms of violence have a few things in common. They involve damage across socially constructed boundaries between populations whose public representatives describe them as differentiated by inherited, encompassing cultures. They often involve claims for political autonomy or independence on grounds not only of distinct culture but also of prior claims to certain territories. They typically increase in situations of rising uncertainty across the boundary, which can happen for a number of different reasons:

- overarching political authorities lose their ability to enforce previously constraining agreements binding actors on both sides of the boundary;
- those same authorities take actions that threaten survival of crucial connecting structures within populations on one side of the boundary while appearing to spare or even benefit those on the other side;
- the declining capacity of authorities to police existing boundaries, control use of weapons, and contain individual aggression facilitates cross-boundary opportunism, including retaliation for earlier slights and injustices;
- leaders on one side of the boundary or the other face resistance or competition from well-organized segments of their previous followers;

• external parties change, increase, or decrease their material, moral, and political support for actors on one side of the boundary or the other.

Change and variation in these circumstances help explain Gurr's findings. Between 1986 and 1995, for example, major powers including the United States and the United Nations responded to the weakening of central authority in the Warsaw Pact, the Soviet Union, and Yugoslavia by signaling increased support for claims of leaders to represent distinct nations currently under alien control. That signaling encouraged leaders to emphasize ethnic boundaries, compete for recognition as valid interlocutors for oppressed nations, attack their ostensible enemies, suppress their competitors for leadership, and make alliances with others who would supply them with resources to support their mobilization. All those moves in turn generated what Gurr and collaborators coded as ethnopolitical violence. International authorities then grew less receptive to new claims for autonomy and independence as they saw how much violence attended those claims and how little formal autonomy reduced the violence. But by that time arms dealers, mercenaries, drug runners, diamond merchants, oil brokers, and others who benefited from weak central political control had moved in to take advantage of supposedly ethnic conflicts, and even to promote them.

Whether violence under these circumstances takes the form of dispersed resistance, coordinated destruction, brawls, opportunism, or something else, however, depends on organizational processes that vary dramatically from one social setting or period to another. Weak generalizations concerning effects of boundary construction and uncertainty provide no substitute for close analysis of social processes on local ground.

NOTES

1. Chesnais, *Histoire de la violence en Occident*; Rummel, *Death by Government*; Tilly et al., "State-Incited Violence, 1900–1999," pp. 161–225.
2. Van Creveld, *Technology and War from 200 B.C. to the Present*; van Creveld, *The Transformation of War*; Kaldor, *New and Old Wars*.
3. Gurr, ed., *Violence in America*; Gurr, *Minorities at Risk*.
4. Groups included were publicly identified ethnopolitical minorities having at least 100,000 members in countries of at least 500,000 total population when, according to standard reports, members of those minorities both a) received systematic differential treatment and b) had movements, parties, committees, and/or militias that claimed to speak on their behalf. Gurr's group used case reports to grade the presence or absence of certain kinds of activity involving such groups over five-year periods, locating each case at the highest value reached during the period. The scale for "rebellion," for example, ran:
    - (0) none reported;
    - (1) political banditry, sporadic terrorism, unsuccessful coups by or on behalf of the group;
    - (2) campaigns of terrorism, successful coups by or on behalf of the group;

    (3)   small-scale guerrilla activity, or other forms of conflict;

    (4)   guerrilla activity involving more than one thousand armed fighters carrying out frequent armed attacks over a substantial area, or group involvement in civil, revolutionary, or international warfare that is not specifically or mainly concerned with group issues;

    (5)   protracted civil war, fought by military units with base areas.

    My well-trained students have a field day criticizing both the basic definitions and the crudity of these measures, but generally curb their contempt when they start trying to do better on their own.

5. Beissinger, "Nationalist Violence and the State: Political Authority and Contentious Repertoires in the Former USSR," *Comparative Politics* 30: (1998) 401–433.

6. Gurr, *Minorities at Risk*, pp. xiv–xv.

7. Brubaker and Laitin, "Ethnic and Nationalist Violence," p. 446.

BIBLIOGRAPHY

Beissinger, Mark. "How Nationalisms Spread: Eastern Europe Adrift the Tides and Cycles of Nationalist Contention." *Social Research* 63 (1996): 97–146.

―――. "The Relentless Pursuit of the National State: Reflections on Soviet and Post-Soviet Experiences." In *Global Convulsions: Race, Ethnicity, and Nationalism at the End of the Twentieth Century*, edited by Winston A. Van Horne. Albany: State University of New York Press, 1997.

―――. "Nationalist Violence and the State: Political Authority and Contentious Repertoires in the Former USSR." *Comparative Politics* 30 (1998): 401–33.

―――. "Event Analysis in Transitional Societies: Protest Mobilization in the Former Soviet Union." In *Acts of Dissent: New Developments in the Study of Protest*, edited by Dieter Rucht, Ruud Koopmans, and Friedhelm Neidhardt. Berlin: Sigma, 1998.

Botz, Gerhard. *Gewalt in der Politik. Attentäte, Zusammenstösse, Putschversuche, Unruhen in Österreich 1918 bis 1934*. Munich: Wilhelm Fink, 1976.

―――. *Krisenzonen einer Demokratie. Gewalt, Streik und Konfliktunderdrückung in Österreich seit 1918*. Frankfurt: Campus Verlag, 1987.

Brass, Paul R. *Theft of an Idol: Text and Context in the Representation of Collective Violence*. Princeton: Princeton University Press, 1997.

―――, ed. *Riots and Pogroms*. New York: New York University Press, 1996.

Braud, Philippe, ed. *La violence politique dans les démocraties européennes occidentales*. Paris: l'Harmattan, 1993.

Brockett, Charles D. "Measuring Political Violence and Land Inequality in Central America." *American Political Science Review* 86 (1992): 169–76.

Brubaker, Rogers, and David D. Laitin. "Ethnic and Nationalist Violence." *Annual Review of Sociology* 24 (1998): 423–52.

Button, James W. *Black Violence: Political Impact of the 1960s Riots*. Princeton: Princeton University Press, 1978.

Chambliss, William J. "State-Organized Crime—The American Society of Criminology, 1988 Presidential Address." *Criminology* 27 (1989): 183–208.

Chesnais, Jean-Claude. *Histoire de la violence en Occident de 1800 à nos jours*. Paris: Robert Laffont, 1981.

Cioffi-Revilla, Claudio. *The Scientific Measurement of International Conflict: Handbook of Datasets on Crises and Wars, 1495–1988 A.D.* Boulder: Lynne Rienner, 1990.

―――. "The Long-Range Analysis of War." *Journal of Interdisciplinary History* 21 (1991): 603–30.

Clark, Samuel, and James S. Donnelly Jr., eds. *Irish Peasants: Violence and Political Unrest, 1780–1914*. Madison: University of Wisconsin Press, 1983.

Cohen, Youssef, Brian R. Brown, and A. F. K. Organski. "The Paradoxical Nature of State Making: The Violent Creation of Order." *American Political Science Review* 75 (1982): 901–10.

Conley, Carolyn A. *Melancholy Accidents: The Meaning of Violence in Post-Famine Ireland.* Lanham, Md.: Lexington Books, 1999.

Copland, Ian. "The Further Shores of Partition: Ethnic Cleansing in Rajasthan 1947." *Past & Present* 160 (1998): 203–39.

Courtwright, David T. *Violent Land: Single Men and Social Disorder from the Frontier to the Inner City.* Cambridge: Harvard University Press, 1996.

van Creveld, Martin. *Technology and War from 200 B.C. to the Present.* New York: Free Press, 1989.

———. *The Transformation of War.* New York: Free Press, 1991.

Daniel, E. Valentine. *Charred Lullabies: Chapters in an Anthropography of Violence.* Princeton: Princeton University Press, 1996.

Davenport, Christian. "Multi-Dimensional Threat Perception and State Repression: An Inquiry into Why States Apply Negative Sanctions." *American Journal of Political Science* 3 (1995): 683–713.

Des Forges, Alison, et al. *Leave None to Tell the Story: Genocide in Rwanda.* New York: Human Rights Watch, 1999.

Dudley, Leonard M. *The Word and the Sword: How Techniques of Information and Violence Have Shaped the World.* Oxford: Blackwell, 1991.

Fatton, Robert. *Predatory Rule: State and Civil Society in Africa.* Boulder: Lynne Rienner, 1992.

Fein, Helen. "Accounting for Genocide after 1945: Theories and Some Findings." *International Journal on Group Rights* 1 (1993): 79–106.

———. "Revolutionary and Antirevolutionary Genocides: A Comparison of State Murders in Democratic Kampuchea, 1975 to 1979, and in Indonesia, 1965 to 1966." *Comparative Studies in Society and History* 35 (1993): 796–823.

Gilje, Paul A. *Rioting in America.* Bloomington: Indiana University Press, 1996.

Gould, Roger V. "Collective Violence and Group Solidarity: Evidence from a Feuding Society." *American Sociological Review* 64 (1999): 356–80.

Grimshaw, Allen D. "Genocide and Democide." In *Encyclopedia of Violence, Peace, and Conflict*, vol. 2, 53–74. San Diego: Academic Press, 1999.

Grimsted, David. *American Mobbing, 1828–1861: Toward Civil War.* New York: Oxford University Press, 1998.

Gurr, Ted Robert, ed. *Violence in America*, 2 vols. Newbury Park: Sage, 1989.

———. *Minorities at Risk: A Global View of Ethnopolitical Conflicts.* Washington: United States Institute of Peace Press, 1993.

———. *Peoples Versus States: Minorities at Risk in the New Century.* Washington: United States Institute of Peace Press, 2000.

Gurr, Ted Robert, and Barbara Harff. *Ethnic Conflict in World Politics.* Boulder: Westview, 1994.

Hair, P. E. H. "Deaths from Violence in Britain: A Tentative Secular Survey." *Population Studies* 25 (1971): 5–24.

Homer-Dixon, Thomas F. *Environment, Scarcity, and Violence.* Princeton: Princeton University Press, 1999.

Husung, Hans-Gerhard. *Protest und Repression im Vormärz: Norddeutschland zwischen Restauration und Revolution.* Göttingen: Vandenhoeck & Ruprecht, 1983.

Jacobs, David, and Robert M. O'Brien. "The Determinants of Deadly Force: A Structural Analysis of Police Violence." *American Journal of Sociology* 103 (1998): 837–62.

Johnson, Larry C. "The Future of Terrorism." *American Behavioral Scientist* 44 (2001): 894–913.

Jones, Bruce. "Intervention Without Borders: Humanitarian Intervention in Rwanda, 1990–1994." *Millennium. Journal of International Affairs* 24 (1995): 225–49.

Kaldor, Mary. *New and Old Wars: Organized Violence in a Global Era.* Cambridge, UK: Polity, 1999.

Kalyvas, Stathis N. "Wanton and Senseless? The Logic of Massacres in Algeria." *Rationality and Society* 11 (1999): 243–85.

———. "The Logic of Violence in Civil War: Theory and Preliminary Results." *Estudio/Working Paper* 2000/151, Instituto Juan March de Estudios e Investigaciones, Madrid, 2000.

Khawaja, Marwan. "Repression and Popular Collective Action: Evidence from the West Bank." *Sociological Forum* 8 (1993): 47–71.

Koopmans, Ruud. "Explaining the Rise of Racist and Extreme Right Violence in Western Europe: Grievances or Opportunities?" *European Journal of Political Research* 30 (1996): 185–216.

Kraska, Peter B., and Victor E. Kappeler. "Militarizing American Police: The Rise and Normalization of Paramilitary Units." *Social Problems* 44 (1997): 1–18.

Laitin, David. "The Cultural Elements of Ethnically Mixed States: Nationality Re-formation in the Soviet Successor States." In *State/Culture: State Formation after the Cultural Turn*, edited by George Steinmetz. Ithaca: Cornell University Press, 1999.

———. "Language Conflict and Violence: The Straw that Strengthens the Camel's Back." In *International Conflict Resolution After the Cold War*, edited by Paul C. Stern and Daniel Druckman. Washington: National Academy Press, 2000.

Lake, David A., and Donald Rothchild. "Spreading Fear: The Genesis of Transnational Ethnic Conflict." In *The International Spread of Ethnic Conflict: Fear, Diffusion, and Escalation*, edited by David A. Lake and Donald Rothchild. Princeton: Princeton University Press, 1998.

Lewis, Michael. *Rioters and Citizens: Mass Protest in Imperial Japan.* Berkeley: University of California Press, 1990.

Licklider, Roy, ed. *Stopping the Killing: How Civil Wars End.* New York: New York University Press, 1993.

Mamdani, Mahmood. *When Victims Turn Killers: A Political Analysis of the Origins and Consequences of the Rwanda Genocide.* Princeton: Princeton University Press, 2001.

Mason, T. David. "Nonelite Response to State-Sanctioned Terror." *Western Political Quarterly* 42 (1989): 467–92.

Mason, T. David, and Dale A. Krane. "The Political Economy of Death Squads: Toward a Theory of the Impact of State-Sanctioned Terror." *International Studies Quarterly* 33 (1989): 175–98.

Mayer, Arno J. *The Furies: Violence and Terror in the French and Russian Revolutions.* Princeton: Princeton University Press, 2000.

McAdam, Doug, Sidney Tarrow, and Charles Tilly. *Dynamics of Contention.* Cambridge: Cambridge University Press, 2001.

Myers, Daniel J. "Racial Rioting in the 1960s: An Event History Analysis of Local Conditions." *American Sociological Review* 62 (1997): 94–112.

Nirenberg, David. *Communities of Violence: Persecution of Minorities in the Middle Ages.* Princeton: Princeton University Press, 1996.

Nordstrom, Carolyn, and JoAnn Martin, eds. *The Paths to Domination, Resistance, and Terror.* Berkeley: University of California Press, 1992.

Olivier, Johan. "State Repression and Collective Action in South Africa, 1970–84." *South African Journal of Sociology* 22 (1991): 109–17.

Perry, Elizabeth J. "Rural Violence in Socialist China." *China Quarterly* 103 (1985): 414–40.

della Porta, Donatella. *Social Movements, Political Violence, and the State: A Comparative Analysis of Italy and Germany.* Cambridge: Cambridge University Press, 1995.

della Porta, Donatella, and Gianfranco Pasquino, eds. *Terrorismo e violenza politica.* Bologna: Il Mulino, 1983.

Reiss, Albert J. Jr., and Jeffrey A. Roth, eds. *Understanding and Preventing Violence.* Washington: National Academy Press, 1993.

Rule, James B. *Theories of Civil Violence.* Berkeley: University of California Press, 1988.

Rummel, R. J. *Death by Government.* New Brunswick: Transaction Publishers, 1994.

Sant Cassia, Paul. "Banditry, Myth, and Terror in Cyprus and Other Mediterranean Societies." *Comparative Studies in Society and History* 35 (1993): 773–95.

Schmid, Alex P., and Janny de Graaf. *Violence as Communication: Insurgent Terrorism and the Western News Media.* Beverly Hills: Sage, 1982.

Scott, James C. "The Moral Economy as an Argument and as a Fight." In *Moral Economy and Popular Protest: Crowds, Conflict and Authority*, edited by Adrian Randall and Andrew Charlesworth. London: Macmillan, 2000.

Stanley, William. *The Protection Racket State: Elite Politics, Military Extortion, and Civil War in El Salvador.* Philadelphia: Temple University Press, 1996.

Sugimoto, Yoshio. *Popular Disturbance in Postwar Japan.* Hong Kong: Asian Research Service, 1981.

Tambiah, Stanley J. *Leveling Crowds: Ethnonationalist Conflicts and Collective Violence in South Asia.* Berkeley: University of California Press, 1996.

———. "Friends, Neighbors, Enemies, Strangers: Aggressor and Victim in Civilian Ethnic Riots." *Social Science and Medicine* 45 (1997): 1177–88.

Taylor, Christopher C. *Sacrifice as Terror: The Rwandan Genocide of 1994.* Oxford: Berg, 1999.

Thomson, Janice E. *Mercenaries, Pirates, and Sovereigns: State-Building and Extraterritorial Violence in Early Modern Europe.* Princeton: Princeton University Press, 1994.

Tilly, Charles. "Revolutions and Collective Violence." In *Handbook of Political Science*, edited by Fred I. Greenstein and Nelon W. Polsby. Vol. 3, *Macropolitical Theory.* Reading, Mass.: Addison-Wesley, 1975.

———. "European Violence and Collective Action since 1700." *Social Research* 53 (1985): 159–84.

———. "Police, Etat, Contestation." *Cahiers de la sécurité intérieure* 7 (1991): 13–18.

———. "Contentious Conversation." *Social Research* 65 (1998): 491–510.

———. "Power—Top Down and Bottom Up." *Journal of Political Philosophy* 7 (1999): 306–28.

———, ed. "Violence." *Social Research* 67, no. 3 (2000).

Tilly, Charles, et al. "State-Incited Violence, 1900–1999." *Political Power and Social Theory* 9 (1995): 161–225.

Tong, James. *Disorder under Heaven: Collective Violence in the Ming Dynasty.* Stanford: Stanford University Press, 1991.

Uvin, Peter. *Aiding Violence: The Development Enterprise in Rwanda.* West Hartford, Conn.: Kumarian Press, 1998.

Viola, Lynne. *Peasant Rebels under Stalin: Collectivization and the Culture of Peasant Resistance.* New York: Oxford University Press, 1996.

Volkov, Vadim. "Violent Entrepreneurship in Post-Communist Russia." *Europe-Asia Studies* 51 (1999): 741–54.

de Waal, Alex. *Famine Crimes: Politics and the Disaster Relief Industry in Africa.* Bloomington: Indiana University Press, 1997.

Waldmann, Peter. *Ethnischer Radikalismus. Ursachen und Folgen gewaltsamer Minderheitenkonflikte.* Opladen: Westdeutscher Verlag, 1989.

Walter, John. *Understanding Popular Violence in the English Revolution: The Colchester Plunderers.* Cambridge: Cambridge University Press, 1999.

White, Robert W. "On Measuring Political Violence: Northern Ireland, 1969 to 1980." *American Sociological Review* 58 (1993): 575–85.

Zimmerman, Ekkart. *Political Violence, Crises and Revolutions.* Cambridge, Mass.: Schenkman, 1983.

CHAPTER TWO

Private Armies
and the Decline of the State

Ulric Shannon

Around the world today, people are taking up arms and fighting under banners that look nothing like flags.[1] To an extent unprecedented in the modern era, war is being waged by entities other than nation-states across all manner of physical and ideological boundaries; and although the *form* of nonstate conflict varies from one society to another, its collective effect is manifest in an emerging global phenomenon: the erosion of the state's monopoly over the use of violence.

In the wake of the Cold War, a postmodern discourse has emerged questioning the relevance of the state, a 350-year-old institution challenged as never before by realities of global scale such as supranational governing regimes, economic integration, "universal culture," population movements, and environmental degradation. To date, the role of armed force has insufficiently been considered as part of this discussion, an oversight that events may soon place squarely on the world's security agenda. For, although they are seldom viewed as fruit of the same tree, the most pressing security threats of the post–Cold War era stem from the demise of what historian Martin van Creveld calls "trinitarian warfare": the force, born at Westphalia, that for three centuries has informed conflict with the principle that "It is the government that directs, the army that fights, and the people who watch, pay, and suffer."[2]

These distinctions are increasingly being blurred by the rise of nonstate violence, a phenomenon with which current strategic thinking is not equipped to cope. One illustration is current American defense doctrine, about which military theorist Steven Metz has written:

> The orthodox position within the Army and the Department of Defense holds that the strategic environment of 2020 will be much like that of 1997. Sovereign nation-states will remain the most important political units. Warfare will continue to be Clausewitzean as nation-states build militaries on a

core of professionals and use them to promote or protect national interests.… While the orthodox position anticipates dramatic improvements in
the effectiveness of militaries able to capitalize on the revolution in military
affairs made possible by information technology, war will remain essentially
political, episodic, violent, state-centric, and *distinct from peace.*[3] (Emphasis
in original.)

On a global scale, however, terrorists, mercenaries, guerrillas, warlords, militias, and other irregular armed forces are exacting a heavy toll from besieged populations and betraying the impotence of national governments—a helplessness
stemming from the fact that, as one analyst writes, "we are legally and behaviorally
prepared to fight only other legal-basis states—mirror images of ourselves—at a
time when state power and substance is declining worldwide."[4]

Ironically, despite the very immediate nature of this problem, one must journey two generations into the past to find the decentralization of armed force
treated not as a mere dialectic issue but as one of threat. During the 1930s, the
landmark work of German political scientist Carl Schmitt established a definition
of individual security that provided for the state's exclusive right to the legitimate
use of force. Recognizing that the capacity for violence could be vested only in the
state, and that once this monopoly was usurped the state essentially lost all meaning, Schmitt presciently framed the current problem of subnational force by
observing that "If within the state there are organized parties capable of according
their members more protection than the state, then the latter becomes at best an
annex of such parties, and the individual knows whom he has to obey."[5] This loyalty, based as it is on fear as opposed to democratic choice, has profound consequences on a society's definition of itself, on the notion of citizenship, and on the
ability of individuals to influence collective decisions.

There are sufficient examples to suggest that various societies have already
been affected by the rise of armed nonstate groups. In India, tea farmers in the
Assam region have assembled an eight-thousand-member private army to protect
their interests against two major separatist insurgent groups responsible for a
wave of kidnappings and extortion; in Pakistan, large areas beyond the commercial center, Karachi, are controlled by drug barons; in Cambodia, army generals
have apportioned important swaths of territory among themselves, which they
administer as local warlords; in Guatemala, wealthy landowners have hired entire
paramilitary units to safeguard their position of privilege; in the Philippines, the
Moro Islamic Liberation Front has hired foreign mercenaries to attack government soldiers.[6]

Beyond these disparate examples, two cases stand out in terms of the consequences that private armed groups can visit on the security of individuals and on
their perception of the state: the use of professional mercenaries in Sierra Leone
and the rise of "narco-militias" in Colombia. These two examples, presented here

as case studies, demonstrate that where institutional weaknesses allow it to thrive, subnational force is eroding the legitimacy of the state as a guarantor of security and economic development and is accelerating the incidence of violent power contention. This is not to suggest a unicausal explanation for state failure, which is both idiosyncratic and overdetermined, but rather to probe the degree to which armed nonstate actors can reinforce existing national pathologies. As yet, this condition has been endemic principally in the developing world; but as borders become increasingly porous, the need to renationalize the means of coercion—though it will likely be termed otherwise—is likely to emerge as a pressing global security imperative.

Professional Mercenaries

The consecration of trinitarian warfare was supposed to eliminate the market in private military force, and it very nearly did. Beginning in the 1860s, a series of conferences in Europe formalized the interdiction of medieval practices in martial affairs in order that war be fought only by duly constituted armies, on behalf of states.[7] So tolled the bell for mercenary soldiers, long reviled, in the words of Sir Walter Raleigh, as "seditious, unfaithful, disobedient destroyers of all places and countries whither they are drawn as being held by no other bond than their own commodity."[8] While gradually going the way of the duel, mercenaries in the modern era have lingered on the fringes of parapolitics, possessed neither of the capabilities to affect the outcome of war nor the legitimacy to be used in good conscience.

In the developing world, however, the end of the Cold War has breathed new life into the profession by creating a power vacuum where superpowers once competed for the strategic balance and by loosing a torrent of professional soldiers made redundant by global military downsizing.[9] As a result, several "security consultancy" firms based in the United Kingdom and South Africa have acquired significant capabilities and begun wading into the brutal resource wars of sub-Saharan Africa, marketing their services to the factions most able to pay.

In recent years, the most prominent company has been Pretoria-based Executive Outcomes (EO). Perhaps the most competent mercenary outfit ever assembled, EO was praised by the *Independent* of London in 1997 as "the most deadly and efficient force operating in sub-Saharan Africa today" with the exception of the South African army.[10] (Although EO nominally ceased operations in 1999, most observers believe the company is merely in the process of mutating into a new corporate identity and that its influence should still be spoken of in the present tense.)[11]

Executive Outcomes' staff of forty officers and two thousand troops is drawn from the ranks of the South African National Defence Force and consists largely of white soldiers from the apartheid era who could not abide the army's new look when it was integrated following the election of Nelson Mandela in 1994. They are highly disciplined, extensively trained, and battle-hardened, and have access to hardware that would unnerve many an African defense force, including Russian-made Mi-17 and Mi-24 helicopter gunships, a radio-intercept system, casualty evacuation aircraft, and fuel-air explosives. (This last weapon, which disperses fuel vapor over a one-mile radius and ignites it, is considered the deadliest form of conventional bombing, and has been described as "Eighty percent nuke for size and no international outrage.") Executive Outcomes owns two Boeing 727s for troop transport as well as Russian MiG-23 fighter-bombers. This private air force allows EO to field personnel from Johannesburg International Airport to any-where in the world within seventy-two hours.[12]

The emergence of a private actor with "national" capabilities carries dire impli-cations for the integrity of the state in the developing world; this is evident both in the recent performance of mercenary outfits and in the token efforts made by the South African government to curtail EO's operations—efforts that seem designed, deferentially, to limit EO's domestic activities without hindering the firm's foreign marketability. It has apparently not been lost on Pretoria that EO's continuing close ties to the South African intelligence community give the firm considerable potential to undermine the ruling ANC, not to mention that EO's leaders are past masters in the practice, from apartheid days. Given the prevailing reactionary mindset among these Afrikaners, fears persist in the government coalition that "EO represents the so-called 'Third Force' of the old regime that came close to wrecking the country's transition."[13] As a result, the Mandela government has evi-dently come to view the mercenary firm's foreign adventurism as an opportunity to externalize this "third force," at the expense of other African countries.

If the South African state can feel its sovereignty sufficiently threatened to occasion such an uncharacteristically cynical attitude, one can only ponder EO's possible impact on any number of much weaker African states. To date, EO's record suggests that it has compromised the state as an institution both through its lien on the already-meager resources of several African countries and through its challenge to their citizens' ultimate loyalty. The mercenary outfit's most publi-cized operation yet, in Sierra Leone, serves as a cautionary tale in this regard.

In April 1995 the National Provisional Ruling Council (NPRC) of Sierra Leone approached Executive Outcomes for a lifeline. The NPRC, or "government" (for lack of a better word, since it did little governing), had assumed power three years earlier in a coup and was in the throes of a civil war with the Liberian-based Revolu-tionary United Front (RUF). The RUF had emerged to oppose government corrup-tion but had quickly mutated into an apolitical band of thugs with a propensity for violently terrorizing the population of Sierra Leone in its quest for control of the country's lucrative diamond trade. By the spring of 1995, RUF fighters controlled the diamond fields and were within twenty kilometers of the capital, Freetown.

Over the next twenty-two months, the NPRC signed three separate contracts with EO for a total of $35 million. Though officially hired for "training" services, EO's contingent of 250 troops actually engaged in most of the government's offensives, for which the Sierra Leone Military Forces lent only a support role commensurate with their lean capabilities.[14] Together they succeeded in driving away the rebels, and less than a year later the country witnessed its first presidential election in twenty-three years.

The irony of former apartheid soldiers taking up arms to defend the clan chiefs of Freetown and help reassert their monopoly over the diamond trade was not lost on everyone; but EO's motives were best understood in the light of the particular affinity of modern mercenary outfits for resource wars in weak states. Invariably, the governments most likely to patronize mercenary companies are those of impoverished countries dependent on a single source of revenue—usually minerals such as diamonds and copper, or oil. This is an economic model tailor-made for oligarchic control, which usually implies a political tradition of undemocratic governance in the service of elites. The result is often that security—a necessary adjunct of unhindered resource exploitation—is also treated as an exclusive resource and is therefore parceled out to the benefit of areas relevant to the ruling clique—either the main centers or a particular region; control is inevitably lost over the hinterland, and the notion of territorial sovereignty, whether over people or resources, quickly becomes illusory.

Mercenary firms have identified these weaknesses and have marketed short-term solutions through complex and often clandestine networks of subsidiary resource-exploitation companies that act as middlemen between themselves and patron states, financing mercenary operations in exchange for mineral concessions. Executive Outcomes, for example, is but one component of a major conglomerate of at least thirty-two security and mining corporations, all connected in nebulous ways. (It is worth noting that many Executive Outcomes officials earned their stripes under apartheid in the Civil Co-operation Bureau, a department of the South African National Defence Force responsible for establishing front-companies to circumvent trade sanctions against Pretoria.)[15]

The practice of trading armed might for mining rights is hotly denied by the mercenary firms, who have been stung by accusations of having essentially recolonized their client states. These denials ring hollow in the case of Sierra Leone, however, where the hiring of Executive Outcomes came at the urging of Branch Energy, a British mining firm now owned by Vancouver-based Diamond Works Inc. While EO and Branch Energy have striven to obscure their corporate links, their symbiotic relationship is such that, according to Jeffrey Moag of the U.S. National Security News Service, "Everywhere EO goes, Branch Energy is picking up a diamond concession."[16] In the case of Sierra Leone, a sizable portion of the country's diamond fields was relinquished to Branch Energy, against the advice of the Minister for Mines, a mere four months after being recaptured from the RUF.[17]

The danger with this kind of barter is that over a prolonged period of conflict, vulnerable regimes may mortgage their nation's already-compromised sovereignty by relinquishing their only source of revenue to foreign companies. The full implications of such arrangements become evident when the fighting stops— however momentarily—and society begins again to coalesce; according to UN Special Rapporteur Enrique Bernales Ballesteros, "Once a greater degree of security has been attained, the firm apparently begins to exploit the concessions it has received by setting up a number of associates and affiliates ... thereby acquiring a significant, if not hegemonic, presence in the economic life of the country in which it is operating."[18] At last count, the acreage ceded to mining companies by the government of Sierra Leone amounted to over one-third of the country's landmass.[19]

Even more important, perhaps, is the impact the hiring of private force has on how citizens perceive the state as an institution; in this regard, EO's controversial record in the field is a cause for concern. On the positive side of the ledger, the company's presence in Angola from 1992 to 1995 is widely credited with compelling the rebel UNITA faction to sue for peace, however briefly; similarly, EO's campaign in Sierra Leone shifted the balance of power sufficiently that it forced the RUF insurgents to the bargaining table, making elections possible and enabling the resettlement of over eight thousand displaced persons.

Although these truces proved to be tragically ephemeral—the battle was subsequently rejoined in both countries, with devastating vigor—Executive Outcomes did not hesitate to capitalize on these purported successes and anoint itself an "upholder of international order and promoter of global peace."[20] Observers on the ground, however, took a more jaundiced view of the mercenary firm. One British journalist qualified the enthusiasm for EO's work, stating, "Wherever they went, civilians stopped dying. The trouble was that they only went where the payoff was high."[21] A doctor from Médecins sans Frontières was more categorical, describing the mercenaries as "racist killers with no interest in the country," the sight of whose helicopters over Freetown was a sign to prepare for a flood of wounded civilians.[22]

Despite the brutality of Executive Outcomes' campaign in Sierra Leone, however, the Afrikaner mercenaries were—and are still—considered heroes by Freetown's ruling elite and, to a lesser extent, the population as well. At the height of the conflict, the local diamond traders approached the government and threatened to leave the country, wealth in tow, if the contract with EO was allowed to lapse. When the head of a teachers' union was quoted describing the mercenaries as "hard-core apartheid attack dogs" in a local newspaper, both the speaker and the newspaper's editor were thrown into jail.[23] While this pressure was being exercised by an aristocracy mindful of its tenuous hold on power and privilege, Executive Outcomes' presence was "sold" to the locals as a munificent gesture; said one mercenary of the elites, "They tell the people we are Africans and that Mandela has sent us. I don't want to confuse them." The tactic worked, according to an American journalist: "Many felt so indebted to the soldiers of Executive Outcomes, whom they rather fantastically imagined had come in a gesture of pan-African generosity, that they prayed for them at mosque. The South African mercenaries, camped on a nearby hilltop overlooking Koidu, were unreservedly hailed by the chiefs, the businessmen, and the street people as saviors."[24]

One can only speculate as to how such adulation, juxtaposed against the utter fecklessness of the Sierra Leonean state, would further erode the capacity and will of individual Sierra Leoneans to take ownership of their political destinies. In a situation where governance is a fig leaf covering a winner-take-all scramble for valuable commodities, political freedom is often reduced to a barter system for ensuring one's personal security. In the case of Sierra Leone, where the most benign force at work was the protection provided collaterally by mercenaries serving an oligarchy, the people came to see an arrangement that left their collective economic weal in the hands of foreigners as preferable to having to rely on one another. In such an environment, a country's entire social and economic agenda becomes predicated on the continued presence of an outside force, irrespective of how ruinous the long-term consequences of its involvement may be. And when the saviors leave, as Executive Outcomes did in January 1997 when the Sierra Leone government proved incapable of acquitting EO's steepening bill, there is no indigenous presence left to fill the void and this social order collapses.

The most eloquent indictment of the fleeting stability provided by private military companies firms is the complete backslide into civil war witnessed in Sierra Leone and Angola in the wake of their interventions, when it became manifest that the presence of mercenaries had likely contributed to the further hollowing-out of vital state institutions. Yet, while one might expect the Pyrrhic nature of the victories won by EO's patrons to leaven the popularity of mercenary services, several factors suggest that the role of private soldiery will grow in the coming years. The first is the growing perception of personal and collective insecurity in the developing world (particularly Africa) and the sense of order and stability that mercenary outfits sustain. Increasingly, demographic realities are moving large numbers of people into the seemingly ever expanding territory beyond the dominion of accountable authorities. In Sierra Leone, where the police often lack gasoline for their vehicles, one resident commented that "the government has no writ after dark"—an admonition that resonates throughout the continent.[25] One German diplomat has gone so far as to suggest that "In the twenty-first century German ambassadors heading for Africa may again be authorized to sign treaties of cooperation with whatever coastal kings or leaders are able to assert some sort of control over the interior."[26]

Another factor is the growing acceptance—if not endorsement—of the services companies such as EO provide, by Western governments eagerly effecting a retrenchment from the developing world. In the aftermath of disastrous humanitarian interventions in Somalia and Rwanda, in which practically all Western nations involved suffered either human casualties or severe political fallout, the will to personally safeguard human security in the Third World has evanesced. The fact that the UN has been largely unsuccessful in its more recent peacekeeping efforts in Africa—having been marginalized in Angola and the Democratic Republic of Congo, and placed on the defensive in Sierra Leone by RUF attacks in May 2000—has also reduced the scope for multilateral action.

Mindful of EO's ostensibly successful missions in the area, Western security establishments have begun debating privately the possibility of outsourcing selected interventions to mercenary firms. During a November 1996 meeting at the U.S. National Security Council devoted to the creation of a humanitarian corridor for fleeing Rwandan Hutu refugees, some consideration was given hiring Executive Outcomes. In June 1997 leaders from mercenary firms including Executive Outcomes and Sandline International were invited to a conference on private armies held by the Defense Intelligence Agency, the Pentagon's intelligence arm; on the possibility that mercenaries might be contracted to conduct humanitarian interventions, one participant commented that "There was a consensus among government officials and the companies that this sort of activity is going to greatly increase during the next few years."[27] Finally, no less a figure than UN Secretary-General Kofi Annan has consulted with British mercenary firm Defence Systems Limited about protecting refugees on the Rwandan-Congolese border.[28]

Western security establishments have not been alone in entertaining notions of mercenaries as peacekeepers; surprisingly, certain humanitarian organizations such as UNHCR have become quiet proponents of mercenary outfits after seeing their work and even benefitting from their services. In Sierra Leone, Executive Outcomes aided in the resettlement of thousands of displaced persons and was credited with demobilizing units of child soldiers. According to one journalist, the mercenaries "were referring youngsters [to juvenile centers] from the areas they'd secured up-country. It was the first tangible evidence of EO activity a visitor to Sierra Leone was likely to encounter and it did the company credit."[29] Executive Outcomes also found itself escorting aid agencies into the treacherous interior, making it possible for them to do their work.[30]

But this shortsighted enthusiasm for mercenary companies neglects the profound consequences that previous missions have had on security in the affected areas and beyond. As the civil wars in Sierra Leone and Angola rage on, it has become clear that the highly debatable merits of mercenary services are far outweighed by their tendency to protract and widen existing conflict. The UN itself has noted that "the presence of mercenaries in armed conflicts tends to make them longer-lasting, more serious and bloodier."[31] This merely compounds the effects of another fundamental paradox of the use of private force, namely the powerful incentive that mercenary outfits have to sustain the conditions of instability that create the demand for their services. This prolonging effect on conflict will only spread as a multitude of other mercenary firms enter the African market, each less professional than the last. (At present, there are over a hundred mercenary outfits in Africa, and their presence has been felt in twenty countries on the continent.)

In sum, the threat posed by mercenary firms lies less in their capacity to visit death and destruction on their opponents than in their ability to position themselves as more credible guarantors of stability than the weak, compromised states they claim to serve. In the end, it is on this level that private armies have the most deleterious effect on long-term individual security. According to British journalist Jeremy Harding, the greatest supporters of private security conglomerates "are probably vulnerable civilians whose environment [they have] secured against armed conflict … people who are less concerned with the idea that their nation-state may have become a job-lot than they are with physical safety, food, and livelihood."[32] The point was driven home in a recent UN report on the illicit diamond trade in Sierra Leone, which concluded that mercenaries were still active in the country, trading arms for diamonds, but this time in the service of the RUF. Yet the fact that EO's spiritual successors were actively working to undermine the government and stripping the country of its main source of income did not deter the people of Sierra Leone, the report stated, from fervently wishing that a private military company could be contracted to bring about a solution to the conflict.[33]

The capacity of mercenaries to provide a fleeting sense of security entrenches short-term thinking about the welfare of both citizen and state. By contriving to keep sovereign control of a country's resources out of its government's hands, mercenaries make it impossible for an informed polity to pursue options for economic stabilization; this limits the capacity of states to move beyond a model of simple subsistence typified by a zero-sum struggle for limited commodities, and consider measures that could address both the root causes of resource insecurity and the requirements for regaining sovereign control of legitimate coercion. One is left to conclude that if the civil society of a besieged state can be conditioned by war to so readily accept these troubling terms and seek its salvation from a neo-colonial foreign corporation, Carl Schmitt's notion that "protection of life is the ultimate reason of the state" takes on bleak overtones.[34]

Narco-Militias

As in Africa, South American and Asian countries have also been plagued by resource wars stemming from a decline of state control over the means of violence; and although this reality does not yet have the scope nor the texture that it does in places like Sierra Leone, its influence on security, development, and the viability of the state is just as real, if not as immediate. In Colombia it is not mercenaries but the growing prevalence of drug enterprises, and the guerrilla movements and paramilitary units that flourish as parasitic kin, that is to blame for the increasing currency of civil violence and for the government's powerlessness to set its own agenda. But as with mercenaries, this impotence has a self-perpetuating effect manifest in ever-more-brazen challenges to the sovereignty and relevance of the state. Since symptoms of an emerging narco-militia problem have appeared elsewhere (Central and Southeast Asia, for example), the Colombian case serves as a cautionary tale bespeaking the need for states to assert and consolidate their control of the means of coercion.

Never a country blessed with great institutional strength, Colombia has shown how an influx of drug money into a state that has abdicated its sovereign right to impose order can occasion the violent disarticulation of a society. Born of a tradition of elite rule in which security was apportioned in relation to personal economic imperatives (chiefly those of mining companies), modern Colombia long ago desisted from any attempt to extend state authority beyond the major cities or to define the notion of citizenship—and attendant rights and responsibilities—of Colombians in the lawless hinterland. Into this man-made environment of subsistence and survival, the massive flood of drug profits of the last three decades has created a situation where citizens are faced with competing "governments," the struggle between which has completely riven Colombian society.

Between 1970 and 1995 the annual proceeds of the narcotics trade rose from $1.8 million to as much as $7 billion,[35] allowing a class of criminal nouveau riches to rise from endemic poverty and in the process highlight the state's failure to discharge the social contract. This has led one scholar to term Colombia a "quasi-state" that has capsized in the face of social demands occasioned by the modernization process.[36] For the average Colombian citizen, that has reduced democratic choice to an exercise in clientele politics centered on the primacy of the provider, the latter measured against his ability to control (or mete out) violence and dispense basic services.

Over time, the map of Colombia has come to reflect these Faustian choices. In terms simply of territorial control, drug lords are by far the country's largest landowners, controlling over seven million acres of farmland. Rural Colombia is ruled by a loose alliance of medium-sized cocaine enterprises and right-wing paramilitary groups, whose protection of the drug trade is merely the modern face of a practice established by mining interests at the country's founding. These militias, who may number over one hundred and boast some five thousand members, have, according to Oxfam, "superceded the official Colombian army in recent years as the front-line force against the guerrillas." The paramilitaries have forced scores of Colombians from their homes in communities that are thought to be giving support to the guerrillas, contributing to what may be the third-largest internally displaced population in the world; they are also believed responsible for half the political killings in Colombia.[37]

Elsewhere in the country, insurgent guerrilla armies totaling more than fifteen thousand troops thrive on a notionally ideological regime of informal taxation and even more informal quasigovernance.[38] The largest such group, the Fuerzas Armadas Revolucionarias de Colombia (FARC), is believed to earn between $500 million and $3 billion annually from its levies on the drug trade and extortion from businesses and landowners, and has humbled Colombia's armed forces in a number of skirmishes.[39] While affirming their socialist credentials and maintaining a semblance of interest in promoting a representational system for all Colombians, the rebels have gradually corrupted their stated democratic principles and instead built an economic empire around the pillars of crime, violence, and fear. In recent years the rebels have subsumed their social mission to the point of working with the paramilitaries to harmonize their competing fee schedules for drug shipments.

The vulnerability of the Colombian state in the face of these *forces vives* has been manifest in the pervasive sense of insecurity among the population, which now reaches into the cities; evidence of this is the phenomenal growth of Colombia's private security industry, whose ranks now outnumber those of the national police by a factor of four. Even more significant, however, are the agreements the government has been forced to conclude as a means of containing the violence. These include a 1991 pact renouncing domestic war tactics (a commitment the rebels and paramilitaries have not felt incumbent upon *them*) and a constitutional amendment prohibiting the extradition of Colombian nationals to the United States—one of the few effective weapons against the drug cartels—repealed only in 1997.[40] In May 1999 the Colombian minister of defense and a significant portion of the army command resigned when President Andres Pastrana announced that an area of forty thousand square kilometers in southern Colombia would be ceded indefinitely to the FARC guerrillas as a peace offering.[41]

While the emergence of a de facto guerrilla state the size of Switzerland within Colombia's borders has sparked much debate, it is merely one example of the widespread development of parallel governance by irregular forces in the country. This has been evident in the ability of armed groups to impose a particular version of social and economic order in their areas of operation—the feature most emblematic of stateness, and one that has eluded the Colombian government. For example, until the 1980s a movement of landless peasants had, for several decades, agitated for land reform and the redistribution of unused estates. When their demands began to include territory coveted by the drug cartels, however, the peasants were made privy to the level of coercive capacity residing in the hands of the cartels and their death squads. In 1989, therefore, the Congress of Peasant Organizations declared that, for fear of reprisals, they would cease their demands for land redistribution in areas where narco-traffickers exercised territorial control.[42] In a truly medieval relationship, observers noted, small landowners were shielded from rural discontent by the cartels' feudal practice of "exact[ing] tribute in exchange for the regulation of public order and the protection of the market."[43]

The drug kingpins were nearly successful in securing such tribute from the Colombian government itself—a move that would have consecrated the death of the state—when they twice offered, in 1988, to settle the Colombian national debt in return for immunity from prosecution.[44]

This attempt to construct a particular social and economic model around the principle of unfettered personal exploitation of a collective resource—land— essentially rejected the notion of citizenship, insofar as it defined an individual's right to life and security as a function of his acquiescence. The narco-militias' calculations were not entirely blind to the need for a veneer of democratic engagement, however, and over time their challenge to the state came to rely on a base of popular support. In the late 1980s, drug kingpin Pablo Escobar earned his share of public adulation by launching a highly publicized "Medellin Without Slums" campaign, in which he underwrote the construction of some 450 homes, installed electricity and running water, built clinics, churches and soccer fields, and gave money to widows. Escobar's perceived legitimacy was such that he was even elected to the national Congress.[45] It is perhaps understandable that citizens would acquiesce to an economic model based on crime when the narcotics trade has been credited with directly improving the income and standard of living of 100,000 poor peasants and urban slum dwellers, and indirectly those of 400,000 relatives; the influx of cocaine dollars into Medellin, according to one scholar, has effectively bailed out that city's failing textile trade.[46]

The emergence of private actors more accomplished than the government in providing basic services and in controlling the means of coercion outside the major cities has driven home, for many Colombians, the purely notional character of the "state" based in Bogota. For them, the rise of subnational armed groups has meant the reign of an atomized form of authority as violent as traditional statist tyranny but in many ways more insidious. According to one scholar, "The lack of liberty and fear for personal safety that are characteristic of authoritarian government amount to the same thing, but the coercion is simply being employed, in the case of Colombia, by groups other than the government."[47] The qualitative difference, however, is that unlike statist despotism the violent competition between these groups narrows the range of options available to individuals for ensuring their security, insofar as mere compliance with a prevailing faction may be insufficient for survival in the context of a winner-take-all scramble for resources.

In his study of the history of civil violence in Colombia, Alejandro Reyes notes that the population has experienced the greatest terror during phases of parity between power contenders, be they narco-traffickers, guerrilla movements, or the state itself.[48] James Zackrison, of the U.S. Office of Naval Intelligence, concurs, writing that "Where the FARC is stronger ... the cartels pay taxes and protection money. Where the cartels predominate ... the FARC leaves the traffickers alone. Where neither has the upper hand ... a continual state of combat exists."[49] Thus, during periods of, and in areas of, unchallenged domination by one side or the other, the incidence of violence has been less frequent—suggesting, to paraphrase Hannah Arendt, that genuine power indeed goes unexpressed.

Private armies elsewhere in the world have not proven quite so amenable to such a pragmatic apportionment of spheres of influence, preferring instead to commingle with legitimate society and challenge state sovereignty in more subtle ways. For example, warlord armies in Serbia have infiltrated the common culture with a particularly hoary brand of ethnic scapegoating, allowing them to position themselves as the most dynamic force in a country where civil society has, in the process, been utterly criminalized; in Central Asia, meanwhile, the post-Soviet era has seen private militias mutate into national armies without losing any of their affinity for rape and plunder nor their contempt for civilian control.[50] This suggests that the eclipsing of a state need not be as absolute as it has been in Colombia, and that the problem of private force may soon require that we candidly address, as a global security issue, the schizophrenic features of numerous failed and failing states. Less clear, amid calls to renationalize the means of violence (a controversial issue in its own right), will be the ultimate fate of the state where the institution is already under assault.

Conclusion

The state is generally seen as the once and future basis of the international system. There has been little consideration of the possibility that a world dominated by nonstate entities is the more historically relevant condition of global power relations, one artificially suppressed for three centuries and now ready to reemerge. It would be useful, therefore, to remember that in the two hundred years that followed the Treaty of Westphalia, the state was a purely Western idea spanning no more than 3 percent of the earth's surface; aside from European colonies, the state only began to appear elsewhere in the twentieth century.[51]

The growth of nonstate violence suggests we are gradually entering a post-Westphalian age, where conflicts will increasingly take the form of those witnessed in the medieval period before state structures were erected to keep religious warfare in abeyance. This kind of conflict is typified by a breakdown in the familiar distinctions between soldier, civilian, and state, a collapse with more than theoretical repercussions on individual security. Human Rights Watch has commented on the rise of private militias in Nagorno-Karabakh in terms that apply to all subnational armies:

> These fighters are not real soldiers in the professional sense. Typically, they serve in loose units out of personal loyalty, or for booty, or revenge on specific individuals, or a desperate hope of protecting or regaining their territory. These are, significantly, armed formations without ... the disciplinary

backbone of professional armies. There [is] no one to insist on discipline among the ordinary soldiers even of a strictly military, prudential nature.... The result is a "disordered warfare" ... high technology coupled with improvisation, weapons of great firepower which yet lack adequate control mechanisms and humanitarian points of view.[52]

Paradoxically, it is as a remedy for precisely this kind of random menace that private force gained great currency in the first place. It is difficult, admittedly, to fault a Colombian or Sierra Leonean for tending toward alternate providers of security in the presence of an impotent state and in the face of threat from without or from within. In this environment as well, it is understandable that citizens might vest their political loyalty and their economic destinies in private armed groups if they were convinced that those forces advocating popular representation and accountability were unable to provide for their protection.

Along the way, however, the distinction between security and commodity has been lost, creating a self-replicating dynamic that assigns private force to alleviate human insecurity only to deepen its root causes. As a result, these private armed groups are able to position themselves, where self-interest so motivates them, as guarantors of social and economic stability, and to selectively challenge the state for the heretofore unquestioned loyalty of its citizens; in an increasing portion of the world, this is a battle for hearts and minds that the state is losing.

NOTES

The views expressed in this article are personal and do not necessarily reflect those of the Government of Canada.

1. A statement meant to expand on (and also challenge) Samuel Huntington's assertion that "In the post–Cold War world flags count.... People are discovering new but often old identities and marching under new but often old flags which lead to wars with new but often old enemies." Samuel P. Huntington, *The Clash of Civilizations and the Remaking of World Order* (New York: Touchstone, 1997), p. 20.

2. Martin van Creveld, *Nuclear Proliferation and the Future of Conflict* (New York: The Free Press, 1993), p. 20.

3. Steven Metz, "Which Army After Next? The Strategic Implications of Alternative Futures," *Parameters: US Army War College Quarterly* (fall 1997). Online at carlisle-www.army.mil/usawc/Parameters/ 97autumn/metz.htm.

4. Ralph Peters, "The Culture of Future Conflict," *Parameters: US Army War College Quarterly* (winter 1995–96). Online at carlisle-www.army.mil/usawc/Parameters/1995/peters.htm.

5. Carl Schmitt, *The Concept of the Political* (New Brunswick, N.J.: Rutgers University Press, 1976), p. 52.

6. Sanjoy Hazarika, "Tea Farmers in North India Plan to Field Private Army," *Winnipeg Free Press*, November 4, 1992; Robert Kaplan, *The Ends of the Earth: A Journey to the Frontiers of Anarchy* (New York: Vintage, 1996), pp. 328, 414; David Isenberg, "Soldiers of Fortune Ltd.: A Profile of Today's Private Sector Corporate Mercenary Firms," Center for Defense Information, November 1997, online at www.cdi.org/issues/mercenaries/merc.html.

7. Van Creveld, *Nuclear Proliferation*, p. 19.

8. Anthony Mockler, *The New Mercenaries* (New York: Paragon House, 1987), p. 37.

9. Between 1987 and 1996, the world's active military forces declined from 28.3 million to 22.7 million. See Bonn International Centre for Conversion, *Conversion Survey 1998: Global Disarmament, Defence Industry Consolidation and Conversion* (Oxford: Oxford University Press, 1998), p. 39.

10. Cited in David Baines, "Mercenary-Mining Links Disclosed," *Vancouver Sun*, April 10, 1997.

11. In December 1998 Executive Outcomes announced on its now-defunct website (www.eo.com) that it was ceasing operations as a result of domestic legislation imposed by the South African government; in January 1999, however, published reports indicated that EO's offices remained staffed. Given the resilience and business acumen of modern mercenary organizations—most are incorporated in fiscal and legal shelters such as the Isle of Man and the Caribbean—there is little doubt that EO will reemerge, perhaps with a new (nominal) base of operations. See "Can Anyone Curb Africa's Dogs of War?," *The Economist*, January 16, 1999, p. 41.

12. Hardware described in Elizabeth Rubin, "An Army of One's Own," *Harper's*, February 1997, p. 47, and Isenberg, "Soldiers of Fortune, Ltd.," p. 9. Fuel-air explosives described in David Shukman, *Tomorrow's War: The Threat of High-Technology Weapons* (New York: Harcourt Brace & Co., 1996), p. 10.

13. David R. Shearer, *Private Armies and Military Intervention*, Adelphi Paper 316 (Oxford: Oxford University Press/IISS, 1998), pp. 54–55.

14. Ibid., pp. 49–53.

15. Jeremy Harding, "The Mercenary Business: 'Executive Outcomes,'" *Review Of African Political Economy* 71 (1997); 88.

16. Cited in Kirsten Sellars, "Old Dogs of War Learn New Tricks," *New Statesman*, April 25, 1997, p. 25.

17. Capt. Reginald Glover, cited in "To Buy a War," *The Fifth Estate* (Canadian Broadcasting Corporation), originally aired on November 3, 1997.

18. United Nations, Economic and Social Council, *Report on the Use of Mercenaries as a Means of Violating Human Rights*, September 23, 1996. Online at www.unhchr.ch/html/menu4/garep/392a51.htm.

19. "To Buy a War."

20. Sellars, "Old Dogs of War Learn New Tricks," p. 26.

21. Harding, "The Mercenary Business," pp. 92–93.

22. Cited in Rubin, "An Army of One's Own," p. 48.

23. Harding, "The Mercenary Business," p. 93.

24. Rubin, "An Army of One's Own," p. 48.

25. Robert Kaplan, "The Coming Anarchy," *The Atlantic Monthly* 273, no. 2 (1994): 44.

26. Cited in Kaplan, *Ends of the Earth*, p. 67.

27. Cited in Ken Silverstein, "Privatizing War: How Affairs of State Are Outsourced to Corporations Beyond Public Control," *The Nation*, July 28–August 4, 1997, p. 12.

28. Damian Lilly, "The Privatization of Peacekeeping: Prospects and Realities," in *Peacekeeping: Evolution or Extinction?*, United Nations Institute for Disarmament Research, 1999. Available at www.unog.ch/unidir/e-df0-3.htm.

29. Harding, "The Mercenary Business," p. 92.

30. In Angola, furthermore, EO claims that the UN "semi-officially" requested—and received—its logistical assistance, smoothing the way for peacekeeping activities. See Sellars, "Old Dogs of War Learn New Tricks," p. 28.

31. United Nations, Economic and Social Council, *Report on the Use of Mercenaries as a Means of Violating Human Rights*, January 17, 1996. Online at www.unhcr.ch/refworld/un/chr/chr96/thematic/27-mer.htm.

32. Harding, "The Mercenary Business," p. 87.

33. United Nations, *Report of the Panel of Experts (Appointed Pursuant to UN Security Council Resolution 1306 (2000), Paragraph 19, in Relation to Sierra Leone)*, December 2000, p. 29.

34. Schmitt, *Concept of the Political*, p. 88.

35. Estimates of Colombian drug profits vary wildly. Francisco Thoumi places them in the $2 to $5 billion range, while more recent journalistic accounts suggest a value of from $3.5 to $7 billion. Thoumi, "The Economic Impact of Narcotics in Colombia," in *Drug Policy in the Americas*, ed. Peter H. Smith (Boulder, Colo.: Westview Press, 1992).

36. Patricia B. McRae, "The Illegal Narcotics Trade in Colombia: Power Contender to the State and National Security?" *Conflict Quarterly* (spring 1993): 10–11.

37. Figures on paramilitaries in ibid., p. 16. "Who's Who in Colombian Conflict," Oxfam UK, online at www.oxfam.org.uk/campaign/cutconflict/html/ body_who_s_involved. html. *The Economist*, April 17, 1999, p. 29.

38. James L. Zackrison and Eileen Bradley, "Colombian Sovereignty Under Siege," *Strategic Forum 112*, Institute for National Strategic Studies, May 1997, p. 2.; *The Economist*, April 10, 1999, p. 51.

39. *U.S. News and World Report*, May 11, 1998. Online at www.usnews.com/usnews/ issue/980511/ 11colo.htm. Zackrison and Bradley, "Colombian Sovereignty," p. 1.

40. Alvaro Camacho Guizado, "Drug Trafficking and Society in Colombia," in *Drug Trafficking in the Americas*, ed. Bruce M. Bagley and William O. Walker III (Coral Gables, Fla.: University of Miami, 1994), p. 99.

41. *The Economist*, May 29, 1999, p. 60.

42. Alejandro Reyes, "Drug Trafficking and the Guerrilla Movement in Colombia," in Bagley and Walker, *Drug Trafficking*, p. 125.

43. Ibid.

44. Kimberley L. Thachuk, "Justice, Drugs and Corruption in Colombia" (paper presented at the Illinois Conference on Latin American Studies, October 30–November 1, 1997), p. 10.

45. Thachuk, "Justice," p. 4.

46. McRae, "Illegal Narcotics Trade," pp. 16, 20.

47. Thachuk, "Justice," p. 5.

48. Reyes, in "Drug Trafficking," p. 126.

49. Zackrison and Bradley, "Colombian Sovereignty," pp. 2–3.

50. Chris Stephen, "King of the Serbian Jungle Is on the Prowl for Votes," *The Globe and Mail* (Toronto), December 18, 1993; Charles H. Fairbanks Jr., "The Postcommunist Wars," *Journal of Democracy* 6, no. 4 (1995): 26.

51. Martin van Creveld, *The Transformation of War* (New York: The Free Press, 1991), p. 193.

52. Helsinki Watch, *Report on the War in Abkhazia*, Human Rights Watch Arms Project 7:7 (1997), p. 11.

CHAPTER THREE

State Violence
and LGBT Rights

Mark Ungar

A global wave of democratization has swept away authoritarian regimes around the world since the 1980s, but left many nondemocratic practices intact. Amid continuing political uncertainty and economic change, one of the practices many new democracies are either unable or unwilling to alter is state violence. This tendency usually appears quickest when an upstart minority group demands its long-denied rights. In countries throughout the world, one such minority are lesbian, gay, bisexual, and transgender (lgbt) people. While there was just a scattering of lgbt organizations outside the West just twenty years ago, today they are found in eighty-six countries around the world,[1] where their challenges to laws, practices, and prejudices touch the rawest of nerves. Homophobia is deeply engrained in both society and the state, which often regard lgbt people as a health hazard, a threat to public morality, and a cultural imposition from decadent Western society. Leaders of many countries have called lgbt people everything from foreign agents to animals. Yet most of these countries have constitutions that pledge to protect the basic rights of all citizens and to prevent violence against them. Whether the state can keep such a pledge—even with a politically weak and socially despised part of society—is thus the flash point of state violence and the ultimate test of constitutional democracy.

State violence comes in many different forms. Discrimination by state agencies based on gender, race, and ethnicity is commonplace, as are torture and imprisonment of political troublemakers. Physical attacks on the urban poor and rural laborers, along with environmental destruction of indigenous peoples' lands, are forms of state violence against economically vulnerable groups. Violence against lgbt people, however, highlights the three principal, closely related types of state violence: "legal" violence, "semilegal" police violence, and extrajudicial violence. First, the state itself is saturated with violence. The courts, the prisons, and other government institutions allow discriminatory and violent practices against individuals in their charge. Second, most new democracies' police agencies are armed with edicts, military laws, "extraordinary" operations, and other provisions that encourage and allow them to carry out unaccountable "semi-legal" violence against lgbt and other people. Third, minorities such as lgbt people are a primary target of extrajudicial killings, torture, hate crimes, and harassment by death squads, vigilante groups, and individuals. Though rarely sponsored by the state, such activities are often directed by off-duty officials and either ignored or tacitly encouraged by a government with a constitutional responsibility to do the opposite.

These types of state violence exist in every region of the world and have survived through every kind of political and economic change. In the past, most repression grew out of government attempts to eliminate political enemies and subdue populations. As the state expanded and modernized, such violence became more efficient and routine. And for many new democracies, it has continued into the present, evolving from explicit policies carried out by designated security forces to a more unaccountable array of actions taking place behind democracy's cloak of legitimacy. Though usually less systemic and brutal than before, it is more amorphous and difficult to link to specific officials. From South America to East Asia, democratizing countries are grappling with powerful authoritarian legacies of repression, police power, and weak judiciaries. Political transition has sparked violent clashes between new freedoms and long-standing state practices, as the promise of democracy threatens to be engulfed by a resurgence of conflict and intolerance. Amid widespread privatization, spending cuts, and globalization, violence has become both an outlet of societal prejudices and an attempt by embattled nation-states to regain their footing.

Homophobia is a trip wire of these contemporary forms of state violence. Though lgbt organizing precedes democratization in many countries, prior to the 1980s groups in the developing world limited themselves to cultural events and to helping individuals. Democratic transitions then provided the freedoms of association, participation, and speech to take this work into the political arena, where it was further encouraged by the international lgbt movement and some favorable domestic court rulings. Many groups attained victories way out of proportion to their size and longevity. Eastern European organizations succeeded in getting long-standing antigay laws rescinded, for example, in a time of tremendous legal and political transformation.[2] But this shift into political activism and public visibility sparked backlashes. As nationalism and ethnic identities grew stronger and as countries were whipsawed by economic problems, the three types of state violence have built on and justified each other. Governments and political parties—stoked by the inflammatory rhetoric of religious and community leaders—found attacks on lgbt people to be politically beneficial. And lgbt communities found that they could not count on progressive parties, state agencies, or societal organizations to counteract this trend.

This chapter looks at the causes, patterns, and politics of anti-lgbt state violence—on all three levels—in three world regions where it has become a highly charged issue: Southern Africa, Eastern Europe, and Latin America. With nascent lgbt organizations bumping up against the limits of tolerance, stirring up political agitation and repressive practices, these regions are displaying the evolving nature of state violence.

Legal Violence

The most deeply rooted kind of state violence occurs within the state's own institutions. Arbitrary detention, poor legal aid, inhumane prisons, and biased courts all amount to a systematic "legal" state violence. Homosexuality itself is illegal in eighty-five countries. It is punished with death in eight of them,[3] and draws a prison term of ten years to life in seven, three to ten years in eleven, and up to three years in ten others. In most of the remaining countries, it carries variable and arbitrarily enforced punishments.[4] Even in countries without such laws, anti-lgbt discrimination pervades the judicial system, from harassing indictments and unfair trials, to singling out for abuse in the judicial and penitentiary systems. In Chile, for example, prison officials used only ten needles when they forcibly drew blood for HIV tests from thirty-seven gay inmates in August 1996. Overworked or corrupt prosecutors and public defenders often do not adequately represent lgbt clients.[5] In Azerbaijan, when the president pardoned ten thousand criminals in May 1998 in honor of the eightieth anniversary of the first Azeri state, he did not include in the amnesty those convicted of homosexuality. Throughout the world, in addition, lgbt people are rejected and fired from public-sectors jobs. The conservative PAN (Partido de Acción Nacional) mayor of the Mexican city of Aguascalientes fired all gay public employees in August 2000, for example, while the government of Thailand has tried to prevent gay teachers from working in the public schools.

Antigay laws are often grouped together with measures against other social ills. The Bar Association of Macedonia voted in 1995 to ban homosexuals and alcoholics from becoming lawyers, for example, and the same year Bulgarian television banned programs from depicting homosexuality, drug addiction, and prostitution. In Lebanon a human rights group and an Internet provider were put on trial in September 2000, under the Lebanese Military Code, for protecting a gay group's website. Throughout Latin America lgbt groups have been denied legal recognition because they offend public "morals." Efforts against antigay laws usually fail, such as the 1994 appeal against Nicaragua's antigay law.[6] When they do succeed, as in Ecuador or Ireland during the 1990s, they take years of political and court action.

Such legal violence often begins at the very top. In Africa, inflammatory anti-lgbt remarks by heads of state have become more common as many of the region's long-ruling leaders face economic problems and challenges to their rule.[7] Political openings have led to increased visibility of lgbt communities, which have been inspired by the success of South Africa's lgbt movement. In that country lgbt activists allied early on with the African National Congress and led the promulgation in 1995 of the world's first national constitution to prohibit discrimination based on sexual orientation. In the rest of southern Africa, though, the official response to such visibility has been more repression. In Swaziland the formation of the lgbt group GALESWA prompted the country's leaders to call homosexuality everything from "satanic" to a "sickness."[8] In Zambia the establishment of the Lesbian, Gay, Bisexual, and Transgender Association (LEGATRA) led to the country's president to call homosexuality "un-African" and the vice president to declare that LEGATRA would never be allowed to register as a recognized legal entity. In September 1998 the home affairs minister threatened to arrest the organization's leaders under the penal code's description of homosexuality as an "offense against morality."

In Zimbabwe, President Robert Mugabe has called gays "immoral," "repulsive," and "worse than animals." Asserting that homosexuality was a "Western perversion unknown in African culture," he has declared that gays have "no rights at all" and should be "hand[ed] over to the police" and jailed. When members of the group Gays and Lesbians of Zimbabwe (GALZ) tried to participate in the country's annual international book fair in 1995, and again the following year after winning court support, they were physically attacked. Since then, the country's press has hammered away at the lgbt community, several top leaders called for the castration of homosexuals, and a minister warned that the police will shut down GALZ for being an illegal organization.[9] In 1998 GALZ's cofounder was arrested on trumped-up sodomy charges. As they have spread throughout the region, such attacks have forced lgbt people to defend themselves in organizations ill-prepared to do so.

This legal repression is part of the histories of nearly every world region. Defined as a medical condition in 1869, "homosexuality" first shifted from a behavior to a public identity in Western Europe during the industrial revolution and the advent of the modern state. In the preindustrial era homosexual relations were either part of specific religious rituals or occurred within very limited community boundaries. The rise and spread of capitalism, which brought urbanization and the growth of the labor class, broke such traditional relations and increased the level of societal interaction. To reassert control, the Western state promoted the nuclear family and repressed subversive notions such as women's rights and homosexuality.

Efforts by the state to control society also occurred in the rest of the world, where colonialism re-enforced many cultures' homophobia and wiped out other cultures' tolerance of it. In Latin America, antigay violence extended back to the Aztecs, who executed with brutal methods men who had homosexual relations,[10] while some religions in Africa associated them with witchcraft. In other societies, from South Asia to North America, individuals who did not fit into either gender role were given positions of honor as priests or judges. In most areas, though, homosexuality was tolerated as part of religious ceremonies and premarital relations, such as in some Mesoamerican nations and in the vodun regions of West Africa. But it was rarely acknowledged, and few men identified as "homosexuals" involving physical attraction to members of the same sex. These subtle accommodations were broken by the emerging dominance of the modern state and of European imperialism. During the expansion of Islam through Africa and Asia, for example, the middle-class religious establishment came down against homosexuality in its attempts "to safeguard or promote traditional values in the face of" an increasingly powerful military elite publicly engaging in prohibited practices such as homosexuality.[11] Unable to stamp out such behavior, though, Islamic states resigned themselves to the continuation of homosexuality and prostitution, which allowed "the Islamic patriarchy system to withstand the stress of its inherent contradictions."[12] But in the nineteenth century Western colonialism and the introduction of Western mores broke this "secret equilibrium"[13] with laws and strong condemnations of homosexuality. After independence, the postcolonial authoritarian regimes in the Middle East have institutionalized these antigay policies into their laws. In every other region of the world, abetted by cultural attitudes such as Spanish machismo,[14] such laws are justified by assertions that homosexuality is an imposed "Western" behavior, when in fact antihomosexual laws are the real legacy of the West. Although strongly supported by the religious establishment of Sri Lanka, for example, the country's laws that allow for twelve years imprisonment for homosexuality came from the 1883 British penal code.

Semilegal Violence

In many democracies, state officials' views of individual rights and public order often run contrary to those of the constitution. To get around such conflicts, officials often use constitutionally dubious predemocratic laws that stayed on the books despite a formal transition to democracy. When adopted by police agencies, this approach leads to a "semilegal" violence that is justified by written laws but falls outside the constitution. Police forces in most countries are trained better for subduing rather than protecting the population,[15] and are bound by "few, if any, occasions in which anyone has a legal right to resist police use of force, even if police use it improperly."[16] Such power is boosted by the weakness of the two institutions that are supposed to oversee the police—the legislature and the judiciary—and by the widely held belief that violations of constitutional civil rights are necessary to control crime and maintain social order. When political and societal uncertainty is high, when structures and rules are new, when crime is rising, and when officers expect antagonism from citizens—all conditions common in new democracies—governments tend to give security forces even wider leeway and allow continuation of many of the violent practices fine-tuned during the predemocratic era.

In such environments, semilegal police violence against lgbt people is usually based on vaguely worded laws, regulations, and practices. They include medical and psychiatric "treatment" with psychotropic drugs in Eastern Europe and the former Soviet Union, "hooliganism" and public order laws in Asia, police edicts in Latin America, and sodomy laws and crimes against "morality," "nature," and "public order" everywhere. Even when such "laws" are formally rescinded, they often continue in practice.[17]

In Eastern Europe, for example, police still draw up "pink lists" of known and "suspected" homosexuals, and carry out harassing investigations such as home searches and telephone monitoring, and raid bars on pretenses such as searches for illegal drugs. In February 1998 Moscow police raided the city's main gay club, where they beat patrons and threatened to "shoot all you faggots."[18] In Bulgaria nonuniformed police raid organizations that publish gay material, supported by the general attorney's assertion that homosexuality endangers national morality. In the March 1997 raid on the "Flamingo Center," they beat the head of the organization and his family.

Those taken to police stations are often tortured in order to extract "confessions" and the names of other people, or just as a form of intimidation. In Albania in 1994 the police arrested and beat three gay activists, one to the point of unconsciousness, in an effort to extract from him the name of their organization's president. In Romania many of those arrested under Article 200 of the penal code, which punishes homosexuality with up to three years in prison, are beaten with truncheons and slammed against tables, to force them to sign confessions. The discrimination that comes with being "out" prevents these victims from seeking redress, further widening the police's realm of impunity.

In contemporary Latin America, despite the spread of democracy, ongoing semilegal police violence is the most serious problem facing that region's lgbt people. As one of society's most "undesirable" populations—popularly associated with AIDS, prostitution, the degradation of street life, and the breakdown of morality—lgbt people have faced the brunt of police repression. Such repression of undesirables is a long-established practice. It dates back to the colonial era, starting as a means to control peasants and indigenous people, then evolving to repress leftists and unionists in the first half of the twentieth century, and most recently becoming an instrument against the poor, immigrants, youth, and lgbt people. Particularly targeted by police are transvestites and transsexuals, hundreds of whom have been assaulted, raped, and killed in police stations throughout Latin America. Economic pressures and skyrocketing crime have led governments to resurrect predemocratic laws originally used to crack down on political unrest, as well as to ignore growing practices such as police killings of delinquents, often under the guise of "shoot-outs." In Mexico, although federal law and a few state laws mention homosexuality only in reference to the corruption of minors, lgbt people are repressed through "morality" ordinances, such as the federal penal code Article 201 regulating "Transgressions Against Morality and Public Decency." These regulations give the police wide leeway to harass, detain, and sometimes kill homosexuals. At least twenty-four gay men, most of them transvestites, were murdered between 1990 and 1995, and in most of these cases there was evidence of either police complicity or direct police involvement. A majority of the killings of fifteen men in Chiapas state between 1991 and 1993 involved weapons reserved for the exclusive use of the military and police agencies.[19]

In Venezuela, one of the region's oldest democracies, this pattern is exemplified by the country's Law of Vagabonds and Crooks (LVM: Ley de Vagos y Maleantes). Enacted in 1939 by a military regime, the law allows the "preventative" detention of anyone that has not committed a crime but is deemed a "threat to society." The law's wide and vague definition of such "vagabonds" ranges from individuals without a "legitimate" profession to those "who habitually walk the street … fomenting idleness and other vices." Like police edicts in other countries, the LVM does not have the due process protections of ordinary penal law. While penal law deals with specific criminal acts, the LVM focuses on precriminal character decided in a highly subjective manner with no presumption of innocence. Unlike normal penal laws, in addition, the LVM can be handled entirely by executive and police officials. Although the investigation and first-instance decision is made by first-instance courts or the judicial police (PTJ: Policía Técnica Judicial), the state governor officially sentences LVM detainees, and "competent authorities," usually from the executive branch's Justice Ministry, can then prolong confinement if the prisoner's "correction" has not "been obtained." The law is used frequently against homosexuals because a person charged under the LVM three or more times— common for those netted in police bar raids—can be incarcerated for up to three years. So while the LVM "of course violat[es] sacred constitutional rights, [it] allows for the immediate way to deal with those who are considered scourges."[20] About a hundred of the approximately five hundred people arrested each year under the law are held without any hearing, and many are sent to the notoriously inhumane El Dorado prison in the Amazon without knowledge of the judges presiding in their cases. The government's lack of interest in modifying the LVM reflects a consensus that the executive branch needs such laws to free its criminal policy from a cumbersome judiciary. [21]

This gap between law and practice, at the heart of police treatment of lgbt people, is rooted in the friction between enacted police power and the actual physical and legal powers of police agencies. In a democracy elected officials have the sole constitutional authority to create laws, juridical norms, regulations, prohibitions, orders, authorizations, and other measures to restrict rights and "to impair actions or deeds contrary to law"[22] as "necessary for the common good."[23] Thus, "police power" would belong to the legislative branch, while the police would simply be the set of agencies that carries it out. But in most countries these rules have been formulated and controlled since independence by authoritarian executives, making it difficult for democratic legislatures to wrest back police power and reform undemocratic law enforcement regulations. Many measures that affect individual liberties continue to be administered by executive agencies such as interior ministries, and can be supplemented by a "general delegation" of police power to the executive in situations such as an absence of implementing norms.[24]

In the process of implementing criminal laws, police agencies themselves often redefine, reinterpret, and reformulate them to the point where the police's physical and administrative powers become the de facto "police power." This usurpation is rooted in the police's unique role: few other agencies carry out government policy with such constant, direct, and dangerous interaction with the citizenry. The police thus shape the protection and interpretation of civil and political rights, such as through monitoring political protests, and the inability of many police forces to handle such tasks easily triggers the recourse of violent tactics. Even attempts by legislators to delineate or clarify police functions can generate serious frictions between police power and the police's powers, with clashes erupting over jurisdiction, accountability, arrest and criminal investigation procedures, how much it is to be reactive to criminal acts and how much it is to be proactive to prevent them, and coordination between street police and judicial police and between forces of different geographic jurisdictions. All these frictions are particularly acute in new or weak democracies, since most regulations must be created from scratch or overhauled through an arduous reform process. Increasing coordination carries political risks, since police agencies are not used to sharing power, for example, while many "public order" measures spark conflict with a society eager to curb police abuse. Despite the extensive political change throughout the world in recent decades, as a result, "by and large, the same kind of [police] mechanisms continue to be used."[25] In addition to a high level of distrust, low accountability over individual officials, and pressure on the police to be effective, the institutional disarray of most democracies gives the police more power and impunity. Time limits on detention should be defined by those with police power, for example, but what good are limits regularly exceeded by police because there are no judges available to take the cases?

Since the transition to democracy, such conditions have characterized the wide range of municipal, state, military, intelligence, and judicial forces in nearly every Latin American country. There are several causes for the continuation of such patterns. First, by their sheer power, the police have been able to carry forward past practices into the democratic era, often encouraged or at least ignored by elected regimes worried about appearing weak on public order and crime. In

Chile, for example, the democratic regime succeeding Augusto Pinochet in 1990 largely left the powerful *Carabinero* national police force intact, despite its role in the seventeen-year-old dictatorship. After the fall of Venezuela's military regime in 1958, the democratic government made the police central in its ample use of executive power to control crime, the leftist insurgency, and a highly politicized society, with pressure put on judges to jail guerrilla suspects and to curtail due process guarantees.[26]

Such power has also been bolstered by the increases in crime and by growing concern about drug trafficking. With the regional average of thirty homicides per 100,000 people at six times the world average, and with about twenty-four assaults per minute, Latin America has been strengthening its police forces. Calling crime a national security problem, for example, in 1998 the Peruvian government adopted ten anticrime decrees, many based on antiguerrilla measures that had been causing rights abuses. These laws endanger basic rights and accountability by transferring many enforcement powers from civilian courts and the National Police to military courts and the notoriously abusive National Intelligence Service (SIN), prohibiting courts from calling police officers who interrogate suspects, and allowing immunity or penalty reductions for those providing information. These decrees will also increase arbitrary and biased prosecutions, as Decree No. 895 has done by creating the crime of "aggravated terrorism" and giving the police power to detain suspects for up to fifteen days and military tribunals to try civilians charged with the crime. The growth of drug trafficking and of antinarcotics operations in response since the 1980s has revived a militarized approach to internal order, in addition, with new drug laws proving particularly immune to legal oversight such as searches without a warrant. Bolivia's 1988 antitrafficking Law 1008 violates many basic rights and fosters discrimination,[27] for example, while external funding of its new Special Narcotics Trafficking Force makes police reform unlikely.

The power of police agencies is further bolstered by their controls over criminal investigation. The law has "conferred great power to police officials to shape the legal proceedings that should be decided by the judge,"[28] and police officials have de facto control over most criminal procedures. Many countries have moved away from the European model of limiting the powerful judicial police agency to preliminary inquiries. Police often also continue as an auxiliary after the information is turned over to the judge, with all police actions having force of proof unless proven false. In the process, officials often destroy evidence, defy court orders, protect accused officials, "use false witnesses, invent facts, . . . bring false charges against innocent persons,"[29] and shake down suspects for money. Many say that detainee access to legal support puts the police at a disadvantage because they believe that public defenders advise detainees to withhold incriminating information. "In the activities of the police pre-trial, judicially speaking, there are no controls, except for the presence" of the *fiscal* (an attorney general official) in detainee statements to the police.[30] Even on the rare occasions when *fiscales* are actually present, they often are in one part of the station while forced confessions and other abuses occur in secret basements. Overburdened judges, meanwhile, "tend to base [their] decisions on police actions without an investigation of them and without a deep conviction regarding the veracity or falsehood of the facts."[31] In contrast to the slow judiciary, the police have "a constant, intense, sustained, efficient, and vast investigative activity"[32] and display "blunt resistance . . . to obey[ing] judicial decisions."[33]

Such authority, finally, is further bolstered by long-standing institutional weaknesses such as inadequate training, poor discipline, and vague definitions of infractions.[34] In such environments, officers develop hostile views. In one study, police agents justified the use of violence by a person's behavior or attitude in 83 percent of the cases and the need to have "control" in 45 percent.[35] Combined with new laws, such demeanors do not bode well for treatment of such an unpopular group as the lgbt community. In Ecuador police used their authority in July 2000 to detain and beat gay pride marchers in the city of Guayaquil. Even if a homosexual were willing to formally accuse the police of such violence, there is little chance of follow-up. In fact, the many reports sent by lgbt groups to judicial police authorities have not even been acknowledged.

Extrajudicial Violence

Killings, disappearances, hate crimes, intimidation and other types of violence perpetrated by individuals, "death squads," and other loosely formed groups are a serious and growing problem throughout the world. Members of minority ethnicities, immigrants, homosexuals, suspected criminals, prostitutes and other marginalized people are all targets. The state's denial of such actions or negligence in investigating them only encourage more violence and can cause its mutation into new forms. New studies are beginning to get a handle on understanding this phenomenon in the contemporary world,[36] but have yet to detail emerging patterns of such violence against specific groups.

As a group, lgbt people are consistently and widely victimized by extrajudicial violence. Even in cities as cosmopolitan as Prague, gay men are regularly beaten by skinheads and others. When chased out of cities, many lgbt people are beaten and isolated by the hometowns to which they return. In several Eastern European countries bombs have destroyed gay bars and right-wing parties have attacked lgbt individuals. When a bomb exploded outside a gay club in the capital of Latvia in February 1995, for instance, the main suspect was a member of an extremist party that called for action against homosexuals. The openness of violence attests to the social tolerance of it. In September 2000 three gunmen blocked the exit of a crowded Johannesburg bar while other assailants opened fire inside.

A lack of police protection and investigation, of course, only encourages such violence. The chair of Moscow's Triangle group, an umbrella lgbt organization, reports that "homosexuals are a prime target for continuous attacks, killings, theft, blackmail, and extortion, because they are still more afraid of the police than they are of the bandits."[37] Even when reported and documented, extrajudicial violence is usually hard to investigate because of perpetrators' clandestine methods and choice of tactics. After the office of *Sister Namibia*, a magazine affiliated with the country's lgbt movement, was torched in July 2000, for example, investigators were too slow to gather incriminating evidence.

Government disregard for anti-lgbt violence is also blatant in Latin America. Murders of gay men are often categorized as "sex crimes" by the authorities, as with the July 1992 killings of five well-known Mexican gay men. Equally as common is inadequate investigation. The Mexican Human Rights Commission denounced the slow investigation of the murders of the five Mexican men, while police in Guatemala have not adequately investigated the 1997 drive-by shootings of five transvestites. Similarly, seven gay transvestites were killed between April and June 1998 in El Salvador, and, despite warnings by the killer of more deaths and bomb threats to the lgbt group Between Friends, the National Civilian Police did not initiate any official investigation and regarded each killing as an isolated incident.[38] In Brazil approximately 1,600 lgbt people have been murdered since 1980.[39] One of them was a city councilman in the state of Alagoas who was abducted, tortured, and decapitated in 1992. Renildo dos Santos had been receiving death threats since he came out as a bisexual on local radio, but received no help from the judges and other authorities to whom he reported these threats, even after being shot and wounded. The city council, meanwhile, stripped him of his seat for committing acts "incompatible with Parliamentary decorum."[40] Only 5 percent of police officials accused of antigay killings in Brazil have gone on trial.

Economic change and uncertainty aggravate extrajudicial violence against lgbt people. Lesbian activists in Peru in the mid-1980s claimed that people cared less about others' sexual orientation because they were too occupied with making ends meet. But the opposite is more likely, as downturns spur action against immigrants and other minorities. Although the world is growing wealthier, it is growing more unequal, causing frustration by the majority of those not benefiting from improvements. And, as with political agitation, it is not just a downturn that creates violence, but change in general. Some of the biggest jumps in antigay violence, in fact, occur in countries undergoing the most traumatic economic change, such as South Africa and Belarus. And as entire economies and labor markets heave themselves into a new global order, such change has become the norm.

The Politics of State Violence

Each of these three types of violence are fueled not only by each other, but by the political environments in which they occur. Most broadly, anti-lgbt state violence reflects shifts in state-society relations caused by the declining power of the nation-state in a rapidly integrating and decreasingly ideological world. Losing ground amid disillusion with traditional political organizations and loosening allegiances to governments, both state officials and societal leaders will tap into popular stereotypes and frustrations. More and more opportunities for corruption and economic gain lead them to cooperate or work with groups that engage in extrajudicial actions, with growth industries such as drug trafficking creating tight links between state officials and criminal elements in the societies they govern.

Taking advantage of the freedoms and political opportunities opened up by democratization, lgbt communities have made great strides in countries around the world. Antigay laws have been rescinded in every region, while greater discussion and debate in many countries is gradually increasing societal acceptance of lgbt people. But anti-lgbt violence is often immune to such progress. In Brazil, for example, there are dozens of lgbt groups and most of the provincial constitutions specifically mention rights based on sexual orientation, representing a level of protection unknown even in Europe. But killings of homosexuals have only gone up, with the 125 murders in 1996 being an increase of 12 percent over the previous year's rate. In Mexico political openings over the past few years have led to an unprecedented level of political organizing and successes by lgbt groups and their allies, but there are still approximately 125 murders of gay men each year.

In post-Communist Eastern Europe strong ties with Western Europe and a high level of urbanization and education have generated a visible lgbt community with media access and significant political influence. But the growth of nationalism, the increasing power of religious organizations, and deep economic and ethnic divisions in many of these countries have led to a backlash stronger than the lgbt movement itself. In Poland the church lobbied successfully against the inclusion of provisions that protect the rights of lgbt people in the new constitution. In Belarus government officials attended an antigay university conference and, in September 2000, banned a gay pride march. When Romania's new and sympathetic government proposed a legislative repeal of Article 200 in June 1998, a sweeping majority of leftists and conservatives in the House of Deputies rejected the measure, using the opportunity to condemn homosexuality in general and to rally the backing of the country's Orthodox Christian Church.[41] Since then the country's Christian Orthodox Students Organization has worked to put an antigay measure on the ballot; in contrast, only one of several gay groups formed since the end of Communist rule still survives, and that one only because of the efforts of expatriates.

Croatia is another country in the region where politics have generated the three forms of anti-lgbt violence. The country's first lesbian and gay organization, LIGMA, was founded in the early 1990s, energized by its work with refugees and its contact with international organizations. A lack of funding, political harassment by the government against all nongovernmental organizations, cultural and societal pressure, and internal ethnic divisions among its members, however, all led to the group's disintegration by 1993.[42] LIGMA's cofounder was arrested, beaten, and confined to a psychiatric hospital. Most problematic was the fact that the group was housed by a small political party which itself came under pressure from the increasingly authoritarian government of President Franko Tudjman. Feminists, homosexuals, Muslims, and other sectors of society that did not fit into or adequately promote the government's strong brand of nationalism were regarded as subversives at worst and outsiders at best. Some Croatian gay and lesbian activists redirected their efforts in the fight against AIDS, at first with some support from the Ministry of Health, but budgetary problems and the lack of political will led to curtailment of this work as well. Despite the political freedoms accompanying the fall of Communism and independence from Yugoslavia, Croatia has backtracked into state repression and cultural intolerance.

In many countries hopes of breaking the cycle of state violence rests on the political capabilities of the lgbt movements. But these movements are usually weak and divided into a wide variety of groups—gay men, lesbians, bisexuals, transgender people, and transvestites—each with its own separate identities and communities. Differences among these groups can be marked; middle- and upper-class gay men tend to focus on AIDS and on antigay laws, for example, while working-class lesbians emphasize economic and other forms of discrimination.[43] The concentration of lgbt organizing in urban areas reflects and further accentuates differences in the levels of tolerance and economic status between gays and lesbians in large cities and those in small towns or rural areas. Age can also be divisive, with older people being far more reluctant to be out in public. Lgbt people in countries beset by divisions of ethnicity, religion, race, or geography, finally, have a harder time establishing effective organizations.

Coalitions with political organizations and parties, essential to mounting any serious challenge to state violence, are usually weak. This weakness stems from several conditions, among them the lgbt movement's unique dependence on people willing to be "out" to society. Because most lgbt activists try to minimize the risks to their lives, their groups become centered on the one person or handful of people who are willing to be public. Such a lack of visible figures makes the community appear small, scaring off support from established political organizations. State repression itself can fuel such a tendency. In general, "if organizations with a strong sense of urgency see themselves embattled, they often tend toward oligarchic leadership patterns," and if political networks "are confined to small circles of trust, as is often the case in politically repressed societies, they may immunize them against dominant influence and even support daring action, but they may well not be sufficient to" develop the practical experience and political skills required for effective political action.[44] Only when lgbt groups are able to ally with major political parties can they hope to achieve durable change. In countries such as Mexico, Argentina, and Hungary, support by ruling or strong opposition parties is making a dent in lgbt violence. A prolonged but successful fight in 1999 by the Ukrainian group Nash Mir to gain legal recognition became a model for similar efforts, such as in Panama the following year.

But in most countries lgbt concerns are ignored even by most human rights groups, which may support them in private but do not want to expend valuable political capital on them. Such alienation often boosts the factions of lgbt groups that favor protest over cooperation. Groups committed to peaceful work often get channeled into AIDS work, which has more legitimacy, acceptance, and urgency. Since July 1999, for instance, the Nigerian rights group Nigeria Alliance Rights has been able to insert promotion of lgbt freedom in the context of its growing AIDS organizing around the country.[45] This work usually does not mark those involved as homosexuals, furthermore, and international AIDS organizations are a better source of funding and expertise than lgbt ones.

Even without such divisions, the question of identity is problematic for any country's lgbt community. Like other social and political movements, the lgbt movement rotates around formation of and changes in identity, which spill over into and shape political strategies. Each sector of the community continually struggles with and develops its identity, always questioning but never fully deciding who it does and does not cover. Amid such debate over the very nature of sexual orientation,[46] such layered identities complicate the strategies adopted by lgbt groups. Demonstrations, cultural events, and the use of symbols build lgbt identity and express it to society[47] but often compete with contrary trends such as materialism and individualism. One of the most common complaints by lgbt activists around the world, in fact, is over the extent to which socializing outstrips activism and economics overwhelms politics. As regions such as Eastern Europe democratize amid neoliberalism, lgbt individuals in urban areas can have their identity and community without the dangers of being "out" to society. Upper- and middle-class men, who usually have the most political power within the lgbt community and benefit most from the new economic order, thus become disengaged from those in the community more vulnerable to state violence.

Involvement by the growing international lgbt movement also affects legal violence by lending credence to charges of Western meddling, but the contacts, technology, organization, and other resources they provide are invaluable. More and more, groups around the world are tapping into international organizations to put pressure on their governments. The first known established gay liberation group was founded in Berlin in 1897, followed in subsequent decades by organizations in Britain, the Netherlands, Scandinavia, and the United States. But it was New York's 1969 Stonewall riots, in which the mostly transvestite patrons of a bar fought back against a routine police raid, that led to the modern lgbt movement. After Stonewall, groups formed throughout the West, followed by organizations in Latin America in the late 1970s, in Africa and Asia in the 1980s, and Eastern

Europe in the 1990s. But many of these organizations were formed by activists with experience in the West, and at a time when the international movement was already firmly rooted in a Western model. These groups' international activity is channeled primarily through the three international organizations: the International Lesbian and Gay Association (ILGA), centered primarily in Europe,[48] the U.S.-based International Gay and Lesbian Human Rights Commission, and the human rights organization Amnesty International.[49]

Although these organizations incorporate non-Western groups, they are based primarily on Western concepts of sexual "orientation" and political strategies focusing on civil and political rights. Such strategies work in the West and in some international forums, and also help lay the groundwork for long-term acceptance, but cannot be easily duplicated elsewhere and often incite state violence in the short run. A $1,000 grant from the Norwegian government to the Zambian groups LEGATRA in 1994, for example, angered Zambian government and religious officials and propelled them into a fresh round of anti-lgbt threats. A concerted campaign by an alliance of national and international organizations against Romania's Article 200 led to the freedom of several people jailed under the law, for example, but not to an elimination of the law itself.

Just as lgbt groups are reaching across borders, in addition, so too are anti-lgbt movements. Antigay laws and demonstrations in the Caribbean and Africa, for example, are partly a result of both antigay British colonial legal legacies as well as increased contacts among these countries. In Latin America the current spread of evangelical churches and their strong antigay message are increasing homophobia throughout that region.

Conclusion

Legal, semilegal, and extrajudicial violence against lgbt people in many of the world's new democracies result from the potent combination of authoritarian legacies, weak governments, unaccountable police forces, and deeply rooted societal homophobia. These elements manifest themselves as questionable laws, "public order" measures, threatening political rhetoric, abusive law enforcement, and extrajudicial activity—which all reinforce and stimulate each other. Roberto Gómez, a Latin American gay rights activist, had been harassed, sexually abused, fired from jobs, and arrested eight times before he began a small rights group in his home country. "What more," he asks, "did I have to lose?"[50] But the steady police violence and legal impediments directed against his group eventually forced him to flee the country—leaving its waning lgbt movement that much worse off. Even in an era of democracy, his condition reveals both the range of obstacles faced by lgbt people and their determination to end them.

When a government is unable to uphold a society's standards of "morality" through constitutional measures, it will continue to do so through unconstitutional ones. When unpopular leaders need a good diversion, homosexuality will continue to be one of the most convenient ones. And as long as the struggle for lgbt rights continues to get caught up in politics and legal debates, violence against lgbt people will continue to happen.

NOTES

1. International Lesbian and Gay Organization, ilga@ilga.com, December 2000.
2. Russia, Belarus, Georgia, Moldava, and Ukraine decriminalized same-sex relations in the early 1990s, while Kazakhstan followed suit in 1997 and Kyrgyzstan in 1998. However, homosexual acts between men remain crimes in Armenia, Azerbaijan, Tajikistan, Turkmenistan, and Uzbekistan. In addition, the Chechen Republic, Ichkeriya, a part of the Russian federation, has considered its own separate criminal code which would punish consenting same-sex acts by caning and possibly death.
3. These countries are Mauritania, Sudan, Saudi Arabia, Yemen, Qatar, Kuwait, Iran, and Afghanistan. Each of these countries practices a strict interpretation of Islamic *shari'a* law.
4. Many other countries are employing homophobia in high-level political actions, such as the charges of sodomy against the finance minister in Malaysia and the trial of the former president in Zimbabwe.
5. Such actions, of course, are not limited to the developing world. In the United States, during the trials of several people sentenced to death, inflammatory homophobic attacks were used by the prosecution, and, in one case, by the defense. Amnesty International, *Breaking the Silence* (New York: AI Press, 1994), p. 41.
6. Article 205 of Nicaragua's penal code says that "anyone who induces, promotes, propagandizes or practices in scandalous form sexual intercourse between persons of the same sex commits the crime of sodomy and shall incur one to three years' imprisonment."
7. Kenya's president, Daniel arap Moi, said that homosexuality "is against African norms and traditions." "Africa: Undercover Homosexuality in Kenya," *Exit Newspaper,* South Africa, September 1998.
8. New Jersey: Magnus Hirschfeld Center for Human Rights, press release, March 26, 1998. These attacks caused GALESWA's founder to lose his job. In Namibia the president's "condemnation" of homosexuals prompted the formation of the Rainbow Project, which then allied itself with the women's association, Sister Namibia. See Niko Kisting, *Report from Namibia,* Rainbow Project Internet Report, May 1997.
9. "Police have no basis to ban GALZ," editorial by Tinokkumbira Kurarama, *The Daily Gazette,* Harare, Zimbabwe.
10. Salvador Novo, *Las Locas, El Sexo, Los Burdeles* (Mexico City: Novaro, 1972), p.12.
11. Bruce W. Dunne, "Homosexuality in the Middle East: An Agenda for Historical Research," *Arab Studies Quarterly* 12, nos. 3&4 (summer/fall 1990): 67.
12. Ibid., p. 69.
13. Abdel-wahab Bouhdiba, *Sexuality in Islam* (London: Routledge & Kegan Paul, 1985), p. 193.
14. See Ian Lumsden, *Homosexuality, Society, and the State in Mexico* (Toronto: Canadian Gay Archives, 1991), pp. 61–62.
15. Many see the character of government and police action to be "virtually indistinguishable. It is not an accident that dictatorial regimes are referred to as 'police states.' Police

activity is crucial for defining the practical extent of human freedom." David Bayley, *Patterns of Policing* (New Brunswick: Rutgers University Press, 1985), p. 189.

16. Carl B. Klockars, "A Theory of Excessive Force and Its Control," in *Police Violence*, ed. William A. Geller and Hans Toch (New Haven: Yale University Press, 1996), p. 2.

17. Prior to the repeal of the main antigay laws in 1992, China regularly convicted homosexuals of "hooliganism" and sent them to be "reeducated at labor camps," sometimes through electric shock therapy. It continues to persecute lgbt people who attempt to organize into groups. Such conditions are common even in many stable democracies. In Turkey transsexual activists are routinely detained under a law against "insulting the memory of Mustafa Kemal Atatürk," the founder of modern Turkey. In December 1989 the owner of a cultural center in which other transvestites held a press conference was arrested under the penal code's Article 536, which prohibits "the illegal distribution of leaflets in public places." Gary Wu, director of the International Chinese Comrades Association, interview by the author, August 15, 1997.

18. "Black Nights for Russia's Gays," *Sydney Morning Herald*, February 14, 1998.

19. "Psicosis en Chiapas por la Cacería de Homosexuales," *Proceso* 852, Mexico City, March 1, 1993, p. 26. Such violence was coupled with antigay actions by mayors of the rightist National Action Party (PAN) in cities such as Guadalajara and Monterrey.

20. José Fernando Nuñez, who introduced legislative and judicial reforms to strengthen the LVM, interview by the author, April 25, 1995.

21. María Antioneta Acuñade, President, Association of Public Defenders, interview by the author, May 1995.

22. León Duguit, *Manuel de droit constitucionnel: theorie general* (Paris: Ancienne Librairie Thorin et Fils, 1907), p. 498.

23. José Roberto Dromi, *Policia y Derecho* (Buenos Aires: Ediciones UNSTA, 1985), p. 793.

24. Guido Zanobini, *Corso di Diritto Amministrativo, Tomo I* (Milano: Dott. A. Giuffrè, 1958–1959), p. 54.

25. Bayley, *Patterns of Policing*, p. 174.

26. José M. Rico, *Crimen y Justicia en América Latina* (México: Siglo Veintiuno Editores, 1985), p. 115.

27. A study of Bolivian drug trafficking courts shows that Law 1008 involves restriction of many economic and civil rights as well as discrimination in arrests and prosecution against young, male, indigenous migrant agricultural workers, while avoiding the heads of drug networks (Roberto Laserna, "Las Drogas y La Justicia en Cochabamba: Los 'Narocos en el País de Culpables," XVIII International Congress of the Latin American Studies Association, March 10, 1994). Since 1988, however, some of Law 1008's more draconian provisions have been eliminated. Judges in other countries stepping up antitrafficking efforts also believe that drug laws discriminate against the poor.

28. Luis Gerardo Gabaldón, "La Policía y el Uso de la Fuerza Física en Venezuela," in *Justicia en la Calle*, ed. Waldmann (Medellín: Konrad Adenaver Stiftung, 1996), p. 186.

29. "La Ley Antidroga es una Patente de Corso de Jueces y Policías," *El Nacional*, September 9, 1988.

30. Saúl Ron Brasch, Superior Court Criminal Judge, interview by the author, March 22, 1995.

31. Thamara Santos Alvins, *Violencia Criminal y Violencia Policial en Venezuela* (Maracaibo: Instituto de Criminologia de la Universidad de Zulia, 1992), p. 86.

32. Esteban Agudo Freytes, "La Policía Técnica Judicial," in *Conferencia de los Jueces* (Caracas, 1983).

33. Saúl Ron Brasch, Superior Court Criminal Judge, interview by the author, March 22, 1995.

34. Venezuela's primary disciplinary code considers the undue use of arms and the mistreatment of detainees to be principal infractions, but does not define either one. The "lack of a clearly defined conception regarding" police duties enhances the discretion of individual officials. Article 282 of the penal code allows agents to use arms in cases of legitimate defense and of defense of the public order, but these conditions are only vaguely defined as "not trespassing the limits imposed by the law." Former police commissioner Rafael Briceño Muñoz, in O. de Pimentel, "Víctimas y Victimarios," *El Diario de Caracas,* June 4, 1989, p. 20. Police impunity extends to pretrial investigation against state officials charged with "exceeding the exercises of their functions." In Venezuela about two-thirds of such investigations are against police officers. They last anywhere from six months to over six years, and sometimes are never completed. Such delays make it highly difficult to produce witnesses and evidence by the time of the trial, resulting in a conviction rate of police officers of just 6 to 19 percent. In similar murder charges, convicted police officials receive an average sentence five and a half years shorter than do convicted civilians.

35. Gabaldón, "La Policía y el Uso de la Fuerza Física en Venezuela," pp. 269–81.

36. See Bruce B. Campbell and Arthur D. Brenner, eds., *Death Squads in Global Perspective* (New York: St. Martin's, 2000).

37. Wockner International News #62, Internet report, July 6, 1995.

38. Fox News–Reuters Ltd., "Seventh Gay Transvestite Killed," June 5, 1998; "Salvadoran Gay Community Targeted," Amnesty International news release, June 22, 1998.

39. Luiz Mott, *Epidemic of Hate* (Bahía, Brazil: Grupo Gay da Bahía, 1996), p. 53; "Violations of Human Rights and Murders of Gay Men, Lesbian, and Transvestites in Brazil," press release, Grupo Gay da Bahía, February 3, 1999.

40. Amnesty International, *Breaking the Silence,* p. 13.

41. Similarly, the debate over discriminatory laws in Cyprus, brought about by pressure from Europe on Cyprus to conform to European rights standards, led to antigay attacks and demonstrations. "Better Naïve Than Gay, Says Archbishop," *Cyprus News,* October 14, 1998.

42. Author interviews with LIGMA members, Zagreb, Croatia, August 1993.

43. Individuals within the groups often change their own identities, furthermore, and many separate their personal identity from their public activism. Fragmenting the community further are differences between "social constructionists," who view their sexual orientation as a product of social norms, and "essentialists," who view it as a characteristic derived at birth, like race. Each perspective generates distinct political strategies. While social constructionists emphasize cultural differences and experiences, essentialists use traditional human rights concepts to demand from the state the same kinds of protections afforded to other minorities.

44. Dietrich Rueschemeyer, "The Self-Organization of Society and Democratic Rule: Specifying the Relationship" (prepared for the 1997 Annual Meeting of the American Political Science Association, August 1997), p. 6–7. Of the fraction of the lgbt community involved in political activity, there is the further tension between the predisposition to protest against the government and the need to sometimes cooperate with it.

45. Behind the Mask, www.mask.org.za, a website of the lgbt movement in Africa.

46. See Edward Stein, ed., *Forms of Desire: Sexual Orientation and the Social Constructionist Controversy* (New York: Garland, 1990); Steven Epstein, "Gay Politics, Ethnic Identity: The Limits of Social Constructionism," *Socialist Review* 93/93 (1987).

47. See Eduardo Canel, "New Social Movement Theory and Resource Mobilization: The Need for Integration," in *Organizing Dissent: Contemporary Social Movements in Theory and Practice* ed. W. Carroll (Toronto: Garamond Press, 1992).

48. Founded in 1978, ILGA organized around the goals of overturning homophobic laws, stopping rights violations through lobbying and public campaigns, supporting local groups, and participating in international forums. Although ILGA grew out of meetings held by Western European groups dominated by men, by the mid-1980s it had became more international and gender-balanced.

49. AI has been active on this issue since its 1991 decision to work on behalf of individuals imprisoned because of their homosexuality. AI members in twenty countries have created committees to work with the international structure to investigate rights violations and incorporate lgbt rights in the organization's missions, publicity, and campaigns.

50. Personal communication, December 2000.

CHAPTER FOUR

Globalization, Weak States, and the Death Toll in East Asia

Bridget Welsh

O n the morning of July 30 in the small marketplace of Labuan in West Java, as shoppers gathered around a shop to sell gold and silver, a man screamed out "*pencuri*"(thief)![1] In an instant, an angry mob rushed forward and a youth used a cutlass to attack the man thus accused. Egged on by the crowd, the youth decapitated the *pencuri* without a moment's hesitation. As members of the mob stepped forward to inspect his handiwork, the youth strutted away, leaving behind the dead body. Within minutes, everyone moved on to shop as if nothing had happened. A few hours later, when the crowd had completely dissipated, a policeman arrived to make arrangements for the body. When asked why the policeman had not arrived earlier, he replied: "Violence is normal now. There was nothing I could do.... I am one man, while they are many."

Unfortunately, the policeman's remarks were correct; violence has become more frequent in Indonesia and in East Asia as a whole.[2] Over fifty thousand people were killed in the region in the last two years in vigilante killings, ethnic conflicts, and through state repression, a sharp increase over previous years.[3] Yet, the policeman's actions were also disturbing. By not responding to the crime until it was over, the policeman showed that he was unwilling to protect the rule of law. In a subsequent interview, he argued that the mob's actions were justified. As he described, the rise in vigilante killings was due to Indonesia's current poor economic conditions, which resulted from the 1997 financial crisis, and an inability of the government to meet social demands. Indirectly, the policeman tied the death of the murdered *pencuri* to the globalization of financial markets and the resulting inability of some states to address their citizens' basic needs.

This chapter explores the interrelationship among these three factors—globalization, weak states, and violence. "Violence" is defined here only as murder. I suggest that the prevalence of violence in East Asia is the product of changes in state power, which in turn have been influenced by globalization. Specifically, I argue that "weak" states—"states that lack the capacity to meet the demands and rights of citizens and improve the standard of living for the majority of the population"—have contributed to the high death toll in the region.[4] In other words, states that lack capacity, accountability, and professionalism—components essential for state strength—exacerbate the social conditions that underscore tensions and push states to resort to repression to protect their power. In the process, weak states promote violence. I further suggest that the globalization of the world economy has made the situation worse by undermining the capacity of states to address social problems and accentuating the inequality that leads to social tensions that can result in violent confrontation. Violence in East Asia has risen in the wake of the financial crisis that began in 1997. As it stands now, the high death toll is likely to continue if steps are not taken to strengthen the region's political institutions.

In order to illustrate the relationship between globalization, state power, and violence, this chapter begins by clarifying the processes that have weakened states in the region. I then lay out the patterns of violence in Asia to show where and how frequently citizens are killed. It becomes clear that violence in the region varies considerably, but has become increasingly ethnic in character. Moreover, despite the broader democracy in Asia as a whole, governments continue to use force to maintain their power through state repression, particularly the systematic killing or "disappearance" of citizens. To demonstrate the tie between state power, globalization, and violence concretely, I examine three case studies in detail: vigilantism in Indonesia, the use of the death penalty in China, and ethnic conflict in the southern Philippines. Each of these cases decisively shows that "weak states" contribute to violence and that globalization has played a prominent role in increasing violence in these countries.

Violence, State Power, and Globalization

Following in the line of other scholars that emphasize state-society relations in their studies of the causes of violence, I argue that state power has played a critical role in the prevalence of violence in the region.[5] Simply put, "weak" states foster violence, while "strong" states deter violence.[6] The distinction between a strong and weak state is often arbitrary. Here, the emphasis is placed on three factors: state capacity, professionalism, and accountability. Of the three, state capacity is the most important. After all, it is the ability of officials in political institutions to carry out policies that allow them to meet social demands, protect political rights, and improve the standard of living for the majority of the population.[7] State strength is thus derived from the ability of its officers to collect information, their expertise, their access to funds and the use of routine procedures and checks that provide for the efficient and fair implementation of policy initiatives.[8] These features allow officers to increase social equality, enforce the rule of law, promote economic growth, and improve social welfare in general.

State power is also closely related to professionalism and accountability. Professionalism involves the hiring and training of individuals who devote their lives to developing expertise within a particular job. These professionals develop an ethic, an esprit de corps, which inspires them to perform at a high standard. Strong states are comprised of professionals, who motivate lower-level bureaucrats and provide policy guidance. Often, however, professionalism can lead to the protection of state interests at the expense of society. This was often the case with military regimes in the developing world. Military officials in Indonesia from 1966 through 1998, for example, used their training to maintain order at all costs and suppressed the rights of thousands of individuals through state repression. Thus, professionalism must be counterbalanced with accountability, which refers to the ability of citizens to examine and correct officials' behavior. Officials must not only have expertise, but must be checked in their power. These checks, against corruption and arbitrary use of authority, must become routine. More often than not, this occurs within a democratic regime, where governments regularly face elections, but it may also occur in an authoritarian regime where accountability has become routine, such as in Singapore.

The tie between state power and violence thus unfolds as follows: Since strong states address citizens' demands, protect rights, and are often "developmental" (geared toward the promotion of public welfare by the promotion of economic growth), they dampen the tensions that foster social conflicts and thus deter violence.[9] Moreover, because "strong" states operate with accountability and professionalism, they do not need to rely on state repression to maintain their authority. In contrast, often corrupt and captured by privileged groups in society, "weak" states lack the characteristics that promote the well-being of their citizens and protect the rule of law. Consequently, social conflicts are not resolved and often erupt violently because the political institutions cannot channel social conflict. More often than not, "weak" states exacerbate social conflicts through perpetuating inequality, failing to protect citizens' rights, and being persistently unable to provide them with a basic standard of living. "Weak" states thus rely on state repression to keep control.

Although there is extensive variation in Asia, states have been weakened recently by globalization. This transformation has taken place in many different spheres of life, from information flows to financial markets. The focus here is economic interconnectedness, specifically the rise of market forces and the resulting prominence of foreign capital and the private sector.[10] It has been accompanied by lower trade barriers, rapid transfers in capital, greater foreign investment, and increased standardization of products and services. In contrast to the glorification of this change, perhaps best described by Thomas Friedman's *The Lexus and the Olive Tree* (1999), this process is seen to weaken states while at the same time creating more problems for them to address as social inequalities widen and poverty deepens.

The weakening of states has occurred on many levels. On a macro level, "interconnectedness" has led to a greater acceptance of market forces and displaced states. Through the 1990s the role of the private sector expanded in Asia and replaced the state as an engine of economic growth and protector of social welfare. From the developed economy of Japan to Communist China, market forces have usurped the role played by political institutions. In Malaysia policy makers adopted pro-market initiatives to attract foreign capital and stimulate growth. In Korea the government reduced education spending. In Thailand the government reduced funding to support agriculture. These are just a few of the many changes. The power of the "developmental" state has dissipated, as the scope of public involvement by state officials in the economy has narrowed. The connection between globalization and the weakening of states in East Asia has intensified in the last three years as a result of the region's financial crisis, which served to deepen the connection between Asian economies and capital flows.[11]

This macro transformation of the state's role has had concrete micro consequences for state power. Opting for higher-paid jobs in the private sector, educated elites are no longer attracted to government work. This has undermined state expertise. State "bashing," in the form of antibureaucratic diatribes, such as those that have become prominent in Japan, has destroyed morale among state officials. While corruption has been a long-standing feature of Asian politics, the scope of corruption, especially among top political leaders and the higher echelon of bureaucrats, has widened with greater links to the private sector. The use of "favors" to win contracts or the ownership of a newly privatized company has increased. Not only has this practice decayed professionalism within states, but it has also undercut states' capacity to implement policies and promote social equality. At the same time, traditional prescriptions to address social welfare, like public spending on education and infrastructure development, have been discredited. This has created a policy vacuum, as officials search for new measures that are seen to promote a more market-oriented environment. Perhaps most important, however, the dominance of the private sector has curtailed the state's access to resources used to distribute social benefits. The downsizing of the public sector has cut back the funds available for officials to promote social welfare. From reduced expertise, morale, and professionalism to policy vacuums (both real and perceived) and reduced funds, globalization has debilitated states.

The negative effects of globalization in East Asia were most intensely manifested in the last three years with the onset of the financial crisis in the summer of 1997. Before this crisis, Asia had become much more closely integrated into the world economy. With its vibrant markets and robust industrializing economies, from Japan and Korea to Singapore and China, Asian economies expanded "miraculously" with an average of 5 percent GDP growth annually. Until the 1980s economic integration took the form of greater foreign investment and rapid growth throughout the region. In the 1990s regional integration deepened and foreign capital continued to play a pivotal role in growth, especially in the manufacturing sector. Yet, the region experienced an expansion of its financial markets, which led to the growth of the banking sector and stock markets and, ultimately, greater portfolio capital flows.[12] Often without adequate local knowledge, investors poured in funds to newly established stock markets and other business ventures, not recognizing the differences among countries or understanding the patterns of corruption and inequality that had accompanied globalization. Rich in capital, Asia was considered to be the center of future world economic prosperity in 1995.

This rapidly changed two years later, however, when the Thai government decided not to use its national reserves to support its overvalued currency.[13] Financial analysts and investors, who had already begun to reevaluate their optimistic assessments of many of the region's economies, lost confidence in Asia.[14] This loss of confidence led to the downward spiral of Asian currencies, massive capital flight, bankruptcies, and the decline of growth in the region as a whole. Reflecting the speed of globalization, this downturn occurred rapidly and decisively. Indonesia was the worst-hit, with a 13.7 percent contraction of its economy in one year. At the core of this crisis were problems with the management of private capital. High debt, risky property ventures, and shallow portfolio investments all undermined these countries' financial stability. Unlike economic crises in Latin America, which were often provoked by public debt and poor management, the Asian financial crisis represented a "globalized" crisis, in which the interconnectedness of economies allowed for market forces to wreck havoc on disadvantaged parties. Western banks were bailed out by the IMF, while local investors, especially those not favored by regional governments, faced bankruptcy. With currency devaluations, middle-class wealth evaporated. For those at the margins, poverty deepened. According to the International Labor Organization, poverty in Indonesia nearly doubled from 64 million people to over 129 million.[15] In less than twelve months, thirty-two years of economic growth in Indonesia was wiped out.

States, already weakened by globalization, became even more vulnerable. Western critics of the region, best exemplified by the IMF and World Bank, harped on the problems within states and advocated the prescriptions used in Latin America, such as public spending reductions and better state fiscal management. These organizations centered on lack of transparency of Asian markets and advocated a greater role for market forces. These measures did not address the roots of the crisis, however, and created more difficulties in the region. Poverty remained high and social inequalities widened further. The market-oriented IMF initiatives weakened states further by forcing reductions in spending and destroying morale among state officials. While the calls for greater accountability were a much needed corrective on practices of corruption, the IMF measures undermined the capacity of bureaucrats to implement and formulate policy prescriptions to address the crisis by creating a deeper policy vacuum and even more limited access to resources. This change occurred as the social effects of the crisis intensi-fied. While Asian economies have rebounded last year, their economies have not returned to precrisis levels. The scars of the crisis—weaker states, greater poverty and social inequality—have not healed. Globalization continues to undermine state power and promote social conditions for conflict.

Overview of Violence in Asia

Today, East Asian states are faced with a dilemma: social demands remain high, yet the acceptance of a state-led response and the states' ability to address social prob-lems has declined. Lacking needed capacity, "weak" states have contributed to the prevalence of violence in the region. It is important to realize that violence in Asia is not new. Millions of people were killed by Mao in China between 1949 and 1976 and Pol Pot in Cambodia in the late 1970s, among other travesties. Social conflicts have raged throughout the modern era in Cambodia, the Philippines, Indonesia, to name but a few countries. Today the level of violence in Asia remains shock-ingly high. As the region has developed economically through the 1990s, violence has not waned. If fact, over the last three years violence has become more promi-nent as old conflicts have been rekindled and new conflicts have emerged. From accounts of the killings in East Timor to the continued civil war in Burma and new violence in the Moluccas, Asia remains in strife.

The overview below focuses on developments in the last three years and com-pares changes in the prevalence of violence over the last decade, as globalization has intensified. As a heuristic device, I distinguish between two types of violence in Asia: social conflict, involving the killing of citizens by other citizens, and state repression, the systematic murder of citizens by state officials, especially the mili-tary and police. These types of violence are manifested in a variety of forms, from ethnic and class warfare and regime challenges to "disappearances" and the impo-sition of the death penalty. In all of these forms, state power plays a pivotal role, either as a protagonist involved in violence or through the inability of state offi-cials to channel tensions or address the problems that perpetuate social divisions.

Table 1 outlines the major social conflicts, which have resulted in the over-whelming majority of deaths. Of all the forms of social conflict, the most promi-nent involves ethnic differences. Ethnic tensions are at the root of the separatist struggles throughout East Asia. Those in Indonesia have received the most atten-tion. Triggered by the downfall of Suharto in May 1998, which resulted directly from the Asian financial crisis and the state's failure to resolve mounting economic woes, groups in the outlying islands used available political space to demand greater local autonomy. By relying on repression to quell such rebellions, the response of the Indonesian state typifies the behavior of a weak state described above. For example, pro-Indonesia (largely Muslim) forces (trained and supported by the Indonesian army) retaliated against the majority Catholic population in East Timor, who voted overwhelmingly for independence in August 1999. The number of people killed will likely never be known. Some observers have estimated that over five thousand people died in the months before the referendum, before the worst of the crisis set in. Over half the people in the country were forced to flee their homes in the ensuing postreferendum chaos.[16] Even after the arrival of UN peacekeepers in September 1999, 100,000 refugees remained in West Papua and sporadic violence is regularly reported. Violence in the separatist movements in Aceh and West Papua (formerly known as Irian Jaya) has also escalated since 1998. The *Jakarta Post* (January 11, 2001) reports that one person is killed every eleven hours in Aceh. Human rights organizations estimate that at least three thousand people have died in this northeast province in the last three years. The degree of violence in West Papua has not reached these levels, but has been increasing as demands for greater autonomy by its residents have been rejected by pronationalist forces in the center of Indonesia, Java. The failure of the Indonesian state to clarify the scope of local autonomy in these areas has added to the violence.

Ethnic minorities in other parts of East Asia have also challenged states. In Tibet the struggle for independence has continued ever since the Chinese invaded over fifty years ago. Yet, here as well there is a marked change in the interaction between the state and society in the era of globalization. In 1999 the Chinese government carried out one of its most repressive responses to the pro-independence movement, arresting and killing many activists. This blatant repression stands in contrast to the systematic effort to restructure the composition of Tibetan society, which has deepened in the last decade as Chinese migrants have relocated to the area. Clearly, the policy of forced assimilation has denied local Tibetans' demands for their own culture and autonomy. The Chinese state in Tibet has remained weak and turned to repression to assert its control. The conflict in the northwest province of Xinjiang between Muslim Uighur separatists and the Han-Chinese government is less well known, yet has taken on a similar form. With bombings in major cities and the deployment of troops in the provincial capital of Kashgar, tensions between the Chinese state and Muslim rebels have escalated in the last three years. The exact number of deaths is not known. As Central Asian countries support the rebels and the demands for local autonomy go unmet, the Chinese hold on the province has weakened and violence is likely to increase. In the southern Philippines, where the Moro National Liberation Front and other splintered factions are fighting the central government, conditions are very similar. Unable to peacefully channel social conflict, the Filipino state has responded with force, which, in turn, has provoked terrorist attacks in the nation's capital, Manila, that have reportedly killed nearly a hundred people. In the upland areas of Burma (also known as Myanmar) fighting between ethnic minorities and the military (SLORC) government escalated in 1997–1999. The Karen and Shan tribes, who control the lucrative drug-producing areas, have used child soldiers to fight

TABLE 1. SOCIAL CONFLICTS IN ASIA 1998–2000

	CENTERS OF CONFLICT	LEVEL OF VIOLENCE	OVERALL ASSESSMENT
Burma	Fighting in the north continues between the SLORC regime and Karen fighters and other ethnic minorities; political tensions high	High; exact figures unknown	Violence remains high as fighting has intensified; increase in violence
Cambodia	Conflict with the Khmer Rouge and the government	Moderate	Tensions have eased in the last year; decrease in violence
China	Northwest Province of Xinjiang and Tibet fighting for autonomy	Moderate	Tensions remain high; increase in violence
East Timor	Fight for independence has led to backlash by Indonesia-sponsored opponents to freedom movement	Extremely high; exact figures unknown	Tensions remain high, although violence has decreased
Indonesia	Riots in Indonesia in 1998; separatist conflicts in East Timor, Aceh, West Papua; ethnic conflicts in Moluccas and Java	Extremely high, estimated over 15,000 deaths; exact figures unknown	Violence continues to be high in the outer islands; violence levels consistent
Japan	No major problems	Low	Minimal social conflict
Laos	Conflict between the government and religious groups	Low; exact figures unknown	Tensions remain high
Malaysia	Tensions over trial of former Deputy PM	Low	Tensions remain high
North Korea	Extensive social hardship as a result of economic crisis	Low; exact figures unknown	Situation improving with closer ties to south
Papua New Guinea	Fighting between government and opposition in Bougainville	Moderate, over 100 killed; exact figures unknown	Tensions have eased; violence levels consistent with previous years
Philippines	Conflict between the New People's Army and Moro National Liberation Front and government in south	Moderate, over 100 killed; exact figures unknown	Tensions remain high
Singapore	No major problems	Low	Minimal social conflict
South Korea	Industrial conflict tied to economic crisis	Low	Situation improving with economic growth
Taiwan	No major problems	Low	Minimal social conflict
Thailand	Conflict between the government and refugees in the north	Low; exact figures unknown	Tensions remain high
Vietnam	Conflict with flooding victims and political opponents	Low; exact figures unknown	Tensions remain high

Source: Based on data presented by Amnesty International, Human Rights Watch/Asia, and U.S. Department of State Reports, 1997–2001. **Note:** "Tensions" refers to the character of the relationship between the government and opposition groups in the state. The poorer the relationship, the higher the tension and greater the possibility of violence.

Burmese troops, who refuse to grant autonomy to the region. Although a cease-fire was reached last year, the Burmese state continues to use state repression to maintain control over the area (and access to drug revenue), in the form of forced labor and disappearances. In all four conflicts, the respective states have failed to improve the standard of living of ethnic minorities and systematically discriminate against them.

Violence along ethnic lines has also developed in the last few years beyond separatist disputes. Fighting broke out in the Moluccas in Indonesia in 1999, where over five thousand Christian and Muslim residents have died in a de facto civil war since 1999.[17] This was a direct response of the Asian financial crisis and weakening of the Indonesian state. With funds pouring in from other parts of the region to support the Muslim minorities in these areas, the fighting has persisted, despite the efforts of local leaders to improve relations. Indonesian state officials—based in Java, over five hundred miles away—remain inept in handling the conflict. In fact, some analysts report that Javanese military officers are supporting the Muslim rebels, who are perceived to be less well-off than their Christian neighbors.

The inadequacies of state power are equally evident in broader social conflicts in Asia. In Indonesia the military remains the country's only powerful institution, yet it lacks accountability and is inclined to use repression to maintain order. With the removal of Suharto from power in 1998 in Indonesia the potential for violence looms. The transition of power in Indonesia was tainted with military-inspired violence. The military promoted instability to maintain itself in power. By hiring thugs to use force in the riots opposing the regime, the military opened the door to the eventual anti-Chinese bloodbath that killed over a thousand people. Although the scope of violence has been narrower in other countries, the struggles between opposition groups in Laos, Papua New Guinea, Malaysia, and China and their respective states have also involved violence. Governments have minimized the death toll by arresting opposition activists, often killing or arresting an individual as an example to other opponents. In all of these examples, weak states have contributed to violence.

In fact, in some East Asian countries conflicts have spread outside of their territories. In northern Thailand, for example, the military has used force to contain the refugees fleeing from Burma, often killing suspected Shan and Karen fighters. Domestic problems, resulting from weak states in the era of globalization, have placed pressure on neighboring countries.

Although citizens are active participants in violence in the region, state repression also remains high, as shown in table 2. Four East Asian states—Burma, China, Indonesia, and North Korea—have reportedly killed over five thousand of their citizens in the last three years through disappearances, the systematic killing of groups, and extrajudicial killings. With over six thousand known deaths, China is perhaps the worst offender. Even states in democratic regimes, like the Philippines, are not exempt from this practice. The Filipino army has been fighting the Moros for years and "disappearances" occur regularly.

The acceptance of violence as a means to maintain authority in Asia is deeply rooted. For most of the region's leaders, violence is an accepted means to impose political authority. No policy manifests this acceptance better than the widespread use of the death penalty. Although this practice is codified and is part of the rule of law, it is nevertheless violent since it involves the systematic killing of citizens. As such, it is included as a form of state repression and listed in table 2. States that rely heavily on the death penalty to address crime demonstrate ineffectiveness in addressing the social problems that cause crime, from poverty to discrimination. Over 75 percent of East Asian countries studied use the death penalty. China kills the most individuals per year, reportedly over a thousand, while the small city-state of Singapore kills the largest proportion of its convicts.

Amnesty International estimates that Singapore executed nearly forty people between 1998 and 1999. These countries are not alone. Japan, Taiwan, and the Philippines—all democratically elected regimes—also join the ranks of states that use violence as part of their rule of law. In fact, the Philippines, under the leadership of former president Joseph Estrada, recently reintroduced executions, despite the opposition of the country's powerful Catholic Church. The widespread use of the death penalty shows the extent to which states in East Asia resort to violence to maintain their authority, even under the rubric of existing laws.

Case Studies

So far, the overview has described the relationship between weak states and violence, and in some cases tied this directly to globalization. To better illustrate the relationship among this set of factors, I delve into three case studies: vigilantism in Indonesia, the use of the death penalty in China, and the ethnic conflict between Muslims and the Christian-dominated government in the southern Philippines. Each of these cases shows how the changing international environment has affected domestic political institutions and resulted in rising levels of violence.

Vigilantism in West Java, Indonesia

This chapter began with an account of vigilantism in West Java. What was more shocking than the mob murder of the suspected thief was the increasing prevalence of this practice. Vigilantism has evolved recently. It emerged out of a growing social conflict among citizens and suspected criminals, and the inability of the Indonesian state to address crime. Newspaper reports of vigilante killings in West Java began to surface in 1998, the year the crisis most severely effected Indonesians. They became more frequent in 1999. By last year vigilante killings were occurring regularly, with an average of two deaths reported weekly in the *Jakarta Post*.[18] The *Far East Economic Review* reports that the Jakarta morgue receives one victim of vigilante justice every other day and has set up a special unit to handle

TABLE 2. STATE REPRESSION IN ASIA: 1998–2000

	FORMS OF REPRESSION	LEVEL OF VIOLENCE	OVERALL ASSESSMENT
Burma	Death penalty; extrajudicial killings; disappearances	Exact figures unknown	Highly repressive
Cambodia	No death penalty; extrajudicial killings in 1998	Exact figures unknown	Moderately repressive
China	Widespread use of the death penalty and conflict with separatist groups	Over 2,000 executions reported; exact number unknown	Highly repressive
East Timor	No death penalty	No executions	Minimally repressive
Indonesia	Death penalty; disappearances in Aceh, West Papua; extrajudicial killings throughout Indonesia	Over 1,000 disappearances/killings reported; no known executions; 27 sentenced to death in 1999; 30 death row prisoners in 1998	Highly repressive
Japan	Death penalty	6 executions in 1998, 5 in 1999; 99 death row prisoners in 1999	Minimally repressive
Laos	Death penalty	No executions	Minimally repressive
Malaysia	Death penalty	1 execution in 1999; 6 sentenced to death 1998	Minimally repressive
North Korea	Death penalty	Reports of executions, yet exact number unknown	Highly repressive
Papua New Guinea	No death penalty	None	Low
Philippines	Death penalty; extrajudicial killings	Exact number of killings unknown; over 1,000 on death row; over 400 sentenced to death in 1998; 6 executions in 1999	Moderately repressive
Singapore	Death penalty	5 sentenced to death in 1998; 28 executions in 1998; 11 executions reported in 1999	Minimally repressive
South Korea	Death penalty	No executions in 1998 and 1999; 37 on death row in 1998	Minimally repressive
Sri Lanka	No death penalty; extrajudicial killings; disappearances	Over 500 disappearances; exact number of deaths unknown	Moderately repressive
Taiwan	Death penalty	32 executions in 1998, 24 in 1999	Moderately repressive
Thailand	Death penalty	17 known executions in 1999; over 100 on death row	Minimally repressive
Vietnam	Death penalty	200 sentenced to death in 1999, 8 executed; 53 sentenced to death in 1998, 18 known executions	Moderately repressive

Source: Based on data presented by Amnesty International, 1998–2001.

the beaten and charred, unidentifiable bodies.[19] Today in the nation's capital, Jakarta, market stalls are stocked with kerosene cans, with ready access for mobs to attack suspected criminals. But the exact level of vigilante killings in Indonesia is not known. The government does not record these statistics and newspaper reports only scratch the surface of this phenomenon. A conservative estimate suggests that there were over 250 vigilante killings in West Java in 2000.

Vigilante killings tend to follow the same format. One or a handful of suspected criminals—usually of theft—are attacked by an angry mob in a crowded space—usually a market. The mob uses accessible weapons—fists, cutlasses, and kerosene—to kill the suspect(s) and impose immediate "justice." The cries for mercy are ignored, including the screams from burning the victims alive. Most of the victims are male and outsiders, new migrants to the area without a social network in the village or city neighborhood. In some instances the killings are the product of rising gang activity, which has become more common in the last three years. Without fail, the police avoid intervening in vigilante "incidents." And, as a testimony of the public execution, the body usually remains in public view long after the killing.

Indonesia has a troubling history with violence, especially in periods of political uncertainty. In 1965, when General Suharto ousted President Sukarno, over 100,000 people were slaughtered in the conflict between Muslims, the army, and suspected members of the PKI (Indonesia's Communist party). Some claim that nearly one million people died. At issue were ideological differences between the two men and conflict between the PKI and Muslims over land redistribution. To this date, little is known about why the violence occurred in such magnitude. Geoffrey Robinson's study of the 1965 massacre in Bali suggests a number of reasons that are relevant to the current situation.[20] He argues that a tradition of violence and class conflict accounted for the scope of the conflict. He suggests that an acceptance of violence as a means of interaction, stemming from the civil war with the Dutch and the prominence of the military in everyday life, and a sharp class divide, which distinguished the richer Muslims from the poorer PKI members, underscored the response.

These features—common use of violence and a class divide—are still present in contemporary Indonesia. Suharto's New Order (1966–1998) government continued the tradition of using violence to impose its authority. The army, ABRI, was the backbone of the regime. In fact, the withdrawal of military support for Suharto in May 1998 tipped the balance against the former general. Similarly, although Indonesia has a relatively high level of social equality—with a Gini coefficient of .36 in 1995—a small handful of Chinese businessmen and Suharto's family members control over 75 percent of the economy.[21] This difference has maintained a sharp class divide. It is not surprising that Chinese businesses were targeted in the riots that surrounded the regime transition in 1998 that killed over a thousand people.

Yet, neither of these reasons helps us understand recent vigilante violence in Indonesia. The answer to the rise of vigilantism lies in the actions of the state, or rather its inactions. Indonesia typifies the weak state, which has been hard-hit by globalization. Above, I described the extent of the economic downturn and resulting poverty. Yet, I did not capture the full impact on the Indonesian state as a whole. Public spending in Indonesia began to sharply decrease in the early 1990s, including funds for human development. These measures were an extension of the state's effort to become internationally competitive and attract foreign capital, an effort to integrate Indonesia into the global economy. By 1995 the Indonesian state was becoming less effective in addressing poverty than it had in the two previous decades, as spending in education and infrastructure, for example, were declining. In 1998, after the onset of the financial crisis, the Indonesian government further reduced spending. Suharto adopted the fiscally conservative measures advocated by the IMF, including the removal of subsidies on basic commodities. These measures reduced the funds available to state officials. At the same time, the demands associated with the crisis placed technocrats in a difficult position. Lacking their own policy initiatives, they turned to the IMF for policy prescriptions, which proved disastrous. By 1998 the Indonesian state had been incapacitated and discredited, as the crisis worsened.

In May of that year Suharto was forced to resign, opening the way to a transition to democracy. The greater accountability, however, was not accompanied with substantial changes to Indonesia's political institutions. The coercive apparatus, notably Indonesia's army, changed its name from ABRI to TNI. Yet, it continued to use force to quell opposition in East Timor and other outlying areas. On Java itself, the military hired thugs to threaten opponents and destabilize Indonesia's newly democratic regime. Known in some cases as "ninjas," these thugs/gangsters, equipped with weapons and dressed in dark clothing, hid their identity as they used violence to kill and rob in their destabilizing effort. This practice provoked reprisals by ordinary citizens. It is not a coincidence that the majority of vigilante killings are of outsiders. Today's vigilantism is an extension of efforts to protect property from outside threats. The lack of accountability of Indonesia's military has sown the seeds of vigilantism.

Two other dimensions of Indonesia's weak state further explain Indonesia's recent vigilante violence: a lack of economic vision and a weak rule of law. Since 1998 the Indonesian economy has slowly rebounded, reaching 5 percent growth last year. This growth is not seen to be the result of state initiatives. The successive governments of B. J. Habibie (1998–1999) and Abdurrahman Wahid (1999–2001) have been perceived as largely ineffective in addressing economic problems. Reforms have been piecemeal. Technocrats remain discredited. The Indonesian bureaucracy lost the luster it once had and remains rudderless in its search for policy solutions.

The state's economic impotence has been compounded by the persistence of economic woes that are exacerbated by globalization. Poverty remains high three years after the crisis. The World Bank estimated that 31.7 percent of the population currently lives in absolute poverty. Unemployment and underemployment remain high, especially in the country's manufacturing center of West Java. The divide between the rich and the poor remains as wide as before the crisis, although most of the wealth, especially Chinese wealth, remains in foreign banks. For those at the margins, like shoppers in the Labuan market, survival remains a daily struggle.

The struggle has been made more difficult by the frayed fabric of Indonesia's legal institutions. Human Rights Watch/Asia has highlighted the problems of accountability, lack of staff, inadequate training, and corruption in Indonesia's legal system in the past few years. The judiciary has yet to develop the credibility it needs to protect citizen rights. In no instance is this more clear than in the handling of the corruption charges against Suharto and his family members. No one was imprisoned for their pilfering of over $5 billion from state coffers. Corruption has continued to shape state-society relations, tainting even democratically elected governments. Indonesia was ranked by the International Center for Transparency the eightieth worst country for its corruption practices in 2000, among the world's most serious offenders. On the ground, police officers cannot handle rising crime. With only 200,000 for a population of 220 million, the police force is small. Many officers lack training and resources. As in Labuan, they turn a blind eye to vigilante attacks out of fear and an understanding of their own ineffectiveness. Under these circumstances, it is not surprising that vigilante killings have become common.

Death Penalty in China

Despite the impression that China is fundamentally different from other countries in the region, there are some striking similarities with conditions in Indonesia; here, too, globalization and a weakening state have contributed to violence. Globalization has followed a similar course in China in the 1990s, with greater integration into the global economy and an increased prominence of market forces. As Thomas Moore notes, China has become one of the world's most important trading economies, moving from being ranked thirtieth by the World Economic Forum in 1977 to eleventh in 1998.[22] This process began in the early 1980s under the leadership of Deng Xiaoping and has extended through the 1990s as China has privatized public enterprises (SOEs) and sought entry into the World Trade Organization.[23] The country's markets have been flooded with expensive Western goods, from Coca Cola to Calvin Klein Jeans, as Chinese products have gained easier access to foreign markets. Although growth dropped with the onset of the Asian financial crisis below 8 percent for two years, China was buffered from most of the debilitating effects of the crisis, due to its size, lower dependence on foreign capital, and isolation policies. The transformation of China's economy has been profound. With the promise of cheap labor, China has become one of the most attractive centers for foreign investment in Asia.

The economic reforms have been accompanied by political changes. While the

Chinese state remains strong (especially when compared to state power in Indonesia and the Philippines) and officials and government leaders have been able to harness many of the economic changes for their personal benefit, the Chinese state has become weaker, in part due to globalization.[24] On a macro level, the state has been displaced by market forces. To date, this has not seriously affected the power of officials to control economic policy, yet it has limited the scope of bureaucratic expertise and reduced the number of ministries. The changes on a micro level are more significant. The state's backbone, the Chinese Communist Party (CCP), no longer attracts the educated elite to the extent that it did in the past. These elites have turned to the private sector and left a less capable bureaucracy. With less expertise, professionalism has declined and corruption has become rampant. Of the eighty-five countries ranked, Transparency International rated China the fifty-second worst country in the world last year for its corruptive practices. The country's ratings have become increasingly worse over the decade. The government has yet to institutionalize checks on the arbitrary use of power by state officials. The growing lack of expertise, professionalism, and accountability in China's political institutions is only part of the weakness of the state. With market reforms, public spending, especially for basic subsidies and social welfare programs, has been reduced to make the economy more competitive internationally. These cutbacks have left officials without funds to implement programs. Moreover, these reductions have involved the decentralization of the federal programs to provincial and local authorities and incapacitated the federal government. While these changes have made local institutions stronger, they have not contributed to greater accountability or more effective prescriptions to solve local problems. As power has moved from the center to the provinces, the abuses of power have been relocated, not reduced. From the CCP to the state planning agencies, Chinese political institutions have become less adept at meeting the needs of its citizens.

This change in state power in the era of globalization has taken place as income inequalities have widened and demands for greater political representation have increased.[25] The World Bank estimates that there are 270 million people living in poverty in China. Regional distortions between the richer coast and poorer inland areas have intensified, with poverty levels skyrocketing in the rural areas. Cutbacks in the public sector have led to rising unemployment in the cities. With a Gini coefficient of .46, social inequality in the country as a whole remains high and has been progressively increasing. These problems have created political demands for greater attention to social welfare. Since the Tiananmen Square massacre in 1989, the Chinese state has largely used force to dampen these tensions. Yet, pressure groups in the form of new political parties, religious groups like the Falun Gong, as well as traditional peasant and worker organizations have continued to protest conditions. The Chinese state, especially at the national level, has proven less adept at handling these conflicts.

It is in this context of a weakening state and greater social problems that there has been an increasing dependence on coercion, especially from the center, and increase in violence. The most known manner in which the Chinese government has used state repression is the death penalty. This policy was introduced by the center, but is carried out by both national and local officials. Today China carries out over 70 percent of world executions every year, more than the rest of the world put together. Amnesty International reports that over twenty-five thousand have been killed in the 1990s and estimates that over fifteen hundred individuals are executed every year. Many are killed in groups to coincide with national holidays, often in public view. The exact number of executions is not known.

As public pressure to address social problems has grown in the last few years, the Chinese state has imposed the death penalty more frequently. In April 1996 the government introduced the "*Yanda*" or "strike hard" program. This initiative declared its commitment to the death penalty as part of the effort to reduce crime: "Any crime which the law regards as serious should certainly receive serious penalties, and any crime which is punishable by the death penalty according to the law, should certainly receive the death penalty. This will assure the healthy progress of strike hard. Hu Jintao, Secretary of the CCP Central Political Bureau." At the same time, the government called on officials to use the death penalty more often: "After launching concentrated attacks, public security organs and procuratorial and people's courts must step up preliminary hearings, collection of evidence and tracking of criminal histories; and work hard to achieve the goal of quick approval of arrest, quick prosecution and quick trials."[26] This led to greater use of the death penalty, often one day after a suspect's arrest.

The death penalty in China is imposed for a wide range of crimes, including hooliganism, petty robbery, drunk driving, and drug possession. The list includes sixty offences. The majority of sentences in the last few years have involved economic crimes, corruption, embezzlement, tax fraud, and robbery. In 1998, for example, Luo Feng, a manager of the Beijing computer company, was sentenced to death for allegedly embezzling 3.9 million yuan ($485,000) and accepting bribes. He was found guilty even though the amount of money allegedly embezzled was inaccurate and one of the charges was dropped. In another case in Sichuan, the Chinese government reportedly executed a nineteen-year-old boy for stealing 60 yuan ($7.5). Most of those executed are poor and lack effective legal representation. In many cases those executed are targets of political officials. Individuals closely connected to the CCP, especially the higher ranks, are rarely killed.

The common use of the death penalty in China is tied to the weakening of the state, outlined earlier. The government introduced the "strike hard" campaign to divert attention from widespread corruption within the ranks of the state. The use of a harsh penalty for corruption allows the government to claim it is addressing the problem, yet it does not increase professionalism or accountability, the root of the misuse of resources. Stiff penalties do not improve standards or make checks on the arbitrary use of power more acceptable. Rather, they entice officials to find alternative ways to avoid prosecution and encourage individuals in the state to target political opponents. The bottom line is that corruption has not decreased. In fact, it has become more entrenched.

On another level it may seem that the use of the death penalty has allowed the state to gain credibility in addressing social problems, especially crime. Yet, its arbitrary and biased imposition has failed to make this measure an effective deterrent. Crime levels remain high, especially crimes tied to the globalized economy and rising social inequalities. Ironically, the death penalty in China is being used to attack the results that the state fostered.

Ethnic Conflict in Mindanao, Philippines

In the southern Philippines a similar dynamic is taking place where the state has created conditions for violent conflict and has had to resort to repression to control it. Last year, fighting between the Christian-led central government and the Muslim rebels intensified in the southern island of Mindanao. After months of negotiations broke down, then-president Estrada sent in the national army to quell the resistance of rebels who had kidnapped seventeen people from the diving resort in Sipadan, Malaysia, and continued to challenge federal Filipino authority. The kidnapping was carried out by different paramilitary groups, led by the Abu Sayaaf faction of the Moro Islamic Liberation Front (MILF) in April 2000. This faction demanded greater attention to the social inequalities on the island and a commitment to broader autonomy. By the end of last year, hundreds of people had died from the ensuing struggle between the Moros and the Filipino government, including four of the foreign hostages. As in China, globalization has exacerbated the conditions that led to the violence, weakened the ability of the state to address the Moro demands, and increased the dependence on state repression to maintain state power.

The conflict between the Filipino federal government and the Moro (Muslim) rebels has its roots in the colonial era and predates globalization.[27] It stemmed from differences over religion conversion, land distribution, and contests for political power among indigenous groups and migrants brought to Mindanao beginning in the 1960s. Tensions came to a head in 1968, when twenty-eight Moro recruits in the Filipino army were killed in a massacre. Moros responded with outrage, prompting greater consciousness of political and economic inequities, and, subsequently, the creation of the Moro National Liberation Front (MNLF). They concentrated their attack on the Christian-led Filipino army instead of the local population. By 1972, when President Ferdinand Marcos declared martial law, a civil war had erupted. Over 100,000 were killed in the early 1970s. Pressured by the Islamic oil-producing countries to reach a settlement, Marcos entered into negotiations with the MNLF. This culminated with the Tripoli Agreement in 1976, which made Mindanao an autonomous region. This agreement, and the subsequent Autonomous Region in Muslim Mindanao (ARMM) initiative introduced by Cory Aquino, dissolved since they failed to address the social inequalities on the island or grant adequate political autonomy to the Moros. It was not until the Fidel Ramos administration (1992–1998) that all sides agreed to end the fighting. Unlike his predecessors, Ramos was committed to improving regional distortions in the economy, especially regarding the southern islands. In 1996 the different rebel groups (primarily the MNLF and MILF) signed the Final Peace Agreement, which was intended to grant greater autonomy to Mindanao and promised attention to ethnic discrimination over land and other state benefits.

With the election of Joseph Estrada in 1998, the political climate changed considerably. The coalition that elected Estrada opposed greater political autonomy for Mindanao. Although Estrada's platform promised greater attention to social inequality, the alliance that backed Estrada did not recognize regional distortions and was not as committed to improving living standards in the south. It was during this period that the Abu Sayaaf kidnapping took place and the fighting resumed. While the new administration negatively affected the political center-periphery relationship with Mindanao, both state power and globalization contributed to the renewed violence. Of the three case studies, the Filipino state is perhaps the weakest. Unlike Indonesia, the state in the Philippines has been weak since independence. Traditionally, political "bosses" (essentially large landowners) gained access to public resources and political power.[28] They maintained their influence by creating private armies and engaged in the systematic pilfering of the country's wealth. The Marcos administration (1969–1986) best exemplifies this practice. His tenure made the word "crony" internationally known. Marcos did little to improve the professionalism of the bureaucracy. Instead, he funded the military to maintain his authority and encouraged corruption through the ranks, including in his own family.

Despite greater accountability as part of a democratic regime, the misuse of state resources by Filipino officials—both politicians and civil servants—has continued. Ramos made a concerted effort to change this practice by improving standards, transparency, and implementing a clear plan for economic development. Yet, the 1998 election of Estrada evaporated these gains. The Filipino state remained weak under his tenure, captured by political elites who use resources to aggrandize their own wealth and solidify their control over the impoverished majority. In 2000 the Philippines was ranked the fifty-fifth worst country for corruption by Transparency International, lower than its previous rankings. The weakness of state power in the Philippines was perhaps best illustrated by Estrada himself. His administration unraveled in 2000, when corruption came to light, and he was forced to resign in January 2001. Although the democratic procedures were effective in ousting Estrada, corruption remains pervasive, even in the ranks of the new Arroyo government. "Bosses" continue to dominate Filipino politics and undermine the professionalism, accountability, and capacity of bureaucrats to implement policies. For the people in Mindanao, these weak political institutions have had serious consequences. The pattern of "bossism" has been replicated on the island, and social inequalities persist. The poverty in Mindanao is higher than in the northern islands.

Globalization has worsened conditions and made violence more prevalent. The Filipino economy is the least developed of the three case studies. Considered a backwater and riddled by poor political leadership, the Philippines did not attract the same level of foreign investment as the rest of the region. Thus, the scope of globalization in the Philippines was much narrower. Its economy did not expand significantly until the Ramos administration. During these years the economy grew impressively, averaging 6 percent growth, and became more market oriented. It was not until the end of Ramos's tenure that the effects of the Asian financial crisis began to set in. Initially, the Philippines was insulated from the crisis.[29] In 1998 its economy grew by .1 percent. It was the only island Southeast Asian economy that registered growth that year. Paul Hutchcroft explains that this success was the result of less foreign capital, Ramos's leadership, and greater fiscal conservatism reinforced by years of economic decline. Yet, it was only a matter of time for the crisis effects to sink in. Without the same level of international credibility or foreign investment, the Estrada government was not able to generate the same level of confidence in the Filipino economy. It shrunk considerably, from 8 percent to 3 percent growth, as foreign investment evaporated. This in turn diminished available state resources and deteriorated the state's capacity to reduce social inequality. With a Gini coefficient of .57 and over forty million in poverty, the Filipino state remains unable to address the needs of its population.

Not surprisingly, the economic and political effects of globalization manifested themselves in Mindanao, where poverty and social tensions increased. It is not a coincidence that the conflict between the Moro rebels and Filipino government intensified under the Estrada administration. The federal government cannot keep the promise to invest in education, provide funds for local infrastructure, and resolve local land disputes. The Abu Sayaaf kidnappings and resulting reliance on the federal military to maintain order are in large part the result of the inherent inability of the Filipino federal government to implement its commitments in the 1996 peace agreement. As was the case in Indonesia and China, violence has corresponded to a weak state and was accentuated by the globalization process.

Conclusion

Each of the case studies shows that weak (or weakening) states and globalization have contributed to the high death toll in Asia. While the states differ substantially, the pattern is consistent. The mobs in Indonesia, the vulnerable political leaders in China, and Muslim factions in the Philippines are more likely to use force to achieve their aims unless there is a concerted effort to strengthen the region's political institutions.

The first step in addressing violence in the region is to tackle the view that states should not be responsible for public welfare. The market does not protect the majority of Asian populations, who are among the poorest in the world. Writing in 1968, Samuel Huntington called for the development of political institutions in order to maintain political order. His study was seen to legitimize the rise of authoritarian regimes throughout the developing world. Yet Huntington drew attention to the important role that states play in protecting political rights. Studies on developmental states and economic development further confirmed the benefits of strong political institutions. Strong "developmental" states increased incomes and social equality, primarily through professionalism and attention to a broad distribution of resources.

In order to reduce violence, there needs to be a move to return to conditions that promote strong "developmental" states. It is necessary to improve standards of professionalism through higher salaries, more recruitment of educated civil servants, and wider acceptance of the benefits of government programs. The attention to improving professionalism, however, must take place in the context of more accountability. Lowering the level of corruption, and respect for rule of law, will only take place in more democratic regimes, where the rights of the majorities are more represented. The death toll will decline with greater professionalism and accountability. It is these factors that are closely tied with improving the economic security of individuals and the protection of basic political rights.

Despite the attention of the role of states in shaping violence, most states, even with greater accountability, will only go so far. There are other contributing factors to violence in Asia that were not explored in detail here, from ethnic identity to international institutions. Further study is necessary to understand what steps can be taken to address these other factors. It is also necessary to examine the dynamic between globalization, state power, and violence in more detail, with greater attention to the effects of the interrelationship of these factors on particular types of violence. In the short term, violence is unlikely to reduce substantially in East Asia. Yet, with steps outlined above and greater appreciation for the other factors shaping violence, perhaps violence can be reduced in the long term.

NOTES

I would like to thank the editors of this volume and Andrew Aeria for comments on this chapter. Errors that may remain are my own.

1. Based on eyewitness account and follow-up interviews in Indonesia, July–August 2000.
2. "East Asia" is defined to include seventeen countries in East and Southeast Asia. These include: Burma (Myanmar), Cambodia, China, East Timor, Japan, Indonesia, North Korea, South Korea, Laos, Malaysia, Papua New Guinea, Philippines, Singapore, Sri Lanka, Taiwan, Thailand, and Vietnam.
3. These numbers are estimates based on reports published by the two leading human rights organizations, Amnesty International and Human Rights Watch/Asia, and U.S. Department of State Reports, 1997–2001.

4. Drawing from Max Weber and Michael Mann, a state is defined as the set of *political institutions* that formulate and implement policy, and includes the coercive apparatus as well as the bureaucracy.

5. See, for example, Brass, ed., *Theft of an Idol*, and Horowitz, *The Deadly Ethnic Riot.*

6. Joel Migdal's *Strong Societies and Weak States* was the first to distinguish between "strong" and "weak" states. The definition developed above is a modification of his thesis.

7. Analysts of state power have made a distinction between "state capacity" and "state autonomy," in which the latter reflects the space available for officers to formulate and implement policies. See Barkey and Parikh, "Comparative Perspectives on the State." While not dismissing the importance of autonomy, the emphasis is placed on the inherent characteristics of political institutions, as opposed to the relationship with specific social groups.

8. These features are a cumulation of factors identified by other scholars. See, in particular, Evans, *Embedded Autonomy*, and Scott, *Seeing Like a State.*

9. A developmental state refers to a set of political institutions that actively engage in the promotion of economic growth through planning and the distribution of state resources. See Woo-Cumings, *The Developmental State.*

10. As David Held et al. have pointed out, there are different views of globalization. These authors identify three approaches: those of the hyperglobalists, the skeptics, and the transformationalists. While not dismissing the alternative approaches, this authors' view of globalization falls more closely into the "hyperglobalist" camp, where the emergence of economic forces has reduced the capacity of states to channel resources and control events within borders.

11. Kim, ed., *East Asia and Globalization.*

12. Vandenbrink and Yue, eds., *East Asia's Financial Systems.*

13. The analysis of the causes of the Asian financial crisis has been extensively debated. See Jomo, ed. *Tigers in Trouble*, Pempel, ed., *The Politics of the Asian Economic Crisis*, and World Bank, *East Asia: Recovery and Beyond* for a range of different views.

14. Space does not permit a richer discussion of the differences among Asian countries. The Asian crisis was most felt in Korea, Indonesia, Malaysia, and Thailand. As such, the present analysis focuses on these countries. Many countries, notably China, India, and Taiwan, were able to successfully buffer the negative effects of the economic downturn.

15. Booth, "The Impact of the Crisis on Poverty and Equity," pp. 128–141.

16. Human Rights Watch/Asia, 1997–2000.

17. Rhode, "Ethnic Violence in the Moluccas"; Dahlby, "Living Dangerously: Indonesia," pp. 74–102.

18. Based on weekly assessments of the *Jakarta Post* from 1998 to 2000. The average was calculated from the "others" category listed in the annual murder statistics.

19. Djalal, "The New Face of Indonesian Justice," pp. 68–71.

20. Robinson, *The Dark Side of Paradise.*

21. The Gini coefficient measures the ratio of income levels of the top 10 percent in relation to the bottom 10 percent. Higher ratios indicate higher levels of social inequality. See Schwarz, *A Nation in Waiting*, and World Bank, *Social Crisis in East Asia.*

22. Moore, "China and Globalization," pp. 105–133.

23. Lardy, *China's Unfinished Economic Revolution.*

24. See Baum and Shevchenko, "The State of the State"; Shambaugh, *The Modern Chinese State*; and Moore, "China and Globalization."

25. Liu Binyan and Perry Link, "A Great Leap Backward?" *New York Review of Books*, October 8, 1998, pp. 19–23.
26. *People's Daily* (China), May 16, 1996.
27. Space does not allow for a richer discussion of the history of this conflict. See McKenna, *Muslim Rulers and Rebels*, for more details.
28. Sidel, *Capital, Coercion, and Crime.*
29. Hutchcroft, "Neither Dynamo nor Domino," pp. 163–83.

BIBLIOGRAPHY

Amnesty International. *Annual Report.* London: Amnesty International, 1997–2001.
———.*China: The Death Penalty Log for 1998.* London: Amnesty International, 1999.
Barkey, Karen, and Sunita Parikh. "Comparative Perspectives on the State." *Annual Review of Sociology* 17 (1991): 523–49.
Baum, Richard, and Alexi Shevchenko. "The State of the State." In *The Paradox of China's Post-Mao Reforms*, edited by Merle Goldman and Roderick MacFarquar. Cambridge, Mass.: Harvard University Press, 1999.
Booth, Anne. "The Impact of the Crisis on Poverty and Equity." In *Southeast Asia's Economic Crisis: Origins, Lessons and the Way Forward*, edited by H. W. Arndt and Hal Hill, 128–41. Singapore: Institute of Southeast Asian Studies, 1999.
Brass, Paul, ed. *Theft of an Idol: Text and Context in the Representation of Political Violence.* Princeton: Princeton University Press, 1997.
Central Bureau of Statistics. 1990, 1995, 2000. Jakarta: Government of Indonesia.
Dahlby, Tracy. "Living Dangerously: Indonesia." *National Geographic*, March 2001, 74–102.
Djalal, Dini. "The New Face of Indonesian Justice." *FEER* 7, no. 13 (2000): 68–71.
Evans, Peter B. *Embedded Autonomy: States and Industrial Transformation.* Princeton, N.J.: Princeton University Press, 1995.
Friedman, Thomas L. *The Lexus and the Olive Tree.* New York: Farrar, Straus, Giroux, 1999.
Held, David, et al. *Global Transformations: Politics, Economics and Culture.* Stanford, Calif.: Stanford University Press, 1999.
Horowitz, Donald L. *The Deadly Ethnic Riot.* Berkeley, Calif.: University of California Press, 2000.
Human Rights Watch/Asia. *Annual Reports.* New York: HR Watch, 1997–2001.
Huntington, Samuel. *Political Order in Changing Societies.* New Haven, Conn.: Yale University Press, 1968.
Hutchcroft, Paul. "Neither Dynamo nor Domino: Reforms and Crises in the Philippine Political Economy." In *The Politics of the Asian Economic Crisis*, edited by T. J. Pempel, 163–83. Ithaca, N.Y.: Cornell University Press, 1999.
Jomo, K. S., ed. *Tigers in Trouble: Financial Governance, Liberalization and Crises in East Asia.* New York: Zed Books, 1998.
Kim, Samuel, ed. *East Asia and Globalization.* Lanham, Md.: Rowman and Littlefield Publishers, 2000.
Lardy, Nicholas R. *China's Unfinished Economic Revolution.* Washington, D.C.: Brookings Institute, 1998.
Liu, Binyan, and Perry Link, "A Great Leap Backward?" In *New York Review of Books*, October 8, 1998, 19–23.
Mann, Michael. "On the Autonomous Power of the State." In *States in History*, edited by John Hall. New York: Blackwell, 1986.
McKenna, Thomas. *Muslim Rulers and Rebels: Everyday Politics and Armed Separatism in the Southern Philippines.* Berkeley, Calif.: University of California Press, 1998.

Migdal, Joel. *Strong Societies and Weak States*. Princeton: Princeton University Press, 1988.

Moore, Thomas. "China and Globalization." In *East Asia and Globalization*, edited by S. Kim, 105–33. Boston: Rowman and Littlefield, 2000.

Pempel, T. J. *The Politics of the Asian Economic Crisis*. Ithaca, N.Y.: Cornell University Press, 1999.

Rhode, David. "Ethnic Violence in the Moluccas." *New York Times Magazine*, forthcoming.

Robinson, Geoffrey. *The Dark Side of Paradise: Political Violence in Bali*. Ithaca, N.Y.: Cornell University Press, 1995.

Schwarz, Adam. *A Nation in Waiting: Indonesia's Search for Stability*. London: Allen and Unwin, 2000.

Scott, James. *Seeing Like a State: How Certain Schemes to Improve the Human Condition Have Failed*. New Haven: Yale University Press, 1998.

Shambaugh, David L. *The Modern Chinese State*. Cambridge: Cambridge University Press, 2000.

Sidel, John. *Capital, Coercion, and Crime: Bossism in the Philippines*. Stanford: Stanford University Press, 1999.

Transition Indonesia Project. *Transition Indonesia Report*. New York: Columbia University Press, 2000.

Transparency International. *Corruption Perception Index for 2000*. Berlin: German.

Vandenbrink, Donna, and Chia Siow Yue, eds. *East Asia's Financial Systems: Evolution and Crisis*. Singapore: Institute of Southeast Asian Studies, 1999.

Weber, Max. *Economy and Society*, Vol. 2. New York: Bedminster Press, 1978.

Woo-Cumings, Meredith. *The Developmental State*. Ithaca, N.Y.: Cornell University Press, 1999.

World Bank. *The East Asian Miracle: Economic Growth and Public Policy*. New York: Oxford University Press, 1993.

———. *World Development Report*. Washington, D.C.: World Bank Publications, 1997.

———. *Social Crisis in East Asia*. Washington, D.C.: World Bank Publications, 1998.

———. *East Asia: Recovery and Beyond*. Washington, D.C.: World Bank Publications, 2000.

CHAPTER FIVE

Political Islam

Inclusion or Violence?

Najib Ghadbian

When Saddam Hussein invaded Kuwait in August 1990, reports had it that even sophisticated political analysts in the United States were perusing the Quran, thinking they would find there the cultural mindset undergirding Hussein's military aggression. True or not, this anecdote shows how ubiquitously Islam is associated with the condoning and even promoting of violence. That said, atrocities carried out "in the name of Allah" in Algeria, and Osama Bin Laden issuing fatwas (religious rulings) urging Muslims to kill Americans and Jews are not mere fabrications of the popular Western stereotype of violent Islam. They are real events and expressions of post–Cold War political conflicts. What is the role of Islam in the various violent conflicts taking place in the Middle East today? Why do some Islamic movements use violence while others do not? How do leaders of Islamic movements theorize the use of violence and why do some of them actually resort to violence? And what is the praxis of Islamic movements in those places in today's world where this struggle over the meaning of Islam and violence is taking its most intense form?

Politics and socioeconomic conditions, not simply religion, are the determining factors in the use of violence. The political environment of repression and dictatorship, together with the use of coercion by most regimes in the Middle East, is conducive to violence and counterviolence by disenfranchised and marginalized groups. Economic disparity is widening and unemployment rising among the semieducated and young people, the bases from which extremist groups draw their members. Both those who use violence and those who reject it find support for their views in Islamic texts, with complex arguments emerging on both sides of the interpretive divide. Is a transition to more representative politics the key to reducing violence? Often the transition to democracy poses such a challenge to the status quo that violence is used to resist it; this is the "transition to democracy dilemma." Given these conditions, how does the issue of Islam and violence play out in the Islamic heartlands, with a special focus on Arab countries?

It is important to note that Islamic movements are not the only political forces in the Arab world, nor should we identify Arab politics with Islamic politics. With the exception of Sudan, where some Islamists share power with the military, Islamic movements are in opposition to political regimes. In some countries they work through the political system and constitute the formal opposition to governments. This is the case of Jordan, Kuwait, Lebanon, Morocco, and Yemen. In other countries such as Egypt and Tunisia, they are not recognized as legal parties. The fact that Islamists are not in power in most cases and they are not allowed to contest for elections in other cases is relevant in understanding why some of them resort to violent means. Most governing elites use political parties' ideas to legitimize their rule and to counter the rising pressure from Islamists. The regimes of Syria and Iraq govern under the banner of the Ba`th party, a pan-Arab nationalist movement founded in the 1930s. Other governments formed centrist parties with no strong ideological coloring, like the National Democratic Party in Egypt and the National Democratic Rally in Algeria. For most monarchies, especially in the Arabian Gulf states, there are no recognized political parties. To sum up, while Islamists are not the only political force in the Arab world, they constitute an important trend within the opposition, with varying strength from country to country.

Political Islam, Not Islam

The dominant view in the West assumes an affinity between Islamic values and the use of violence in the Muslim world, particularly violence of a political nature.[1] As Sheila Carapico observes, "while lynchings, hate crimes, and family violence in America are but individual exceptions to a sound social ethic, 'Islamic terrorism' is portrayed as if it were a religious expression."[2] Political violence, in the Muslim world as elsewhere, is motivated by political considerations. Using quantitative analysis, Jonathan Fox has concluded that there is *no* sufficient evidence to support the stereotype of the Islamic militancy. He did find, however, that religion tends to be a potent issue in conflicts involving Islamic groups.[3] This may seem simple, but it is necessary to state: What we are studying is political Islam, not Islam or Muslims in general. Those Muslims who are the adherents of political Islam are "Islamists." In most cases, an Islamist is someone who calls for the implementation of Islamic law (*shari`a*) in all aspects of life, including the public domain. Islamists have formed movements and organizations in most Muslim countries to pursue their goal of changing their societies by deriving their programs and ideas from the texts of Islam. While Islamists are referred to as "fundamentalists," I do not find this term appropriate, since it is historically connected to specific Protestant movements and carries negative connotations. Political Islam refers to those Islamist individuals and movements who actively seek to implement Islam in the public as well as private realm.

While individuals and groups who subscribe to political Islam agree on the relevance of the principles of Islam to solving contemporary problems, they differ in methods, styles, and substantive issues. One of those major disagreements among Islamists today is about the instrumental use of violence. In the chaos of Algeria, for example, Islamists are deeply divided. While some of those who are taking part in the atrocities are associated with the Islamic Armed Group (GIA), others are part of the coalition government, the Movement of Peace.

There are two important points regarding the distinction between moderate and radical, or extremist, movements. First, this distinction is based, partially, on how such movements deal with the established political order. Moderate movements have opted to bring about change through gradual and peaceful means, while the extremists are ready to use all means necessary to implement their vision of Islam. Second, the moderates as well as the extremists are not monolithic movements, but rather diverse both in terms of their membership and agendas. A good example is the Algerian Islamic Salvation Front that includes several trends from the most extreme to the relatively moderate and pragmatic elements. Another level of the normative and the ideological divergence, even among the radical and extremist movements, could be seen through the scope of their activities. The Islamic group in Egypt, for instance, is involved in the social and economic provisions to the poor, particularly in southern Egypt. The Armed Islamic Group, on the other hand, has only brought atrocity to the Algerian people.

What is the range of differences among Islamists on the use of violence? I identify two general trends regarding the connection of Islamists to violence. The first is that Islamic groups that perpetrate violence are in the minority within the larger current of political Islam; the second is that, despite the variation in the targets of violence, acts of violence are politically motivated.

Islamic resurgence is "the increasing prominence and politicization of Islamic ideologies and symbols in the Muslim societies and in the public life of Muslim individuals."[4] Over the last two decades there has been an increasing politicization of Islam. Following the popularity of Islamic revival, various governments have tried to express their Islamic credentials. For example, the Nimeiri government in Sudan announced in 1984 that it would implement Islamic law (*shari`a*). All Islamic groups want to transform their societies and polities into more "Islamic" ones, but what that means differs widely. Not only are there differences from one country to another, but disagreements exists on a variety of issues within the same country. While some movements and groups, particularly in the Arab world, perpetrate acts of violence, the majority of Islamic movements are pursuing their goals through peaceful means. The moderate Islamic movements preach Islamic ideals, build economic institutions such as investment companies and credit unions, and provide social and educational services. They contest with governments over the control of civil society, and for power when allowed to participate in elections. Moderate Islamists refute extremists from within the religion by "emphasizing Islam's capacity for nonviolent power sharing and, thus, its compatibility with modern democratic procedures such as periodic elections, parliamentary government and entrenched civil liberties."[5]

Taking Egypt as an example, there are two Islamic groups believing in the legitimacy of violence against the political regime: al-Gama`a al-Islamiyya (the Islamic Group) and Jihad. However, Egypt's Muslim Brotherhood, and other moderate Islamic organizations and individuals who work through peaceful means, constitute the mainstream Islamic movement and have much larger memberships than the two radical groups. Carrie R. Wickham studies the causes and consequences of political mobilization in Egypt and documents the work of the Muslim Brothers in professional associations and syndicates. She describes the Brothers' efforts to achieve Islamic reform through institution building and increased participation in the mainstream channels of public life. She concludes that while "the violent acts of armed Islamists have commanded greater media attention, it is the incremental legal activities of Islamists in spheres like the professional associations which have had the greatest impact in reshaping public life."[6]

The rise of Islamic movements in the Arab world over the last twenty years coincided with a move toward democratization throughout the area. Yet the democratization process has stalled in almost every country, particularly in Egypt, Tunisia, and Algeria. Both Egypt and Algeria have employed a very heavy-handed approach to suppress the Islamists who emerged as the winners from the electoral process associated with the political openness. It was no accident that these two countries witnessed increased violence throughout the 1990s, which in Algeria approached full-scale civil war. In both cases, the failure of regimes to carry on with democratization has constituted the context for the new wave of violence.

The use of Islam by violent political groups comes from political, not religious, considerations. From the street guerrillas in Algeria and Egypt and the suicide bombers in Israel and Occupied Territories to the terrorist bombing of embassies, violence in the Arab world is highly politicized. Ali Mazrui suggests that while "Islam may generate more political violence than Western culture, Western culture generates more street violence than Islam."[7] Major cities in the Middle East, like Cairo and Tehran, are much safer, and have lower rates of crimes, Mazrui says, than U.S. and European capitals. With regard to urban street violence, the Middle East is characterized as a safer place than other regions.[8] In comparison, "there is nothing even remotely resembling the anomie and random violence of Lagos, Bogota, or Los Angeles in Cairo, Istanbul, or Casablanca." The same "Islam" that is associated in popular imagination with the use of violence is cited as a factor behind lower crime rates in Muslim cities. "It is a tribute to the social cohesiveness of Muslim societies that this nearly universal plague of the modern world has been relatively mild in the region."[9]

The targets of violence are most frequently the institutions of coercion (e.g., members of the security forces and government officials), underscoring the political nature of the violence. In Israel, the Occupied Territories, and Lebanon, Islamists (Hamas and Islamic Jihad in Palestine and Hizbollah in Lebanon) say that they are fighting foreign occupation. While in their mind the struggle is considered a "war of liberation," the distinction, in the Palestinian case, between military and civilian targets is blurred. Americans, mostly military presence, were the targets of Islamists in Lebanon in the mid-1980s and recently of the groups believed to be associated with the Saudi dissident Osama Bin Laden. Other foreigners, like tourists in Egypt and French civilians in Algeria, have been targeted by the extremist Islamists. Finally, there are the civilian victims of violence who are either caught in the crossfire in all the previous cases or are sometimes used as a political tool between the fighting parties (like in Algeria).

Violent acts occurring in this region tend to receive more attention from the media than the day-to-day social and charitable services provided by Islamists throughout the Middle East. Most people outside the Arab world know Hamas as a producer of suicide bombers, but little is known about the social, medical, and educational services this movement provides to thousands of Palestinians in Gaza and the West Bank.

Explaining Violence by Islamists

When all is said and done, some Islamic individuals and movements employ violence as a means to achieve their political goals. No matter how isolated such acts are, they are committed by individuals and groups who justify it in the name of Islam.

Why do radical and extremist Islamists advocate and perpetrate acts of violence? Analysis of this question leads to a combination of four factors. First, these Islamists exist in political and economic environments characterized by extreme political repression and economic disparity. Second, they espouse a one-sided and distorted understanding of Islam. Third, they function with a distorted, often paranoiac understanding of the world, particularly of "the enemy." A fourth mediating factor that contributed to the radicalization of some Islamists was the massive volunteering of young Islamists around the globe to fight with the Afghan mujahideen in their armed guerrilla struggle against the USSR. Activists with this "Afghani" background contribute in higher proportion to acts of political violence committed by Islamists. The primacy of political motivations in which there is a relationship between political Islam and violence makes it sensible to analyze these motivations.

Political and Economic Contexts

Political authoritarianism, economic crisis, and social anomie have been the dominant realities in the Arab world over the last three decades, despite variations among countries. These are the issues that both moderate and extremist Islamists claim to confront.

After Arab states gained independence one by one, there was a sense of hope among the leaders as well as the peoples of the region. Grievances from within, which had been deferred during the struggle for independence from the colonizer, would surely be addressed. But after sovereignty had been achieved, both traditional and progressive regimes continued to justify authoritarianism, now in the name of the larger tasks of nation building, development, and the restoration of Palestinian rights. By the 1980s, after nearly four decades of authoritarian rule, Islamist groups took up the banner of popular resistance from the nearly defunct left, recruiting their cadres from the young, students, low-level white-collar workers, and the unemployed. These are people whose education gives them aspirations that the system cannot satisfy. Authoritarian political environments, coupled with economic hardship and social anomie, are characteristics of contexts that engender violent groups. The more intense the perception of the discrepancy between aspirations and actual conditions, the greater the potential for political violence—in systems where nonviolent means of political participation are narrow to nonexistent.[10]

The last two decades have witnessed four types of politically motivated violence in the Arab Middle East and North Africa. The first type is armed struggle and counterviolence in response to extreme repression by the region's most despotic regimes: Iraq, Syria, and Libya. The uprising that took place in southern and northern regions of Iraq after the defeat of Iraq in the second Gulf War is an example. While the uprising of the Shi'i and Kurdish communities were popular spontaneous revolts, Islamists were a prominent force among the rebels in the south. A second example is that of the Muslim Brotherhood in Syria. The Brotherhood was radicalized by the police state that President Assad has nurtured since his military coup in 1970. The minority-based authoritarianism of Assad with its severe brutality spawned, in reaction, a violent campaign of assassination attempts and bombings by a small militant fringe of the Syrian Muslim Brotherhood in the mid-1970s. The confrontation escalated to a showdown between the regime and the Muslim Brotherhood that ended when the regime besieged the city of Hama and massacred its residents en masse in 1982, not discriminating, at that point, between Brotherhood members and other Hama citizens.[11]

The second type of political violence has taken the form of conflict between governments and radical Islamists in two countries: Egypt and Algeria. What distinguishes this type of violence from the previous one is the fact that the regimes in these two countries had initiated a process of liberalization, both economic and political, and then either attempted to reverse the process, as in the Egyptian case, or abort it as in Algeria. The genesis of extremist Islamic groups in Egypt goes back to the last days of Nasser, when the state unleashed its apparatus of coercion against Islamists, who suffered imprisonment, torture, and execution. After their release from prison during Sadat's rule, these groups were further radicalized by economic setbacks and the continued lack of meaningful avenues of political participation under both Sadat and Mubarak. It was one of these groups, Jihad, that assassinated Sadat in 1981; several individuals associated with another radical group attempted to assassinate Mubarak in 1995.[12] The second case is Algeria. After embarking on a democratic opening in 1988 only to be astonished by the success of the Islamic Salvation Front (FIS) in the local and then national elections in 1990 and 1991, leaders of the military decided to stop the Islamist parties from being elected to power. They nullified the result of the parliamentary election, banned the FIS as an illegal political party, and arrested its leaders. The political and military suppression of Islamists by the government sparked an all-out civil war which still rages.[13]

The third type of violence is the one fought in the name of national independence and liberation. This is the case of the Islamist and National Resistance movement in South Lebanon in the last few yeas before the Israeli withdrawal from Lebanon, and the Palestinian struggle for statehood. The resort to violence by Islamists among the Palestinians in the Occupied Territories exemplifies this type. Military occupation and displacement by Israel, combined with extreme economic hardship and intense nationalist aspirations, led to the eruption of the *intifada* in the 1980s. While the *intifada* was a popular revolt against occupation, the signing of a peace treaty and the establishing of a Palestinian authority did not end the violence. The continuation of the Palestinian plight and the stalemate in the peace process offered fertile ground for the resumption of violence[14] by many Palestinians, including the military wing of Hamas.[15] If the peace process moves forward, it is likely that Hamas will move into opposition roles vis-à-vis the Palestinian Authority, similar to the Muslim Brotherhood in Jordan and Egypt. One indication of that are the efforts of Hamas leaders to avoid confrontation with the Palestinian Authority, despite harassment by the Palestinian security forces of Hamas members and sympathizers.

The last form of political violence seen in the last few years is the terrorist acts carried out by supporters and sympathizers of Osama Bin Laden. These include the two bombings that targeted American personnel in Saudi Arabia (1995 and 1996), the bombing of the two American embassies in East Africa (1998), and the bombing of the USS Cole Destroyer (2000). The political motivation of Bin Laden, as he articulated it in several interviews with the media, is noticeable in his demands for the withdrawal of the American military forces from Saudi Arabia and the reforming of the Saudi polity, making it more Islamically authentic.

These cases exemplify the way in which repression and violence by political regimes in the region have nurtured an environment in which legitimate political participation is extremely narrow and tightly controlled, if present at all. Brutal state tactics, imprisonment, and torture have radicalized those who do not have a great deal of resources to marshal as alternative responses, including the young, the educated unemployed, and lower-level white-collar professionals. Lately, even

urban violence has been associated with the use of Islamic symbols. Several countries in the Middle East have witnessed "cost-of-living rioting" after the adoption
of drastic measures, such as price hikes on basic commodities as part of economic
structural adjustment programs. Widespread riots took place in Egypt in 1977,
Tunisia in 1978, Morocco in 1982, Sudan in 1985, Algeria in 1988, and Jordan in
1989 and 1997. In both Egypt and Algeria protest was justified using Islamic
terms. In Egypt, three days after announcement of price increases in January 1997,
severe rioting ensued in Cairo and several other cities. The government immediately revoked the price increase. Algeria saw the worst riots in 1988, after the failure of the government in implementing its reformist policies, and was perceived
to be massively corrupt. In their study of the political economy of the Middle East,
Alan Richards and John Waterbury have concluded that "government policies
during the past three decades have fostered a counter-elite of Islamist business
and frustrated educated youth, accumulated potential recruits of the movement
through economic failure, provided them with numerous grievances, and evacuated critical spaces in the political economy."[16]

These factors have created an environment of violence in which we observe the
reactive violence of radical Islamists. The typical extremist Islamist combines a
certain socioeconomic background (young, from provincial towns and cities, with
some education and professional aspirations) with an upbringing stressing
Islamic values.[17]

Interpretation of Islam

The extremist Islamists' understanding and interpretation of Islam is a contributing factor to their acceptance and perpetration of violence. Extremists utilize two
key principles in Islam to justify the use of violence. The first is the centrality of
socioeconomic equity and justice and the second is the doctrine of *jihad* (waging
holy war on behalf of Islam as a religious duty).[18] The principle of social justice is
derived from the many Quranic verses and the sayings of the Prophet Mohammed
urging Muslims to struggle actively in the world for justice and social equity.
Islam's egalitarian ethic has been a mobilizing force for the underdog throughout
history for moderates and radicals alike.

Jihad is invoked by Islamists as a means to social and political justice. Moderates see jihad in a nuanced manner as a spiritual effort toward the good, starting
within oneself and moving toward reform in the society at large. The struggle to
uphold truth and justice does not exclude the use of violence. The difference
between moderates and extremists is that for the first group violence is the last
resort and there are several constraints when violence is to be implemented. The
extremists often overlook the restraints and tend to consider the use of violence a
legitimate means whenever conditions of injustice prevail. Related to the doctrine
of jihad is the concept of martyrdom, or *shahadah*. In the discourse of radical
Islamists one finds a strong emphasis on this concept. Islamic texts are clear about
the nobility of martyrdom; dying for the sake of God is the highest form of sacri-

fice and devotion to God. At the same time, Islam clearly forbids suicide. Martyrdom then is to be understood as taking place when the situation for the community is perceived as desperate, as in a state of war. In fact, most of the Islamic texts on martyrdom have such contexts as the occasion of their narration. For example, in many hadiths the Prophet utters praise of martyrs as consolation to the families of men who died in battle in defense of the community. Other hadiths give women who die in childbirth the status of martyrs too, along with people who die in exile and from epidemic disease, and this status grants paradise, but no one has ever understood that to mean that women should strive to die in childbirth or that people should try to catch epidemic diseases or get exiled. As with jihad, extremists tend to overlook the ways in which Islamic tradition carefully defines the notion of martyrdom. Their simplistic understanding of martyrdom sheds light on why some radical Islamists have resorted to suicide bombings and attacks.

Several extremist groups in the 1970s were influenced by the teachings of Sayyid Qutb, a leading member of the Egyptian Muslim Brotherhood. Qutb was executed by the Nasser regime for an alleged attempt to overthrow the government. Qutb wrote a book while in prison in which he asserted that any political systems that does not implement Islam is in a state of *jahiliyya*, that is, paganism or ignorance. *Jahiliyya* is a loaded term used in the early Islamic era to refer to a specific spiritual ignorance, the pre-Islamic Arabs' ignorance of monotheism. It came to imply moral degeneracy and to be a pejorative term demarcating believer from infidel. According to Qutb, Nasser's regime exemplified *jahili* (pagan) rule, not only because it was not implementing *shari`a* (Islamic law), but because it was torturing pious Muslims for their faith. While Qutb espoused the principle of jihad as a legitimate means to fighting injustice, he did not directly call for the use of violence. To him, jihad meant the education of a generation of Muslims to the ideals of Islam, followed by the peaceable reform of society—a society that would of its own accord wish to form an Islamic state—and subsequently the establishment of an Islamic state.[19]

But the extremists who came after Qutb derived a different conclusion from his starting principles: The struggle to overthrow a corrupt and illegitimate government is a religious duty, a form of jihad, which they defined in a narrow sense as physical violence. The theorist behind the group that assassinated Sadat, Mohamed Abdussalam Faraj, wrote a tract entitled *The Forgotten Obligation*, referring to jihad. According to Faraj, the first task of jihad is "to uproot these infidel leaders and replace them with the comprehensive Islamic system."[20] The idea of justifying the resort to violence against most governments in the Arab world became widely acceptable within the ranks of extremists.

Worldview of Extremist Islamists

The discourses of some extremist Islamists reveal a third factor shedding some light on their resort to violence: their distorted worldview. This goes beyond the usual demonizing of the enemy which all fighting groups and countries do. The first kind of distortion is their lack of realism about their own power in relation to the state. Several cases in which extremist Islamists took arms against "illegitimate and corrupt" regimes show gross miscalculation on the part of the radical Islamists. Armed Islamists in Syria, Egypt, and Algeria have paralleled each other's tendency to underestimate the power of their opponents. Each of these extremist factions believes that "the masses are rallying" behind them and "the security forces will run away when confronted." All it takes is a few brave stalwarts and the age of miracles will return. The ramparts of the state—backed by high-tech surveillance and state-of-the-art military equipment—will presumably come tumbling down before the superior moral purity of the rebels. Although such statements are obviously mouthed for propaganda purposes, they appear at some point to become beliefs on which plans are based, judging by the disastrous tactics that such groups have employed.

In an interview, one of the leaders of Egypt's al-Gama`a al-Islamiyya offers the following reasons why the group uses violence against foreign tourists: "First, many tourist activities are forbidden [by Islam] . . . so this source of income for the state is forbidden." Second, he says that tourism is an abomination because "it is a means by which prostitution and AIDS are spread by Jewish women tourists, and it is a source of all manner of depravities, not to mention being a means of collecting information on the Islamic movement."[21] Not only is he seeing foreign conspiracy behind the Egyptian tourist industry, but he has localized the danger as lying in the sexually predatory woman of the enemy. The idea of the sexually predatory woman, whose otherness is sometimes exacerbated by her being foreign as well, as an important source of danger for the virtuous man dates back to the story of Joseph and Potiphar's wife in Genesis, and to even earlier Egyptian folk tales, and, at one time or another, has received due emphasis in the Jewish, Christian, and Islamic cultural traditions. Here it resurfaces in the discourse of extremist Islamists, and it is the foreignness of the woman as much as her sexual aggressiveness that is emphasized as the source of danger. Xenophobia is an important element of the distorted worldview of the extremists.

This distorted worldview of extremist Islamists has contributed to their receiving a major blow at the hands of the security forces. By 1999 the Egyptian regime succeeded in eradicating the security threat emanating from two Islamic groups, Jihad and al-Gama'a. In a recent article examining the retreat of violence by the extremist Islamic groups in Egypt, Fawaz Gerges quotes the leaders of these groups who told him that they felt "empowered" and "arrogant" and had "lost touch with reality." He concludes that the two groups "failed to appreciate the strength of opposing—local, regional, and international—forces arrayed against them. Most importantly, however, they alienated and antagonized the pacific Egyptian public by relying exclusively on shock tactics to jolt it out of its political slumber."[22]

A second example of the extremists' distorted worldview is provided by Osama Bin Laden. News agencies have reported that Bin Laden, in the aftermath of the American and British military strike against Iraq, urged Muslims to attack U.S. and British citizens and interests to avenge these two countries' air strike on Iraq. The justification given by Bin Laden was that "the British and American people have widely voiced their supports for their leaders' decision to attack Iraq." This is enough to qualify these people, in addition to the Israeli Jews, as legitimate targets.[23]

Distorted worldviews and demonization of the enemy tend to be greatest among those who resort to indiscriminate acts of violence and terrorism. In the case of the extremists among the Islamic currents, the distorted worldview is connected to a very selective and twisted interpretation of Islamic texts. For instance, the members of extremist groups, such as GIA, who kill civilians and commit atrocities ignore totally the Islamic teachings about the sanctity of human life, the prohibition of killing civilians, and the punishment of criminal killing both in this life and in the next. "The expansion of violence to targets that were initially outside of the scope of Islamist grievances—intellectuals, journalists, foreigners, and civilians—can be traced to GIA's anti-system and Manichean worldview, which refused to distinguish between active enemies and neutral observers."[24]

The Afghani Factor

There is another factor which contributed to the radicalization of Islamists and strengthened the tendency among some young Islamists toward violence: the war in Afghanistan. Between 1980 and the mid-1990s thousands of young Muslims, mostly Arabs, volunteered to help the Afghani mujahideen against their Soviet-controlled regime.[25] Infused with Islamic idealism, but without an outlet for it at home, these people saw in the Afghani struggle a good cause, a case of stalwart believers against clear-cut infidels. What better place to put into action the ideals—faith, courage, martyrdom—in which they believed but had little practical chance to implement at home. Many of the young volunteers were escaping the oppression of their own governments and found a safe haven in the guerrilla-controlled areas of Afghanistan. At that time, the United States had an interest in seeing the Soviets lose their foothold in Afghanistan. The Afghan guerrillas received sympathetic press in the West and were called "freedom fighters." After the Soviet withdrawal from Afghanistan, the war changed course to a civil war between the various Afghani factions. Internecine tribal warfare did not make for a very satisfying moral clash between good and evil; many of the volunteer mujahideen dispersed, looking for new battlegrounds. Bin Laden and the street fighters in Egypt and Algeria got their military training and doses of extremism in Afghanistan.

A sometimes overlooked fact about the Afghani war is that "the largest CIA covert aid program in US history financed and armed the most extreme of the *mujahidin* groups."[26] The irony is that some of these groups turned against the

United States. The United States also "has been a factor of major importance in the growth of military capabilities of militant Islamic forces in Egypt and elsewhere."[27] The Saudi government contributed also, funding and facilitating the movement of young Saudis and others to join the freedom fighters. A source close to the Saudi government estimates the number of Saudi nationals alone who participated in the Afghani war to be in the thousands.[28] While a majority of these people went back to resume their normal life, according to the Saudi source, some decided to stay behind and join the ranks of Bin Laden. One cannot underestimate the psychological effect of the Afghan war on those volunteer fighters who decided to go back to their own countries. A point that impressed many who participated in the Afghani war was that the ragtag, low-tech Afghan mujahideen succeeded in forcing a superpower out of their country. This reinforced their belief that militant jihad is an effective way to deal with evil forces, that all it takes is commitment and belief in one's just cause to bring down the vast apparatus of the state, security forces and all.

While Bin Laden continues to operate from Afghanistan, some of his followers join other "Muslim causes" in Bosnia, Chechnya, Kosovo, and Dagestan. The latest attempt to establish an Islamic state in Dagestan, in which some of Bin Laden's followers took part, has escalated into a full-scale invasion of Chechnya by the Russian forces. It is reported that one of Bin Laden's supporters, Khatab, was the mastermind behind the terrorist bombing campaign in several Russian cities. The alleged involvement of Bin Laden supporters in the conflict of Dagestan made it possible for the United States and Russia to work together against Bin Laden. On October 15, 1999, the Security Council decided to impose limited economic sanctions on the Taliban government if it didn't hand over Bin Laden by November 14.[29] The Security Council voted again on December 19, 2000, to impose broad sanctions on the Taliban rulers unless they close "terrorist" training camps and surrender Bin Laden to be tried for the bombing of the two U.S. embassies in 1998.[30]

Conclusion and Prospects

Islam is not synonymous with violence. Political movements deriving their ideology and programs from Islam constitute the major opposition force all over the Middle East. They stand in opposition to authoritarian rulers who suffer from a serious lack of legitimacy. Islamic groups disagree on a variety of issues, including the instrumental use of violence. While some groups do feel the use of violence is legitimate in the fight against injustice and evils, such groups are still in the minority within the popular trend of political Islam.

The debate between extremists and moderates over the question of violence is centered around two points: the usefulness of violence as a means and the religious basis for the justification of violence. For the extremists, oppressive political rulers will not yield until confronted with power, and Islam urges believers to resort to jihad to fight evil and oppression. The moderates see the use of violence as counterproductive and as obstructing the Islamization process by giving justification to regimes for continued repression. The moderates think that armed jihad is the last resort and is restrained by several considerations, including weighing the benefits against the great cost, refraining from excessive violence, and having overall respect and compassion for human life.

How effective and useful has the resort to violence been in the cases we have examined? The answer varies. Under the extreme authoritarian regimes of Iraq, Syria, and Libya, attempts to violently overthrow such regimes not only failed but also were costly for the Islamic opposition movements and more importantly for the civilian populations, as the cases of the Shi`a uprising of 1991 in Iraq and the armed uprising in the Syrian city of Hamah show. The excessive use of violence by these regimes as well as the gross human rights violation, however, have further delegitimized and demoralized these regimes in the long run. What the bloody confrontation taught the opposition, and the public at large in these countries, is that these movements are no match for the security forces, and popular revolt is not likely to bring about regime change.

In the Egyptian and Algerian cases the evidence is less conclusive. In Egypt the larger radical Islamist group, which carried out violent attacks throughout the 1990s, conceded defeat in March 1999 by declaring a unilateral suspension of all armed activities. The defeat of this group was effected as much by the suppression by the security forces as by losing public support, which resulted from the indiscriminate killing and bombing of noncombatant targets such as civilians and tourists.[31] The defeat of radical Islamists in Egypt cannot be considered as a victory to the regime. Many Egyptian activists and scholars have warned the government not to take this conceded defeat as an alternative to carrying out serious political and economic reforms. In a way, the defeat of radical Islamists has meant a triumph for the logic of moderate Islamists who advocate peaceful and gradual change from within. One indication that the weight of the moderate Muslim Brothers has not evaporated was the parliamentary election in October 2000. Despite the usual harassment and obstruction of opposition voters by government forces, the Muslim Brothers won more seats than all the other "legal" opposition parties combined.[32] Algeria is the case that demonstrates what could go wrong when violence persists and none of the fighting factions are capable of achieving a clear-cut victory. The war that the regime started by arresting the leaders of the FIS has degenerated into a Hobbesian state of nature in which everyone seems against everyone else. Not only have there been contradictory reports on who is responsible for the atrocities committed against the civilian populace, but also Islamists have taken three opposite sides. The Society of Peace (formerly known as the Islamic Society Movement) decided to accept the election cancellation and continued to work from within the system. It has participated in every election since then and even joined some cabinets. Its leader, Mahfuz al-Nahnah, ran for the presidential election in 1995 and won about 25 percent of the popular vote. Most other Islamists went underground and engaged in guerrilla war against the government. They formed small factions, the most notorious being the Islamic Armed Group (GIA), believed to be behind the worst atrocities committed in the course of the conflict. A third faction emerged in 1993–94 under the title of Islamic Salvation Army (AIS), claiming to be the military wing of the FIS. By early 1996 GIA turned against AIS. In the summer of 1997 AIS reached an agreement with the government to disband itself and even help the government in its fight against GIA.[33] All the military and political initiatives have failed so far to put an end to violence in Algeria.

One area where one form of violence—armed struggle—has worked is in Lebanon. In the last few years Hizbollah had intensified its military attacks against Israeli forces and its Lebanese proxy, South Lebanon Army (SLA). Despite the image of Hizbollah as a terrorist organization, its targeting of Israeli army and defining its political objective as the liberation of Lebanon from foreign military occupation have augmented the support among most Lebanese and generated international sympathy for the movement's cause. The Israeli early retreat from Lebanon in May 2000 was perceived as a victory to the armed struggle of Hizbollah.[34] The eruption of the second Palestinian *intifada* on September 27, 2000, was influenced by the Lebanese example. While the protest movement began right after the provocative visit of the Israeli opposition leader, Uril Sharon, to the Muslim holy site in Jerusalem, the failure of the Camp David Summit and the continuation of the Israeli military occupation of most of the West Bank nine years after the investiture of the peace process, constituted the background to the recent violence in the Palestinian occupied territories. The Palestinians, according to Chris Hedges, "filled with rage and economic despair, grew impatient with Fatah's conciliation, as well as its nepotism and corruption, and embraced the harsher methods and rhetoric of the Islamists. After all, they argued, such tactics worked for Hezbollah in southern Lebanon."[35]

What are the prospects of a less violent political Islam? If the use of violence is related more to political and economic conditions than to religion, the answer lies not in religion but in addressing the political and economic conditions that breed extremism. The evidence shows a strong correlation, throughout the Arab world, between political suppression and violence. It is not a coincidence that in those countries—Jordan, Yemen, Kuwait, and recently Lebanon—where Islamists are recognized as legal political parties and allowed to participate in the political process, violence by Islamists has been minimal or absent. Those countries that refused to grant Islamists any legal status—Syria, Egypt, Libya, and Algeria after its crackdown on the FIS—have seen their Islamist groups become more radicalized and more likely to use confrontation and violence.

Political openness seems to be conducive to nonviolence. For openness to happen, the people at the top must be responsive to the demand to open the structure of power. This is what makes the presence of a capable political leadership within movements as well as within regimes so crucial. Leaders who are skilled in the art of conflict resolution and compromise are required to steer the process in a manner so that all the players see clearly that they have a stake in it. Take the Lebanese case. The Taif Accord of 1990 formally ended the civil war and gave an avenue for new political forces, especially the Shi`ites, to participate in the political process. Since then even Hizbollah has taken important strides toward transforming itself into a political party working within the system. The withdrawal of Israeli forces from Lebanon is likely to put further pressure on Hizbollah to fight its future wars through the ballot box.[36]

Finally, political Islamic movements are faced with what John Keane calls "the transition to democracy dilemma." This dilemma is simply the choice, for any Islamic movement attempting to transform a non-Islamic state into an Islamic one, between two incompatibilities: principles and power.[37] If an Islamic movement decides to play the democratic game while its opponents—those in power—refuse to abide by the same rules, such a movement is faced with the prospect that it might never achieve governmental power. The closest case of this is the Tunisian Islamic movement, al-Nahdha, which contested in the parliamentary election in 1989. Despite rigged results, the movement came second after the ruling party. It was an alarming sign to the ruling elite, which trumped up allegations of a seditious plot and cracked down massively on the movement. There was no violent reaction from the movement, whose members were subjected to imprisonment or forced to flee into exile. The movement subsequently lost ground and support. If, on the other hand, a movement resorts to violence to fight state suppression, as is the case with the FIS in Algeria, the group is faced with two dangerous outcomes. It does not remain faithful to its professed commitment to pluralism and democracy, and the whole country succumbs to the vicious cycle of violence. The malicious civil war in Algeria has, unfortunately, brought these two fears into reality.

Obviously, there is no easy solution to this transition to democracy dilemma. What might work in one country will not work for another. The argument of some Islamists that violence is the only means to bring down brutal and corrupt regimes is perhaps not without validity. Yet Islamists, both radicals and moderates, have learned the hard way that it is not easy to defeat the security apparatus of the modern state. Other Islamists, influenced by the pacifist and *sufi* traditions and fearing the unintended consequences of violence, maintain that it is better for the believer to be in the oppressed camp than to be in the camp of the oppressor. The examples of Jordan, Yemen, Kuwait, Morocco, and recently Lebanon have demonstrated that including Islamists—no matter how nominal such inclusion—in the political system has spared these countries the viciousness of confrontation between ruling elites and their Islamist challengers. History has repeatedly shown us, however, that those in the position of power are not likely to share power, unless they reach the conclusion that if they do not do so they might lose it entirely. As long as dictators or occupying forces on one side, and their challengers on the other side, think they can monopolize power and resources, violence is inevitable.

NOTES

1. For examples, see James Walsh, "The Sword of Islam," *Time International*, June 15, 1992, p. 18; Denise Bombardier, "Islamic Terrorism: A Growing Peril," *World Press Review*, May 1987; and Daniel Pipes, "The Muslims Are Coming! The Muslims Are Coming!" *National Review*, November 19, 1990, pp. 28–31. For more comprehensive survey and discussion of alarmist views of Islam, see John Esposito, *The Islamic Threat: Myth or Reality?* 3rd ed. (Oxford: Oxford University Press, 1999), and Ahmad Yousef and Ahmad AbulJobain, *The Politics of Islamic Resurgence Through Western Eyes: A Bibliographic Survey* (Springfield: UASR, 1992).

2. Sheila Carapico, "Introduction to Part One," in *Political Islam*, ed. Joel Beinin and Joseph Stork (Berkeley: University of California Press, 1997), p. 30.

3. Jonathan Fox, "Is Islam More Conflict Prone than Other Religions? A Cross-Sectional Study of Ethnoreligious Conflict," *Nationalism and Ethnic Politics* 6, no. 2 (2000): 1–24.

4. Ali E. Hillal Dessouki, "The Islamic Resurgence: Sources, Dynamics, and Implications," in *Islamic Resurgence in the Arab World*, ed. Ali E. H. Dessouki (New York: Praeger Publishers, 1982), p. 4.

5. John Keane, *Reflections on Violence* (London: Verso, 1996), p. 96.

6. Carrie R. Wickham, "Islamic Mobilization and Political Change: The Islamist Trend in Egypt's Professional Associations," in *Political Islam*, ed. Joel Beinin and Joe Stork (Berkeley: University of California Press, 1997), p. 131.

7. Ali A. Mazrui, "Islamic and Western Values," *Foreign Affairs* 76, no. 5 (1997): 130.

8. Alan Richards and John Waterbury, *A Political Economy of the Middle East*, 2nd ed. (Boulder: Westview Press, 1996), p. 259.

9. Ibid., p. 260.

10. Ted R. Gurr, *Why Men Rebel* (Princeton: Princeton University Press, 1970).

11. For an account to the events leading to the Hama confrontation, see Umar Abd-Allah, *The Islamic Struggle in Syria* (Berkeley: Mizan Press, 1983).

12. There are several studies on the radicalization of Islamists in Egypt. One example is Hamied N. al-Ansari, "The Islamic Militants in Egyptian Politics," *IJMES* 16, no. 1 (1984): 123–44.

13. Robert Mortimer, "Algeria: The Dialectic of Election and Violence," *Current History* 96 (May 1997): 231–35.

14. The eruption of the second uprising known as *al-Aqsa intifada*, on September 27, 2000, attests to this view.

15. A good discussion of the context of Hamas's origins can be found in Jean-Francois Legrain, "Hamas: Legitimate Heir of Palestinian Nationalism?" in *Political Islam: Revolution, Radicalism, or Reform?* Ed. John Esposito (Boulder: Lynne Rienner Publishers, 1997), pp. 159–78.

16. Richards and Waterbury, *A Political Economy of the Middle East*, p. 348.

17. Ibid., p. 272.

18. For a discussion of these two points, see Mir Zohair Husain, *Global Islamic Politics*

(New York: HarperCollins College Publishers, 1995), pp. 32–42.

19. Sayyid Qutb, *Ma`alim `ala al-Tariq (Milestones on the Path)* (Cairo: Dar al-Surruq, 1982).

20. For a further discussion of the disagreements between moderate and extremist Islamists, see Najib Ghadbian, *Democratization and the Islamist Challenge in the Arab World* (Boulder: Westview, 1997), ch. 4.

21. "What Does the Gama`a Islamiyya Want? Tal'at Fu`ad Qasim, Interview with Hisham Mubarak," in *Political Islam*, ed. Beinin and Stork, p. 321.

22. Fawaz A. Gerges, "The End of Islamic Insurgency in Egypt?: Costs and Prospects," *Middle East Journal* 54, no. 4 (2000): 593.

23. Quoted by *Reuters*, December 25, 1998.

24. Mohammed M. Hafez, "Armed Islamic Movements and Political Violence in Algeria," *Middle East Journal* 54, no. 4 (2000): 573.

25. See, for instance, Barnett R. Rubin, "Arab Islamists in Afghanistan," in *Political Islam*, ed. Esposito, pp. 179–206.

26. Beinin and Stork, eds., *Political Islam*, p. 11.

27. Ibid., p. 11.

28. "Qissat al-Afghan Asa`oudiyyin" (the Story of the Saudi Afghans), *al-Majallah*, no. 847 (May 5–11, 1996): 19.

29. *Associated Press*, October 16, 1999.

30. Nicole Winfield, "UN Gives Taliban Ultimatum on Bin Laden," *Associated Press*, December 20, 2000.

31. Gerges, "The End of Islamic Insurgency in Egypt?" pp. 592–612.

32. Steve Negus, "Egypt: Election Results," *Middle East International*, no. 638 (November 24, 2000): 14–15.

33. Hafez, "Armed Islamic Movements and Political Violence in Algeria," pp. 573–91.

34. Michael Jansen, "Lebanon's Finest Hour," *Middle East International*, no. 626 (June 2, 2000): 4–6.

35. Chris Hedges, "The New Palestinian Revolt," *Foreign Affairs* 80, no. 1 (2001): 134–35.

36. Beverly Milton-Edwards, "Hizbollah After Withdrawal," *Middle East Insight* 24, no. 4 (July–August 2000): 48.

37. John Keane, "Power Sharing Islam?" in *Power Sharing Islam?* ed. Azzam Tamimi (London: Liberty for Muslim World Publication, 1993), p. 20.

CHAPTER SIX

State Rape

Sexual Violence as Genocide

Lisa Sharlach

There will never be a really free and enlightened State, until the State comes to recognize the individual as a higher and independent power, from which all its own power and authority are derived, and treats him [and her] accordingly.

—*Henry David Thoreau*[1]

Rape is among the most traumatic and the most prevalent of human rights abuses, and it has accompanied warfare since prehistory. Nevertheless, scholars of political violence, if they address rape at all, tend to present it as a consequence of war rather than as a component of it.[2] Examination of the civil wars in Pakistan, the former Yugoslavia, and Rwanda suggests, however, that states may use rape as a policy to maintain social and political inequality. A state dominated by one sex and one ethnic group (or ethnic coalition) may encourage men of the dominant ethnic group to rape women of another ethnic group to keep the subordinate group subordinated. In the worst-case scenarios, the dominant group, frightened by what its members perceive as an onslaught of international and internal movements for democracy and socioeconomic change, harnesses the state apparatus to destroy the subordinated group altogether. This is genocide, and the overtly or covertly state-sanctioned use of sexual violence as a tactic of genocide is the focus of this chapter.

A study of ethnic warfare that omits sexual violence tells only part of the story. It ignores the full extent of the humiliation of the ethnic group through the rape of its women, the symbols of honor and vessels of culture. When a woman's honor is tarnished through illicit intercourse, even if against her will, the ethnic group is also dishonored. The aftereffects of rape—forced impregnation, psychological trauma, degradation, and demoralization—go beyond the rape victims themselves.

The shame surrounding sexual violence complicates investigation of rape's political uses. Recent efforts by human rights and international organizations to document sexual violence against women in wars across the continents provide the necessary scraps with which to quilt together the other part of the story of ethnic warfare in the final decades of the twentieth century. Few political scientists have taken advantage of the emerging resources with which to study rape in political conflict.[3] The absence of systematic study may stem from an assumption that rape is a topic that our colleagues in sociology and psychology rightfully own. Political science is, however, a promising vantage point from which to analyze sexual violence in war because of the discipline's emphasis upon power relations and the institutions that mediate them. This study therefore is of *state rape*, mass rape either perpetrated, encouraged, or tacitly approved by the institutions of the state.

The function of state rape is to inflict sexualized degradation and injury upon women who belong to a less powerful ethnic group. State rape is especially likely in societies in which dominant groups—based on gender, ethnicity, region, or religion—have disproportionate control of the coercive apparatus of the state. The trigger for a campaign of mass rape by the dominant group is the threat of transition toward political and economic equality. Thus, state rape perpetuates the dominant group's hegemony—its preponderant influence in politics and society.

Rape as Genocide

Genocidal rape is not new, but how governments and armies use it is. In ancient times, invading conquerors killed the men and enslaved the women. The rape of the slaves lasted for generations, until the conquerors had completed the genocide through miscegenation. No longer does the conqueror assimilate the females of an ethnic group through generations of enslavement and forcible miscegenation. Since the Holocaust, almost all genocide has occurred in civil, not international, war. The level of the modern state's involvement in genocidal rape has escalated from "toleration" to "encouragement and sanction" to "institutionalization" to "instrumentalization as a tactic serving strategic war aims."[4]

The legal definition of genocide, enshrined in the 1948 *Convention on the Prevention and Punishment of the Crime of Genocide* (hereinafter the "Genocide Convention"), is as follows:

> Genocide means any of the following acts committed with intent to destroy, in whole or in part, a national, ethnic, racial or religious group, as such:
> (a) Killing members of the group;
> (b) Causing serious bodily or mental harm to members of the group;
> (c) Deliberately inflicting on the group conditions of life calculated to bring about its physical destruction in whole or in part;
> (d) Imposing measures intended to prevent births within the group;
> (e) Forcibly transferring children of the group to another group.[5]

Nowhere does the Genocide Convention explicitly address sexual violence. However, rape may fall under Section D of the definition above because forced impregnation of a group's women by men from outside the group results in ethnically mixed offspring. Had these women not been forcibly impregnated by outsiders, they could have delivered babies fathered by men within their own group. Additionally, rape may fit within Section B of the Genocide Convention's definition— rape causes serious physical and/or mental injury to the survivor, and may destroy the morale of her family and community.

The authors of the Genocide Convention debated whether mass killings of people on the basis of political identity—such as partisan or ideological affiliation—should constitute genocide.[6] The final version of the Genocide Convention does *not* encompass crimes against political groups.[7] Thus, it matters greatly whether a specific episode of political violence meets the criteria specified in the Genocide Convention's definition. Genocide warrants, even mandates, intervention by the international community through the auspices of the UN Security Council. Any state may prosecute crimes of genocide by another state, wherever those crimes might have transpired. States do *not* have this right of intervention in another country's internal affairs if the violence that is taking place there does not meet the legal definition of genocide. Political violence, even the slaughter of tens of thousands of people, does not merit international intervention unless the killing is motivated by an intent to destroy an ethnic, religious, or national group.

In the early 1990s news of rape as ethnic cleansing in Croatia and Bosnia-Herzegovina sparked law professor Catharine MacKinnon to denounce rape as a tactic of extermination:

> It is also rape unto death, rape as massacre, rape to kill and to make the victims wish they were dead. It is rape as an instrument of forced exile, rape to make you leave your home and never want to go back. It is rape to be seen and heard and watched and told to others: rape as spectacle. It is rape to drive a wedge through a community, to shatter a society, to destroy a people. It is rape as genocide.[8]

Other legal scholars argue that it is forced impregnation, not rape per se, that constitutes genocide.[9] Forcing females of a targeted ethnic group to conceive is genocidal because those so impregnated cannot bear the offspring of men of their own ethnic group while their wombs are so "occupied." Under this logic, anal rape, oral rape, object rape, rape of prepubescent girls, rape of postmenopausal women, and vaginal rape using a condom or without ejaculation would not constitute genocide because such rape would not result in conception of an ethnically hybrid fetus.

In 1998 the International Criminal Tribunal for Rwanda (ICTR) ended this debate. The ICTR ruled that Jean-Paul Akayesu, the former mayor of Taba Commune, was guilty of a number of crimes of genocide, including rape.[10] The ICTR's decision sidesteps entirely the issue of forced impregnation. Rape may fit within the legal definition of genocide simply because it represents the enemy's intent to destroy.

The expansion of the Genocide Convention's mandate to encompass sociopolitical groups might permit international criminal courts to deem mass rape to be genocide, intended to harm or destroy the female sex in whole or in part, regardless of whether the sexual violence had an ethnically or religiously based motivation. The Genocide Convention should be expanded to include sexual violations of girls and women, even if there is not evidence that the rapists targeted their victims on the basis of racial/ethnic, national, or religious identity. Intent to destroy people on the basis of sex should, in my analysis, merit the same status under international law as the intent to destroy people on the basis of ethnicity, nation, and religion.

Case Studies of State Rape

Bangladesh, the former Yugoslavia, and Rwanda may appear to have little in common. The levels of economic development, the degree of religious heterogeneity, the political cultures, and the patterns of ethnic and class stratification vary tremendously. Similar to all three, however, was potential political liberalization quashed by the eruption of ethnic war. Moreover, in all three case studies, a dominant social group harnessed the coercive apparatus of the state to inflict sexual violence as one tactic in a larger strategy of humiliation, subjugation, and attempted eradication of a less powerful ethnic group.

Admittedly, the structure of this study reflects the methodological sin of selection on the dependent variable. All the cases in this chapter are of state rape; no case study is of a state that does not perpetuate or perpetrate sexual violence to influence power relations. Therefore, it must be emphasized that these three cases are *not* representative of all instances in which men have used rape as genocide. The observations drawn from these cases are not truisms.

East Pakistan, 1971

Pakistan, an Islamic nation, formed after the bloody 1940s Partition from India. The Muslims in predominantly Hindu colonial South Asia wanted self-determination because they feared that their minority voice would not be heard in the postindependence democracy. Pakistan had two noncontiguous regions, West (now simply Pakistan) and East (now Bangladesh), both on the northern border of India. Disgruntled East Pakistanis perceived themselves as exploited by the Western half of the country, which reserved for itself most of the national development projects and the jobs in the military.[11] During 1971 East Pakistanis waged a nine-month war of independence on their territory. East Pakistani insurgents fought Pakistan's national army, which was comprised almost entirely of West Pakistani troops.

The invading West Pakistanis (and their East Pakistani sympathizers) raped between 200,000 and 400,000 women as part of a campaign to destroy East Pakistani Bengalis, an ethnic group that encompasses all castes and includes both Hindus and Muslims.[12] Approximately three million people died. Not all of the casualties were Bengalis, however. Fearing their potential complicity with West Pakistan, the Bengalis themselves killed approximately 150,000 of the five to six million non-Bengalis living in East Pakistan.[13]

The national army raped and killed civilians—men, women, infants, and children—purposefully.[14] War correspondents heard repeatedly from refugees that soldiers killed babies by throwing them in the air and catching them on their bayonets, and murdered women by raping them and then spearing them through the genitals. *Newsweek* concluded that the prevalence of these unusual techniques of homicide of children and women was an indication that the West Pakistani army was "carrying out a calculated policy of terror amounting to genocide against the whole Bengali population."[15]

There is no evidence of a directive from West Pakistan to rape, but there is evidence that senior officers were aware of, encouraged, or themselves participated in the rape warfare. For example, survivors reported that a high-ranking Pakistani officer alluded to the mass rape as a means of subjugating the enemy women. In allusion to the Bengal tigers, he referred to the rape of Bengali women as "taming the tigresses."[16] Additionally, a Bangladeshi political scientist reports that the West Pakistani officers showed pornographic films in the barracks in East Pakistan to encourage their weary soldiers to rape.[17] Moreover, when India's army intervened on behalf of East Pakistan to force the West Pakistani army to surrender, an Indian journalist notes that a West Pakistani soldier shouted:

> "*Hum ja rahe hain. Lekin beej chhor kar ja rahe hain.*" (We are going. But we are leaving our Seed Behind.). He accompanied it with an appropriately coarse gesture. Behind that bald statement lies the story of one of the most savage, organized and indiscriminate orgies of rape in human history: rape by a professional army, backed by local armed collaborators. It spared no one, from elderly widows to schoolgirls not yet in their teens, from wives of high-ranking civil officers to daughters of the poorest villagers and slum dwellers. Senior officers allowed, and presumably encouraged, the forced confinement of innocent girls for months inside regimental barracks, bunks and even tanks.[18]

The rapists inflicted degradation, physical and psychological trauma, and/or death upon the Bengali women. After rape, soldiers might murder the victims by forcing a bayonet between their legs.[19] Soldiers kept some captives in their bar-racks.[20] Women and girls in detainment suffered gang rape and torture, such as being tied to the window bars by their hair. A captive who displeased the soldiers might be murdered—shot or speared up the vagina.[21]

The majority of the rape survivors had contracted syphilis, gonorrhea, or both.[22] These venereal diseases, left untreated, would cause many of the rape sur-vivors to be ill and/or sterile for the remainder of their lives. Additionally, the rapes inflicted psychological harm. One survivor of sexual enslavement relates that of the six hundred women with whom she was detained in Syedpur, many developed mental illnesses.[23] Even those Bengali girls who evaded the rapist sol-diers by hiding or by fleeing from place to place suffered nine months of fear. An act of such physical and psychological violence may fall within the domain of Article II, Section B of the 1948 Genocide Convention if one can demonstrate the rapist's intent to harm the victim because of her ethnic affiliation.

In addition to causing injury, the rapes were genocidal in that they caused the forced impregnation of some group members by outsiders. Twenty-five thousand pregnancies due to the 1971 raping is a standard estimate.[24] Soldiers allegedly told their victims that "They must carry loyal 'Pakistani' offsprings instead of 'bootlick-ers of India or the Hindus' in their wombs."[25] Moreover (and providing additional evidence of the military leaders' coordination of a rape campaign), a Pakistani major in occupied East Pakistan wrote to another, "'I have not been astonished that Rashid has controlled and made pet the Bengali women/their next generation must have to be changed/ perhaps oneday [sic] you or me will be found there.'"[26]

An International Commission of Jurists concluded that Pakistani officers turned a blind eye when enlisted men raped, and in some cases themselves sexu-ally enslaved Bengali girls.[27] In sum, the rapes of 1971 were not simply the mis-chief of errant young soldiers, but were coordinated by some of the senior officers of the state to facilitate the defeat the secessionist Bengalis.

Civil War in Yugoslavia
Bosnia-Herzegovina, 1990–1995

Rape was a tactic to influence political power relations during the civil war in the former Yugoslavia. Estimates of the number of rape victims range from ten thou-sand to sixty thousand.[28] Most of the rapists were ethnically Serbian men; most of the victims were Muslim women.[29] The sexual violence, according to Amnesty International's monitors, "has been carried out in an organized or systematic way with the deliberate detention of women for the purpose of rape or sexual abuse."[30]

Croatia and Bosnia-Herzegovina's secessions from Yugoslavia and the war with Serbia and Montenegro that ensued have been well publicized, and need not be reiterated here. Ethnic cleansing entailed killing, raping, or abducting everyone who was not Serbian within days or hours.[31] News of mass rape in towns nearby caused entire villages to flee, thus facilitating their occupation by Serbs. The fighting in Bosnia-Herzegovina killed approximately 200,000 and displaced half of the entire population.[32] Seventeen thousand of the fatalities and 34,000 of the wounded were children.[33]

Some believe that international observers avoided using the term "genocide" so as to absolve themselves of responsibility for intervening on behalf of the victims. Those who argue that the Serb and Bosnian-Serb aggression against Muslim civilians in Bosnia-Herzegovina constituted genocide point to the fact that Serbs killed Muslims simply on the basis of their ethno-religious identity; Serbs intentionally attacked civilians, and high-level Serb officers authorized at least some of the killing. Croats and Muslims also committed war crimes during this conflict. However, there is no evidence that during the 1990s either Croats or Muslims perpetrated genocide.

In February of 2001 the ICTY (International Criminal Tribunal for the former Yugoslavia) convicted three Bosnian Serb men for gang-raping Muslim women detained in the war. For the first time an international court condemned "sexual enslavement" as a crime against humanity.[34] To understand the court's difficulty in substantiating charges of genocide, one must note that Serbian politicians during and after the war practiced what some suspect was a well-rehearsed strategy of refutation of any involvement in rape, forced expulsion, torture, or killing of Croats and Muslims. This tactic of denial at every level—from Banja Luka to Belgrade—has left international prosecutors with little evidence of the *intent* to destroy an ethnic or religious group that is necessary to meet the Genocide Convention's criteria for genocide.[35]

The Serbian nationalists' cover-up of the ethnic cleansing campaign was brazen. Serb officials called the notorious detention camp Trnopolje an "Open Reception Center" and "an El Dorado for them [the Muslims]. They think this is a guaranteed way to go abroad. Many people have closed their houses and apartments in order to come here."[36] The Serbian government, military, and Orthodox Church denied that any detention centers existed on Serbian territory, much less that rape transpired in them. The state-run television warned that anyone spreading such lies would face prosecution. When the Serb leaders could not deny that violence had taken place—the destruction of an estimated six hundred mosques in the summer of 1992, the shelling of Srebrenica at the conclusion of a peace agreement,[37] the mortar fire upon a Sarajevo market that killed sixty and wounded two hundred—the Serb leaders denied responsibility. Instead, they charged that the Muslims (or the UN) had perpetrated the violence themselves as a ploy to win international sympathy for the Muslim-Croat alliance.[38]

A skeptic might dismiss the Serb rapes in their campaign to expel the members of Bosnian and Croatian households from the region as akin to looting—an unfortunate yet inevitable fact of war. The skeptic might argue that rape is a spoil, not a strategy, of war. He or she might add that rape in war represents self-gratification for a pent-up soldier, not military policy. However, the "boys-will-be-boys" and "women-are-booty" explanations do not explain the mass rape of girls and women in the *official* detention centers. Here, interrogators might rape to torture those women they suspected of lying.[39] Some of the detention centers held only women; the survivors and refugees referred to them as "rape camps."[40] Serb forces invading Foca sent women to what had been a high school, an athletic arena, and to private residences. They interred sexual slaves in what had been taverns or restaurants, innocuously renamed "Nymph's Tresses," "Laser," "Coffeehouse Sonja," and "Fast Food Restaurant."[41] In one large arena turned "rape camp" in Doboj, soldiers allegedly detained between 2,000 and 2,500 women and girls between May and June of 1992.[42]

The apparent objective of at least some of the rape in detention was not sexual gratification alone, but impregnation. Soldiers intentionally detained some women they impregnated until abortion was no longer possible.[43] Serb forces allegedly bused some of those visibly pregnant back to the front lines in vehicles "often painted with cynical comments about the babies to be borne."[44]

Disgrace of the victims and by proxy the men to whom they were related was another motive, one inextricable from and closely related to the tactic of impregnation by Serbs. The rapists denigrated their Muslim victims with epithets that fused images of Muslim inferiority and extinction: "'Fuck your Turkish mother,' 'Death to all Turkish sperm,'"[45] "'You should not bear a Balija, you should rather bear Serbs.'"[46]

Serbian leaders deny that such assaults took place, much less that they issued a directive to rape. In 1992 President Radovan Karadzic stated that his army "did not commit a single crime, rape, or attack against civilians."[47] Karadzic also said, "The lies about the organized rapes of Muslim women are shameful, lacking all basis in fact and going beyond all bounds of human decency."[48] The following year Karadzic conceded that there had been eighteen isolated incidents of rape in Serb-held territory, but he insisted that allegations of a rape policy were "propaganda" from "Muslim Mullahs."[49] In 1997 the state-run television announced that investigation of claims by Muslim women of rape by Serbs had proven that all such reports were false.[50] In 1999 the Milosevic government's official press reported that a Jewish-American lobbyist had confessed to persuading the *New York Times* to print fictional allegations of mass rape by Serbs on behalf of his clients, the president of Croatia, the leader of the Muslim-Croat alliance in Bosnia-Herzegovina, and the Kosovo Albanians.[51] In November 2000, after sixteen Bosnian-Muslim women from Foca gave testimony before the ICTY of repeated rape during their detention (lasting up to two years) in the Partizan sports hall, the lawyer for the three accused Bosnian Serbs explained that the alleged detention centers were merely "collection centers" to which the women fled for their own protection and from which they had been free to leave at any time.[52] Moreover, Serbian leaders charged that the international press overlooked the rapes perpetrated by Croat and Muslim men. Authorities, to prove that Serbian women and girls had suffered rape, released the hospital files of those raped by the enemy to foreign journalists.[53]

Nevertheless, many believe that the rape was a Serbian political strategy.[54] Indicators of a plan include: (1) in noncontiguous parts of Bosnia-Herzegovina soldiers raped educated or upper-class women first and ordered family members to commit incest; (2) the rapes happened across Bosnia-Herzegovina simultaneously and accompanied the fighting; and (3) many rapes took place within official detention centers.[55] Moreover, witnesses reported that Karadzic's advisors spoke of rape as part of the cleansing of the town of Foca.[56] Finally, Alija Delimustafic, formerly the Bosnian minster of the interior, claimed to have secretly recorded orders to rape issued by Velibor Ostojic, a minister to Karadzic.

However, prosecutors are unable to secure evidence of a Serbian government-issued rape plan that is strong enough to hold up in court. During the war crimes trials, the ICTY did establish the complicity of Foca's chief of police, Dragan Gagovic, in rape. His office was adjacent to the Partizan Sports Hall, a detention center for women, children, and the elderly. A group of detainees spoke to the chief of police to complain of rape. The next day, under the ruse of taking her statement, Gagovic orally, anally, and vaginally raped one of the complainants. In the summer of 1996 the ICTY indicted Dragan Gagovic for knowledge of the detention centers and what transpired in them.[57]

Kosovo, 1999

Kosovo is a symbol of Serbian nationalism. In the 1990s, however, ethnic Albanians in Kosovo outnumbered Serbs nine to one.[58] Upon becoming president in 1989, Milosevic banned the Albanian language, removed Albanians from their jobs in the civil service, and dismantled the existing Albanian legislature. These moves sparked a militant Albanian insurgency, which the Serbian government tried to repress. In 1999 Serb forces killed an estimated ten thousand Kosovar Albanians and forcibly displaced over 1.5 million.[59] In early June of 1999 the United Nations Population Fund reported that Serb men were raping Albanian women fleeing Kosovo.[60] The survivors felt that commanding officers were responsible.

Rape in Kosovo was systematic and sometimes took place at the direction of commanding officers.[61] The Serb forces—official or paramilitary—trucked some women to detention centers, where rape was only one form of torture inflicted upon them. Captors released the raped and brutalized Albanian women after several hours or several days.[62] A Serbian commander in the town of Pec kept a list of the soldiers' names to ensure that each had his turn to go to the Hotel Karagac to rape the detainees there.[63]

Moreover, troops staged rapes before the victims' families or in public to shame not only the victim but also her kin and the community.[64] Investigators suspect that the troops raped in plain sight and later publicly bragged about the assaults so that news of the sexual terrorism would spread and frighten Albanian residents out of Kosovo.

Researchers believe that the nearly one hundred reports of rape obtained from survivors and direct witnesses represent only a fraction of the total.[65] Many of the Albanian women killed were probably first raped.[66] The Yugoslav authorities were aware that their paramilitaries had raped in Bosnia-Herzegovina, but they again relied upon paramilitaries in Kosovo without taking precautions to prevent sexual assault.[67]

Serb officials once again deny that any rape by their men occurred. The Serbian state-run media instead depicted the Serbs in Kosovo as victims, and blamed the fighting—and rape—upon Albanian "terrorist hordes" trained by U.S. and German instructors.[68]

Rwanda, 1994

Rwanda had experienced several episodes of ethnic conflict between the Hutu and the Tutsi, who had been the economic and political elite before and during colonialism. The Hutu rebelled against the Tutsi in 1959 and took control of the state the following year, which caused many alarmed Tutsi to flee Rwanda. The Hutu ruling party, Parmehutu, discriminated against the Tutsi that remained in a variety of ways, such as instituting quotas for the number of university and civil service seats that Tutsi might occupy.[69] The Tutsi expatriates periodically tried to reenter Rwanda, and each such attempt caused the Rwandan Hutu to attack those Tutsi within Rwanda. In 1990 the RPF (the Rwandan Patriotic Front, the army of the Tutsi in exile) invaded Rwanda. The French and Belgians helped the Hutu government to drive the RPF away before it reached Kigali, the Rwandan capital.[70]

In the early 1990s both the international community and emerging Rwandan social movements pressured the Hutu government to find a solution to the Tutsi expatriate problem and embrace multiparty democracy.[71] The Arusha Accords that President Habyarimana reluctantly consented to in 1993 promised reconciliation with the Tutsi. Threatened, and viewing Habyarimana's action as capitulation, Hutu extremist leaders drew a plot to exterminate Rwanda's Tutsi.

The state-controlled RTLMC radio announced on April 3, 1994, that residents of Kigali were likely to hear "a little something" involving RPF weapon fire within the next three days.[72] The following day a prominent Hutu announced before a gathering that included UN representatives that the only acceptable solution to the Tutsi problem was to eliminate them from Rwanda altogether. Others well-placed in the government informed the head of an African nongovernmental organization that the RPF would kill Habyarimana before the following Friday, the swearing-in date for the new government. On April 6, 1994, near the Kigali airport, air missiles struck down a plane carrying President Ntaryamira of Burundi, President Habyarimana, and everyone else aboard. An OAU-sponsored panel of experts observed, "(R)adio station RTLMC immediately blamed the Belgians, among others, [*sic*] Since then, virtually every conceivable party has been accused of the deed." [73]

The death of Habyarimana was also the birth of the three months of slaughter that killed an estimated one million Rwandans, most of whom were Tutsi.[74] Few of the Hutu extremists were well-armed, and an international force, a foreign national army, or a combination of the two probably could have prevented the genocide. Belgium, France, the United States, and other world powers, however, refrained from calling the extermination of Tutsi "genocide"—perhaps to avoid an unpopular and costly intervention such as the one in Somalia. Some suggest that Western leaders did not deploy their soldiers to protect Rwandan civilians because they did not want to risk a few white lives for many black ones.

Hutu men raped Tutsi women across the country during the genocide.[75] The UN estimates that in this tiny country there were between 250,000 and 500,000 rapes.[76] Leaders ordered the informal militia known as the *interahamwe* (literally, "those who stand together") not to spare Tutsi women and children. Men often raped before they killed; some of the rape victims who survived the spring of 1994 had been left for dead.[77]

In some areas of postwar Rwanda, almost all the Tutsi women who remain from before 1994 are rape survivors.[78] One explains that a Hutu during the mass slaughter might capture an attractive Tutsi woman for what Rwandans euphemistically refer to as "marriage."[79]

Leaders planned the genocide carefully, but it is uncertain whether they planned the mass rapes. Some believe that rape in Rwanda was systematic, premeditated, and used intentionally as a weapon of ethnic conflict to destroy the Tutsi community and to render any survivors silent.[80] One survivor interviewed by the author disagreed; she said that the raping began spontaneously as recompense for those *interahamwe* who were especially prolific killers.[81]

Unlike in the former Yugoslavia, there seems to be no evidence of the Hutu men's intent to impregnate the enemy's women by rape (although pregnancy was sometimes a consequence).[82] However, a uniquely Rwandan component of rape as genocide was the deliberate transmission of HIV. According to witnesses, Hutu rapists said that they had HIV and wanted to give it to their victims so that they would die slowly and gruelingly from AIDS.[83] The majority of rape survivors do test positive for HIV.[84] In Rwanda protease inhibitors (to control HIV) are not available, and HIV left untreated for five to fifteen years almost always results in AIDS-related death. In essence, the intentional transmission of HIV is protracted genocide.[85]

One similarity to the war in the Balkans, however, is that Hutu rapists denigrated their victims because of their ethnic identity. Examples gathered by Human Rights Watch include: "You Tutsi women are too proud;" "We want to see how sweet Tutsi women are;" "You Tutsi women think you are too good for us;" "We want to see if a Tutsi woman is like a Hutu woman;" and "If there were peace, you would never accept me."[86] A survivor relates, "Before he raped me, he said that he wanted to check if Tutsi women were like other women before he took me back to the church to be burnt."[87]

The International Criminal Tribunal for Rwanda ruled in the case of Jean-Paul Akayesu, the former mayor of Taba Commune, that rape was a component of the genocide.[88] The court noted that the killers raped Rwandan women because of their ethnic identity: "The rape of Tutsi women was systematic and was perpetrated against all Tutsi women and solely against them."[89] The tribunal has also prosecuted a woman, Pauline Nyiramasuhuko, for encouraging her subordinates (including her son) to rape Tutsi women. Nyiramasuhuko, at the time of the genocide, was the Rwandan minister of family and women's affairs.[90]

Conclusion

State rape is especially effective against groups that shame not the rapist, but the raped. In such societies, rape diminishes the social standing of the victim and her kin. Family honor may be linked with female chastity, and a raped woman brings disgrace upon her family and her community. In newly independent Bangladesh, Sheikh Muhibur Rahman tried to lesson the stigma surrounding rape victims (which was so strong that it caused husbands to leave their wives and parents to abandon their daughters). Rahman valorized the rape survivors as *biranganas* (war heroines), set up rehabilitation centers on their behalf, and offered rewards to men who would marry them. Nevertheless, few proposals were forthcoming. Some of the *biranganas* committed suicide; others fled to West Pakistan, where their shame would be a secret.[91] Similarly, the Bosnian Muslim rape survivors, in addition to coping with the rape-related injuries and trauma, face a culture in which a raped woman is forever dishonored. Muslim religious leaders there also urged bachelors to marry the rape victims, but few did.[92] Likewise, the Kosovar Albanians do not perceive raped women and girls to be innocent victims; the death of the family member defiled by rape may seem the only way to restore the family's honor.[93] A common saying is that a good woman should commit suicide if she has been raped.[94] Finally, Rwandans today also shun the rape survivors. The popular perception is that the survivors prostituted themselves to spare their own lives. In Rwanda the physiological and psychological complications of rape, that the rape victims became pariahs, and the destitution of those widowed, orphaned, or abandoned in the genocide led many rape survivors to say that they would rather have been killed.[95]

The methods of state rape vary. Soldiers may rape women before murdering them, they may attempt to dilute an ethnic community's bloodline by raping and impregnating its women, or they may intend for the mass rapes to demoralize the surviving members of a community. Rwandan Hutu men used the HIV virus as a weapon of genocide against some Tutsi women. Top-level leaders, rather than prevent or prosecute such acts, ignored them or, in the case of Yugoslavia, denied that they even happened. Neither the Pakistani, nor the Serbian, nor the Rwandan Hutu government issued a formal directive during the civil war to rape women of the insurgent ethnic group. Nevertheless, their agents—and, in some cases, commanding officers—encouraged and/or engaged in rape as part of a strategy of subjugation or eradication of a people that had attempted to upset a politically and economically inequitable status quo.

NOTES

Portions of this chapter appear in a paper presented at the 1999 meeting of the Association of Genocide Scholars and in Lisa Sharlach, *Sexual Violence as a Political Weapon: The State and Rape* (Lynne Rienner Publishers, forthcoming). The Institute on Global Conflict and Cooperation and the University of California Davis Pro Femina Research Consortium funded this research. I am indebted to Lesley Mandros Bell, Matthew Hoddie, Dave Massengale, and especially Howard Sharlach for their assistance.

1. Henry David Thoreau, "On the Duty of Civil Disobedience," in *Social and Political Philosophy*, ed. John Somerville and Ronald E. Santoni (New York: Anchor Books, 1963), p. 301.
2. Ruth Seifert, "The Second Front: The Logic of Sexual Violence in Wars," *Women's Studies International Forum* 19, nos. 1–2, (1996): 35–36.
3. Inger Skjelsbaek, *Sexual Violence in Times of War: An Annotated Bibliography* (Oslo, Norway: PRIO International Peace Research Institute, 1999).
4. Helen Fein, "Genocide and Gender: The Uses of Women and Group Destiny," *Journal of Genocide Research* 1, no. 1 (1999), p. 49.
5. *Convention on the Prevention and Punishment of the Crime of Genocide*, December 9, 1948, Article II.
6. Ervin Staub, *The Roots of Evil: The Origins of Genocide and Other Group Violence* (Cambridge: Cambridge University Press, 1989), pp. 7–8.
7. Frank Chalk, "Redefining Genocide," in *Genocide: Conceptual and Historical Dimensions*, ed. George Andreopoulos (Philadelphia: University of Pennsylvania Press, 1994), pp. 48–53.
8. Catharine A. MacKinnon, "Rape, Genocide, and Women's Human Rights," *Harvard Women's Law Journal* 17 (1994): pp. 11–12.
9. Siobhan K. Fisher, "Occupation of the Womb: Forced Impregnation as Genocide," *Duke Law Journal* 46 (1996): p. 125.
10. *The Prosecutor versus Jean-Paul Akayesu*, Case No. ICTR-96-4-T, September 2, 1998, Count 12.
11. R. J. Rummel, *Death by Government* (New Brunswick and London: Transaction Publishers, 1994), p. 316.
12. Rounaq Jahan, "Genocide in Bangladesh," *Century of Genocide: Eyewitness Accounts and Critical Views*, ed. Samuel Totten, William S. Parsons, and Israel W. Charny (New York and London: Garland Publishing, 1997), p. 296; R. J. Rummel (*Death by Government*, p. 329) writes that West Pakistan was guilty of genocide against Hindus and mass murder of Bengalis; P. C. C. Raja, "Pakistan's Crimes Against Humanity in Bangladesh," FBIS-NES-97-351, "India: Commentary Raps Pakistan for Crimes Against Bangladeshis," December 19, 1997 (originally broadcast by Delhi All India Radio General Overseas Service in English, December 17, 1997); Urvashi Butalia, "A

Question of Silence: Partition, Women, and the State," in *Gender and Catastrophe*, ed. Ronit Lentin (London and New York: Zed Books, 1997), p. 264; Amita Malik, *The Year of the Vulture* (New Delhi, India: Orient Longman, 1972), p. 152.

13. Jahan, "Genocide in Bangladesh," p. 299; Rummel, *Death by Government*, pp. 331–35.

14. Malik, *The Year of the Vulture*, pp. 140–54.

15. *Newsweek*, June 28, 1971, in Fazlul Quaderi, *Bangladesh Genocide and the World Press* (Dacca, Bangladesh: Begum Dilafroz Quaderi, 1972), p. 158.

16. Sultana Kamal, "The 1971 Genocide in Bangladesh and Crimes Committed Against Women," in *Common Grounds: Violence Against Women in War and Armed Conflict Situations*, ed. Indai Lourdes Sajor (Quezon City, Philippines: Asian Center for Women's Human Rights, 1998), p. 272.

17. Abul Hasanat, *The Ugliest Genocide in History; Being a Resume of Inhuman Atrocities in East Pakistan, Now Bangladesh* (Dacca, Bangladesh: Muktadhara, 1974), p. 64.

18. Malik, *The Year of the Vulture*, p. 154.

19. *Newsweek*, June 28, 1971, reprinted in Quaderi, *Bangladesh Genocide*, p. 158.

20. Susan Brownmiller, *Against Our Will: Men, Women and Rape* (New York: Fawcett, 1993), p. 82.

21. Kamal, "The 1971 Genocide," p. 273.

22. Hasanat, *The Ugliest Genocide*, p. 77; Brownmiller, *Against Our Will*, p. 75.

23. Kamal, "The 1971 Genocide," p. 274.

24. Brownmiller, *Against Our Will*, pp. 79, 84.

25. Kamal, "The 1971 Genocide," p. 272.

26. In Shumi Umme Habiba, "Mass Rape and Violence in the 1971 Armed Conflict of Bangladesh: Justice and Other Issues," in *Common Grounds*, p. 260.

27. International Commission of Jurists, Secretariat, *The Events in East Pakistan, 1971* (Geneva: International Commission of Jurists, 1972), p. 40.

28. Charlotte Bunch and Niamh Reilly, *Demanding Accountability: The Global Campaign and Vienna Tribunal for Women's Human Rights* (New Jersey and New York: Center for Women's Global Leadership and the United Nations Development Fund for Women, 1994), p. 36.

29. Amnesty International, *Bosnia-Herzegovina: Rape and Sexual Abuse by Armed Forces* (New York: Amnesty International, 1993), p. 4.

30. Ibid.

31. Seada Vranic, "Mass Rape in Bosnia: Breaking the Wall of Silence," www.cco.caltech.edu/~bosnia/articles/serbmedia.html (January 13, 1999). Serb captors also inflicted sexual torture upon Croatian or Muslim males. Amnesty International, *Bosnia-Herzegovina*, p. 5; J.L.M. Commission 1994, 5, 8; (J.L.M.) Commission of Experts' Final Report (S/1994/674), Parts I and II, United Nations Security Council, May 27, 1994, www.his.com:80/~cij/commxyu3.htm#II.I; Fein "Genocide and Gender," p. 55.

32. U.S. Department of State, "Background Notes: Bosnia-Herzegovina," Bureau of European Affairs, August 1999, www.state.gov/www/background_notes/bosnia_9908_bgn.html (June 18, 2000).

33. U.S. Department of State, "1999 Country Reports on Human Rights Practices," February 25, 2000, www.state.gov/www/global/human_rights/1999_hrp_report (April 2, 2000).

34. Jerome Socolovsky, "Serbs Convicted of Rape, Torture," *Associated Press*, February 22, 2001. International law permits the prosecution of crimes against humanity even if they took place in the absence of war.

35. Norman Cigar, *Genocide in Bosnia: The Policy of "Ethnic Cleansing"* (College Station, Tex.: Texas A&M University Press, 1995), p. 87.

36. Ibid., p. 90.

37. Eric Stover and Gilles Peress, *The Graves: Srebrenica and Vukovar* (Zurich, Berlin, and New York: Scalo, 1998), p. 116.

38. In Cigar, *Genocide in Bosnia*, pp. 93–94.

39. International Criminal Tribunal for the Former Yugoslavia (Press Office), "Gang Rape, Torture and Enslavement of Muslim Women Charged in ICTY's First Indictment Dealing Specifically with Sexual Offenses," June 26, 1996, www.haverford. edu/relg/sells/indictments/gagovic.html.

40. In 1994 the author worked in Croatia for the World University Service-Austria, Zagreb Office and Unaccompanied Children in Exile.

41. Maria B. Olujic, "Women, Rape, and War: The Continued Trauma of Refugees and Displaced Persons in Croatia," originally published in *Anthropology of East Europe Review* 13, no. 1 (1995), condor.depaul.edu/~rrotenbe/aeer/aeer13_1/Olujic.html (January 14, 1999).

42. Alexandra Stiglmayer, "The Rapes in Bosnia-Herzegovina," *Mass Rape: The War Against Women in Bosnia-Herzegovina*, ed. Alexandra Stiglmayer (Lincoln, Nebr.: University of Nebraska Press, 1993), p. 118.

43. (J.L.M.) Commission of Experts' Final Report. Also Stiglmayer, "The Rapes in Bosnia-Herzegovina," pp. 134–35.

44. Ruth Seifert, "Rape in Wars: Analytical Approaches," *Minerva: Quarterly Report on Women and the Military* 5.11, no. 2 (June 30, 1993): p. 17.

45. Stiglmayer, "The Rapes in Bosnia-Herzegovina," p. 109.

46. State Commission for Gathering Facts on War Crimes in the Republic of Bosnia and Herzegovina, "War Crimes Against Women," March 1993, gopher://gopher.igc.apc. org:70/00/peace/yugo/crimes/so/38 (April 6, 2000). Bosnia-Herzegovina used to be part of the Ottoman Empire, and many of the Muslims have some Turkish ancestry. "Balija" is a derogatory reference to a Muslim.

47. In Cigar, *Genocide in Bosnia*, p. 88.

48. In Stiglmayer, "The Rapes in Bosnia-Herzegovina," p. 163.

49. Roy Gutman, "Evidence Serb Leaders in Bosnia OKd Attacks," *Newsday*, April 19, 1993, www.haverford.edu/regl/sells/rape2.html (November 8, 1999).

50. Paris AFP, "Bosnia-Herzegovina: UN Demands Airtime on Bosnian-Serb TV to Refute 'Lies,'" August 13, 1997, FBIS Transcribed Text Document Number FBIS-EEU-97-225.

51. According to the Ministry, the U.S. lobbyist disclosed, "Everything functioned perfectly, placing the Jewish organizations on the side of 'Bosnians,' that was an excellent bluff. We were in position to make the Serbs look like Nazis in public." Serbian Ministry of Information, "Media Lies, Propaganda War Against Serbs and a Warning to Jews," April 17, 1999, www.serbia-info.com/news/1999-04/17/10982.html (June 24, 2000).

52. Moreover, the defense's brief stated that the sixteen Muslim women provided testimony so coherently that "it is obvious that there are no permanent psychological and psychiatric consequences suffered by any of these witnesses." Jerome Socolovsky, "Serb Defense: Women Lied About Rape," *Associated Press*, November 21, 2000.

53. Lepa Mladjenovic, "Ethics of Difference: Working with Women War Survivors," in *Common Grounds*, ed. Sajor, p. 351.

54. Stiglmayer, "The Rapes in Bosnia-Herzegovina," pp. 148, 154; Human Rights Watch Women's Rights Project, *Human Rights Watch Global Report on Women's Human*

Rights (New York: Human Rights Watch, 1995), p. 11; Amnesty International, *Bosnia-Herzegovina*, p. 4; (J.L.M.) Commission of Experts' Final Report, I.G.1; personal communication with young refugee women, Zagreb, June–July, 1994.

55. (J.L.M.) Commission of Experts' Final Report, IV. E.3, 8.

56. Roy Gutman, "Evidence Serb Leaders in Bosnia OKd Attacks," *Newsday*, April 19, 1993, www.haverford.edu/regl/sells/rape2.html (November 8, 1999).

57. International Criminal Tribunal for the Former Yugoslavia, "Gang-Rape, Torture, and Enslavement," The Hague: Netherlands, 1996.

58. *Washington Post Online*, "Kosovo: The Jerusalem of Serbia," July 1999, www.washingtonpost.com/wp-srv/inatl/longterm/balkans/overview/kosovo.htm.

59. U.S. Department of State, "Executive Summary," *Ethnic Cleansing in Kosovo: An Accounting*, December 1999, www.state.gov/www/global/human_rights/kosovoii/homepage.html (June 18, 2000).

60. Some witnesses report that there were needles in the victims' arms and froth on their mouths. OSCE (Organization for Security and Cooperation in Europe), "Kosovo/Kosova: As Seen, As Told," 1999, http://www.osce.org/kosovo/reports/hr/part1/index.htm (June 19, 2000).

61. Almost all of the rapes in Kosovo were gang rapes. Human Rights Watch, "Federal Republic of Yugoslavia: Kosovo: Rape as a Weapon of 'Ethnic Cleansing,'" 2000, www.hrw.org/reports/2000/fry/Kosov003-06.htm#TopOfPage (April 12, 2000).

62. Amy Bickers, "Kosovo/Sex Crimes," transcript of *Voice of America* broadcast No. 2-250174, June 3, 1999.

63. U.S. Department of State, "Documenting the Abuses," *Ethnic Cleansing in Kosovo: An Accounting*, December 1999, www.state.gov/www/global/human_rights/kosovoii/document.html (June 18, 2000).

64. OSCE, "Kosovo/Kosova."

65. Reports exist of rape by ethnic Albanians of Serbian, Albanian, and Roma women subsequent to the entry of NATO troops in Kosovo. Human Rights Watch, "Federal Republic"; U.S. Department of State, "Documenting."

66. OSCE, "Kosovo/Kosova."

67. Human Rights Watch, "Federal Republic."

68. Miroslav Markovic, "KFOR: U.N. Peacekeeping Mission or a New Fraud for the Serbs," Serbian Ministry of Information, June 29, 1999, www.serbia-info.com/news/1999-06/29/12974.html (June 24, 2000).

69. Alain Destexhe, *Rwanda and Genocide in the 20th Century*, trans. Alison Marschner (New York: New York University Press, 1995), p. 44.

70. Guy Vassall-Adams, *Rwanda: An Agenda for International Action* (Oxford, U.K.: Oxfam, 1994), p. 21.

71. Destexhe, *Rwanda and Genocide*, p. 29.

72. Philip Gourevitch, *We Wish To Inform You That Tomorrow We Will Be Killed With Our Families* (New York: Farrar, Strauss, and Giroux, 1998), p. 110.

73. International Panel of Eminent Personalities to Investigate the 1994 Genocide in Rwanda and the Surrounding Events, "Special Report," July 7, 2000, www.oau-oua.org/Document/ipep/report/Rwanda-e/EN-III-T.htm (December 3, 2000).

74. Felicite Umutanguha Layika, "War Crimes Against Women in Rwanda," in *Without Reservation: The Beijing Tribunal on Accountability for Women's Human Rights*, ed. Niamh Reilly (New Jersey: The Center for Women's Global Leadership, 1995), p. 38.

75. Catherine Bonnet, "Le viol des femmes survivantes du génocide au Rwanda," in *Rwanda, un génocide du XXe siécle*, ed. R. Verdier, E. Decaux, and J.-P. Chrétien (Paris:

Editions L'Harmattan, 1995), p. 19; Elizabeth Royte, "The Outcasts," *New York Times Magazine*, January 19, 1997, p. 38.

76. Binaifer Nowrojee, "Shattered Lives: Sexual Violence during the Rwandan Genocide and Its Aftermath," New York: Human Rights Watch, 1996, p. 24.

77. Nowrojee, *Shattered Lives*, p. 35.

78. Layika, "War Crimes Against Women in Rwanda," p. 39.

79. Interview of anonymous survivor, AVEGA, Association des venues du genocide d'avril (Association of Widows of the April Genocide), Kigali, Rwanda, November 10, 1998.

80. Bonnet, "Le viol des femmes survivantes du génocide au Rwanda," p. 2.

81. Interview of anonymous survivor, AVEGA.

82. Interview of Alice Karekezi, Special Monitor for Women's Human Rights at the ICTR, Arusha, Butare, Rwanda, November 12, 1998.

83. Interview of Chantal Kayitesi, AVEGA, Kigali, Rwanda, November 10, 1998; United Nations High Commission on Human Rights, "Fundamental Freedoms," p. 18.

84. Interview of staff member, Rwandan Women's Net, Kigali, Rwanda, November 11, 1998. Of course, a survivor may have contracted HIV before or after being raped.

85. Layika, "War Crimes Against Women in Rwanda," p. 40; Interview of staff member, Rwandan Women's Net, Kigali, Rwanda, November 11, 1998.

86. Nowrojee, *Shattered Lives*, p. 18.

87. Ibid., p. 43.

88. Bill Berkeley, "Judgment Day," *Washington Post Magazine*, October 11, 1998, pp. 10–15.

89. UN Press Office, "Rwanda International Criminal Tribunal Pronounces Guilty Verdict in Historic Genocide Trial," Press Release AFR/94L/2895, September 2, 1998, http://www.un.org/News/Press/docs/1998/19980902.afr94.html (September 16, 1999).

90. "U.N. Charges Rwandan Woman with Rape," *Associated Press*, August 12, 1999.

91. Santi Rozario, "Disasters and Bangladeshi Women," in *Gender and Catastrophe*, ed. Lentin, p. 264.

92. Slavenka Drakulic, "The Rape of Women in Bosnia," in *Women and Violence: Realities and Responses Worldwide*, ed. Miranda Davies (London: Zed Books, 1994), p. 181.

93. Carol J. Williams, "Kosovo Rape Victims Face Society's Harsh Judgment," *The Sacramento Bee*, May 30, 1999.

94. OSCE, "Kosovo/Kosova."

95. Nowrojee, *Shattered Lives*, pp. 49–59.

PART TWO

Identities, Adversaries, and Democratic Values

CHAPTER SEVEN

From Protest to Retribution

The Guerrilla Politics of Pro-life Violence

Carol Mason

Finding an accurate vocabulary with which to discuss pro-life violence was not easy in the 1990s, when "life" became in some antiabortion circles a justification for killing rather than an argument against it.[1] Michael Bray, author of *A Time to Kill*, and Paul deParrie, editor of *Life Advocate* magazine, are two pro-life leaders who publicly defend killing for life on biblical principles.[2] After the first political killing of an abortion provider, Dr. David Gunn, by Michael Griffin in 1993, another statement that claimed murdering abortionists is "justifiable homicide" was written by Paul Hill, with the help of Bray.[3] This "defensive action statement" was signed by thirty pro-life leaders and circulated to the media a year before Hill himself fatally shot two men outside a Pensacola clinic. Since Hill's crime, Bray and other pro-life organizers have hosted an annual White Rose Banquet, where letters by Hill and other incarcerated pro-life felons are read, and cars parked outside sport "EXECUTE Murderers/Abortionists" bumper stickers.[4] For these pro-life leaders, it is not a contradiction to kill for life.

However, pro-life organizations denounce all violence, and many pro-lifers I have personally spoken with have told me that those who commit antiabortion violence are not "real" pro-lifers. Many have insisted that they deplore violence, which they say is antithetical to the principles of the pro-life movement. They speak with a conviction that I recognize and respect as a heartfelt aspect of witnessing their faith. But witnessing is only one form of pro-life discussion. It is an oral, performative discourse designed to spur religious conversion, to proselytize. I have witnessed a lot of witnessing, and I am grateful for those pro-lifers who have shared with me their life stories and their views. My analysis, however, is based more on primary pro-life texts written by and for the pro-life community. These texts, unfettered by the compulsion to proselytize, supply accurate vocabulary with which to discuss pro-life violence, and insights with which to analyze it.

Read symptomatically, pro-life texts in the 1990s articulate an acceptance of violence that is not generally acknowledged beyond militants such as Bray and

Hill. This chapter focuses not on the calls for violence they wrote, but on a text describing a strategy designed to work within the system to restore "respect for life" through legislation and litigation. This text, an underground manual circulated in 1992 by Mark Crutcher, is called *Firestorm: A Guerrilla Strategy for a Pro-life America.*[5] Like many confidential pro-life strategies before it, including campaigns delineated in the *Abortion Buster's Manual, Closed: 99 Ways to Stop Abortion, The Army of God* manual, and "No Place to Hide," *Firestorm* seeks not to outlaw abortion, but to stigmatize and demoralize those who provide and seek abortions through sabotage and harassment. Unlike the strategies preceding it, however, *Firestorm* seeks to carry out this sabotage and harassment only with "guerrilla legislation." Like pro-life murder, "guerrilla legislation" seems to be an oxymoron.[6] "Legislation" is a formalized and painstakingly slow legal process, or the collection of state-sanctioned laws procured by such a process. "Guerrilla" action is radical, random, often violent and illegal. But in coining the phrase "guerrilla legislation," *Firestorm* calls into question these general assumptions and hints at a relationship between pro-life violence and pro-life legal strategy.

In *Firestorm*, "guerrilla legislation" refers to both a collectivity of pro-life laws and the litigious and legislative processes by which pro-lifers can propose, pass, and enforce those laws. The very idea of "guerrilla legislation" indicates an ideological relationship between pro-life violence and pro-life litigation and legislation. Instead of viewing pro-life violence either as "lunatic fringe" behavior or as a reasonable resort to force necessitated by a repressive state prohibiting peaceful protest, we can situate pro-life trends in violent tactics in the context of trends in legal strategy. Such contextualization demonstrates how pro-life violence and pro-life litigation or legislation function together politically, even if they are not orchestrated. Pro-life litigation and legislation capitalize on pro-life violence, and, as primary pro-life texts reveal, pro-life ideology accommodates violence not only implicitly and in practice, but also explicitly and in principle.

Trends in Illegal, Violent Tactics

How pro-lifers came to use violent means to protest abortion has been detailed by journalists and scholars.[7] Few, however, have considered the historical trends within that violence. Since the first political killing of an abortion provider by Michael Griffin, pro-life violence has become more and more like guerrilla warfare. In particular, there are three trends that suggest a definite shift from protest to guerrilla warfare.

First, pro-life assassins no longer fit the description of religious martyrs, protesters, or proselytizers. Assassins are no longer confronting abortion providers face to face, as Michael Griffin approached David Gunn.[8] Neither are they hoping to serve as a martyr as Paul Hill hoped to, sacrificing his freedom (and possibly his life) to challenge pro-choice laws (specifically the new Freedom to Access Clinic

Entrances act) and "save babies." Recently, anonymous snipers shoot from undisclosed locations. Gunmen and bombers alike flee the scene after attacking, not standing their ground as either political protestors or religious exemplars. The trend is to be fugitive guerrillas, not martyrs. This is true of alleged assassins Eric Rudolph, James Kopp, and anonymous snipers who have taken aim at doctors in their homes of upstate New York and Canada.

Second, most recent bombs are made to kill and maim people, not only to destroy buildings that house clinics.[9] Unlike the bombings in Pensacola in 1984, later bombings (in Atlanta and Alabama, for example) were designed to detonate while people are at the clinic. When two bombs are planted at a clinic, they are set so that one will go off or be detected first, and the other will detonate when police or paramedics have arrived on the scene to investigate the first bomb.[10] The objective is sabotage not just of facilities, but of personnel. This is especially evident with bombs that have nails or shrapnel in them; when they detonate, small metal shards or spikes are propelled through the skin of anyone in proximity.

Third, civil disobedience in the form of "direct action" has given way to domestic terrorism. Direct action tactics such as clinic blockades have been replaced by more underground activities such as butyric acid attacks and anthrax scares, in addition to the bombs and snipers. One explanation for this is that a repressive, unfair government has prevented pro-lifers from protesting peacefully with laws such as the Freedom to Access Clinic Entrances, or FACE. Pro-lifers have been forced to take illegal, violent action, according to this explanation. But the FACE law went into effect in 1994, after David Gunn was murdered and George Tiller, an abortion provider in Kansas, had been shot. To argue that lethal force was made neccessary because of the FACE laws ignores basic chronology and cannot account for the desire to cause bodily harm, which is evident in shootings, antipersonnel bombings, and butyric acid attacks.

Just as much as snipers or bombs, the butyric acid attacks and anthrax scares indicate a definite shift to terrorism and guerrilla warfare. Both terrorism and guerrilla warfare translate the element of surprise into a sustained psychological fear derived from the arbitrary and irregular nature of attacks. In 1998 butyric acid attacks were launched on a wide scale. From May 18 through May 23 the highly toxic chemical that can cause severe nausea and irritation of eye, throat, nose, and skin was spilled or injected in ten clinics in Florida. From July 6 through July 8 eight more clinics were hit with the acid in New Orleans and the Houston area.[11] These concentrated attacks aim to deter clinic employees from working and to force clinic owners to spend a lot of money in removing the toxic residue from both personnel and clinic walls and floors. Although rashes of butyric acid attacks occur simultaneously, not all clinics are targeted each time and it is impossible to predict which clinics will be doused in the future. Prior to 1998, according to the National Abortion Federation, seventy-nine incidents of butyric acid vandalism caused damage totaling $863,050.

Anthrax scares are also deployed arbitrarily and irregularly. Anthrax is classified as a biological weapon, a deadly bacteria that can be sealed in an envelope or left on any surface. In October 1998 seven clinics in Indiana, Kentucky, and Tennessee received letters that claimed "You have just been exposed to anthrax." As a result of coming into contact with such letters, employees and patients of a clinic in Indianapolis, as well as two police officers and a postal worker, were scrubbed down by special hazardous chemicals emergency crews.[12] In February 1999 another rash of anthrax scares occurred, this time at clinics in Missouri, Washington, and West Virginia. Approximately thirty firefighters and employees "were quarantined and washed down with bleach" in one location; in another, the building was evacuated.[13] All of these incidents were hoaxes; the bacteria was not used.

Not knowing when an anthrax scare, butyric acid attack, sniper, or bomb will hit is, to say the least, unnerving. Since 1990, 150 incidents of arson, thirty-nine clinic bombings, and more than a hundred cases of assault and battery are on record. Since 1993 seven people have been murdered and fifteen attempted murders have occurred.[14] The psychological terror these efforts induce is accompanied by the financial sabotage they procure. The cost of rebuilding facilities, cleaning hazardous chemical spills, replacing staff, paying hiked insurance rates, and increasing security is extraordinary.

Such trends in illegal, violent tactics—snipers, bombs, biological weapons, and chemical warfare—are not elements of protest. They are more accurately described as sabotage waged by guerrillas. According to *Merriam-Webster's Collegiate Dictionary*, a guerrilla is "a person who engages in irregular warfare especially as a member of an independent unit carrying out harassment and sabotage." This definition of "guerrilla" is an accurate description of illegal, sometimes lethal, pro-life violence. But it also accurately describes *legal* pro-life strategy.

Trends in Legal Strategies

Despite its military-apocalyptic title, *Firestorm: A Guerrilla Strategy for a Pro-life America* is an eighty-six-page manual that delineates the rationale for and components of a legal and nonviolent strategy. It is not a well-known text, because like most underground pro-life manuals it is kept a secret to ensure that the strategies promoted work without interruption or detection. Written and circulated by Mark Crutcher in 1992, *Firestorm* is emphatically "<u>CONFIDENTIAL</u> and is intended to be used only by those people to whom it was directly sent" (87).

The intended audience for *Firestorm* are those who want "to win" the "battle" for "an America which protects its unborn" (1). *Firestorm* relinquishes the goal of reversing *Roe v. Wade* and outlawing abortion and, much like another underground manual titled *The Army of God*, seeks instead to increase the financial and psychological costs of providing or obtaining abortions until it is no longer feasible.[15] Unlike the overt promotion of violence in *The Army of God,* however,

Firestorm seeks to do it legally—that is to say, by breaking no laws and by promoting pro-life legislation and litigation. Proposing a "steady stream of regulatory legislation that's specifically designed to run [doctors] out of business," *Firestorm* emphasizes "a requirement that all abortions have to be done by licensed physicians," and "mandatory malpractice insurance, or proof of financial responsibility" (50).

Unlike publicly distributed writings of Crutcher's, this underground manual predicts much of the legal maneuvering and illegal terrorism that has characterized antiabortion politics in the 1990s.[16] For example, *Firestorm* predicts that pro-life assassinations will occur; a year later, Dr. David Gunn was killed. It also predicts the proposed prohibition of "abortions done late in pregnancy" three years before bans on late-term or so-called partial birth abortions were introduced in Congress. *Firestorm* is not an exact blueprint for pro-life legislation, much less its relation to violence. But the legal strategies described in it resemble guerrilla warfare in design and effect.

Like trends in illegal pro-life violence, plans for legal guerrilla campaigns reject the idea that "it's OK to martyr yourself for the unborn," and are designed not to appear as part of an orchestrated strategy (1). Both guerrilla warfare and what *Firestorm* refers to as "guerrilla legislation" are executed as isolated incidents. To this end, Crutcher created Life Dynamics Incorporated (LDI) as a front organization for the monitoring of separate "guerrilla campaigns." Rather than creating "another national organization with its own state affiliates," Crutcher emphasizes that LDI should legally operate as and be seen as "a 'company' that provides education and support materials to existing state groups who want to make a commitment to this guerrilla campaign" (83). This appearance masks the organization's roles in orchestrating the guerrilla campaigns detailed in *Firestorm*. *Firestorm* explains five guerrilla programs labeled G-1 through G-5 ("G" for guerrilla), and LDI is bound to "coordinate all the activities outlined in G-1 through G-5." Other duties of LDI, as conceived in 1992, are:

b) develop and produce the "hard products" necessary to carry-out those activities (ad slicks; post-cards; operating manuals; training materials; videos; etc.);

c) develop sales and marketing strategies for each of the G-3 regulatory legislation proposals, and educate state leaders in those strategies. LDI will also provide the educational tools needed to teach the "business approach" needed for some of the G-2, G-4, and G-5 activities;

d) become a central clearing house to constantly monitor the guerrilla campaign in every state. LDI will identify what works and what doesn't, and track the abortion industry's defense tactics;

e) see that [G-1 through G-5] is carried-out as evenly as possible from state to state. (82–83)

The individual "guerrilla programs" are specifically designed to appear to be working as independent campaigns. But the ulterior motive is to achieve an optimal, culminating impact: "We don't want one state's guerrilla program getting too far ahead of the others. That would simply become a warning to the abortion industry in other states of exactly what our future intentions are for them" (83).

As a front organization, LDI is designed to use other pro-life organizations under the guise of serving them. LDI is publicized as a clearinghouse of educational materials, but *Firestorm* reveals that the real agenda is to be a "clearing house to constantly monitor the guerrilla campaign." Reports of LDI's activities have sounded the alarm that a new antiabortion strategy is afoot, noting its propensity for sneakiness. For example, one journalist emphasizes the shady dealings in his reportage:

> In March 1993, Life Dynamics, under the guise of an abortion rights advocacy group called "Project Choice," took a survey of physicians who provided abortions about their personal fears and misgivings about the procedure, then released the findings to the media. In April 1993, the group published a book of crude jokes and cartoons about abortion providers. It then mailed copies to half of the medical students in America. But Life Dynamics' latest project, pushing malpractice suits, may prove the most controversial.[17]

LDI is often described as controversial and dangerous. In general, reporting on LDI does not portray the organization in favorable light. But neither does it offer any indictment of LDI as the front organization for a larger "guerrilla strategy" called Firestorm.

Although media have reported that LDI is a "self-proclaimed center of a guerrilla movement," they seem to have accepted this idea as only a military metaphor.[18] *Firestorm's* description of LDI as the cover for a decentralized and clandestine "guerrilla strategy" is not a rhetorical trick. It indicates, rather, a desire to make pro-life action as decentralized and leaderless as possible. *Firestorm's* description of guerrilla "operatives" or "agents" conveys the intention to rely on a loosely knit coalition of individuals, not a massive, unified movement compelled by majority consensus.

> Of course, in some states the agent might be an independent pro-life organization that's not affiliated with any particular national organization. In fact, an agent could probably even be just an individual who wants to make the guerrilla campaign a reality in his or her area. The responsibilities of FIRESTORM agents would be to assemble a team of pro-life organizations (referred to as operatives) within their state who agree to assume responsibility for one specific part of the guerrilla campaign (G-1 through G-5).

What we want is a coalition of specialists who focus their efforts in one area. Once this team of operatives is created, the agents would then be responsible for coordinating and monitoring their activities. (84)

In claiming that "the agents would then be responsible for" executing certain plans, *Firestorm* also implies that culpability for those actions would rest entirely on those individual agents. The activities cannot be traced back to LDI, Crutcher, or any donors or employees.

In this way, *Firestorm* deploys a guerrilla strategy comparable to leaderless resistance, popularized in the 1990s throughout the militia movement.[19] Leaderless resistance consists of a cell-based structure of organizing, not a central leadership or hierarchy. Its advantage is to thwart suspicions of conspiracy and to make acts of terrorism appear as isolated incidents. Both guerrilla warfare and guerrilla legislation reduce the likelihood of leaders or strategists being held accountable for the consequences of pro-life action, and give pro-life actions the appearance of being the work of individuals or small groups motivated only by their own conscience. Firestorm is thus a strategy designed with a built-in disavowal of any culpability. No one can be held accountable for cumulative results of individual cases of litigation or regulatory legislation sponsored by lawyers and politicians unaffiliated with LDI. *Firestorm*, therefore, remains valuable not as proof of conspiracy but as an articulation of the dynamic among pro-life legislation, litigation, and violence.

Pro-life Litigation, Legislation, and Violence Working Together

Firestorm provides a good vocabulary with which to describe the ulterior consequences, if not ulterior motives, that pro-life litigation and legislation procure. It allows us to see how neatly the illegal and the legal strategies line up in the social control of abortion providers, girls, and women. The following examples of malpractice lawsuits and regulatory laws demonstrate how pro-life litigation, legislation, and violence function together for devastating political impact.

One of LDI's main efforts is called ABMAL, short for abortion malpractice. In 1993 Crutcher mailed a seventy-two-page guide on how to litigate abortion malpractice to four thousand lawyers.[20] Because Crutcher has always insisted upon and operated under secret affiliations, there is no telling who are the six hundred lawyers and five hundred expert witnesses Crutcher says he has recruited. In fact, although attendance records proved otherwise, three lawyers completely denied having attended LDI's seminar on how to profit from abortion malpractice litigation.[21] It is therefore also impossible to say what lawsuits are direct results of Firestorm and its front organization, LDI. It is not, however, difficult to determine the political impact and consequences of them.

Like pro-life assassinations of doctors, pro-life malpractice suits do not seek to eliminate all abortion providers. The political objective is to sabotage the medical practices of doctors not on a systemic basis, but at random. Just as doctors are arbitrarily targeted by pro-life snipers and assassins, doctors are randomly taken to court. Not knowing when a lawsuit will hit may have the similar psychological effect of not knowing when a bullet will hit.

Psychology aside, the tactic of pro-life malpractice lawsuits can wear down doctors financially. Even if Firestorm fails to achieve its goal of discouraging insurance companies from "writing abortion malpractice coverage at any price," significant hiking of insurance rates or the cost of legal defense can run doctors out of business. This is the case of Dr. Bruce Steir, who was forced to relinquish his medical license when he was faced with "three legal battles at once: the battle to retain his license, the battle to prove he was not negligent, and the battle to stay out of jail."[22] Because he could not financially fight all three battles, he reluctantly surrendered his license. Dr. Steir produced $250,000 bail to stay out of jail while facing abortion-related murder charges.

Unlike pro-life malpractice suits that seek compensation due to emotional damages—which are largely seen by legal experts as "frivolous"[23]—the case against Dr. Steir involves the death of a woman whose uterus was perforated during a second-trimester abortion. Significantly, the death was initially reported as an accident by the county chief medical examiner. Controversy then ensued as the examiner *changed* the cause of death and Dr. Steir was arrested under the charge of second-degree murder. What convinced the examiner to change the cause of death from "accident" to "murder" was a report filled with inaccurate testimony and hearsay. The examiner was later convinced by refutations of the report, and testified that had he not been given the misinformation, he would not have changed the cause of death to murder. Proven to contain false and inflammatory statements, the report was produced by a consumer protection agency called the Medical Board of California, in conjunction with a pro-life activist who connected the patient's survivors with a pro-life attorney.

To avoid the charge of second-degree murder, the conviction of which would carry a mandatory prison term of fifteen years, Steir accepted a plea bargain, pleading guilty to involuntary manslaughter. In spring 2000 he was found guilty and sentenced to six months in jail. He was released two months early for good behavior, financially and emotionally devastated by this fatal incident, "the only death," he said in an interview with a local television reporter, "of a patient of mine throughout the 40 years of my career as a doctor."

In comparison to other physicians whose patients died, Bruce Steir was subject to unusual tactics and standards. An independent study by the ACLU of Northern California compared his case with other disciplinary cases involving California doctors since 1993, concluding that Steir "deserved to lose his license," because of his patient's death, "but he did not deserve to be singled out for criminal prosecution." The report condemns the charge of murder and details the influence of Jeannette Dreisbach, the pro-life activist. Ultimately, the ACLU calls for "openness by the Medical Board as to its policies and procedures; fairness and consistency by the Medical Board in pursuing complaints against doctors; and reofrm of Medical Board's practices or policies that allow bias to influence the agency's actions."[24]

Dr. Steir's case is thus a "hallmark of the effort to use regulatory agencies as a weapon against abortion providers." Targeted Restrictions on Abortion Providers (TRAP) laws have been enacted in thirteen states and pro-life publications have used Steir's case to argue for them, claiming that there is no such thing as "safe abortion."[25] By regularly anticipating and tracking abortion complications and introducing people to pro-life lawyers, Dreisbach and the Medical Board of California are able to increase the numbers of pro-life malpractice suits—even murder charges—which may increase insurance rates for women's doctors.

It certainly increases the stigmatization of doctors, which is one of Firestorm's stated goals. Crutcher's LDI distributed a second graphic book of crude jokes and cartoons aimed at dehumanizing doctors, called "Quack the Ripper." Also, the first edition of a monthly, hour-long, LDI-produced "video magazine" called LifeTalk lists seven examples of penalized and incarcerated abortion providers. Despite the fact that reasons for these legal entanglements range from tax evasion to manslaughter, the seven cases are then interpreted in sweeping terms by Crutcher as evidence of abortion providers' basic incompetence and "stupid life habits."

Doctors are routinely portrayed as incompetent but rich during LifeTalk, and presenting their legal troubles as news items, LDI implies that its promotion of abortion malpractice suits is working. LDI provides an array of abortion malpractice litigation services for lawyers, including client referral networks, legal education materials, depositions and interrogatories, client training, case management, a cocounsel network, expert witnesses and consultants, research collected by "spies" and information on abortion providers and clinic workers, and "abortion animation"—a video created for courtroom demonstrations. These services are detailed on LDI's website, which does not state what Firestorm does: Crutcher's calculated intention to get "these 'chain-store' law firms to start looking upon abortion malpractice as a lucrative field" (64).

One political effect of this sort of promotion of abortion malpractice suits is to create moral outrage that distorts the reality of abortion in America. Abortion is among the safest and most frequently performed surgeries in the United States. An estimated 43 percent of all U.S. women will have an abortion by the time they turn forty-five. Approximately 1.5 million American women obtain abortions each year. According to the Alan Guttmacher Institute, "The risk of abortion complications is minimal; less than 1% of all abortion patients experience a major complication, such as serious pelvic infection, hemorrhage requiring a blood transfusion or major surgery." "The risk of death associated with childbirth is about 10 times as high as that associated with abortion."[26] Psychologically, too, abortion is shown to cause few adverse reactions. C. Everett Koop, the pro-life surgeon general of Ronald Reagan's cabinet, oversaw a study that concluded that women did not suffer psychologically after terminating their pregnancies.[27] These facts indicate that hundreds of thousands of women terminate pregnancies safely and sanely every year, but this reality is shrouded by pro-life promotion of malpractice suits.

Another political effect of pro-life malpractice is to make the defense of abortion as an option for women synonymous with the defense of the medical profession. From a historical standpoint, this equation makes for some strange bedfellows. Historically, progressive women and the medical profession have been at odds. In fact, the outlawing of abortion throughout the United States, especially through the 1860s, was in large part due to the professionalization of male physicians who wanted to delegitimize women who provided abortions as well as midwifery skills.[28] A century later, in the 1960s, the medical profession was still seen as progressive women's enemy, since hospitals and doctors did not fight for repeal of abortion laws, but only for their reform. Feminists and other progressive women sought to undo the mystification of their own bodies that the medical profession had institutionalized. By "demystifying" the female body and the simple procedure of abortion, ordinary women launched a self-help movement that defied both the law and the medical establishment. In the Chicago area an underground women's collective called Jane operated from 1969 to 1973, providing eleven thousand safe, affordable, and successful abortions.[29] Pro-life malpractice suits play on this history of women's struggle to break free from the male-oriented and male-dominated medical profession, attempting to channel the distrust and anger derived from any actual medical mistreatment of women to pro-life causes.

But if *Firestorm* is any indication of pro-life legislation and litigation in general, the goal is not to stop the medical mistreatment of women. In fact, it is not even to outlaw abortion, according to Crutcher (34). It is to create a matrix of individual pieces of regulatory and punitive legislation that work in concert to prevent (sometimes forcibly) people from obtaining or providing abortions. Some legislation proposed in *Firestorm* has been put into effect since 1992. For example, what *Firestorm* proposes as "a requirement that women obtaining an abortion must be a resident of the state" prefigures the 1998 Child Custody Protection Act prohibiting minors seeking abortions to cross state lines.[30] *Firestorm* also proposes prohibitions to "abortions done late in pregnancy" three years before the term "partial birth abortion" was created by pro-life strategists, then opposed in Congress.[31]

These two pieces of pro-life legislation fused (as guerrilla strategies are apt to do) in the case of a pregnant twelve-year-old girl who was the victim of incestuous rape by her seventeen-year-old brother. The girl and her family, recent immigrants to Michigan from India, remained completely anonymous throughout the trials to obtain an abortion for the girl. Her pregnancy went undetected for reasons that are not described fully in any media account, but which certainly may include the taboo of incest, cultural differences, and communication problems. A doctor apparently did not find the girl's complaints credible; consequently he misdiagnosed her symptoms until she had gestated for twenty-eight weeks. Because Michigan law prohibits abortions after the twenty-fourth week, the family had to appeal for permission for the abortion. The judge not only denied the request and "made the girl a ward of the court until a psychiatric examination was performed," but "prohibited the girl from leaving the state, blocking her parents' efforts to take her to Kansas for a late-term abortion." Thus two pro-life guerrilla strategies—bans on late abortions and prohibiting pregnant minors to cross state lines for abortions—were teamed up to delay the abortion for two additional weeks. Once the travel ban was lifted and the girl was returned to her parents' custody, they drove to Kansas to terminate her pregnancy.[32]

In the case of this anonymous twelve-year-old, the culminating effects of guerrilla pro-life legislation amount to more than just being denied an abortion. Pro-life guerrilla legislation also denies recourse from rape, especially from the rape of young women. In particular, bans on late-term procedures may affect young women and girls who may not know they are pregnant until the second or third trimester. They deny it themselves and hide it from others. Incest and rape are pernicious for girls because they are too young to recognize or understand manipulation and coercion when it is part of their daily family or community life. Even in cases that do not involve rape, it is clear that compulsory pregnancy—enforcing the condition of pregnancy against the will of a woman—is the order of the day for some communities that use legislation as justification for vigilante action.

Take for example the situation of a fifteen-year-old girl in Blair, Nebraska. In 1995 she was prevented from having an abortion, despite having the full support of her parents. It was her boyfriend's family that orchestrated a pro-life intervention by enlisting the aid of a pro-life deputy sheriff, a pro-life doctor, and a pro-life county prosecutor. According to the *New York Times*, the house of the girl's parents "was violently invaded by the boyfriend, his parents and friends; their daughter was taken from them in the middle of the night by law-enforcement officers determined to stop her from having an abortion; she was put into foster care, and, finally, she was ordered by a judge not to abort the pregnancy."[33]

The girl's family filed a suit after leaving their hometown of Blair, detailing in the complaint the invasion, kidnapping, and harassment. Remarkably, there was no denial of the actions. No one, according to the *New York Times* "appeared to dispute the facts of the case. Rather the issue here appeared to center on whether the actions taken by a community strongly opposed to abortion were an acceptable use of the legal system or an example of anti-abortion extremism."[34] More precisely, this is an example of pro-life guerrilla strategy, of combined illegal forced entry and sanctioned law enforcement (court orders) to impose compulsory pregnancy.

As these cases of the twelve-year-old in Michigan and the fifteen-year-old in Nebraska attest, the distinction between what is illegal pro-life activity and what is legal pro-life activity becomes ambiguous as guerrilla mentalities and strategies are focused on girls. The line separating protection from coercion, loving support from manipulation, and pro-life proselytizers from pro-life predators gets very thin. This thin line is blurred in a pamphlet by Terra Vierkant, circulated in 1996. The front page of the pamphlet reads: "Twelve and Pregnant ... What Choices Does She Have? Too Young to Bear?"[35] It describes how to compel a pregnant girl to reject abortion as an option. The job entails describing the "side effects" of abortion and enlisting other pro-lifers to show the family members the medically inaccurate pro-life movie *The Silent Scream*.[36] This convinces the girl's father not to drive her to the clinic. Then, a pro-lifer keeps "in close contact with" the girl day after day until she reverses her original decision to have an abortion and commits to going through with the pregnancy. For months, the pro-lifer continues the relationship until the girl, now thirteen, delivers a baby.

What gives the pro-lifer permission to play such an active role is reportedly a call from the girl's mother, who knew of her child's pregnancy only because the pro-life "parental notification" laws were in effect in 1985. Again, pro-life legislation permits activity that extends beyond the traditional means of proselytizing or witnessing one's religious convictions. Such legislation gives license to pro-lifers who are increasingly warlike in their attitudes and calculating in their strategy. Part of this calculation is the recirculation of misinformation about so-called side effects of abortion—myths that should have been nationally discredited by Surgeon General Koop's report. Another part of this calculation involves the *missing information* about the girl and her circumstances. Just as there is no discussion in the pro-life pamphlet of what kind of psychological toll it takes on a thirteen-year-old to become a mother, there is no discussion of how she got pregnant in the first place. In this regard, the pamphlet follows a general trend in abortion politics to eschew discussion of the only briefly mentioned "cases of rape and incest" and to ignore the relationship between abortion and rape or incest.

What some women are taught as raped girls is reinscribed in the midst of pro-life assassinations and bombs: some people deserve the random acts of terror that are forced on them. A sophisticated understanding of how blaming the victim works seems to have been eradicated in the so-called postfeminist 1980s and 1990s; no women want to present themselves as victims. But that thirteen-year-old in Michigan is a victim. She is not only a victim of an incestuous family, but of a pernicious legal system which, armed with guerrilla pro-life legislation, would deny her abortion as a recourse from rape, impose compulsory pregnancy, and enforce mandatory motherhood.

The rape of teens, incestuous or not, provides another opportunity for pro-lifers to place unintended consequences "squarely in the realm of calculated results." As in the case of the twelve-year-old in Michigan and the twelve-year-old featured in the pro-life pamphlet, while it may be no one's intention that these girls get pregnant, it serves as an opportunity to draw from and reinforce the pro-life guerrilla legislation that regulates abortion, such as parental notification laws, interstate travel bans, and late abortion bans. *Firestorm* makes no apologies about calculatedly using the misfortunes of girls and women as opportunities to further pro-life guerrilla strategy. Ironically, to exploit these opportunities and, by extension, the girls and women themselves, Firestorm employs strategies that ostensibly are designed to fight for women's rights.

According to Crutcher's own words, Firestorm's focus on women's rights is not genuine; it is a ploy to hide the real agenda and confuse opponents. "They are evidently so accustomed to our arguments being focused only on the unborn baby, for us to voluntarily talk about the woman catches them totally off-guard" (75). That is not to say, however, that it is pro-lifers who should propose regulatory "guerrilla" legislation. In fact, Crutcher prescribes that "pro-life organizations should not allow themselves to be publicly identified with this, or any other guerrilla type legislation" (59). All guerrilla "legislation should be sold as 'pro-women' and/or 'consumer protection' legislation" (57).

For example, in proposing a "requirement that all abortion related counseling be done by people not employed by people in the abortion industry," Crutcher explains that "We simply sell it as consumer protection that would prohibit any medical-related counseling from being done by people who might financially profit from the decision being discussed. Our goal would be to sneak this legislation through and once it's passed do whatever is necessary (lawsuits?) to see it applied to abortion counseling" (51). Here the link between punitive lawsuits and preemptive, regulatory legislation proposed as consumer protection for women is made clear. Like the abortion malpractice cases and other pro-life litigation, regulatory laws appear to be made for the benefit of women as reproductive health care consumers. But *Firestorm*'s promotion of callous disregard for women is never very disguised, as is evident in Crutcher's explanation for this strategic switch away from fetal protection to women's protection: "When it comes to regulatory legislation, always keep in mind that, generally speaking, it is not necessarily designed to directly protect the baby, but the mother. . . . While it may sound crude, the reality is that an abortionist has to go through the mother to get to the baby. And like it or not . . . her case is easier to make in the legislature" (62). It is even easier when women, not men, are spokespersons for the pro-life cause. *Firestorm* blatantly insists, "in all cases make sure the person delivering the message is female" (70). In *Firestorm*, if not in pro-life politics generally, protecting women is an undenied ruse.

Unfortunately, it is a ruse that may prove effective. Take for example the case of Deborah Gaines, who sued the Brookline, Massachusetts, clinic where pro-life assassin John Salvi III killed two clinic workers and injured six others in 1994. Gaines's case reflects pro-life guerrilla tactics described in *Firestorm*, and illustrates how pro-life violence and punitive legislation against abortion clinics function together.

According to legal statements, Deborah Gaines was scheduled to have an abortion at PreTerm the day John Salvi hit, December 30, 1994. After his attack inside the clinic, he chased Gaines outside, which terrorized her to the point of never being able to terminate her pregnancy.[37] Suffering from posttraumatic stress, Gaines decided to avoid abortion clinics, hence abortion, and consequently delivered a baby girl many months later. She sued the clinic because they did not provide her, as a patient, with enough security from the likes of Salvi. Gaines demanded financial compensation for mental anguish and the "wrongful birth" of her daughter, without whom Gaines had planned to finish her GED and gain independence from the welfare program.[38] Eventually the Brookline clinic owners settled out of court.

To stunning effect, this case reflects the strategy in *Firestorm*. It positions the woman as a reproductive health care consumer whose protection and rights are the ostensible foci of the lawsuit. It aims punitive and regulatory legislation at the clinic owners and clinic personnel, not at abortion itself. Couching the case in terms of "wrongful birth," the prosecutors appear to have a callous view of the baby and seem to be privileging the mother. This too is a reflection of Firestorm's aim to catch abortion rights advocates "off guard" by focusing on the woman side of the mother-fetus dyad that has characterized the abortion debate.

Crutcher may or may not have been behind the Gaines case, but LDI certainly is responsible for having contacted employees of the Brookline clinic three years after Salvi's attack, urging them to "turn in their employer for tax and safety violations." Letters from LDI were sent to the homes of employees, warning them of "potential illnesses" they could get "by working at an unsafe abortion clinic."[39] Like Gaines's case, the letters appeal to a desire for security and protection of those working in or benefiting from abortion clinics. LDI's emphasis on workers' protection in the letters to clinic employees is a variation on Firestorm's stated intention to pose lawsuits and regulations in terms of women's protection.

Firestorm's emphasis on women's "protection" is revealing in another way. It foreshadows the demand for governmental protection that women are now forced to make in the wake of lethal pro-life violence. As Deborah Gaines's case shows, protection for women may be couched in legal terms of consumer rights, but the protection she really needed was from a man with a gun, a guerrilla for life. The emphasis on "women's protection" that pro-life legislation touts has gained more applicability as the years have passed, as pro-life violence has become guerrilla warfare, and as those who provide or seek abortions have apparently had no recourse other than asking the government to protect them from bombs, assassins, anthrax, and acid.

Conclusion: The Logic of Killing for Life

As pro-life violence became guerrilla warfare in the 1990s, pro-lifers conducted their own ruminations about how law, justice, and violence relate. Veteran pro-lifer and law professor Charles Rice wrote an article, "Can the Killing of Abortion-ists Be Justified?" In keeping with a vibrant tradition of pro-life scholarship,[40] Rice uses sophisticated, natural law arguments to conclude that "The use of violence in the pro-life cause must be utterly rejected."[41] This emphatic rejection, however, is tempered within the general discussion. Rice argues that the "use" of violence should be rejected because it is, in 1994, politically and strategically disadvanta-geous and morally unjustifiable since pro-lifers are *not yet* to the point of no other recourse. Rice's rejection of the "use" or application of violence, however, does not preclude the acceptance of violence at a later time or in different circumstances. In this article, as in others, pro-life violence is never rejected in principle.

Five months before "Can the Killing?" appeared, Rice saw another of his pro-life discussions of lethal violence in print: "The Death Penalty Dilemma."[42] Rice bases this discussion of capital punishment also on natural law, which is the cor-nerstone of Catholic Thomist thought. St. Thomas Aquinas believed that "divine law, revealed through grace, perfects, but does not overturn, the human law that is based on natural reason."[43] Moreover, for those who subscribe to natural law, "recourse to violence poses no problems, since natural ends"—derived by natural reason perfected through the revelation of divine law—"are just."[44] Natural law normalizes violence, in the sense that "recourse to violent means is as justified, as normal as a man's 'right' to move his body to reach a given goal."[45] Drawing from natural law, Rice delineates several justifications for capital punishment, claiming that it is not "unjust to execute a murderer" because it may deter other murders from occurring, and because "retribution," though not vengeance, is a "sound principle of natural law and common sense." Punitive violence is commonsensical to Rice when murder is the offense.

Rice's critique continues: "Murder should be stigmatized as the crime of crimes" because it devalues life, which is defined as the dominion of God. Only God can give life, and only God can take life away. It is therefore not a contradic-tion for the government, on behalf of God, to execute a murderer: "The state derives its authority from God who is the Lord of life." The death penalty, says Rice, "promotes respect for innocent life." On these grounds, Rice makes punitive violence seem not only natural and commonsensical, but also an obvious comple-ment to antiabortion politics: "Capital punishment is obviously a 'right to life' issue," he says. Like the banning of abortion, "the imposition of capital punish-ment can be seen as a means to restore respect for innocent life." Rice advocates state-sanctioned killing for life because he sees it as ultimately sanctioned by God.

Rice takes for granted that his readers believe both that abortion is murder and that abortion providers are murderers. With these unexamined assumptions intact, the article approves punitive violence such as capital punishment not only as retri-bution, but as a commonsensical, obvious, and natural way to deal with "abortion-ists or more conventional killers." Killing for life is hardly a contradiction, accord-ing to Rice's logic; it is tantamount to restoring respect for God as Lord.

Rice's article makes explicit what is implicit in other pro-life discussions based on natural law: it naturalizes and normalizes violence as retribution for challenging God's dominion over life. Many early pro-life arguments were made on the basis of natural law, some written by Rice and others, most notably by John Noonan, who edited the *Natural Law Forum*, published from 1956 to 1968 by Notre Dame Law School, where Rice is a professor.[46] Rice's pro-life critique of violence is therefore not important because it is particularly original thinking or in any radical way a departure from erudite pro-life arguments. Rice's article is important because of when and where it appeared.

"The Death Penalty Dilemma" appeared in the April 4, 1994, issue of *The New American*, a magazine of the John Birch Society. It was published just a month before a similarly themed pro-life discussion appeared in another right-wing magazine. In May 1994 the cover story of *Life Advocate* examined the April 1994 trial of Rachelle "Shelley" Shannon, who shot Dr. George Tiller in August 1993. A sidebar to the article discusses Paul Hill and his "defensive action statement." About two months after Shannon's conviction, in July 1994, Hill became a pro-life assassin. Later that year, in December, John Salvi also killed for life. In Salvi's apartment was a copy of Rice's article from *The New American*.[47]

The fact that Salvi had Rice's article in his apartment does not suggest Rice's intention to promote violence, or that it incited Salvi to kill. But in the context of Rice's logic of natural law, Salvi's—and others'—attacks may be understood functioning not as a protest of the "violence" of abortion, but as retribution for the violation implicit in that so-called violence. Guerrilla warfare and "guerrilla legislation" aimed at those seeking or providing abortions constitute retribution for challenging God's dominion over life. In this way, pro-life retribution through guerrilla strategies is not as much a punishment for an individual's infringement of God's law, as a way to restore the order of God.[48] In this light, the acts of killing for life—like the strange notion of "guerrilla legislation"—are revealed not as an oxymoron, but as a logical consistency and a political manifestation of religious retribution.

NOTES

1. Research compiled for this chapter was made possible by a fellowship from the Bunting Institute. I am also indebted to Jacqueline Soohen and the Radcliffe Research Partnership Program. Throughout this essay I use the term "pro-life" rather than "antiabortion" to signify right-wing agendas that go beyond the curtailment of reproductive freedom. What the "life" of "pro-life" means is contingently defined in right-wing writings; and assassinations of abortion providers have especially brought the phrase into question. A thorough examination of this topic comprises my book *Killing for Life*, forthcoming from Cornell University Press.
2. On deParrie, see Mark O'Keefe, "Anarchy in the Name of God," *The Oregonian*, Sunday, January 24, 1999. On Bray, see James Risen and Judy L. Thomas, *Wrath of Angels* (New York: Basic Books, 1998), chap. 4.
3. Risen and Thomas, *Wrath of Angels*, p. 347.

4. Ibid., p. 370.
5. This manual is archived in the library of Political Research Associates of Somerville, Massachusetts. Thanks to Jean Hardisty and Chip Berlet for their help.
6. Thanks to Steve Waksman and especially Liette Gidlow for bringing to my attention the complexities of this phrase.
7. See Risen and Thomas, *Wrath of Angels*. Also Jeffrey Kaplan, "Absolute Rescue: Absolutism, Defensive Action and the Resort to Force," in *Millennialism and Violence*, ed. Michael Barkun, (London and Portland, Oreg.: Frank Cass, 1996); Faye Ginsburg, "Rescuing the Nation: Operation Rescue and the Rise of Anti-Abortion Militance," in *Abortion Wars: A Half Century of Struggle, 1950–2000*, ed. Rickie Solinger (Berkeley: University of California Press, 1998).
8. Risen and Thomas, *Wrath of Angels*, p. 340.
9. Christina Nifong, "Bomb Signals New Strategy," *Christian Science Monitor*, February 2, 1998.
10. Karen Foerstel and Andy Soltis, "Six Injured in Abort-Clinic Bomb Blasts," *New York Post*, Friday, January 17, 1997. See also the June 9, 1997, U.S. Department of Justice, Federal Bureau of Investigation press release, which reads, "there were secondary bombs designed to explode after law enforcement personnel arrived on the scene." These articles pertain to three bombs detonated in and around Atlanta, Georgia, in 1997 and 1996.
11. See the Abortion Rights Activist website for chronologies of pro-life violence, including butyric acid attacks, www.cais.com/agm/main/ytd98.htm.
12. "Anthrax Scare," *The Body Politic*, November 5, 1998.
13. "'Pro-life' Murder: Charleston Clinic Threat," *The Charleston Gazette*, February 26, 1999.
14. These figures are from Sharon Lerner, "Blight to Life," *Village Voice*, October 28–November 3, 1998.
15. The *Army of God* manual, which has no publication date or author listed, discusses "babies rescued through the increased cost of killing."
16. Joseph Scheidler's book *Closed: 99 Ways to Stop Abortion* (Lewiston, N.Y.: Life Cycle Books, 1985), which details legal ways to interfere in abortion provision, is a more moderate version of the anonymous, underground *Army of God* manual, which delineates how to make bombs and other weapons of destruction for pro-life purposes. In a similar way, Crutcher has publicly circulated more openly a few, selected, toned-down ideas from *Firestorm* as *Access: The Key to Pro-life Victory* and as *Lime 5*.
17. Mark Ballard, "The New Abortion Front," *Texas Lawyer*, April 22, 1996.
18. Ibid.
19. Louis Beam, a former Grand Dragon in David Duke's Texas Klan and then a member in the Aryan Nations, delivered in 1992 the finer points of leaderless resistance to 150 participants in a militia meeting in Estes Park, Colorado. See Martin A. Lee, *The Beast Reawakens* (Boston: Little, Brown and Company, 1997), p. 348.
20. Vivienne Walt, "Group Offers Case in a Kit; New Tactic vs. Abortion Docs." *Newsday*, September 6, 1993.
21. Ballard, "The New Abortion Front."
22. Letter to National Abortion Federation members from Feminist Women's Health Center, Chico, California, March 17, 1998.
23. Ballard, "The New Abortion Front."
24. Phyllida Burlingame, *Unfair Prosecution of Abortion Providers: Bias by the Medical Board of California*, American Civil Liberties Union of Northern California, 2000.

25. Ibid.
26. These statistics are from the Alan Guttmacher Institute. For additional compelling information on the safety and frequency of abortion in America, visit their website: www.agi-usa.org.
27. On Koop, see Ballard. Additional studies that indicate abortion as having no psychological damage include: Nada Stotland, "The Myth of the Abortion Trauma Syndrome," *Journal of the American Medical Association* 268, no. 15 (October 21, 1992): 2078–79. Nancy Adler et al., "Psychological Factors in Abortion: A Review," *American Psychologist* 47, no. 10 (October 1992): 1194–204.
28. On the criminalization of abortion in the United States, see the following: Carroll Smith-Rosenberg, *Disorderly Conduct: Visions of Gender in Victorian America* (New York: Oxford, 1985); James C. Mohr, *Abortion in America: The Origins and Evolution of National Policy, 1800–1900* (New York: Oxford, 1978); Faye D. Ginsburg, *Contested Lives: The Abortion Debate in an American Community* (Berkeley: University of California Press, 1989); Kristen Luker, *Abortion and the Politics of Motherhood* (Berkeley: University of California Press, 1984).
29. For history of the illegal abortion service called Jane, especially with regard to the self-help movement, see Ninia Baehr, *Abortion Without Apology: A Radical History for the 1990s* (Boston: South End Press, 1990). See also Laura Kaplan, *The Story of Jane: The Legendary Underground Feminist Abortion Service* (New York: Pantheon, 1996)
30. Nell Bernstein, "Law Creates a New Class of Children: Isolated, Illegal," *San Jose Mercury News*, July 19, 1998.
31. Sharon Lerner, "The 'Partial' Ploy: How the Anti-choice Campaign Against a Nonexistent Procedure Threatens Roe," *Village Voice*, September 23–29, 1998.
32. Ilaina Jonas, "Girl, 12, in Incest Case Has Abortion," *Pittsburgh Post-Gazette*, August 1, 1998.
33. Tamar Lewin, "Nebraska Abortion Case: The Issue Is Interference," *New York Times*, September 25, 1995.
34. Ibid.
35. The pamphlet was printed and distributed by Pro-life Action Ministries, St. Paul, Minnesota.
36. See *The Facts Speak Louder*, Planned Parenthood's response to the film.
37. DeNeen L. Brown, "Deborah's Choice," *Washington Post*, September 27, 1998.
38. Alison Fitzgerald, "Woman Sues Abortion Clinic for 'Wrongful Birth,'" *The Charlotte Observer*, September 1, 1998. Brian MacQuarrie, "'Wrongful Birth' Suit Raises Fears for Children," *Boston Globe*, September 5, 1998.
39. "Clinic Workers Get 'Chilling' Mailing," *Boston Herald*, February 28, 1997.
40. For an earlier discussion of retribution and "retributive justice" with regard to both capital punishment and "respect for life" as manifested in antiabortion campaigns, see Thomas J. Higgins, "Why the Death Penalty?" The article appeared in the Catholic magazine *Triumph* in February 1973, just a month after the Supreme Court decision of *Roe v. Wade*.
41. Charles E. Rice, "Can the Killing of Abortionists Be Justified?" *The Wanderer*, September 1, 1994. Reprinted on the Internet at www.trosch.org.
42. Charles E. Rice, "The Death Penalty Dilemma," *The New American*, April 4, 1994, pp. 23–24.
43. Elizabeth Mensch and Alan Freeman, *The Politics of Virtue: Is Abortion Debatable?* (Durham, North Carolina: Duke University Press, 1993), p. 35.
44. Jacques Derrida, "Force of Law: The 'Mystical Foundation of Authority,'" in *Decon-*

struction and the Possibility of Justice, ed. Drucilla Cornell, Michel Rosenfeld, and David Gray Carlson (New York: Routledge, 1992), p. 32.

45. Ibid.

46. Mensch and Freeman discuss natural law and the Catholic tradition with regard to antiabortion arguments in *The Politics of Virtue*, p. 31.

47. Chip Berlet, "John Salvi, Abortion Clinic Violence, and Catholic Right Conspiracism," *Political Research Associates*, March 19, 1996.

48. The ultimate objective of retribution such as capital punishment is to restore a particular order, rather than to punish a particular individual. See Walter Benjamin, "Critique of Violence," in *Reflections: Essays, Aphorisms, Autobiographical Writings* (New York: Schocken Books, 1986).

CHAPTER EIGHT

Violence, Nonviolence, and the U.S. Civil Rights Movement

Sally Avery Bermanzohn

Many people associate the U.S. Civil Rights movement with nonviolence. But violence was central to the dynamics of southern civil rights. White racist brutality pervaded the experience of African Americans, who debated a wide range of strategic responses and often protected themselves using armed self-defense.

Official histories belittle the role of violence. Many historical accounts deify Martin Luther King Jr. as leading a biblical struggle. Coretta Scott King portrayed her slain husband as "an instrument of a Divine plan and purpose." Pulitzer Prize–winning biographies emphasized biblical themes through their titles, which compared King to Christ (*Bearing the Cross* by Garrow) and Moses (*Parting the Waters* by Branch).[1] In contrast, this chapter analyzes King as a master politician who deeply understood the use of terror by southern racists, and who developed nonviolent resistance as a practical strategy.

Martin Luther King Jr. was not a pure pacifist. As a young man in divinity school he thought that an armed revolt was the only way to end segregation.[2] As an adult he wrote that sometimes violence could be justified if it was the only means of resisting tyranny. In the last years of his life, he spoke out against the U.S. war in Vietnam and in support of (armed) national liberation movements.[3] King called himself a "practical pacifist" because he understood that in the segregated South violent conflicts inevitably meant black losses. He realized that a nonviolent strategy could enable African Americans to take the moral upper hand, gain white liberals' support, and increase pressure on the federal government to thwart violent racists. King and other civil rights activists skillfully utilized the unique factors that were favorable at that time, including the Cold War, democratizing movements in Africa, and the spread of television in the United States.

The main theme of this book is that the exercise of state power is key to the politics of violence. The civil-rights-era South is a clear example. Before the 1960s the U.S. Constitution's "guarantee" of equal rights was a sham for southern blacks.

Ku Klux Klan terror and lynch murder bolstered segregation, while federal, state, and local governments perpetuated racist violence by failing to punish it. Only federal action, beginning with the Supreme Court's 1954 *Brown v Board of Education of Topeka* decision, and the pressure of a massive grassroots civil rights movement, dismantled segregation. Integration was a regime change for the South, overturning an old regime that centered on disenfranchising black citizens.[4] To stop integration, the Ku Klux Klan grew in the 1950s and early 1960s, along with new organizations, such as White Citizens Councils. White supremacists were responsible for more than one thousand documented violent incidents between 1956 and 1966, including bombing, burning, flogging, abduction, castration, and murder. Few were punished for these crimes.[5] The breakthrough came in 1964: Congress passed the first significant civil rights law since Reconstruction, and President Johnson finally ordered the FBI to act against Ku Klux Klan violence. Piven and Cloward argue that thwarting racist brutality was the most significant victory of the Civil Rights movement, stating, "in the South the deepest meaning of the winning of democratic rights is that the historical primacy of terror as a means of social control has been substantially diminished."[6]

Ignoring or marginalizing violence is a noteworthy phenomenon in recent political discourse. John Keane in *Reflections on Violence* criticizes "the paucity of reflection" on the "the causes, effects and ethico-political implications of violence."[7] Civilization is the opposite of violence, requiring people to settle differences and disputes by peaceful means, yet brutality plagues modern societies. The pattern of violence in society reveals the structure of actual power. The powerful often ignore violence when the victims are poor and/or powerless. Mobs attack racial, religious, or sexual minorities when they feel entitled and believe they can get away with it. The dynamic is similar when men batter women, or adults batter children. How government defines crime, and how law enforcement and the judicial system implement the law, affects the prevalence of violence. Authorities perpetuate it when they ignore it, or brutalize those in their custody. Violence grows when the powerful give excuses for it, such as the view that vigilantes provide useful social control through terror.

Keane argues that violence sometimes plagues a population to the point that the community "passes over into the category of uncivil society."[8] In the Old South, good manners often honey-coated a brutal reality. A duality existed between what John Hope Franklin called the "two worlds of race" maintained by "intimidation, terror, lynching, and riots."[9] White southerners prided themselves on their "civility," their personal grace, courtesy, concern. But William Chafe, in *Civility and Civil Rights*, points out that for African Americans there was "the other side of civility—the deferential poses they had to strike in order to keep jobs, the chilling power of consensus to crush efforts to raise issues of racial justice. As victims of civility, blacks had long been forced to operate within an etiquette of race relations that offered almost no room for collective self-assertion and independence. White people dictated the ground rules, and the benefits went only to those who played the game."[10] Moreover, for blacks any "violation of the game" risked brutality that lurked just beneath the smiles and pleasantries. As Robert Williams wrote in 1962, "in a civilized society the law is a deterrent against the strong who would take advantage of the weak, but the South is not a civilized society."[11]

This chapter analyzes the dynamics of violence and politics in the American South during the Civil Rights movement. The first part analyzes the pre-1960 relationship between racist terror, southern government, and federal policy, exploring how blacks in the rural South defended themselves when they had no governmental recourse. The second part traces the development of Martin Luther King Jr.'s nonviolent resistance, and the long struggle to force the federal government to fight the racist violence. John Keane argues that the strategy of nonviolent resistance cannot be understood in isolation from the use of force in society. For example, Gandhi used nonviolence, according to Keane, to "forcibly obstruct the British imperial government."[12] King's strategy can be understood as an activist approach that *forcibly* ended segregation and established black political rights.

White Violence, Government Complicity, and Black Self-Defense

Until the mid-1960s, the U.S. government allowed racist terror to exist in the South. Lynching is mob murder in defiance of law and established judicial procedures; after Reconstruction it became commonplace in the South. Between 1882 and 1968, newspapers reported 4,742 lynch murders in the United States. Seventy-three percent of the victims (3,445 individuals) were black. Eighty-one percent of the lynchings (3,848) occurred in twelve southern states.[13] A lynch tradition cannot exist without the complicity of authorities. Local and state officials, including police, jailers, mayors, and others, often facilitated, or at least did not impede, racist mobs. Whites who opposed violence or advocated equality of the races could themselves become targets. Violence threatened anyone who violated the social order, in economic relations such as buying or selling land, or social relations by having black friends or lovers of a different race.

Getting the state to protect black lives and punish racist murderers dominated the efforts of civil rights groups for most of the twentieth century. Ida B. Wells-Barnett in 1909 argued for federal enforcement of civil rights, stating, "Lynching is color-line murder ... it is a national crime and requires a national remedy."[14] That same year, blacks and whites founded the National Association for the Advancement of Colored People (NAACP), which campaigned for federal antilynching legislation for six decades. Congress failed to act: antilynching bills passed the House of Representatives in 1922, 1937, and 1940, but Senate filibusters by southern Democrats defeated each of them. Federal authorities maintained a hands-off policy, viewing racist violence as a matter for southern states to handle.

Many southern whites abhorred violence. By the 1920s many business leaders opposed lynching because it created a "bad business climate" and spurred blacks to migrate north.[15] In the 1930s thirty thousand white women joined the Association of Southern Women for the Prevention of Lynching to lobby against the brutality that white men committed in the name of protecting white women.[16] Some southern political leaders with concerns about their national reputations spoke out against violence, although overall politicians allowed it to continue.[17]

Public opposition to mob murder led to a decline in lynching as a public spectacle in the 1920s. But violence continued in more subtle forms. Lynching became secretive. Those blacks deemed "uppity" had "accidents" or "disappeared." Legal violence increased, including police brutality and prison conditions so lethal many healthy prisoners succumbed. All-white-male juries condemned black-on-white crimes, while acquitting white-on-black crimes.[18] Zangrando writes about the change in the tactics of violence:

> Worried that outside pressure might produce a federal antilynching law, some southern whites found it wise to suppress the news of mob violence ... select committees might be assigned to abduct, torture, and kill victims without public fanfare ... Further masking the realities was the phenomenon of "legal lynchings," whereby officials consented in advance to a sham court trial followed promptly by the prisoner's execution.[19]

The structure of violence varied from place to place, varying by tradition and personality of the authorities. In southern cities, blacks developed their own institutions including churches and civic organizations that were independent of whites. In the rural South, however, many blacks continued to be economically dependent on whites, and terror continued.[20]

Washington set the tone of the country's response to violence. Presidents occasionally spoke out deploring a particular atrocity, but the federal government maintained a hands-off policy from the fall of Reconstruction until 1964. National leaders brushed off racist brutality as a problem for state and local authorities.

Black Self-Defense

Defending one's life is a fundamental human instinct. When government fails to protect people, they will do what they can to protect themselves. Rural African Americans' recourse was self-reliance, defending themselves. Many blacks in the rural South used weapons to hunt and to defend their homes and families. People did not openly discuss armed self-defense but they widely practiced it. James Forman, a 1960s civil rights leader wrote about the prevalence of "self-defense—at least of one's home." Forman noted that in rural areas "there was hardly a black home in the South without its shotgun or rifle."[21]

To analyze the dynamics of violence and armed self-defense, I interviewed two dozen African Americans who grew up poor in the rural South before civil rights. All discussed the threat of violence in their lives. Three of them, Ronnie Johnson, Willena Cannon, and Thomas Anderson, gave detailed descriptions of the impact of violence on the lives of their families. Ronnie Johnson comes from a large family in southern Mississippi.[22] He explained that "behind the front door of every house was a couple of shotguns and rifles. A drawer had shells in it. In the bedroom was another shotgun." Johnson discussed the elaborate measures his family took to protect themselves:

> For my family, the greatest fear was a surprise attack by a group, by the Klan, that would have overwhelming force and drag people from the house. To protect themselves, families like mine tried to have a lot of sons, and teach them how to use weapons. My kinfolk lived in houses that were within shouting distance of each other, so they could gather in time of need. Our house was at the end of a long road that led off the main highway, and everyone kept dogs in the yard. By the time anyone got down that road, everybody knew who they were, what they were, and why they were coming. This close network provided a common defense for ordinary occasions. But if a concerted effort came against one family, then it could be a shoot-out.

Johnson explained that the county law enforcement included only a few individuals, the sheriff and a couple of deputies. They made the rounds, in the tradition of southern civility, acting friendly to keep the peace. "The sheriff seemed real concerned about my grandmother, who he had known all his life," he explained, "but that same sheriff could put on a Klansman's hood." If a white man felt a black violated the social order, whites could form a mob to "take care of the uppity nigger." Law enforcement might or might not be part of the group when it went after an individual. Sometimes the group wore hoods, other times they did not cover their faces. Often they were hooded to protect the identity of the sheriff, landlord, or factory owner in the group.

Blacks' possession of arms deterred white violence. Describing a rural Georgia county in the early 1960s, Melissa Fay Greene writes in *Waiting for Sheetrock*, "one of the reasons for relative peace between the races was that they both were equally armed and each side knew it."[23] Ronnie Johnson agrees, but adds a crucial point: "Everybody held their own ground. It was mutual respect, but only to a certain degree—'cause the other side always had more force."

Yet the possession of firearms could not always protect African Americans from violence. A surprise attack by a mob of whites could leave blacks powerless to defend themselves. Willena Cannon grew up in Mullins, South Carolina, in the 1940s–50s, in a sharecropping family.[24] In 1949, as a small child, she witnessed the Klan murder of her neighbor. White men trapped her neighbor in a barn because he was dating a white woman, a consensual relationship that was well known in the area. The sheriff appeared and talked to the Klansmen. But rather than setting the black man free, the sheriff quickly left the scene, stating it was "the people's business," not his. "The people" were white; black lives were expendable, not "the business" of the sheriff. Willena, her sister, and neighbors watched in horror as the white men set the barn on fire, and stopped anyone from saving the man. The incident terrorized Willena for years. "I heard the man in the burning barn holler," Willena remembered, "and that screaming went on in my nightmares for a long time." No newspaper ever reported the incident. It was a secret lynching that never became a statistic.

Lynchings, such as the one witnessed by Willena Cannon, relied on fear as the means of social control. As Smead writes in *Blood Justice*, "the black victim became the representative of his race and, as such, was being disciplined for more than a single crime. Indeed the guilt or innocence of the victim was always far less important than the act of the lynching itself. The lynch mob, in its deadly act, was warning the black population not to challenge the supremacy of the white race."[25]

Authorities reinforced the terrorism by signaling their indifference to white-on-black crimes. For poor rural blacks, legal recourse did not exist. To survive in this environment, Willena's mother taught her children to show no sign of resistance, fearing any protest might lead them to "disappear." "People were afraid of appearing arrogant," explained Ronnie Johnson, "but at the same time they had to survive and protect themselves." Blacks were caught in a double bind. They had good reason to not appear "uppity," yet wanted to communicate that if attacked they would fight back. Any disagreement could jeopardize a black person, and most were especially vulnerable because they were economically dependent on working for whites. Getting fair price for farm labor was a challenge; whites could retaliate for a black getting a good price, or for a black complaining about getting cheated. The Johnson family depended on hiring themselves out to whites, and he remembers working in cotton: "I remember getting on a cotton truck with my family and uncles riding to the fields. Only my grandfather and my grandmother would talk to the white person who owned the property. They worried that the younger folks weren't used to negotiating and would appear arrogant. The elder people did all the talking, and collected all the money, and made all the decisions."

Some individuals deliberately cultivated a reputation for readiness to fight if attacked. Thomas Anderson grew up on a farm in South Carolina in the 1930s, one of six children born to impoverished sharecroppers.[26] He remembered "the Ku Klux Klan going into people's houses, dragging them out, beating them, hanging them." One of the victims was his cousin. "They drug him out, hung him from a tree, and started shooting. They shot at him 'til there was nothing left but the rope." Anderson's anger overwhelmed his fear. "Being a kid, I was searching myself. Is this the way it's gotta be?" he asked himself. He resolved, "It won't happen to me. Nobody will ever do me the way I don't want them to do. They will have to kill me first." He kept a proud, cool exterior, and learned to use a gun. Thomas Anderson made sure that everyone in the county, white and black, knew that he was an expert marksman. His philosophy was "armed self-defense. You don't go after nobody. But if they come after you, you protect yourself."

Tensions Mount in the 1950s

The tensions between violent racists and civil rights fighters increased throughout the 1950s. Black servicemen had fought and died for the United States in World War II, yet state laws and terror continued to disenfranchise southern blacks. As the United States emerged as a global power, it became harder for the federal government to maintain its hands-off policy toward the South. Racist violence and segregation became embarrassing for U.S. foreign policy. [27] In 1954 the Supreme Court found segregated education unconstitutional in a case argued by the NAACP. The unanimous *Brown v Board of Education of Topeka* decision placed the Constitution squarely on the side of black political rights. But the southern power structure yielded nothing. Across the South political leaders declared they would defy the Supreme Court rather than implement integration. "Constitution or no Constitution, we will keep segregation in Mississippi," Governor Ross Barnett declared defiantly. "I call on every official in the state of Mississippi, every citizen, to use every Constitutional and legal means …"—he paused, took a breath, and added emphatically—"*every possible way.*" [28]

Encouraged by the actions of state political leaders, white violence became more audacious. In 1955 two white men in Mississippi killed a fourteen-year-old boy for "talking fresh to a white woman." Unaware of Mississippi's social order, Emmett Till made a fatal error. He was a young teen from Chicago, vacationing with relatives in Mississippi. He told his cousins about his integrated school, and his friends including white girls. Then he said "bye baby" to a white woman in Mississippi. That night two men took Till from his uncle's home, beat him, and threw his battered body into the river. Despite overwhelming evidence, a Mississippi jury (all white men) let the murderers free. The murder of Emmett Till sent shock, fury, and fear through black communities. Ronnie Johnson recalled: "I never will forget the day they pulled Emmett Till's body out of the river. They found him about a half a mile from where we lived. That night all my aunts and uncles came over to our house. The fear, the whispers, the anticipation: what should we do?"

Till's young age and the mild nature of his offense shocked the Johnson family. A few days later, Ronnie's teenage uncle came home from his gas station job covered with blood. A local white man didn't like the way he pumped gas, jumped out of the car, and hit him in the face, breaking his nose. Ronnie's father and uncle grabbed weapons and went to revenge the attack. They knew who the white man was and where he lived, but couldn't find him that night. Despite the family network and elaborate methods of self-defense, Mississippi had become too dangerous for Ronnie Johnson's father and mother. Quickly, they picked up and left the state.

Outrageous acts against blacks continued. In 1957 Klansmen in Birmingham, Alabama, decided to prove themselves worthy as KKK leaders by "cutting a nigger." They seized a thirty-four-year-old black man, a World War II veteran, interrogated him about voting rights, school desegregation, and that "nigger-loving Communist named Earl Warren." Then they castrated him.[29] In 1959, when Mack Charles Parker, a black man, was waiting trial for raping a white woman, he was dragged out of his jail cell by hooded white men and murdered. The FBI investigation found that the local police and jailers cooperated with the murderers. Yet a state jury acquitted the white men.[30]

Despite the Supreme Court's landmark decision outlawing segregated education, southern schools remained segregated, and violence maintained the color line. The NAACP filed lawsuits, including a successful one in Arkansas, where the federal court ordered the desegregation of Little Rock High School. Under court order, nine black students were to enter Little Rock High School in September 1957. Instead, Governor Orville Faubus defied the federal government and directed the National Guard troops to prevent the students from entering the building. A mob of several hundred whites gathered in front of the school. A local newspaper editor told the Justice Department: "The police have been routed, the mob is in the streets, and we're close to a reign of terror."[31]

Daisy Bates, president of the Arkansas NAACP, led the campaign to desegregate Little Rock High School. She received many threats to her life and her home was firebombed, but local law enforcement refused to arrest the perpetrators. Bates appealed to federal authorities, who responded that they had "no federal jurisdiction" to protect her. A black neighbor told Bates, "I doubt whether the Negroes are going to take much more without fighting back. I think I'll take the rest of the day off and check my shotgun and make sure it's in working condition."[32] President Eisenhower reluctantly sent federal troops to protect the nine students. Troops remained in Little Rock the entire school year.

The inaction of local and state authorities encouraged the Ku Klux Klan, whose ranks swelled to fifty thousand in the early 1960s. Wherever civil rights activity developed, Klan violence followed. Bombing became the weapon of choice, as violent racists targeted the homes of scores of "uppity" blacks and "moderate" whites, as well as churches, synagogues, integrated schools, and local government offices. The bomb that killed four little girls in a Birmingham church in 1963 was the twenty-first bomb in eight years detonated against blacks in that city alone, which became known to many as "Bombingham."[33]

As opposition to the KKK grew, white segregationists developed new organizations that attracted more middle-class membership. White Citizens' Councils sprang up across the South in the 1950s, holding rallies of up to ten thousand people. Though the Citizens' Councils claimed to use economic pressure, rather than violence, to stop integration, often their membership and activities overlapped with the Klan (for example, the Alabama Klansmen who castrated the black man were also members of the Citizens' Council). Some referred to the councils as the "uptown KKK."[34]

State governments established state agencies dedicated to maintaining segregation. The Mississippi State Sovereignty Commission, from 1956 through 1977, "used spy tactics, intimidation, false imprisonment, jury tampering and other illegal methods … to maintain segregation at all costs." The commission gathered intelligence on sixty thousand people, one out of every thirty-seven people in Mississippi. Arkansas, Louisiana, Alabama, and Florida created similar state investigative commissions. In Mississippi, none of the documents released in 1998 showed a direct connection between the Sovereignty Commission and the deaths of civil rights advocates. But the documents do include plans for using violence. For example, there were multiple discussions of "taking care of" individuals who tried to integrate Mississippi colleges, including having their cars hit by a train or engineering an accident on the highway.[35]

Hovering above the state governments' efforts to thwart African Americans' civil rights was the FBI. Since its origin in 1908, the FBI had been active in the South, as in the rest of the country. But J. Edgar Hoover, who headed the bureau from 1919 to 1972, interpreted his mission as hunting down communists, weeding out anti-American activity, and not protecting civil rights. In 1939, after 4,692 people had died in documented lynchings, Hoover directed the FBI to carry out formal investigations of mob murders. However, he opposed federal antilynching legislation in a 1956 confidential report to President Eisenhower, because he did not see violence against blacks as a significant problem, and he saw the Civil Rights movement as led by subversives.[36] Thus the FBI gathered information on violence, but punishment required action by local authorities. Racist violence was not Hoover's concern, and he repeatedly dismissed it as a "local issue."[37] James Forman expressed the view of many activists in the South: "The FBI was a farce. It wasn't going to arrest any local racists who violate any and all laws on the statute books. Instead it would play a game of taking notes and pictures."[38]

Although no African American was immune to violence, activists received the most threats. Many individual NAACP leaders and lawyers responded by carrying revolvers. Daisy Bates, head of the Arkansas NAACP who led the Little Rock High School desegregation, kept a handgun in her car, and displayed it to scare off white adolescents who threatened her.[39] NAACP lawyers J. L. Chestnut and Orzell Billingsley carried guns as they pursued legal cases in rural Alabama.[40] Vernon Dahmer, president of the Hattiesburg MS NAACP, died using a shotgun to defend his family and home, after the KKK firebombed it.[41]

When Martin Luther King Jr. emerged as a leader during the 1955 Montgomery bus boycott, he received the typical response to civil rights activists. His life was threatened and his home bombed. And in the tradition of the South, after whites firebombed his house, blacks armed themselves and surrounded King's house to protect him.[42]

Martin Luther King Jr.: Nonviolence as Practical Strategy

How does one fight for equal rights when any action, any small gesture, risks brutal retaliation? Blacks rallied against the Klan in Harlem in 1949, but in the South similar tactics were suicidal. In this fearful environment, NAACP court cases dominated the fight for racial justice. But by the mid-1950s, as southern politicians flagrantly defied the Supreme Court, many blacks questioned the effectiveness of the legal strategy. For example, Connie Lane, a lifelong resident of Greensboro, North Carolina, was twenty-two years old when the Court ruled segregated education unconstitutional in 1954. But nothing changed for her, and she felt great frustration toward the NAACP, which she described as "this grand organization, something for the bourgeoisie black folks, the doctors, the lawyers—not for ordinary people, not for me."[43] She and other African Americans argued over tactics. Was there an alternative to the NAACP's legal strategy? What was the best way to gain equal rights? How could blacks avoid violence directed against them? Anger and fear vied for the upper hand. There were no easy answers.

Martin Luther King Jr. described the debate in the black community:

During the fifties, many voices offered substitutes for the tactics of legal recourse. Some called for a colossal blood bath to cleanse the nation's ills ... But the Negro of the South in 1955 assessing the power of the force arrayed against him, could not perceive the slightest prospect of victory in this approach. He was unarmed, unorganized, untrained, disunited, and most important, psychologically and morally unprepared for the deliberate spilling of blood. Although his desperation had prepared him to die for freedom if necessary, he was not willing to commit himself to racial suicide with no prospect of victory.[44]

King grew up in the South, fearful of white violence. The first time police arrested King, which was during the Montgomery bus boycott, "panic seized him ... King gave in to visions of nooses and lynch mobs."[45] King appreciated that blacks' own institutions, their churches, civic groups, schools, were weak compared to the coercive powers arrayed against them. Even where blacks made up a substantial part, or even a majority, of the population, they faced what Morris termed "the iron fist of southern government."[46]

Twentieth-century urbanization gave many African Americans more independence in southern cities. People working day jobs for white bosses in a city were not as vulnerable as those living and farming on a white man's land. City folk built churches and paid the salaries of their ministers, making their Reverends economically dependent on them, rather than the white community. Martin Luther King Jr. was an example of this type of minister, who could speak the mind of his congregation without fear of economic retaliation.

But violence was another matter. As a young man, King assumed that blacks would have to use violence to win equal rights. He wrote: "When I was in theological school I thought the only way we could solve our problem of segregation was an armed revolt."[47] He met pacifists, but felt they had "an unwarranted optimism concerning man." He felt many were self-righteous. He never joined a pacifist organization. Instead, he was searching for a "realistic pacifism."[48] Mahatma Gandhi's philosophy sparked King's interest because of its efficacy. According to Gandhi, "the moral appeal to the heart and conscience is, in the case of human beings, *more effective* than an appeal based on threat of bodily pain or violence."[49] Gandhi criticized passive nonviolence and advocated aggressive resistance. King felt that Gandhi's philosophy was "the only *morally and practically* sound method open to oppressed people in their struggle for freedom." He described Gandhi's nonviolent resistance as "one of the most potent weapons available."[50]

It is one thing to study Gandhi in school and quite another to apply the principles to a different time, place, and circumstance. Blacks in the American South faced very different conditions than those in the anticolonial struggle in India. Would nonviolence work? Or would it just subject black people to more violence? Tactics were a matter of life and death for activists. Many blacks saw nonviolence as passive and ineffectual, as acceptance of the status quo. On the other hand, they realized that any use of arms could be used as an excuse for increased white violence against them. In college and divinity school King determined through lengthy discussions with his classmates that support from white liberals was possible, if it could be mobilized. Placing the freedom movement on the high moral ground was necessary to gain support outside the black community.

Nonviolent Resistance Strategy Evolves during Montgomery Bus Boycott

Suddenly in 1955 questions about movement strategy were no longer theoretical, as King found himself thrust into the leadership of a mass movement. On December 1, 1955, Rosa Parks refused to give up her seat on a bus to a white man, and police jailed her for violating state segregation laws. Her friends in the Women's Political Council decided to organize a bus boycott, and black ministers elected a twenty-seven-year-old newcomer named Martin Luther King Jr. as the spokesperson. [51]

White officials criticized the bus boycott for having similar tactics to the White Citizens' Council.[52] King wanted to distinguish blacks' constitutional demands for equality from the violent tactics of the Klan and White Citizens' Council. In a speech on the first night of the boycott, King stated: "There will be no crosses burned at any bus stops in Montgomery. There will be no white persons pulled out of their homes and taken out on some distant road and murdered. There will be nobody among us who will stand up and defy the Constitution of this nation.... We are not here advocating violence.... The only weapon that we have in our hands this evening is the weapon of protest."[53] King advocated nonviolence, not passivity. King often used the word "militant" or "coercion" to describe his tactics. In one speech, for example, he stated, "Not only are we using the tools of persuasion—but we've got to use the tools of coercion."[54] In the midst of battle, he developed nonviolence civil disobedience as a practical method to cope with segregationists' violence. King wrote in *Our Struggle: The Story of Montgomery* that the boycott developed a way "to continue our struggle while coping with the violence it aroused."[55]

King was aggressive in negotiations with the white city leaders, breaking a historical pattern of black leaders caving in because of fear. The boycott continued for a year, and the unity of the black community was remarkable. Unlike court battles that depended on a few brave plaintiffs and their lawyers, the boycott depended for its success on black working people, the maids, the day laborers, for a year every day finding ways other than the bus to get to work.

White racists attacked the homes of the boycott leaders, including the homes of King, Abernathy, Shuttleworth, and Gratz, as well as churches and other locations. The KKK marched trying to intimidate the boycotters. Ten thousand attended the White Citizens' Council rally in the Montgomery Colliseum, the largest segregationist rally of the century. But with worldwide interest aroused by the new medium of television, the more violence the blacks endured, the more the press covered the boycott. Terror lost its effectiveness. It took its toll on the victims, but it could no longer derail the movement for equality.

Nonviolent resistance emerged as a strategy in the day to day activities of the boycott. Taylor Branch points out that "nonviolence, like the boycott itself, had begun more or less by accident." It took six more years for King to fully develop this strategy.[56]

King struggled deeply within himself to provide nonviolent leadership. He knew that as a leader, he was a target for violent whites. His home was assaulted three times, and people protected him with arms. There were weapons inside King's home. Civil rights leader Bayard Rustin visited King in the middle of the boycott, and saw guns in the King household. At one point, Rustin "shouted to stop someone from sitting on a loaded pistol that was lying on the couch."[57] Reverend Glenn Smiley, a follower of Gandhi who visited King to advise him on nonviolent resistance, advised King to "get rid of the guns around his house." King talked intensely to Smiley, describing his fears about violence. He told Smiley, "Don't bother me with tactics . . . I want to know if I can apply nonviolence to my heart."[58]

King knew that nonviolent resistance was a strategy that could fail and lead to great bloodshed. John Keane points out that "renunciation of violence" can sometimes result in "tragic annihilation."[59] As a leader King felt responsible if a demonstration provoked violence against the demonstrators. Mass leaders often face moral dilemmas as they make choices on how to proceed, and King criticized people who saw nonviolent resistance as a pure and simple moral stand. He said, "I came to see the pacifist position not as sinless." King criticized self-righteous advocates of peace, stating that "the pacifist would have a greater appeal if he did not claim to be free from the moral dilemmas that the Christian nonpacifist confronts."[60]

Not all African Americans agreed with King's nonviolent strategy, but it caught on because it was effective. It spurred millions into action and rallied support from around the country and the world. It was the most practical method available at that time to deal with racist violence. Some civil rights activists followed King's strategy, even though they themselves personally disagreed with nonviolence. Ella Baker, a leader who worked for NAACP in the 1940s and with King in the 1950s, was not a pacifist. She explained: "I frankly could not have sat and let someone put a burning cigarette on the back of my neck. . . . If they hit me, I might hit them back."[61] Connie Lane, a Greensboro activist, explained that she disagreed with King's philosophy: "I never could get into all this passive resistance, somebody hits you, you fall down on your knees and start praying." She paused, then added, "but I appreciated what Dr. King was doing."[62]

A major challenge to King's strategy came from Robert Williams of Monroe, North Carolina. Williams served in the army in World War II and the Marines in the Korean War. When he returned home to North Carolina, the local NAACP chapter elected him their president. In 1957 a Klan motorcade attacked the house where the Monroe NAACP was meeting, and Williams and others shot at them. The KKK backed off. Williams's NAACP chapter led a variety of civil rights struggles, including a successful campaign to free two boys, ages seven and nine, who were incarcerated for playing a children's kissing game with white girls. In 1959 Williams helped a black woman bring suit against a white man who assaulted her, tore off her clothing, and tried to rape her. Williams's frustration rose to the boiling point when the all-white-male jury quickly acquitted the white man. It was yet another example of the double standard of the South. In the name of protecting white women, white men lynched black men and boys, but at the same time felt entitled to violate black women. Just after the verdict, a furious Williams declared on the courthouse steps, "The Negro in the South cannot expect justice in the courts. He must convict his attackers on the spot. He must meet violence with violence, lynching with lynching." For this statement, Williams was kicked out of the NAACP.[63]

An intense debate ensued on the strategy of Robert Williams versus that of Martin Luther King Jr. In *Southern Patriot* in 1961 King stressed nonviolent resistance as aggressive action against segregation. In an opposing article, Williams advocated armed self-defense, stating: "In a civilized society the law is a deterrent against the strong who would take advantage of the weak, but the South is not a civilized society; the South is a social jungle; it had become necessary for us to create our own deterrent. . . . We would defend our women and our children, our homes and ourselves with arms."[64]

Williams' words reflected the sentiment of many. But Williams had broken an unwritten rule about armed self-defense: he publicly advocated it. James Forman, leader of the Student Nonviolent Coordinating Committee (SNCC), pointed out that "self-defense was something people should do and not proclaim." While Forman sympathized with Williams's anger and disillusionment, he also criticized him for openly advocating armed self-defense, which he thought "was a warm invitation for the police to crack down."[65] Forman described the tremendous energy that Robert Williams put into just defending his home; night after night Williams and his supporters had to stay up all night, prepared for an armed attack by the Klan.

Civil rights groups criticized Williams, but upheld the right to self-defense. Williams's phrase "meeting violence with violence, lynching with lynching" was roundly criticized because it could be interpreted as a strategy of violence, a justification for blacks lynching whites. The NAACP and King wanted to clearly demarcate themselves from that view. But while criticizing Williams, they affirmed the right of self-defense. As they removed Williams from membership, the NAACP stated, "We do not deny but reaffirm the right of an individual and collective self defense against unlawful assaults."[66] King blasted Williams for the "advocacy of violence as a tool of advancement, organized as in warfare, deliberately and consciously." He critiqued Williams's approach as one with "incalculable perils," arguing that nonviolent mass action was a constructive alternative. At the same time, King defended the right of self-defense, stating it was accepted as "moral and legal" by all societies. He acknowledged that pure nonviolence "cannot readily or easily attract large masses, for it requires extraordinary discipline and courage."[67] King's nonviolent strategy won the public debate. And nonviolent resistance continued to coexist with armed self-defense.

King was a "practical" pacifist not a "pure" one. In 1967–68 he spoke out against the Vietnam War saying, "These are revolutionary times. All over the globe men are revolting against old systems of exploitation and oppression.... The shirtless and barefoot people of the earth are rising up as never before."[68] He sympathized with the national liberation movements who were using force of arms.

The Movement Forces the Federal Government off the Fence

In the early 1960s civil rights activists continued to face violence, and the federal government continued its hands-off policy. In 1961 black and white Freedom Riders rode on public buses through the South, integrating public facilities. The FBI knew that the Klan planned a "baseball bat greeting" for the Freedom Riders in Alabama, but failed to protect them from a brutal beating. The FBI also stood by while police beat people trying to exercise their right to vote. In 1962 Fanny Lou Hamer, a forty-five-year-old Mississippi country woman who would become a nationally recognized civil rights leader, tried to register at the county courthouse. She was arrested, evicted from her home, and shot at.[69] But violence did not stop the movement, as sit-ins, marches, and voter registration drives spread across the South.

Pressure on Washington to end segregation and violence mounted. The failure of the government to protect the exercise of constitutionally protected rights became increasingly embarrassing in the context of the Cold War. The Soviet Union used the South's brutality to batter the U.S. image abroad. Moreover, American national interests found King's nonviolence useful in international relations. The United States promoted King's leadership as an alternative to the armed national liberation struggles in Africa and other parts of the world. For example, the United States Information Agency made a video of the 1963 March on Washington, which they showed around the world as evidence of peaceful progress in race relations in the United States.[70] But that required that there be actual progress in the South. Such progress depended on the federal government doing something it had failed to do for almost a century: dismantle the stranglehold of white supremacy on local and state governments and punish racist violence.

The mounting pressure came to a head in June 1964. Civil rights activists organized Freedom Summer, attracting northern white and black students to come south to work on voter registration and other issues. In June the Ku Klux Klan lynched three young civil rights workers, James Chaney, Andrew Goodman, and Michael Schwerner in Neshoba County, Mississippi. A deputy sheriff drove one of the two cars of Klansmen. The murders of the young men, one black and two white, became international news. Finally a president took action: President Johnson directly ordered J. Edgar Hoover to stop the Klan. As a result the FBI added a counterintelligence program (COINTELPRO) against the Klan to its programs against civil rights activists, the Black Panthers, and Vietnam War protesters. It was the only COINTELPRO initiated under pressure from outside the bureau and the only one directed at right-wing groups.[71]

Thus in 1964, as the Ku Klux Klan marked its ninety-eighth year of working to undermine the U.S. Constitution, the FBI determined that the Klan was "essentially subversive." The bureau's "war on the Klan" lasted until 1971, when it was disbanded along with the other COINTELPROS. The FBI focused on infiltrating Klan organizations, and by the late 1960s there were two thousand FBI informants in racist hate groups, comprising perhaps 20 percent of total Klan membership. Sometimes it was unclear whose side the informants were on. One man on the FBI payroll talked about murdering all black people. Another informant was part of the carload of Klansmen who murdered civil rights worker Viola Liuzzo.[72]

Conclusion

Nonviolent resistance combined with armed self-defense in the Civil Rights movement to pressure government to do its job: protect people's rights regardless of race. Government actions curtail or encourage violence. In the United States, from Reconstruction until the height of the Civil Rights movement, the federal hands-off policy toward the South had fostered violence against blacks. Even in the late 1950s and early 1960s whites could brutalize blacks and get away with it. Particularly in rural southern counties, African Americans often had no recourse to government protection. Many maintained arms to defend themselves and their homes, but this was not always effective, because violent whites had the power of local and state institutions behind them.

African Americans bent on civil rights coped with the violence used against them in various ways. Many activists routinely carried handguns to protect themselves, as they faced harassment and sometimes murder. When the Montgomery bus boycott launched massive protest action, Martin Luther King Jr. argued for the boycotters to be nonviolent to differentiate themselves from the tactics of the Ku Klux Klan and White Citizens' Council and to win the support of white liberals. King gradually developed nonviolence into a strategy in the late 1950s and early 1960s, which helped the Civil Rights movement grow in size and effectiveness. Pacifism coexisted with armed self-defense: both King and the NAACP officially upheld the right to defend oneself and one's home.

The Civil Rights movement both inspired and drew inspiration from democratic movements around the world. During the Cold War, in the new medium of television, massive nonviolent resistance galvanized national and international attention, as the Civil Rights movement demanded that the Constitution be enforced throughout the country. U.S. leaders found King's nonviolent strategy useful in foreign diplomacy because it could be promoted as an alternative to armed national liberation movements. In the 1960s, faced with both international pressure and the growing size and scope of the Civil Rights movement, the federal government finally acted to thwart racist violence in the South. In a dramatic policy shift, LBJ in 1964 ordered J. Edgar Hoover to use the FBI to undermine the Ku Klux Klan, not just gather information on it. The federal government thus began to break the link between violent racists and southern local and state government, a central victory for civil rights.

Federal involvement, despite its serious shortcomings, was decisive in beginning to cut the link in many places between vigilantes and local law enforcement. There have been exceptions, including police complicity with Klan murders in Greensboro in 1979, and police brutality that plagues the country to this day. Racist violence continues in illegal hate crimes, and in legal forms such as the high rates of incarceration and the use of the death penalty. But the Civil Rights movement, by forcing authorities to punish violent racists, took a major step in breaking the white supremacist grip on power.

As John Keane suggests, strategies of social change may be evaluated based on whether they create or strengthen pluralistic peaceful society. Sometimes the use of arms can be constructive, as it was in the American Revolution and in many other national liberation movements. Pacifism, too, can be effective or counterproductive based on how it is practiced: sometimes it has disarmed people who then face increased bloodshed. Keane finds that Gandhi's movement in India "used nonviolence as a means of contesting illegitimate power, for the purpose of strengthening civil society."[73] In the same way, King's nonviolent resistance forced the U.S. government to guarantee civil rights. The Civil Rights movement succeeded, not because of its nonviolence, but because it was combined with armed self-defense to make the South less violent and more democratic.

NOTES

1. Coretta Scott King, *My Life with Martin Luther King, Jr.* (New York: Holt, Rinehart and Winston, 1969), p. 293. David J. Garrow, *Bearing the Cross* (New York: Vintage Books, 1988); Taylor Branch, *Parting the Waters: America in the King Years 1954–1963* (New York: Simon and Schuster, 1989).
2. Garrow, *Bearing the Cross,* p. 43; King, *Stride Towards Freedom* (London: 1958), pp. 91–3.
3. Adam Faircloth, "Martin Luther King, Jr. and the War in Vietnam," in *The African American Voice in U.S. Foreign Policy Since World War II,* ed. M. L. Krenn (New York: Garland, 1998), p. 257.
4. Herbert Shapiro, *White Violence and Black Response* (Amherst: University of Massachusetts, 1988).
5. "The Ku Klux Klan," SPLC, 1988, p. 23. Unpunished crimes in Mississippi include the murder of Charles Moore in 1964, Ernest Avants in 1966, Benjamin Brown in 1967, Wharlest Jackson in 1967, and Rainy Pool in 1970. The suspected Klansmen were never arrested and still remain unpunished (see Stephanie Saul, "Their Killers Walk Free," *Newsday,* December 15–20, 1998). Other crimes are being punished three decades after they occurred. For example, in 1998 a Mississippi court convicted the man responsible for the 1966 murder of NAACP leader Vernon Dahmer (*Associated Press,* August 21, 1998), and in 1994 a court finally convicted the man who assassinated NAACP leader Medgar Evers (*New York Times,* March 18, 1998).
6. Frances Fox Piven and Richard A. Cloward, *Poor People's Movements* (New York: Vintage Books, 1979), p. 182. Piven and Cloward criticize scholars, including leftists, for "the tendency to ignore this gain."
7. John Keane, *Reflections on Violence* (New York: Verso, 1996), p. 6.
8. Ibid., pp. 70–71.
9. John Hope Franklin, *Race and History* (Baton Rouge: Louisiana State University Press, 1989), p. 149.
10. William H. Chafe, *Civilities and Civil Rights* (Oxford:Oxford University Press, 1981), p. 8.
11. Robert F. Williams, *Negroes with Guns* (Detroit: Wayne State University Press, 1998, reprinted from 1962), p. 26.
12. Keane, *Reflections on Violence,* p. 64.
13. Robert L. Zangrando, *The NAACP Crusade Against Lynching: 1909–1950* (Philadelphia: Temple University Press, 1980), pp. 6–7.
14. Shapiro, *White Violence,* p. 120.
15. Steward E. Tolnay and E. M. Beck, *A Festival of Violence: An Analysis of Southern Lynchings, 1882–1930,* (Chicago: University of Illinois Press, 1992), p. 5.
16. Jacqueline Hall, *Revolt Against Chivalry: Jesse Danial Ames and the Women's Campaign Against Lynching* (New York: Columbia University Press, 1991).
17. Smead, *Blood Justice,* p. xi.

18. Zangrando, *NAACP Crusade*.
19. Ibid., p. 4.
20. Aldon D. Morris, *The Origins of the Civil Rights Movement* (New York: Free Press, 1984), pp. 1–12; Tolnay and Beck, *A Festival of Violence*.
21. James Forman, *The Making of Black Revolutionaries* (Seattle: Open Hand Publishing, 1990), p. 376.
22. I interviewed Ronnie Johnson on October 15, 1998, in Brooklyn, New York. Johnson's uncle, Rev. Aaron Johnson, a civil rights activist who lives in Greenwood, Mississippi, was interviewed by Richard Rubin, "Should the Mississippi Files Have Been Reopened?" *New York Times Magazine*, August 30, 1998, pp. 30–37.
23. Melissa Fay Greene, *Waiting for Sheetrock* (New York: Fawcett Columbine, 1991), p. 202.
24. I interviewed Willena Cannon on November 1, 1989, in Greensboro, North Carolina. See Bermanzohn, "The Greensboro Massacre: Political Biographies of Four Surviving Demonstrators," *New Political Science* 20, no. 1 (March 1998): 69–89.
25. Smead, *Blood Justice*, p. x.
26. I interviewed Thomas Anderson on August 3, 1990, in Greensboro, North Carolina. See Bermanzohn, "Survivors of the 1979 Greensboro Massacre," (Ph.D. diss., City University of New York, 1994).
27. Smead, *Blood Justice*, p. 127.
28. "Eyes on the Prize: Fighting Back 1957–1962," Public Broadcasting System.
29. Shapiro, *op.cit.* pp. 410-11.
30. Howard Smead, *Blood Justice: The Lynching of Mack Charles Parker* (Oxford: Oxford University Press, 1986).
31. Shapiro, *White Violence*, p. 415.
32. Ibid., p. 415–16.
33. Kenneth O'Reilly, *"Racial Matters": The FBI's Secret File on Black Americans, 1960–1972* (New York: Free Press, 1989), p. 79.
34. Shapiro, *White Violence*, pp. 410, 434, 468.
35. *New York Times*, March 18, 1998.
36. Branch, *Parting the Waters*, pp. 180–82.
37. O'Reilly, *Racial Matters*, p. 5.
38. Forman, *Black Revolutionaries*, p. 353.
39. Daisy Bates, *The Long Shadow of Little Rock: A Memoir* (New York: David McKay and Co., 1962).
40. J. L. Chestnut, *Black in Selma: The Uncommon Life of J. L. Chestnut, Jr.* (New York: Farrar, Straus and Giroux, 1990), p. 110.
41. *New York Times*, April 5, 1998.
42. Branch, *Parting the Waters*, p. 165.
43. I interviewed Connie Lane on March 10, 1992, in Greensboro, North Carolina.
44. Martin Luther King Jr., *Why We Can't Wait* (New York: Harper and Row, 1964), p. 24.
45. Branch, *Parting the Waters*, p. 160.
46. Morris, *Civil Rights Movement*, p.3.
47. Garrow, *Bearing the Cross*, p. 43.
48. Martin Luther King Jr., "Pilgrimage to Nonviolence," in *Nonviolence in America: A Documentary History*, ed. Staughton Lynd (New York: Bobbs-Merrill Co., 1966), pp. 386–90.
49. Mahatma Gandhi, *Non-Violent Resistance* (New York: Shocken Books, 1951), p. iii (emphasis added).

50. King, "Pilgrimage to Nonviolence," p. 390.
51. Branch, *Parting the Waters*, pp. 123–27.
52. This same line of reasoning is used by David Duke in the 1980s–90s, and the Association for the Advancement for White People.
53. Branch, *Parting the Waters*, p. 140.
54. Ibid.
55. Shapiro, *White Violence*, p. 394.
56. Branch, *Parting the Waters*, p. 195.
57. Ibid, p. 179.
58. Ibid., pp. 179–80.
59. Keane, *Reflections on Violence*, p. 88.
60. Lynd, *Nonviolence in America*, p. 389.
61. Susan G. O'Malley, "Ella Baker," in *Encyclopedia of the American Left*, ed. Mari Jo Buhle et al. (Chicago: University of Chicago Press, 1992), p. 82. In 1960, as the sit-in movement of black youth spread across the South, Ella Baker became the advisor to the Student Nonviolent Coordinating Committee. When SNCC debated over whether to take up voter registration in the deep South or to focus on nonviolent resistance, Baker pushed them to combine the two. She thought that nonviolent resistance could be an effective tactic in gaining voting rights in the deep South, explaining that when students "went into these deeply prejudiced areas and started voter registration, they would have an opportunity to exercise nonviolent resistance ... they wouldn't have to abandon their nonviolence. In fact, they would be hard put to keep it up"(p. 82).
62. The author interviewed Connie Lane on March 10, 1992, in Greensboro, North Carolina.
63. Williams, *Negroes with Guns*.
64. Ibid., p. 26.
65. Forman, *Black Revolutionaries*, pp. 150, 374.
66. Shapiro, *White Violence*, p. 460.
67. Ibid., pp. 460–61.
68. King, *Where Do We Go from Here?*, quoted in Faircloth, "Martin Luther King, Jr. and the War in Vietnam," p. 257.
69. O'Reilly, *Racial Matters*, pp. 1–3, pp. 83–90.
70. Forman, *Black Revolutionaries*, p. 336.
71. James K. Davis, *Spying on America: The FBI's Domestic Counterintelligence Program* (New York: Praeger, 1992).
72. O'Reilly, *Racial Matters*, pp. 217–18.
73. Keane, *Reflections on Violence*, p. 64.

CHAPTER NINE

Ethnonational Conflicts, Democratization, and Hate Crime

Roger MacGinty

Introduction

T his chapter makes two points. First, that situations of ethnonational conflict are not characterized by endemic hate crime and intergroup hostility. Instead, significant restraining factors often operate to limit, or at least conceal, the incidence of hate crime. Second, that processes of democratization designed to regulate ethnonational conflict bring few guarantees that hate crime will cease. In fact, the tensions associated with peace processes and transitions toward democracy can lead to increases in hate crime against traditional targets and the selection of new targets.

Definitions

Definitions are complicated by the international scope of the chapter. Terms such as "hate crime," "ethnonational conflict," and "deeply divided society" have contested or imprecise meanings and may not necessarily have universal applicability. The term "ethnonational conflict" is chosen in preference to "ethnic conflict" in order to reflect the complex and multidimensional nature of many protracted intergroup conflicts.[1] Nationalism (as in ethno*nationalism*) is capable of inhabiting a variety of guises and employing various means, including sentiment, hatred, and identity, in order to mobilize people. Ethnicity by itself is rarely, if ever, enough to cause a conflict. Most contemporary violent conflicts tend to have more prosaic origins such as competition for scarce resources. These scarce resources can take the form of economic goods or rights but are often access to political power or recognition of cultural legitimacy. Protagonists may "play the ethnic card" and articulate their cause in terms of ethnicity and identity, but conflict is not intrinsically "ethnic."[2] If a conflict is particularly protracted and infects all aspects of life, it may seem that its roots lie in ethnicity but scratch the surface, and access to political, economic, or cultural power are usually the seminal issues.[3]

A society is deeply divided, according to Nordlinger's classic definition, "when a large number of conflict group members attach overwhelming importance to the issues at stake, or manifest strongly held antagonistic beliefs and emotions toward the opposing segment, or both."[4] Furthermore, the protagonists retain and exercise a capacity for intense violence in a context in which conflict regulation finds limited support and success. But the term "deeply divided society" requires qualification. At times divisions are so entrenched by history, culture, legislation, and physical separation that it is imprecise to refer to one geographical territory as a single society. Despite their physical proximity, it is difficult to argue that Israelis and Palestinians constitute a single society. The term "deeply divided society" can be more accurately applied to Northern Ireland where the two communities share many cultural characteristics but differ on the political issue of allegiance to a unitary Ireland or the United Kingdom. In South Africa, despite ingrained racial fissures, the common bond of the new political dispensation and the lack of political alternatives among the white community mean that the singular "deeply divided society" is appropriate.

For the purposes of this chapter, hate crime is taken as violent or threatening activity on the part of individuals primarily motivated by prejudice. It is recognized that incidents can have multiple or overlapping motivations. Issues of race, religion, economic gain, political persuasion, ideology, self-defense, and personal grudge can all contribute to a single incident. From this point of view, prejudice must be the primary motivating factor. While hate crime need not necessarily relate to a single incident, there is a danger of relativism gone mad in which an entire political or legislative environment is branded as hate crime. Apartheid South Africa provides an obvious example in which the state was based on racist notions of superiority and separation. But for intellectual manageability, it is more useful to attempt to identify specific incidents of violence, intimidation, or speech as hate crime.

Hate crime is very much a label—emotive and condemnatory rather than an objective tool able to delineate with absolute clarity a distinct category of violence or crime. It is not immediately clear how the attribute "hate" changes the crime. The term suggests that the action has an element of prejudice and is, perhaps, gratuitous in its execution. Yet such attributes are impossible to measure and are open to interpretation with victims and perpetrators often holding divergent accounts of the same incident. Actual motives are difficult to ascertain. Hate crime does not actually describe a particular *type* of crime or violence. The physical actions involved in a racially motivated assault and a robbery motivated assault may be largely similar. The key differences lie in the motivation and the subsequent interpretation of such incidents.

Indeed the promotion of "hate" as the monocausal explanation for certain incidents may prevent more sophisticated analyses of the causes of hate crime.

The danger is that "hate" becomes a catch-all label assigned to certain actions and perpetrators and stands in the way of deeper analyses of motivations. Most analysts inhabit (or like to think that they inhabit) a rational world. In this rational world hate is regarded as irrational, as occupying a sphere so far removed from the moral and political universe of analysts that they cannot hope to understand it. The logical extension of this view is that since hate is irrational and incomprehensible in analysts' minds, then there is little purchase in attempting to deal with it in a rational manner. This overdependence on hate as an explanatory factor risks absolving analysts of responsibility for examining deeper motivations however abhorrent they may be.[5]

This problem is reinforced by the attractiveness of the term "hate crime" for media organizations. It allows news stories to be simplified, dramatized, and personalized, often at the expense of precision in terminology or more layered explanations. Many incidents labeled as hate crime are the product of a combination of latent tensions and more immediate triggers—a mix too complex for many media formats. Added to this, governments and nongovernmental organizations can have strong interests in either using the term "hate crime" or preferring alternative labels.[6]

Discussions of hate crime also risk ethnocentrism. Hate crime tends to be a U.S.-based conceptualization with most scholarly literature on the subject emanating from U.S. sources. A number of high-profile U.S. cases of hate crime have made world headlines in recent years, but the phenomenon of hate-motivated violence is by no means restricted to the United States. Other terms are used in other localities. In Northern Ireland the approximation is "sectarian," and in South Africa it is "racial." In much of Western Europe, terms such as "right wing violence" or "neo-Nazi violence" are used.

Moving on from the issue of hate, the term "crime" brings its own problems. The decision of whether or not an action or incident constitutes a crime is subjective, dependent on the jurisdiction and its political context. In other words, the source of the hate crime seems particularly important. Debates on terrorism are instructive in this respect since they often focus on the legitimacy of the violent actor rather than on the nature of the violence itself. A state, the argument goes, cannot be guilty of terrorism (at least within its own borders) because it holds a monopoly of legitimate violence. Since a state makes the laws, its agents are unlikely to contravene those laws, or if they do they are unlikely to be prosecuted.[7] This is regardless of whether or not the state engages in activities that may be described as terrorism. For example, a state might induce terror in a section of its people by using the element of surprise in the timing of its actions and the choice of targets. Yet because terrorism is a social construct the tendency is to label government violence using more legitimate terms such as force.

These issues of the source of the violence, the nature of the violent actor, and the social construction of terminology are at play in relation to hate crime, particularly when viewed in an international context. The international context and the prevailing view of the regime will often determine whether or not a state is regarded as a perpetrator of hate crime. While the term "hate crime" is rarely used in relation to states, it is worth bearing in mind the nature of the violence in deeply divided societies and state reactions to that violence. Many regimes are tempted to use extralegal techniques against violent insurgencies. Robust security measures or emergency legislation, if exclusively targeted against one community, can approximate to hate crime. But other terms are normally used. In the negative sense, persecution, repression, ethnic cleansing, and war crimes may be used, but according to interpretation these may be labeled as "security measures." For example, the Turkish government may class its activities against Kurdish militants as "internal security" measures[8] but these go beyond tactical missions against selected militants to encompass attacks or restrictions on an entire community.[9]

It is much easier to associate hate crime with individuals and groups of individuals rather than organized groupings whether they originate from state or nonstate sources. As will be shown in the section below, the status of the perpetrator often acts as a mask for the real incidence of hate crime in deeply divided societies. Legal sanction, political platform, and historical and cultural status may help insulate organized groupings from accusations of hate crime. This is not to say that they cannot be culpable of hate crime, merely that the connection between individuals and groups of individuals and hate crime is more easily sustained.

Restraints and Masks on Hate Crime in Deeply Divided Societies

Deeply divided societies are rarely the scene of unrestrained hate crime with endemic intergroup violence. Instead, there are often sources of restraint and stability that condition the level and nature of violence. What may seem like unregulated violence is often subject to controls, patterns, and conventions. This section will give brief consideration to four factors that serve to restrict or conceal the incidence of hate crime in deeply divided societies: the source of the hate crime, the stage of the conflict, the monopolization of violence by organized militant groupings, and ethnic segregation.

This argument does not suggest that hate crime does not exist in deeply divided societies. It recognizes that hate crime is often actively and openly pursued as a deliberate strategy. Organizations with ideological motivations, such as the Ku Klux Klan, make little attempt to conceal their racist notions. The ethnic cleansers of the former Yugoslavia were explicit in their use of hate to intimidate people from their homes. Their cousins in Rwanda in 1994 were subject to few restraints. Widespread ethnic cleansing though is usually restricted to certain stages or time periods of a conflict and is facilitated by a wider political and security environment. Full-blown intergroup conflict is rare. Instead, more common patterns are of grudging coexistence, uneasy separation, or the domination of one group over another. In such circumstances, restraints are often in operation to limit the incidence of hate crime.

Source of Hate Crimes

The first controlling factor on the level of hate crime relates to the source of hate crime in ethnopolitical conflicts. Of particular importance is the commonly found overlap between state and nonstate personnel. The traditional view of conventional warfare has been of a strict separation between civilians and a formalized military. Although such a dichotomy is perhaps too rigid even in historical terms,[10] contemporary conflicts have seen a blurring of this distinction. This was illustrated in the former Yugoslavia where regular soldiers and police, part-time militias and civilians not only shared aims but also membership of organizations. It was commonplace for organized intimidation to be carried out by civilians with the tacit support of the regular troops and police.[11] Alternatively, formerly civilian neighbors became members of militias or paramilitary groups in a relatively short space of time. Although state and nonstate actors may be engaged in similar activities, the status of the former group accords its actions a cloak of legitimacy regardless of how abhorrent those actions may be. The broadening of the category of state actors during ethnonational conflicts and the tendency to attribute motives other than prejudice to state actions may conceal the real incidence of hate crime.

The *al-Aqsa intifada* in Israel/Palestine in late 2000 and early 2001 provided a similar example. The disturbances saw incidences of both the Israeli Defense Force and Israeli settlers firing at Palestinian demonstrators and rioters.[12] Members of the Israeli Defense Force are legitimate state agents, mandated to provide security for the Israeli state and its citizens.[13] The settlers, on the other hand, are merely citizens and acting in a private capacity. In a strict sense, and unless firing because of an absolute necessity of self-defense, they were guilty of hate crime while the soldiers were not. In many ways the distinction is technical. Both the settlers and the soldiers carry their arms legally. Often they will share the same cultural and ideological background. Indeed, many settlers are reserve members of the Israeli Defense Force. The key difference, however, lies in the state's power of legitimate naming. It can mandate its officers to act on its behalf while the settlers are acting unilaterally without formal state sanction. States are more capable of masking their motivations in terms other than prejudice, with the blurring of the distinction between state and nonstate actors helping to mask the real incidence of hate crime by state-aligned nonstate actors.

Conflict Stage

A second restraint or mask on the incidence of hate crime is linked to the conflict stage or phase. Conflicts often follow a pattern of intensity, fluctuating according to range of factors. These factors might include the level and type of violence, political initiatives, availability of armaments, and the humanitarian impact of the fighting. Seasonal factors, third-party interventions, and changes at the elite level of protagonists may also affect the intensity of the conflict. The Interdisciplinary Research Programme on Root Causes of Human Rights Violations divides conflicts into a five-stage model.[14] Stage one approximates to a "peaceful stable situation," stage two to a "political tension situation," and stage three to a "violent political conflict." Stages four and five are "low-intensity conflict" and "high-intensity conflict." Each of these stages contains different opportunities for hate crime. Equally, each stage may provide restraints. For example, an accountable legal system and active civil society that may restrain hate crime in a political tension situation may be severely eroded by the low-intensity conflict stage and cease to provide an effective restraint. Yugoslavia in the late 1980s might provide an illustration of the political tension stage in which a mixture of internal and external factors managed to outweigh the centrifugal forces of nationalism. Despite growing tensions, there were sources of restraint on intergroup violence. By the early 1990s, however, when the republic's constituent parts started to secede and when some pursued strategies of aggrandizement, the restraining and civilizing factors were outweighed by more destructive forces.

As violent ethnonational conflicts become more established, the violence tends to become more organized and regularized. In such a situation the opportunities for hate crime may become limited, or hate crime, while continuing, may become masked by more formal military interactions. Conflicts may begin as mainly horizontal violence between communities, often in the form of street disturbances and rioting. Such situations may offer the opportunity for individuals and groups of individuals to attack other individuals and groups of individuals. In other words, the early stage of the conflict cycle may be a permissive environment for hate crime. As conflicts become more established, however, these opportunities may be restricted or masked.

Horizontal forms of violence will often give way to more vertical forms of violence between dedicated and organized combatants such as militant organizations and state forces. In such situations, militant organizations act as violent proxies on behalf of conflicting communities. Horizontal conflict, such as rioting, can reach unsustainable levels.[15] It may be too dangerous for large numbers of people to remain on the streets if firearms are introduced into the conflict, or large-scale rioting may become too disruptive to the entire community. Situations of vertical violence, in which organizations solely dedicated to waging violence monopolize a community's violent response, are more easily sustained. A division of labor spreads the burden of the conflict among the community. This is not to say that hate crime is eliminated in situations of vertical violence. Hate crime may well continue but it may not be as visible, or it may be overshadowed by more intensive and organized violence. For example, a sustained campaign of street violence in the Basque Country in the late 1990s (known as *kale borroka*) received little international press coverage and was overshadowed by more mainstream political violence and efforts to initiate a peace process.[16]

Monopolization of Violence by Militant Groups

A third restraint on hate crime comes in the form of the monopolization of violence by militant organizations in deeply divided societies. Militant organizations, whether state or nonstate, are key regulators of intergroup hostility. They tend to monopolize a community's violent response and are often ruthless toward competitor organizations. Just as states view themselves as the sole custodians of the right to legitimate violence, nonstate guerrilla organizations seek to monopolize violence from within their own group. The Liberation Tigers of Tamil Eelam (LTTE) in Sri Lanka, for example, have a gruesome record of annihilating other separatist guerrilla groups and moderate Tamils.[17] They wish to be regarded as the sole representatives of the separatist cause. This has implications for the incidence of hate crime since more established and disciplined groups may shy away from more gratuitous forms of violence.

The key to a sustained campaign by a militant organization is continued legitimacy. Seemingly sectarian attacks or blatant hate crime risks damaging this legitimacy. In short, hate crime makes for bad politics. While the actions of militant organizations may bear the hallmarks of hate crime, it is often linked with a wider political goal. Depending on the degree of political sophistication in the militant organization, hate crime may jeopardize this wider goal. Furthermore, outright military victory is an unrealistic goal for many guerrilla organizations. They lack the capacity to defeat conventional, standing armies. Thus, the rationale behind their violent campaigns is often "armed propaganda."[18] The real aim is to keep a situation in the headlines in the hope of an international initiative, or raise the costs of occupation to unsustainable levels. Again, the key point is that hate crime is not always the most efficient way for militant organizations to secure their goals. It could even be counterproductive.

Established militant organizations also frown upon lone operators—often a source of hate crime. The Northern Ireland conflict provides few examples of lone operators who were not linked with established paramilitary organizations.[19] So-called loose canons or unguided missiles could jeopardize the dominant militant group's operations and incur disproportionate security responses from state forces. In many conflict situations with established militant organizations, revenge attacks by victims' families are rare. A more likely pattern is for the victims' families to channel their revenge through militant organizations. In a larger organization, personal motivations are then subjugated by organizational goals.

This is not to suggest that militant organizations do not engage in hate crime; many paramilitary killings in Northern Ireland were sectarian. Nor does it absolve all those with a political manifesto of hate crime. But it is worth noting that blatant hate crime is rarely the most effective way for a militant organization to achieve its goals, particularly if it wishes to maintain political legitimacy. In situations in which groups are effectively excluded from the political system, or in which there are few rewards for maintaining political legitimacy, the restraints on hate crime are severely eroded. So too are the motivations to conceal hate crime.

Ethnic Segregation

A fourth restraint on hate crime in deeply divided societies is ethnic segregation. At the macro level, demographic separation is a common way for ethnonational wars to come to an end or reach a less violent phase. Of 110 conflicts recorded in the 1989–99 period, only 20 percent ended as a result of a peace agreement.[20] Short of outright victory for one side or the other, the most common conflict outcome is de jure or de facto partition. Cyprus, Kosovo, and Eritrea provide examples. According to Chaim Kaufmann, "Once ethnic groups are mobilized for war, the war cannot end until the population are separated into defensible, mostly homogenous regions." Attempts at integration are faced with "continuing mutual threats," which "ensures perpetuation of hypernationalist propaganda, both for mobilization and because the plausibility of the threat posed by the enemy gives radical nationalists an unanswerable advantage over moderates in intra-group debates."[21] This is a depressing message and can be countered by reference to stable ethnically mixed polities. Under circumstances of violent ethnonational conflict however, segregation is a common conflict regulation mechanism.

This is often most visible in terms of residential segregation with sharply delineated areas for different communities. Apartheid South Africa was based on demographic engineering and the enforced separation of people. The issue of territory is central to the Israeli-Palestinian conflict, with the city of Jerusalem providing a classic example of almost total residential segregation.[22] In Northern Ireland residential segregation has increased enormously in the last thirty years, to the extent that 50 percent of people live in an area that is inhabited by 90 percent or more of their coreligionists.[23] Physical separation is a simple and indeed universal security measure. It is visible in the form of gated communities in the United States. Here the essential divide is driven by economics, although unspoken racial undertones may exist as well. In deeply divided societies the onus for separation might be more urgent. Pograms, expulsions, and discriminatory legislation governing land ownership and tenancy for certain groups all lead to separation. So too does the sheer insecurity of cohabitation.

Residential segregation holds certain advantages. To a certain degree, it is even "popular." In a deeply divided society, it is often much easier to live within a majority than a minority community. More pertinently, it is often a good deal safer.[24] With residential segregation comes segregation in other activities such as schooling, commerce, and leisure. Education, for example, is almost entirely segregated in Northern Ireland with less than 3 percent of children attending integrated schools where Catholics and Protestants are taught together.[25] While much segregation may initially develop because of the need for physical security, it can lead to a self-generating single-identity community. This is visible throughout Northern Ireland in which the patchwork of Protestant and Catholic communities are often serviced by their own schools, shops, bars, and taxi firms, with separate and often identical services located in each community. It is worth noting that the division is greatest among working-class communities with more integration in middle-class areas. Poverty and lack of opportunity means that many people are restricted in the choice of where they live and they may become trapped in a ghetto or interface area.

In many cases ghettos become institutionalized and even encouraged by the state.[26] If the ghetto becomes large and secure enough, it can offer a high degree of insulation from the conflict. Since opportunities for direct intergroup conflict are diminished, hate crime may be reduced. At a basic level, the absence of the visual stimulus of the "enemy" may help reduce tension. A lack of interaction between protagonists may also prevent opportunistic attacks. To commit a hate crime, perpetrators have to be more dedicated and leave their territory. Security at enclave boundaries often complicates this task. Interface areas on the boundaries of the enclave, shared arterial routes, and town centers become possible areas for conflict and hate crime, leaving the bulk of the enclave area relatively stable.[27] It was noticeable during the *al-Aqsa intifada* that many casualties occurred at checkpoints and on designated roads leading to Jewish settlements.

While physical separation may help limit the incidence of hate crime, it is important to note that territory, particularly when linked with identity, is capable of playing a significant role in inflaming conflict and hate crime. It can act as a rallying point, a refuge, or an aspirational nation-state. In the form of an ancestral homeland, territory provides a link between the past and present—an essential feature in many nationalist mobilizations. It also has the advantage of "compactness" or the ability of a particular piece of territory to identify with a much broader political project such as Zionism in Israel or unionism in Northern Ireland.[28] The use of symbolic messages also makes for low-cost politics, requiring a minimum of articulation and intellectual justification. Instead, the message is articulated through emotion and sentiment and is able to resonate with the symbolic inventory of each group.[29]

Contested territory plays a prominent role in the conflicts in Northern Ireland and Israel/Palestine and has contributed to hate crime. At the macro level, the entire territories are contested. Many Israelis oppose a Palestinian state, while many Palestinians refuse to recognize Israel's right to exist. The legitimacy of Northern Ireland is questioned by those who wish to see a unitary Northern Ireland. Territory is also contested at the local level *within* Northern Ireland and Israel/Palestine. The immediate trigger of the *al-Aqsa intifada* was Israeli opposition leader Ariel Sharon's September 2000 visit to Temple Mount or Haram al-

Sharif, a site holy for both Jews and Muslims.[30] This fed into the broader conflict over Jerusalem itself. According to Natan Sharansky, the organizer of a mass pro-Jewish rally in Jerusalem in January 2001, "The issue of Jerusalem is not a security issue, or a question of borders, it is the very identity of the Jewish people."[31]

The issue of contentious politico-religious parades in Northern Ireland has focused attention on particular stretches of road. The Protestant-unionist Orange Order asserts its right to march down traditional routes. According to its members, this is an expression of religious freedom and civil liberty. The vast majority of the annual twenty-five hundred parades occur in mainly Protestant areas and pass off without incident.[32] Population movements have meant that parades that traditionally passed through mainly Protestant areas now pass through Catholic areas.

From the late 1980s onward the increasingly assertive Catholic population has been more prone to complain against what it regards as sectarian parades that do not have the consent of the local residents. A number of these parades have been inflamed into major flashpoints, capable of generating tension far beyond their point of origin. In these cases, conflicts that are ostensibly about territory contain much broader messages about a (lack of) willingness to share territory space. This space can be physical as well as political or cultural. The conflicts over territory also transmit messages of subordination and dominance. To march through an area without the consent of its inhabitants in the full knowledge that they oppose it is expressive of contempt for the local residents. Equally, to deny fellow citizens of a locality access to a main thoroughfare conveys a lack of respect. If the marches and counterprotests do not constitute actual hate crime, they help contribute to an atmosphere more conducive to hate crime. The summer months of Northern Ireland's marching season are accompanied by dramatic increases in public order offenses, street assaults, and sectarian intimidation encouraged by the general atmosphere of lawlessness.

Democratization and Hate Crime

As democratization in Eastern and Central Europe has shown, the introduction of more plural political systems brings few guarantees that prejudice and prejudice-motivated crimes will be exorcised. In the extreme case, the breakup of Yugoslavia and the horrific violence that ensued was precipitated by a series of referendums. In other words, a key component of a modern responsive democracy hastened a situation in which human and minority rights suffered. One Croatian observer reflected on his decision to vote to break away from Yugoslavia in the 1992 referendum: "We thought that we were opening the door for our children. Instead our grandparents walked in."[33] Disaffected youths in Germany, Hungary, Romania, and the Czech Republic vented their disappointment at economic liberalization on minorities. The phenomenon is neatly summed in the title of Paul Hockenos's book *Free to Hate*.[34] The collapse of authoritarian state structures gave individuals greater freedom. In some cases this has been abused and channeled into prejudice, with extreme nationalists offering quick-fix solutions at the expense of minorities.

The region's violent history, with the repeated redrawing of borders and the mass movements of people, means that it contains many minorities. Kolossov and Trevish calculate that there were nine independent states in eastern and central Europe in 1910 with seventy-seven minorities and subnations. By 1993 the picture had become more complex with twenty-nine independent states and 114 minorities and subnations.[35] An estimated fifty million people belong to ethnic minorities in the region, or 10–15 percent of the total population.[36] This ethnic mix in itself does not point to hate crime and persecution of minorities. But the increase in minorities, often isolated from their core group, the economic pressures of post-Communist transitions, and the varied enforcement of new criminal justice systems can contribute to environments in which hate crime can flourish. The pressures to engage in post-Communist nation building often outweigh the pressures to develop a stable, inclusive multicultural society. It is also worth noting that the existence of right-wing parties, even if they do not hold power, often has a significant restraining influence on mainstream parties. The realities of electoral competition means that mainstream parties may maintain or introduce restrictive legislation on immigration or minorities to guard against accusations of weakness.[37]

Other drawbacks in relation to democratization are evident in relation to ethnonational conflict, the main focus of this chapter. Democracy and democratization have been the clarion-call Western responses to post–Cold War conflict. References to democracy dominate U.S. State Department press statements. The months of January and February 2000 find references to "the restoration of democracy" (Congo), "the successful conduct of democratic elections" (Croatia), "seriously flawed parliamentary elections" (Uzbekistan), and the "struggle to create a democratic society" (Montenegro).[38] George W. Bush's chief foreign policy goals are enunciated simply as "democracy and peace."[39] The United Nations has placed a massive emphasis on electoral assistance programs, providing technical assistance, observers, or reports in sixty-nine states in the 1989–99 period.[40]

Yet the emphasis of many international efforts to encourage democratization has often been on the quantification of democracy rather than on its quality. The rush to have early postconflict elections has often hindered the more long-term task of encouraging a more deep-rooted democracy. The need for any transition from conflict to peace to have popular approval is clear. This might come in the form of a referendum on a peace accord,[41] or the election of a new postaccord government. Early elections can have serious drawbacks though. They risk remobilizing warring factions, with the election regarded as conflict by other means. They may favor narrowly based political parties, primarily organized along ethnic lines with strong links to guerrilla organizations rather than civil society. Early elections might also provide a premature sense of "closure" for the international community. The holding of an election is often taken as a defining moment and as an indicator of a well-functioning democracy. Images of people queuing to vote in a formerly war-ravaged country are incredibly symbolic and risk prompting the international community to conclude that the conflict is over.[42]

The key point is that the mere holding of elections by itself is not enough to ensure that a stable and inclusive democratic society is functioning to the benefit of all its citizens. Many states manage to stage regular elections but are still characterized by a poorly developed civil society, ingrained nepotism and corruption, the systematic exclusion of minorities and women, and the persecution of opposition parties.[43]

Northern Ireland, Israel-Palestine, and South Africa have all undergone processes and transitions in the 1990s that included significant degrees of democratization. Northern Ireland, a territory that already possessed a relatively high level of democracy, saw a peace process that culminated in the devolution of a consociational powersharing administration. Israel-Palestine witnessed a faltering and often violent peace process that led to the granting of limited Palestinian autonomy. The most dramatic change was in South Africa with a transition to majority rule. Both the processes leading to the democratization and the nature of the new political dispensations were marked by increased hate crime.

In all three cases the peace processes were enormous endeavors, attempting to change the very nature of the conflicts, challenging entrenched beliefs, and requiring a sustained engagement with actors previously regarded as enemies. The peace processes operated at multiple levels involving complex mixes of governments, political parties, militant organizations, nongovernmental organizations, and third parties. In all three cases there was a tendency, particularly among those on the extremes, to interpret the peace processes in zero-sum terms. They were regarded as high-stakes, all-or-nothing enterprises in which the risks of failure would be catastrophic.[44] One manifestation of this nervousness was an increase in street demonstrations in all three areas. The South African transition was marked by mass rallies by the African National Congress with counterdemonstrations by the Inkatha Freedom Party and others. Northern Ireland has seen increased tension associated with politico-religious parades and Israel-Palestine has seen a number of street demonstrations and the rekindling of the *intifada*.

Local activists and militants who feel disempowered by elite-level negotiations often regard the street as the arena to vent their anger and display their power (or powerlessness).[45] Street politics associated with peace processes has provided an environment conducive to hate crime and direct intergroup violence unmediated by proxy militant organizations and security forces. Group dynamics are difficult for organizers to control and the public nature of demonstrations means that they are not solely restricted to members of militant organizations who may be subject to strictures and restraints. The number of people charged with security-related offenses actually increased in Northern Ireland after the paramilitary organizations called cease-fires in 1994. The increase is largely accounted for by public order offenses related to parades.[46]

Parades and demonstrations, and state responses to them, often generate further intergroup tension and contribute to an environment permissive to prejudice and hate crime. Given that parades are conducted in public, heavy-handed security responses or clashes between groups often receive extensive media coverage, further contributing to the sense of grievance. An environment of lawlessness provides cover for those who wish to perpetrate hate crime. The marching season in Northern Ireland sees a dramatic increase in the number of incidents of sectarian intimidation.[47]

The pressures caused by peace processes and transitions also spark the phenomenon of spoiler violence and spoiler groups committed to derailing efforts to reach a peace accord.[48] These spoiler groups can be new organizations formed to oppose peace efforts (for example, the Afrikaner Volksfront in South Africa), breakaway factions from long-standing militant groups who are included in the peace process (for example, the Loyalist Volunteer Force in Northern Ireland), or established groups who are excluded from the peace process (Hamas in Israel-Palestine). These groups are often a source of hate crime. They tend to lack the restraint and discipline of more established and mainstream militant groups. While those organizations involved in a peace process are usually subject to a cease-fire, spoiler violence becomes more visible.

The basic aim of spoiler groups is to shock the participants and supporters of a peace process into withdrawing from it. As a result, many spoiler attacks are deliberately calculated to cause offense and thus inhabit the realm of hate crime. While Hamas bomb attacks on Israeli buses may seem like a particularly unsophisticated form of political violence, their essential political aim is to encourage Israelis to become so disaffected with the peace process that they withdraw from it. The ultimate target of the attack is actually the mainstream Palestinian movement under Chairman Arafat. The almost inconsequential nature of the Israeli victims of this violence makes the attacks particularly gratuitous.

The emergence of spoiler groups is just one aspect of the increasingly informal nature of violence associated with peace processes and transitions. Cease-fires by the main protagonists in a conflict may result in a weakening of discipline in militant organizations (and security forces). This can have the implications for the social control and community "policing" roles played by militant organizations that may have regulated criminal activity, including hate crime. A lessening of security and surveillance, and the filtering of weaponry that had been the exclusive preserve of organized groups into criminal hands, contributes to increasing informal violence. As in South Africa and Northern Ireland, the legitimacy of police forces, and thus their ability to deal with criminal activity, might be called into question. Both locations witnessed significant increases in nonpolitical crime after the beginning of their peace processes. For example, in the year after the 1998 Good Friday Agreement was reached, Northern Ireland's crime rate rose by 9 percent, with violent crime rising by 12 percent.[49] Commentators pointed to the development of a "knife culture" following eight fatal stabbings in the Christmas and New Year period in 2000/01.[50] Spiraling crime rates have been even more dramatic in South Africa, with the murder rate increasing from 19,600 in 1993 to 24,600 in 1997.[51] It is important to note that South Africa's crime rates are very much linked to economic deprivation.[52]

The increasing crime rates contain incidences of hate crime both against traditional and new targets. The continuing violence against traditional targets suggests that peace accords are unable to draw a definitive line in the sand. Grievances, a sense of moral outrage, and the desire for revenge can continue regardless of an accord reached among elites. Furthermore, many peace accords do not actually address the central conflict grievance. They demand that protagonists change the manner in which they conduct the conflict but do not challenge the essential character and belief systems of the main actors. The implication is that prejudice, the fundamental source of hate crime, is left intact by the peace process. More seriously, peace processes can actually reinforce mutually exclusive identities. It is possible to argue that those Palestinians loyal to Yasser Arafat have been bolstered by their involvement in the Oslo process. To a certain extent, they have been encouraged and even rewarded for being a particular type of Palestinian while costs were attached to pursuing more extreme versions of the Palestinian cause (the most obvious cost being exclusion from the peace process). While being included in the peace process, moderate, Arafat-aligned Palestinians were able to maintain anti-Jewish prejudices and so hate crime was able to continue.

Similar processes were at work in Northern Ireland. The peace process was based on inclusion, or the principle that those capable of destabilizing a peace accord from the outside must be included in it in order to make it work. Those on the political extremes were accommodated as long as they called cease-fires. Hardline nationalists or unionists were not required to disavow their mutually exclusive brands of nationalism and the accompanying baggage of intolerance. The key point is that neither the Israeli-Palestinian nor Northern Ireland peace processes rest on a reconciliation of conflicting identities. Instead, the focus is on technical issues such as land or mechanisms for governance. Issues of reconciliation, such as addressing prejudice, are regarded as secondary. As a result, despite the implementation of a peace accord, hate crime can continue.

Both South Africa and Northern Ireland saw the emergence of new targets for hate crime. The postaccord periods in both societies saw increased attacks on immigrants. Black African immigrants, particularly from Nigeria, Zimbabwe, Mozambique, and Angola, have been the victims of attacks in South Africa.[53] The postapartheid transition placed heavy emphasis on national integration, with a

specific *Masakhane* or "building the nation together" program designed to promote a new brand of civic nationalism accessible to all South Africans. While this
may have had limited success in forging reconciliation between blacks and whites,
the xenophobia displayed toward blacks from outside South Africa has seriously
dented the hopes for the creation of a new multicultural society. President Mbeki
admitted that South Africa has "not won the struggle against racism,"[54] while
alleged police brutality against immigrants and "new pass laws" against migrants
suggest that official attitudes have not kept pace with the vision for a "rainbow
nation."[55] In a pattern replicated in other transition societies, immigrants have
become easy scapegoats for frustrations at unrealized economic expectations.

Northern Ireland has a tiny immigrant community,[56] yet they have become the
target of attacks in the peace process period. The ostensible reason for many of
these attacks was robbery, although the regularity with which members of ethnic
minorities were targeted and the gratuitous nature of some of the attacks pointed
toward more sinister motives.[57] In many respects ethnic minorities are particularly vulnerable in a society like Northern Ireland that is dominated by two main
(Catholic-nationalist and Protestant-unionist) political and cultural blocks. Without the umbrella of protection offered by the wider communities and their paramilitary groups, ethnic minorities are at risk. Furthermore, a society in which
interethnic prejudice is rife is unlikely to hold tolerant views toward minority
immigrant groups.

Conclusion

A key argument of this chapter is that deeply divided societies are not the scene of
unrestrained hate crime. In the definitions section it was argued that violence,
however abhorrent, normally has a rational basis. The categorization of certain
types of violence as "hate crime" risks writing it off as irrational and unworthy of
sophisticated analysis. Prosaic and practical motivations such as the protection of
economic privilege or the control of territory often lie behind violence rather than
simple prejudice.

It is also important to place hate crime into the wider context of political and
criminal violence in deeply divided societies. A mix of factors including the targeting priorities of combatants and their level of organization will influence the
nature and intensity of the violence. Restraining factors can limit the incidence of
hate crime, for example, the anxiety of combatants to retain political legitimacy in
the eyes of the international community. Other factors, such as the blurred distinction between civilians and the military in situations of ethnonational conflict,
can help conceal or mask the real incidence of hate crime.

Peace accords are often trumpeted as "a new beginning,"[58] but there is often a
dissonance between agreements reached at the elite political level and grassroots

opinion. While a new political accommodation may be engineered in the negoti-ating chamber, it is unlikely that any agreement can be comprehensive enough to address all of the grievances and prejudices that form the basis of the conflict. Fur-thermore, the tensions associated with the passage of a peace process or transition toward democracy can actually inflame conflict between ethnic groups. The result is that hate crime can continue, even in the postsettlement phase of conflicts. Transitions are usually accompanied by high public expectations, particularly in relation to economic rewards. Failure to fulfill these expectations can lead to disil-lusionment and the identification of scapegoats, often from minority or immi-grant communities.

Deeply divided societies are likely to have an enduring culture of violence. While political violence may become more regulated as the result of a peace process, through, say, cease-fires or demobilization programs, more informal sources of violence can continue. This postconflict context is particularly impor-tant and can be conducive to hate crime, despite wider political moves toward democracy. Significant elements of the postconflict context include demoralized police forces undergoing reorganization, the illegal transfer of military weapons into civilian hands, and the frustration of economic expectations. The back-ground of a society relatively inured to violence and dislocation is likely to mean that the targeting of minorities will receive little attention. Over two years on from the conclusion of the Good Friday Agreement (April 1998) Northern Ireland has a powersharing government with an ambitious Programme for Government. Its main paramilitary organizations have maintained cease-fires and the state is engaged in a demilitarization process. Yet a low level of prejudice-motivated attacks persists.[59] Democratization brings few guarantees that hate crime will cease.

NOTES

1. Walker Connor, *Ethnonationalism: The Quest for Understanding* (Princeton, N.J.: Princeton University Press, 1994).
2. See Michael E. Brown's comments on ethnic entrepreneurs in "The Causes of Internal Conflict: An Overview," in *Nationalism and Ethnic Conflict*, ed. Michael E. Brown et al. (Cambridge, Mass.: MIT Press, 1997), pp. 3–25, at pp. 19–20.
3. Rogers Brubaker and David Laitin, "Ethnic and Nationalist Violence," *Annual Review of Sociology* 24 (1998): 423–52.
4. Eric A. Nordlinger, "Conflict Regulation in Divided Societies," *Occasional Papers in International Affairs* 29 (Harvard: Center for International Affairs, 1972), p. 9.
5. Much of this is drawn from a discussion by John R. Bowen on the overdependence on "ethnicity" as an explanatory factor for contemporary conflict. See "The Myth of Global Ethnic Conflict," *Journal of Democracy* 7, no. 4 (1996): 3–14.
6. See James B. Jacobs and Jessica S. Henry, "The Social Construction of a Hate Crime Epidemic," *The Journal of Criminal Law and Criminology* 86, no. 2 (1996): 366–91.
7. States may be tempted to disown agents caught while engaged in extralegal activity saying that they were acting in an individual capacity.

8. See Republic of Turkey website, www.turkey.org.

9. See, for example, "Turkey Bombs Kurdish Shepherds" (August 18, 2000) and "Kurdish Party Officials Detained in Turkey" (June 7, 2000) both from BBC News website.

10. William Eckhart, "Civilian Deaths in Wartime," *Bulletin of Peace Proposals* 20, no. 1 (March 1989): 89–98.

11. Eyewitnesses recalled this pattern of intimidation in Croatia in 1992–95. Author field trip, December 2000.

12. See, for example, reports of four Palestinians being killed in shooting incidents in "US Reported to Be Offering Arafat an Instant Mini-State," *Guardian* (October 28, 2000).

13. The Israeli Defense Force mission statement reads: "To defend the existence, territorial integrity and sovereignty of the State of Israel. To protect the inhabitants of Israel and to combat all forms of terrorism which threaten the daily life." See website www.idf.il/English/doctrine.stm/ (January 2001).

14. See A. P. Schmid and A. J. Jongman, "Violent Conflict and Human Rights Violations in the Mid-1990s," *Terrorism and Political Violence* 9, no. 4 (winter 1997): 166–92, at p. 167.

15. In the 1987–93 period over fifteen hundred Palestinians were killed and twelve thousand were imprisoned for *Intifada*-related offenses. This led to considerable fatigue within in the Palestinian community and raised questions about the sustainability of the *Intifada* in the absence of wider political changes. See John King, *Handshake in Washington: The Beginning of Middle East Peace?* (Reading: Ithaca Press, 1994), pp. 185–6.

16. "A Lot of Local Sabotage," *Financial Times* (February 8, 1997).

17. For example, the newly elected mayor of Jaffna, Sarojini Yogeswaran, was assassinated by the LTTE in May 1998, her husband having met the same fate some years previously. Her successor was, in turn, assassinated. Paikiasothy Saravanamuttu, "Sri Lanka—the Intractability of Ethnic Conflict," in *The Management of Peace Processes*, ed. John Darby and Roger MacGinty (London: Macmillan, 2000), pp. 195–227, at p. 221.

18. Malachi O'Doherty, *The Trouble With Guns: Republican Strategy and the Provisional IRA* (Belfast: Blackstaff Press, 1997), p. 109.

19. The term "paramilitary" is used in Northern Ireland to refer to nonstate guerrilla groups.

20. Peter Wallenstein and Margareta Sollenberg, "Armed Conflict, 1988–99," *Journal of Peace Research* 37, no. 5 (2000): 635–649, at p. 640.

21. Chaim Kaufmann, "Possible and Impossible Solutions to Ethnic and Civil Wars," in *Nationalism and Ethnic Conflict*, ed. Brown et al., pp. 265–304, at p. 279.

22. Scott A. Bollens, "Uncovering the Urban Dimension in Nationalist Conflict: Jerusalem and Belfast Compared," *Terrorism and Political Violence* 10, no. 1 (spring 1998): 1–38, at p. 7.

23. David McKittrick, "Apartheid Deepens in Ulster," *Independent* (London) March 21, 1993.

24. Hastings Donnan and Graham McFarlane explore the motivations for segregation in Northern Ireland—from kinship to intimidation—in "Informal Social Organisation," in *Northern Ireland: The Background to the Conflict*, ed. John Darby (Belfast: Appletree Press, 1983), pp. 110–35.

25. Alan Smith, "Education and the Peace Process in Northern Ireland" (paper presented to the Annual Conference of the American Education Research Association, Montreal, April 1999).

26. Bollens, "Uncovering the Urban Dimension," pp. 7–9.
27. According to Bollens (ibid., p. 4), "Jewish casualties were higher in the city of Jerusalem than elsewhere, with many political murders occurring along the old boundary 'seam.'"
28. Barry A. Turner, ed., *Organisational Symbolism* (Berlin: Walter de Gruyter, 1990), p. 4.
29. Donald L. Horowitz discusses the importance of symbolism in deeply divided societies in *Ethnic Groups in Conflict* (Berkeley, Calif.: University of California Press, 1985), pp. 216–19.
30. "Chief Rabbis Say Israel Must Keep Holy Site," *New York Times,* January 5, 2001.
31. Natan Sharansky, "Record Turnout Expected at Jerusalem Rally," *Jerusalem Post,* January 8, 2001.
32. Neil Jarman and Dominic Bryan, *Parade and Protest: A Discussion of Parading Disputes in Northern Ireland* (Coleraine, Northern Ireland: Centre for the Study of Conflict, 1996).
33. Author's notes, anonymous interviewee, Croatia, December 2000.
34. Paul Hockenos, *Free to Hate: The Rise of the Right in Post-Communist Eastern Europe* (New York: Routledge, 1993).
35. Valdimir Kolossov and Andrei Trevish, "The Political Geography of European Minorities: Past and Future," *Political Geography* 17, no. 5 (1998): 517–34, at p. 524.
36. Géze Jeszenszky, "More Bosnias? National and Ethnic Tensions in the Post-Communist World," *East European Quarterly* 31, no. 3 (1997): 283–98, at p. 290.
37. John Rex, "The Problematic of Multinational and Multicultural Societies," *Ethnic and Racial Studies* 20, no. 3 (1997): 455–77, at p. 469.
38. Taken from www.state.gov.
39. "Bush Foreign Agenda Takes Shape," BBC News website (December 17, 2000).
40. Figures calculated from information found at www.un.org (January 2001).
41. President de Klerk held a referendum on the reform process in South Africa among whites only in March 1992. A referendum on the Good Friday Agreement was held in Northern Ireland and the Republic of Ireland in May 1998.
42. The difficulties of postconflict elections are covered by Timothy D. Sisk, *Powersharing and International Mediation in Ethnic Conflict* (Washington, D.C.: USIP Press, 1996), Timothy D. Sisk and Andrew Reynolds, eds., *Elections and Conflict Management in Africa* (Washington, D.C.: USIP Press, 1998), and Peter Harris and Ben Reilly, eds., *Democracy and Deep-Rooted Conflicts: Options for Negotiators* (Stockholm: International IDEA, 1998).
43. See Julius O. Ihonvbere, "Democratization in Africa," *Peace Review* 9, no. 3 (September 1997): 371–78.
44. This is often evidenced by the apocalyptic language employed by extremists.
45. See, for example, "Jerusalem Braced for Right-Wing Rally," BBC News website (January 8, 2001).
46. The figures can be found on the Royal Ulster Constabulary website: www.ruc.police.uk (January 2001).
47. See, for example, "Litany of Intimidation Growing," *Irish News,* July 28, 1997.
48. Stephen John Stedman, "Spoiler Groups in Peace Processes," *International Security* 22, no. 2, (fall 1997): 5–53.
49. "Shock Rise in Violent Crime Rates," *Belfast Telegraph* June 30, 2000.
50. "Knife Culture Must Be Stopped," *Irish News,* January 8, 2001.
51. "Murder in SA Highlights Crime Problem," *Irish Times,* February 4, 1999.

52. See Pierre du Toit, "South Africa: In Search of Post-Settlement Peace," in *The Management of Peace Processes*, ed. Darby and MacGinty, pp. 16–60.

53. See Alan Morris, "Our Fellow Africans Make Our Lives Hell: The Lives of Congolese and Nigerians Living in Johannesburg" *Ethnic and Racial Studies* 21, no. 6 (November 1998): 1116–36, and "South Africa's New Racism," BBC News website (August 28, 2000).

54. "Racism 'Still Rife' in South Africa," BBC News website (January 8, 2000).

55. "'Too Black' Migrants Jailed in New South Africa," *Guardian*, November 18, 2000.

56. A study by Greg Irwin and Seamus Dunn estimates the combined total of the three main immigrant groups in Northern Ireland (Chinese, Indian, and Pakistani) to be less that ten thousand in a total Northern Ireland population of 1.5 million. See *Ethnic Minorities in Northern Ireland* (Northern Ireland: Centre for the Study of Conflict, 1997).

57. See, for example, "Meeting over Attacks on Chinese Community," BBC Northern Ireland News website (November 1, 2000), "Chinese Victims Forced to Move," *Irish News*, April 4, 2000, "The Alarming Rise in Race-Related Crimes," *Irish News*, April 12, 2000, and "Chinese 'Targeted' in Violent Attacks," *Irish News*, November 20, 2000.

58. *The Agreement: Agreement Reached in the Multi-Party Negotiations* (Belfast: HMSO, 1998), p. 1.

59. "Fears over Escalating Pipe-Bomb Incidents," *Irish News*, January 11, 2001.

CHAPTER TEN

Economics, Violence, and Protest in Venezuela

A Preview of the Global Future?

Margarita López Maya, Luis E. Lander, and Mark Ungar

Introduction

Over the past two decades Venezuela has experienced an economic free fall that has dramatically decreased the quality of life for the majority of the population. As the economy collapsed, violence increased throughout public and private life. This crisis has not only destroyed most achievements of Venezuela's industrial modernization since World War II, but has transformed Venezuela itself. The economy may eventually recover, aided by needed restructuring and high oil prices. But the record level of violence accompanying the economic crisis has taken on a dynamic of its own, indelibly altering the country's politics and society.

The purpose of this chapter is to show how economic change leads to violence—particularly, to increases in violent protest against economic conditions and policies. In an era of globalization, democratization, and inequality, this link between economics and violence is one that could become increasingly prominent. As discussed in the chapters by Ghadbian and Welsh, popular opposition to economic policies and conditions has generated violence and political instability from East Asia to the Middle East. In Latin America citizen agitation against contemporary economic policies has also become a central feature of state-society relations and the future of democracy. The upheavals in Venezuela, rooted in a popular consensus against neoliberal economic policy amid decreasing state power, may be the clearest preview of the future of violent protest throughout the world.

The first section of the chapter describes economic conditions in Venezuela, the causes of the decline of the last two decades, and the policies taken by the government to halt it. The second section then examines the socioeconomic costs to the Venezuelan population for both the economic decline and the adjustments intended to overcome it. The third section describes the largest and most violent popular reaction to the government's economic policies—the massive popular revolt of 1989, known as the *Caracazo*—connecting it with Venezuela's general economic conditions and institutional weakness as well as with the literature on violent protest. The final section turns to popular agitation against these policies in the years following the *Caracazo*, showing how an expanding set of grievances made violent protest a norm in Venezuelan life throughout the 1990s. It describes the confrontational and violent nature of this mobilization, the actors and motivations behind it, and how they all help to define what could be called "the agenda of the poor for the twenty-first century."

Venezuela's Economic Crisis

Although Venezuela's economic troubles were similar to those of other Latin American countries in the 1980s, they were also distinct in many significant ways. First, the Venezuelan economy highly depends on oil. Petroleum-related activities in the 1990s comprised between 16.5 and 22.6 percent of the Gross Domestic Product (GDP). In addition, international oil prices fluctuate widely, which makes it extremely difficult to carry out long-term planning. Second, since World War II Venezuela has adopted an ambitious and expansive state-run model of development. Based on distribution of its massive petroleum earnings, the state built a vast network of administrative agencies, social services, public works, and other programs. This approach led to vast improvements in the living standards of most social sectors. Just as significantly, it also led to the ingrained citizen expectations—far more than in any other Latin American society—that a proactive state can and should guarantee ongoing support and improvement.

In the 1980s both the dependence on oil income and the popular expectations around it prevented Venezuela from responding to the economic crisis engulfing it.[1] At the same time that the country was reeling from a drop in oil prices and from the pressures of its huge external debt, most other governments in Latin America were beginning to adopt neoliberal reforms, based on a reduced state role and an open economy. Not only was Venezuela's crisis more severe, however, but so was its resistance to change. Both the parties and the popular sectors believed that oil would ultimately save them from spending cuts and restructuring, which would be more painful in Venezuela than in other countries because of the size and role of the Venezuelan state. Much of this opposition was directed against International Financial Agencies (IFIs), particularly the International Monetary Fund (IMF), that promoted neoliberal "adjustment" comprised of spending cuts, privatization, currency devaluation, export promotion, and an end to state subsidies and price controls.

But because of the severity of the economic decline, there were nevertheless several attempts to introduce such neoliberal adjustment policies. The first began with the government of Luis Herrera Campíns (1979–84), of the conservative Social Christian party COPEI. A second one was attempted under his successor, Jaime Lusinchi (1984–89), from the other dominant political party, the center-left social democratic Acción Democrática (AD). Still a third was initiated under the 1989–93 administration of Carlos Andrés Pérez, also from AD, and the last of them by the 1994–99 government of Rafael Caldera. All four attempts were characterized by their short duration, and although the first two were far less coherent than their successors, they all faced fierce popular resistance that culminated in their demise. These successive failures make the Venezuelan case a typical example of a society with "adjustment fatigue," which, by the continuation of failed attempts, lost confidence in the capacity of this approach to overcome its economic crisis.

This interruption of adjustment policies accentuated and deepened a decline begun with the exhaustion of the former development model, and also reinforced the social deterioration that began to manifest itself with this decline. Many of those who promote neoliberalism assert that it was not the policies that were at fault, but an inability to sustain them. In particular, they blame the entrenched, corrupt, and short-sighted party leaders who were unwilling to push for unpopular but necessary adjustments.[2] However, neoliberalism's critics argue that Venezuela's economic indicators are proof of this policy's dangers. Although most other countries of the region experienced mixed but clear results from neoliberalism—including the abatement of inflation, increases in unemployment, and sustained annual growth—in the case of Venezuela the results were far more ill-defined. Nevertheless, the empirical data clearly show that the exhaustion of the old approach and the ineffectiveness of adjustment policies came together to create an irrefutable condition of economic and social deterioration.

Although the Herrera Campíns government had some neoliberal orientation, the combination of a boom in oil prices (1979–81) and the sheer momentum of the state's profligate spending habits prevented adjustment policies from being coherently implemented. At the end of its term, however, the government was forced to devaluate the currency. Despite the fact that the 1974 boom of petroleum prices led to increasing income for the rest of the 1970s,[3] the money was still insufficient to pay for the state's economic and social commitments. According to oil economy experts, the Venezuelan development model sustained by oil rent began its inexorable decline after 1979, revealed initially in the stagnation of economic activities.[4] Within a few years, the combination of this stagnation, the government's delays in refinancing the external debt, and the disarray in the international financial markets caused by Mexico's debt moratorium declaration led to a massive capital flight from the country and to the government's decision to devaluate the currency, the bolívar, for the first time in twenty years. More than any other event, the announced devaluation—on "black Friday," February 18, 1983—aroused the collective conscience to the gravity of the country's economic situation.

In February 1984, soon after taking office, the Lusinchi government initiated another set of adjustment policies. Lusinchi announced an economic *paquete* (package) that followed some of the IFIs' policies recommendations. The plan was not a formal accord with the IMF, but a unilateral move by the government to create conditions favorable to obtain a refinancing of its external debt, one of the region's largest. Lusinchi's adjustment plan can be considered heterodox, since it included characteristics of different approaches. In particular, it maintained an active role of the state in investment and regulation, and gave greater priority to redistribution and employment than do orthodox adjustment programs. The specific policies of the February 1984 *paquete* were: a) a devaluation of the bolívar and the establishment of a differenciated exchange regime; b) non-salary means to compensate for the impact on wages and salaries, instead of the traditional pay increases; c) a transportation subsidy for those earning under 3,000 bolivares; d) an opening of the price-control system, which later led to price liberalization; e) increases in the prices of gasoline and other energy products; f) a pledge to reduce state spending.[5] Other nonneoliberal policies, announced at the same time, were geared toward lowering interest rates and stimulating employment and agricultural development.

The government justified the neoliberal policies, considered severe at the time, with the need to make up for past losses and to pay the debt. But the government's "VII Plan of the Nation," announced a few months later, was a muddle of approaches. The plan's most controversial part—swiftly killed by fierce opposition—was to create an "Economic System of Cooperation" between public and private ownership. More coherent were Lusinchi's price and salary policies, intended to readjust the relation between production and sales prices, since Herrera Campíns's devaluation and price controls were discouraging production and private investment. Budget shortfalls also obliged an increase in prices, while devaluation prompted measures to strengthen the competitive edge created by devaluation, before it was blunted by salary and other pressures. In December 1986 Lusinchi decreed a new devaluation, due to the effects of a yearlong drop in oil prices on the balance of payments, which was followed by stepped-up efforts to repay and refinance the debt. But the government also increased state spending to boost its popularity and the chances for its party's victory in upcoming elections. Along with a decrease in international reserves and other economic disequilibria, this approach led Lusinchi to declare a moratorium on debt payment in January 1989, a month before leaving office.

Another packet was announced by Lusinchi's successor, Carlos Andrés Pérez, a few days after his inauguration in February 1989—made necessary by alarming macroeconomic trends. Inflation reached historical highs of 29.46 percent in 1988, international reserves plummeted from $13.7 billion in 1984 to $6.5 billion in 1988, and the current account balance of payments deficit ballooned from $1.3 billion in 1987 to $5.8 billion in 1988. By 1988, in addition, the foreign debt reached the amount of $26.6 billion.[6] These conditions led to a formal agreement between the IMF and the Venezuelan government to adopt an orthodox adjustment program. This agreement's principal points were reduction of state expenditures, salary restrictions, unification of exchange rates, flexible interest rates, elimination of agriculture preferences, postponement of low-priority investment plans, reductions of subsidies, introduction of a value-added tax, adjustment in the rates of state-provided goods and services, including domestic petroleum prices, import liberalization, and the lifting of restrictions on certain international transactions, such as in investment and dividend repatriation. To compensate for the negative effects of these policies on the working class, additional policies included subsidies for basic foodstuffs, new programs aimed at the poorest households, food programs for children, aid for microenterprises, support for health clinics, a restructuring of the social security program, and creation of the Presidential Commission for the Struggle Against Poverty.[7] Despite its obvious importance, this plan was not presented to Congress, nor made public until the IMF agreement was signed. The reaction by an unsuspecting public was one of the most extensive and violent in Venezuelan history, sparking a popular revolt soon after the announcement. The *Caracazo* then fed into two attempted military coups in 1992 and the impeachment of Pérez in 1993. One of the casualties of these convulsions were the policies of adjustment. Soon after being introduced they were politically dead.

The December 1993 presidential campaign, centered on Pérez's neoliberal plans, was won by former president Rafael Caldera. An architect of Venezuela's democracy and once head of COPEI, Caldera bolted his party and stitched together a populist coalition, called *Convergencia* (Convergence), whose 1993 victory was the first time neither AD nor COPEI won the presidency since the transition to democracy in 1958. In its first years the Caldera government feverishly worked to put together a coherent and effective economic plan not determined by neoliberalism. But a international consensus hostile to such plans, along with a financial and bank crisis—one of the country's worst, involving the collapse of most of the country's top banks—forced the government to request IMF aid in 1996. This led to still another adjustment package, known as "Agenda Venezuela," in April 1996. Although the social programs included in the Caldera plan were more extensive and presented far more carefully than in Pérez's plan, in the population's view it was little more than a repeat of it. "Agenda Venezuela" included a set of measures and policies of which the most significant were: an increase in the domestic prices of gasoline and other energy sources, liberation of the public services rates, devaluation of the bolívar as a result of the lifting of the previous currency exchange control implanted during the bank crisis, increase in the value-added tax, privatization of public enterprises, unfreezing of price controls (except for five essential foodstuffs), creation of a banking protection fund, social programs focused on the protection of the most vulnerable social sectors, plans to reduce state spending and to beef up tax collection, progressive flexibility in interest rates, strengthening of the capital, banking, and industrial sectors, and reaffirmation of collective bargaining as the best tool to fix salary encouraging its flexibility. Although not presented as part of the "Agenda," there were also bold changes in the all-important oil policies, with moves toward privatization, increased output, and market determination of prices.

Although popular opposition to the "Agenda" was far milder than that to Pérez's plan—events such as the *Caracazo* did not occur—the fall in international oil prices after October 1997, in part spurred by Venezuela's increased output, played a key role in the collapse of the "Agenda" by the landslide 1998 presidential victory of Hugo Chávez. The army lieutenant-colonel who led a bloody but unsuccessful coup attempt in February 1992, Chávez ran on an antineoliberal platform. His triumph represented a radical political break, expressed most clearly in his displacement of the traditional elites and his adoption of a new constitution. On economic matters, in contrast, Chávez's changes have been decidedly undramatic. The government has respected its agreements with the IMF, but has substantially modified oil policy by rolling back the moves toward privatization and by complying with its agreements in OPEC (the Organization of Petroleum Exporting Countries) and by playing a more active and important role in the organization.

The Social Costs of the Economic Decline

It is impossible to calculate neoliberalism's exact responsibility for the socioeconomic collapse suffered by Venezuelan society in the last twenty years. As described above, all plans were interrupted soon after implementation. These interruptions did not lead to the positive results that its promoters had predicted, but primarily to the deterioration of indicators such as inflation and formal employment. In an overall analysis, in fact, all of the indicators most frequently used to evaluate the social impact of social adjustment programs show negative figures.

The figures of table 1 confirm the erratic nature of the Venezuelan economy since 1979, swinging between spurts of growth and periods of recession. In many of the years with growth above 5 percent, there was a corresponding increase in petroleum activity, but in other years a decrease of petroleum activity did not correspond with a decrease of the GDP. The first years of each adjustment program—1984, 1989, and 1996—brought either decrease (1984 and 1989) or stagnation (1996), followed either by moderate growth (1985 and 1986) or increase and then decrease. In a clear realization of one of the adjustment programs' most important objectives, there was a recuperation of international reserves at the end of the first year of adjustment, which, in the case of Pérez's packet, continued for the plan's duration. But in each of the first years of adjustment there is a significant increase in inflation, followed by a decrease that never returns to previous levels.

Since 1984 the government has proved incapable of lowering inflation to single digits. While we are not able to affirm a direct relation between adjustment and the behavior of the GDP in Venezuela, however, the social impact was clear: increasing unemployment and poverty (see table 2).

Table 2 shows a clear decline in formal public employment, which has been replaced more by informal labor than formal private employment. Hovering around 40 percent over the past twenty years, after 1994 the informal sector jumped to around 48 percent. This rate contrasts with employment patterns during previous declines: between 1969 and 1979 the average annual increase in informal employment barely reached 0.1 percent.[8] Another significant change, as seen in table 3, was in income distribution. The living standards of the majority of Venezuelans deteriorated as the average annual income plunged by nearly 43 percent, from $5,345 in 1979 to $3,049 in 1997. The adjustment plans not only accelerated this fall, but inequality in income distribution as well. During the final adjustment program, in fact, near a third of the national income went to the richest 5 percent of the population.

TABLE 1. SELECTED MACROECONOMIC INDICATORS

YEAR	GDP(IN MILLONS OF BS. 1984)	INCREASE (VARIATION GDP)	INFLATION (VARIATION CPI)*	RATE OF CHANGE (BS./$)**	INTERNATIONAL RESERVES (IN MILLIONS OF DOLLARS)
1979	494,942	1.5	12.83	4.3	8,819
1980	474,205	-4.19	22.89	4.3	8,885
1981	467,395	-1.44	15.94	4.3	11,409
1982	451,781	-3.34	8.52	4.3	11,624
1983	420,099	-7.01	5.85	9.9	12,181
1984	410,067	-2.39	12.08	12.65	13,723
1985	415,349	1.29	11.4	14.4	12,341
1986	431,594	3.91	11.58	22.7	11,685
1987	459,613	6.49	28.08	30.55	9,402
1988	477,564	3.91	29.46	39.3	6,555
1989	460,813	-3.51	84.47	43.05	7,411
1990	492,170	.8	40.66	50.58	11,759
1991	532,605	8.22	34.2	61.65	14,105
1992	559,789	5.1	31.43	79.55	13,001
1993	558,785	-0.18	38.12	106	12,656
1994	544,461	-2.56	60.82	170	11,507
1995	556,831	2.27	59.92	290	9,723
1996	560,184	0.6	99.87	476.5	15,229
1997	590,663	5.44	50.04	504.25	17,818
1998	585,819	-0.82	35.78	564.5	14,853

Sources: Asdrubal Baptista, *Bases Cuantitativas de la Economia Venezolana, 1830–1995* (Caracas: Fundacion Polar, 1997); IESA (www.iesa.edu.ve/scripts/macroeconomia); and authors' calculations of GDP increase and the inflation rate for selected years.
* Annual average.
** At the end of December.

TABLE 2. WORK FORCE 1979–1998

Year	EAP	Unemployment (% EAP)	Formal Sector Public % employed	Formal Sector Private % employed	Informal Sector % employed
1983	5407292	10.3	22.67	36.03	41.3
1984	5716207	13.4	21.78	36.42	41.8
1985	5915573	12.1	20.18	39.52	40.3
1986	6107115	10.3	19.38	39.12	41.5
1987	6321344	8.5	18.86	42.44	38.7
1988	6572049	6.9	18.71	43.19	38.1
1989	6900588	9.6	19.68	40.62	39.7
1990	7154622	9.9	19.85	38.65	41.5
1991	7417929	8.7	19.07	40.43	40.5
1992	7537817	7.1	18.05	42.35	39.6
1993	7546241	6.3	16.8	42.6	40.6
1994	8025928	8.46	16.4	34.29	49.31
1995	8608653	10.22	17.57	33.99	48.44
1996	9024627	12.43	17.13	34.24	48.63
1997	9507125	10.65	16.96	35.57	47.47
1998	9940299	11.01	15.62	34.40	49.98

Source: IESA and authors' calculations for selected percentages.

TABLE 3. EARNINGS OF THE WORK FORCE AND INCOME DISTRIBUTION 1979–1997

Year	Real Annual Income (Bs. 1984)	Income Distribution The Poorest 5% (in Percentage) (1)	Income Distribution The Richest 5% (in Percentage) (2)	Income Distribution Ratio: 1 and 2
1979	42,162	0.62	25.78	41.58
1980	39,051	0.65	24.89	38.29
1981	36,300	0.67	24.26	36.2
1982	33,333	0.71	25.16	35.43
1983	33,192	0.65	26.01	40.01
1984	29,009	0.67	26.19	39.08
1985	28,814	0.63	27.49	43.63
1986	26,811	0.64	27.39	42.79
1987	26,924	0.65	27.71	42.63
1988	25,008	0.69	27.36	39.65
1989	19,630	0.67	27.11	40.46
1990	19,518	0.66	26.02	39.42
1991	20,835	0.61	23.65	38.77
1992	22,019	0.67	26.65	39.77
1993	20,636	0.74	26.64	36
1994	17,866	0.66	28.08	42.45
1995	16,868	0.64	27.01	42.2
1996	14,377	0.57	27.58	48.56
1997	15,299	0.53	28.15	53.11

Sources: Asdrubal Baptista, *Bases Cuantitativas de la Economia Venezolana 1830–1995* (Caracas: Fundacion Polar, 1997); and authors' calculations of the ratio between 1 and 2.

As table 4 shows, this decrease in income was accompanied by a decrease in real social spending, which eroded living standards even more. A state that for nearly a century played a central role in income distribution, funded principally by oil rents, reduced this role, principally in education and health, during the years of the most vigorous implementation of adjustment policies. This reduction made it particularly difficult to reverse the increase in extreme poverty—especially for a growing population. Although not reflected in these numbers, furthermore, the efficiency of state spending also decreased.

The fall in state spending and efficiency, along with population growth and income deterioration, led to sustained increases in both poverty and extreme poverty—particularly during the first year of each adjustment policy. Table 5 defines "households in poverty" as those with per capita family incomes less than double of the cost of the "basic food basket," which is the minimum daily nutrition requirements, and "extreme poverty" as those with per capita family incomes less than the cost of the basic food basket. Based on these definitions, the rates of both poverty and extreme poverty at the end of the 1990s were almost three times their levels at the beginning of the 1980s. Nearly half of all Venezuelan families are poor, and more than a quarter are desperately poor.

TABLE 4. REAL SOCIAL SPENDING (BASE YEAR: 1984) IN MILLIONS OF BS. 1979–1998

Year	Education	Health	Total Social *
1979	16062.34	5230.1	28958.39
1980	15446.57	5702.34	35950.82
1981	19178.86	6128.23	37152.49
1982	17366.44	5277.28	32064.01
1983	16721.77	4721.34	28568
1984	15701.1	5188.4	28413.4
1985	15246.67	5909.9	31018.77
1986	13720.67	6388.34	29227.86
1987	15261.2	6235.83	31297.36
1988	12064.91	5599.36	25354.84
1989	10634.98	4311.55	22869.31
1990	11203.29	5415.77	27772.05
1991	12450.47	5800.05	35269.6
1992	14432.62	7261.76	37541.15
1993	11947.69	4699.53	28136.26
1994	11524.16	3813.45	24426.58
1995	10002.72	3441.03	24693.77
1996	7309.42	2661.04	24460.91
1997	10321.71	4585.02	29686.7
1998	11055.33	4870.05	29248.08

Source: Eleonora Mandato, *El Gaso Social en Venezuela durante el Siglo XX* (Caracas: Impregraf, 1998).
* In addition to education and health, total social spending includes housing, urban development, social security, social development, culture and social communication, and science and technology.

TABLE 5. HOUSEHOLDS IN POVERTY 1980–1997

YEAR	NUMBER OF HOUSEHOLDS	% OF HOUSEHOLDS IN POVERTY	% OF HOUSEHOLDS IN EXTREME POVERTY
1980	2806679	17.65	9.06
1981	2880084	22.82	10.71
1982	3019932	25.65	12.14
1983	3130682	32.65	14.95
1984	3183339	37.58	18.9
1985	3211477	34.77	16.6
1986	3412139	38.88	17.67
1987	3541504	38.84	16.61
1988	3659369	39.96	16.77
1989	3821954	44.44	20.07
1990	3859923	41.48	18.62
1991	3914165	35.37	16.01
1992	4032402	37.75	15.52
1993	4190519	41.37	16.81
1994	4396784	53.65	27.52
1995	4396354	48.2	22.95
1996	4549363	61.37	35.39
1997	4,468,445	48.33	27.66

Source: IESA 2001.

The *Caracazo* and Forms, Nature, and Motivations of Popular Protest

Venezuela's precipitous socioeconomic decline led first to the erosion of the political and institutional system established upon the 1958 democratic transition, and then, at the end of the twentieth century, to its complete overhaul. Institutionalized in the 1961 constitution, Venezuelan democracy was born in 1958 by a set of agreements, among which the "Pact of Punto Fijo" was the most important. This was an agreement signed by the major parties to share power, and it led to a successful two-party system that eventually gained control over all key instruments and institutions of political life. Oil earnings and the defeat of the leftist guerrillas buoyed this arrangement up through the 1970s. At the end of that decade, though, corruption, inefficiency, and stifling party controls led to widespread discontent. The ensuing political upheaval, which has yet to end, has been fueled in part by an increase in violence, both in daily life and in the forms of popular protest.

The most dramatic event of the violent protest cycle developing since the 1980s occurred on February 27, 1989, and the following days. The popular revolt broke out throughout Venezuela, and escalated quickly. The capital as well as most main cities were engulfed in shooting, barricades, road closures, vehicle burning, property destruction, and widespread looting. The revolt lasted five days in Caracas and slightly less in the rest of the country. The cost in material and human losses was very high; the deaths, numbering almost four hundred, were largely of poor residents in the capital.

This unusual and unexpected outbreak of violence has given rise to an impressive output from scholars seeking to understand it. But this literature is focused more on explaining the disturbance's causes than the violent nature of the revolt itself. We argue that these exceptional violent features of the *Caracazo* were due principally to the institutional weaknesses of Venezuelan democracy at the time. After reviewing some conceptual interpretations of uprisings of this nature, we describe in some detail the event in order to support our argument.

In its forms of protest and the predominantly violent nature of the collective actions that took place, the *Caracazo* is reminiscent of the popular uprisings in some Latin American cities in the nineteenth century[9] and also the notorious food riots suffered by European societies during the centuries of transition to modernity: barricades, burnings, stonings, the occupation of streets and premises, looting with proceeds sometimes shared out, sometimes not.[10] According to some of the literature on urban uprisings, actions of the type carried out during the *Caracazo* are characteristic of premodern societies, since in modern societies social unrest is channeled through organized actors using a repertoire of forms of protest predominantly peaceful or conventional in nature, though occasionally confrontational in special circumstances.[11]

Observing the fact that violent forms of protest have grown throughout the world in the last two decades, John Walton and David Seddon have constructed an analogy between the European transitions to modernity and the present situation of many Third World countries. They argue that the latter are going through a societal transition characterized by the passage from paternalist modernization, which in Latin America was promoted by a pro-development populist state, to imposed neoliberalism, led by the international financial agencies.[12] The popular sectors of these societies, like the poor in England in the seventeenth and eighteenth centuries, are seen as having developed a *moral economy* during the modern paternalist phase—that is, a moral code by which they expected to be tied in with the economy, the government, and the wealthy. With this code, the poor feel that they have a right to be protected by the state from the market's rigors and vicissitudes and to be able to obtain at least the minimum resources necessary for survival. Thus, the similarity between past and present forms of protest can be attributed to the fact that when the authorities replace paternalism with laissez-faire, they are seen to betray their moral "agreement" with the poor.

However, authors such as Eckstein acknowledge that uprisings such as the *Caracazo* are shaped by other historical, political, and institutional factors.[13] Piven and Cloward's interpretation of "disruptive action" is particularly useful in this regard. They maintain that disruption of everyday life was practically the only instrument the poor had to pressure the authorities, and that this "is a product of the terrible hardships which they suffer . . . in times of breakdown and stress."[14]

Although it is difficult to anticipate when such action might arise, these authors regard the institutional context as being crucial for an understanding of where such action begins, why some forms of action prevail over others, and why protest can be accompanied by varying degrees of violence. This section, while recognizing that the popular uprising of February 1989 was prompted by international neoliberalism, will show how the reaction of Venezuelan society was influenced, primarily, not by a premodern characteristic, but by its history of protest and the weakness of its institutions.

During the weekend of February 25–26 in 1989, an increase of 100 percent in gasoline prices came into force throughout the country. This increase, part of the macroeconomic adjustment program announced on February 16 by Pérez's government, led to an increase in public transport fares. In an accord with the National Transport Federation (*Fedetransporte*), the Ministry of Transport and Communications (MTC) agreed to a 30 percent rise in public transport fares. However, the Union of Taxis and Minibuses, which was affiliated with the federation, expressed its disagreement with the increase, and on February 27 its president implied that the union would not make its members comply with it.[15]

Protests began around 6:00 A.M. on the morning of February 27 at key points on the capital's public transport system. At the Nuevo Circo bus terminal, the main intercity transportation hub, passengers resisted when public transport drivers attempted to charge fares in excess of the official increase.[16] Similar protests against the fare increase began early that morning in at least eleven other cities around the country, and in at least four more by afternoon. The eye of the gathering storm, however, was Caracas. Shortly after 6:00 A.M., university students occupied Nuevo Circo, whose employees and vendors supported the occupation. As terminal authorities awaited instructions from the MTC, students organized a sit-down to block the terminal's entry road, held up the documents showing the official fares, and denounced the flagrant breach of them. The drivers claimed that they were only following orders from their bosses at the Union of Taxis and Minibuses not to comply with the official 30 percent increase.[17] After the Nuevo Circo throng felt that it had sufficient strength, it spread out to the city's main centers, where, shouting slogans condemning the price increases and Pérez's general economic measures,[18] it built barricades to block off the city's main traffic arteries. After midday another growing crowd gathered in front of the Universidad Central de Venezuela (UCV), exhorting UCV students to join the protest.[19] Around 5:00 P.M., the Metropolitan Police (PM) finally came to confront the students.

At the Francisco Fajardo highway, the crowd blocked each intersection with branches, empty bottle crates, and other objects. It stopped passing trucks thought to be carrying foodstuffs, nonviolently detained the drivers, and distributed the cargo. The PM eventually arrived but had orders to take no action. Also joining into the protests were the city's thousands of motorcycle couriers,[20] who ferried around blockaders, spread news of demonstrations, warned of approaching police patrols, and provided cover on corners and side streets. The Caracas metro shut down at nightfall, and the streets swelled with the thousands of people forced to find their way home. The growing crowds that took to the streets on their journeys home became aware of the size of the protest that was unfolding. Meanwhile, a spillover of people from the Nuevo Circo protest had taken over a major intersection near the headquarters of the Federal District fire department, where they set fire to a bus and prevented firefighters from approaching. Other fires were set at nearby junctions. At every point, men, women, children, and elderly people were shouting protests against Pérez's economic measures. The PM arrived at many areas, firing shots into the air, and late in the afternoon a female UCV student died from a shotgun pellet fired by a policeman in a Central Park building.[21] By 6:00 P.M. the combination of blockades of key arteries, student demonstrations, looting, and the paralysis of public transport together threw the city into chaos.[22]

The same pattern of events unfolded in the towns of Caracas's seaboard and in neighboring Miranda state. Protests paralyzed the country's main port, La Guaira, for days. In Catia La Mar an angry crowd laid huge tires across one of the main avenues, cutting off surrounding slum areas and many towns on Caracas's seaboard. In the bedroom community of Guarenas there were already arson and looting by 7:30 A.M. on February 27.[23] Tension had been rising in Guarenas since the previous weekend, as residents anticipated that the public transport operators would flout the official fare increases, but the government took no precautionary measures. When hundreds of National Guard troops arrived on the morning of the 27th—delayed by huge traffic jams—the city was enveloped by violent protest unsuccessfully contained by a handful of overwhelmed policemen.[24] All commercial premises, police posts, and the transport terminal were subsequently destroyed.[25] This revolt was repeated in cities around the country, such as Barquisimeto, one of Venezuela's most populous: it began with student protests against the increase in student fares, and by public transport users in general, which quickly turned violent and spread throughout the city. But unlike in Caracas, at midday the state governor called out the National Guard. The president attended an afternoon meeting of businessmen in that city, but remained unaware of what was happening or attributed little importance to it.

Looting in the capital and other cities intensified after dusk on the 27th and continued the following day, with crowds ransacking some of the largest downtown department stores.[26] In the early hours the army was ordered to take control of the city,[27] but by then the rebellion had spread to more cities. In Caracas, on the 28th the main avenues were taken over by hundreds of demonstrators, smashing shop windows and doors and seizing everything they could lay their hands on. Among the slogans shouted and scrawled on walls were "The people are hungry," "The people are angry," and "No more deception." Banners were waved and the national anthem sung as people burst into shops, while crowds outside cut off entry routes to the city by lighting huge bonfires in the middle of the main avenues. Particularly vicious attacks were carried out against shops owned by Chinese, Lebanese, and Portuguese immigrants, on the grounds that they caused shortages by hoarding.[28] Armed groups, some in police uniforms with their faces covered by handkerchiefs, reportedly arrived in trucks to take away the entire stocks of shops. Along with food stores, also ransacked were hardware, clothing, and other shops. In some neighborhoods not a single shop escaped destruction, with even their roll-up metal doors ripped apart. Inmates rioted in city prisons, while mental patients from some hospitals were let out. In the south of the city the police used extensive force and the army fired light automatic rifles, a weapon designed for warfare. But officers held back in other areas, in some cases actually siding with or joining in with the people. In one neighborhood, the PM allowed women and children to loot shops while men remained behind barricades.[29]

The situation was very similar in the suburbs and in practically all sizable cities. In Barinas, for example, the two municipal markets were attacked by people protesting the high cost of living and the absence of consumer protections. Protest began with university students setting fire to a bakery, later spreading to residential areas, with an unsuccessful attempt to set fire to a building occupied by AD's Sectional Executive Committee (CES).[30] In Maracaibo, the country's second largest city, housewives, students, workers, and street vendors protested the high cost of living, mobs looted markets and trucks, and public transport drivers stopped work. In Barcelona, a state capital in the country's east, intense disturbances and looting in the morning eased off toward afternoon. But in Puerto La Cruz, the state's tourism capital, disturbances and looting persisted throughout the day and the city had to be taken over by the National Guard. The area's public transport operators introduced a 100 percent fare increase, but after talks regional authorities persuaded them to adhere to the official 30 percent rise.

The government addressed the population for the first time shortly after midday when the interior minister appealed for calm and declared, obviously too late, that violence would not be tolerated. This appeal had little effect, especially because the minister had a fainting attack before he could finish, causing the address to be suspended and attempted again two hours later without a clear explanation for the hitch. Needless to say, this only increased political uncertainty. But later, shortly before 6:00 P.M., President Pérez, accompanied by his cabinet, came on the air to declare the suspension of a raft of constitutional guarantees and the imposition of a curfew from 6:00 P.M. to 6:00 A.M.

This curfew, aided by a brutal wave of repression, especially in Caracas's poor neighborhoods, dampened the violence. In their desperate attempt to control the situation, the army and various police forces vented their anger on civilians. On March 1, for example, the army killed more than twenty people when it fired on a crowd in the Petare area. Looting and shooting continued in several parts of Caracas, but was being carried out by criminal gangs, often armed, rather than by large mobs.[31] In the sprawling poor areas in the west of the city, for instance, the army battled snipers on the rooftops of working-class apartment buildings.[32] The soldiers, most of them inexperienced youths aged around eighteen, fired at the buildings with light automatic rifles, destroying apartments and killing unarmed civilians.[33] The nights of March 1–2 and 2–3 were a nightmare in Caracas's poor neighborhoods. There were police raids on homes, shoot-outs, incendiary attacks, and corpses lying in the streets at the end of each curfew.

In other cities the curfew and militarization brought about a restoration of calm. On the first day there were still pockets of unrest in certain cities, and all commercial activities, schools, and transport remained halted. Signs of normality started to appear on March 3, with hawkers going back on to the street and businesses reopening. In Caracas the cemeteries were crowded with people seeking to bury their dead,[34] and the press continued to publish reports of shoot-outs between snipers, soldiers, and police in western districts of the city. But looting had ceased, and in some cities the curfew was reduced or removed on the night of March 3.[35]

When the dust settled, attempts were made to calculate the toll of dead and wounded, as well as of material losses, but to date the figures remain incomplete and unreliable. The minister of defense soon issued a death toll of 277,[36] but later studies have come up with higher figures. Lists at the Caracas mortuary of Bello Monte, where by law all those who had died in the streets and hospitals of the capital during those days had to be taken, revealed a total of 310 deaths.[37] But this and other estimates do not include deaths in the country's other cities or the corpses not taken to the mortuary. In 1992 a list of 396 dead was drawn up by two human rights organizations, the Network of Support for Justice and Peace, and the Committee of Families of the Victims of February–March 1989 (COFAVIC). Based on information supplied by the families of those who had died or disappeared, this count is the one we consider to be the most accurate.[38]

In other reports, Bello Monte's forensic director said that the first two corpses arrived there at 10:00 P.M. on February 27, which is fairly late, considering that the uprising began before 6:00 A.M. Staff at various health clinics added that very few corpses were brought in that day, the majority of admissions being for wounds sustained during looting. On the other hand, a then-member of Pérez's cabinet stated that on the morning of the 28th they were given a total of 63 fatalities, which would represent 15.9 percent of the number of deaths in the COFAVIC figure.[39] Along with studies of the victims' personal details and of the anatomical location of the firearm wounds, these reports reveal that most deaths occurred after the 28th and that the security forces were responsible for most of them. The majority of victims appeared to be unarmed civilians who were on the streets during the curfew. Eighty-seven percent of the fatalities were men, their average age was twenty-seven, and 83 percent had no previous criminal record[40]; 85.8 percent of the deaths were caused by firearms and 11.9 percent by unrecorded causes. Of 266 corpses with firearm wounds, more than 60 percent died from shots either to the thorax (35.71 percent) or the head (29.32 percent), with 211 having only one shot wound (79.2 percent) and 39 having two (14.66 percent). As for the number of wounded, there are only rough approximations. On March 4 the government reported 1,009 wounded by firearms, 218 by knives or other sharp instruments, and 604 cut by glass.[41] But the casualty hospital in the east of Caracas reported that it alone had treated 575 wounded.[42]

The number of arrests during the *Caracazo* ran into the thousands, and lengthy research would be needed to obtain reliable figures, but by March 1 the press reported that in most cities the number of arrests ranged from one hundred to nearly two thousand.[43] According to a list drawn up by the students' Federation of University Unions, more than a hundred students were arrested in different operations. Some of those detained by the DISIP (the Office of Intelligence and Prevention Services) had been beaten with baseball bats and pieces of metal piping during interrogations.[44] As for material losses, the official inventory for the Caracas metropolitan area recorded the destruction of 900 general stores, 131 grocery shops, 60 supermarkets, 95 hardware shops, 72 stationers, and 850 other assorted stores. In the states of Miranda (excluding the metropolitan area of Caracas), Aragua, and Carabobo, 784 shops were destroyed. The chamber of insurers calculated losses to be in excess of 3 billion bolívares—but only of businesses that were insured. Three-quarters of affected businesses were independent merchants serving poor neighborhoods, and about 35 percent of supermarkets belonging to chains in the metropolitan area were affected.[45]

Despite its extreme violence, the *Caracazo* was in part the culmination of building pressures. In the five years previous to the riots there had been a growth in unconventional forms of protest that were confrontational and violent in nature. Strikes, occupations, road blockades, and other disturbances were increasingly being used by social sectors who were not previously active in the political system: the student movement, neighborhood organizations, street vendors, and civil servant unions in the education, public health, and judiciary sectors. These actors used visibility to make up for the inadequacy of the political parties and the trade unions as structures of representation and mediation in a time of prolonged economic recession, unemployment, and decline in living conditions.[46] These forms of protest reached extremes of "anti-institutionality" with the *Caracazo*, but in fact, emerging actors from the popular sector had already been making them a regular activity.[47]

In the case of the *Caracazo*, however, the disruptive action reached a magnitude, violence, and extent that could not be compared with any previous protest. Most significantly, it bears scant relation to the wave of protests that took place in Venezuela between December 18, 1935, and February 14, 1936, when the death of the dictator Juan Vincente Gómez created an unprecedented configuration of political opportunities, with a temporary power vacuum during that short period suddenly and unexpectedly propelling crowds into the streets. Shops were looted at some points in the nineteenth century, but most looting was carried out on the properties of politicians who had fallen from favor. These actions were tolerated, and even up to a point approved, by the country's emerging leader, General Eleazar López Contreras. And as López strengthened his grip on power, the masses became better organized, focusing their demands on political modernization. But, in general, they responded with violence only when they were violently repressed.[48]

From a comparative standpoint, there are both similarities and differences between this upheaval and the *Caracazo*. In 1935 there was no uncertainty about who was in charge. In 1989, in contrast, even though Pérez had just been elected with a big majority, the violence's first few days were marked by an absence of authority in its various forms: the civil servants responsible for enforcing the agreements with *Fedetransporte* were not visible, and most police forces either did not intervene during the early protests or else maintained that they had orders not to do so. But the most surprising absence—and the most significant in determining the form and scale of the uprising itself—was that of the national government itself, which did not make an appearance until after 1:00 P.M. on February 28.

There is no shortage of testimonies claiming ignorance by the national government of the events unfolding on February 27. Statements made both by ex-president Pérez and by senior members of his government, including the minister of defense, suggest that the government leaders were not ignorant of the situation, but rather did not realize its gravity.[49] Also, the senior leaders of the political parties AD and COPEI claim not to have received any information from the government until the night of the 27th. The trade union leadership, like that of the dominant parties, was also notable by its absence from the streets and even appeared bewildered by what was happening.[50] What country were they living in? Institutionality broke down, opening the way for an unchecked popular rebellion. The government's confusion was subsequently increased by the police and military's violent and extrainstitutional repression, particularly in the capital.

The *Caracazo* was therefore a massive and violent protest carried out by a society which did not have adequate channels for making itself heard by those in power. When it sought to give outward expression to its sense of malaise at the first concrete expression of the macroeconomic package, namely the increase in public transport fares, it found itself in a public area that was totally lacking in controls. As a result the masses turned on the shops, as they had always done in the past when there was a vacuum of authority. They could not head for the houses of overthrown politicians, but surely would have done so if a coup d'état had taken place. But the Armed Forces, as represented by the minister of defense and the High Command, remained loyal to the Pérez regime, thus enabling him to survive. To sum up, the *Caracazo* could have been motivated, as Piven and Cloward assert, by the extreme hardship suffered by the poor, which could be indirectly attributed, according to Walton and Seddon, to the international forces of neoliberalism, but the huge disruption to everyday life in Venezuela which occurred during those days was due primarily to the weakness of the institutions which had been designed to contain and regulate it.

Protest in the 1990s: Violence as a Norm

Even before the Lusinchi years, state and society relations, controlled by the parties, unions, and other associations based on the pacts of the 1958 transition to democracy, became less and less effective. Widespread questioning of the parties, charges of corruption against public officials, and criticisms of the state's role all multiplied, as did the street protests organized by various actors independent of established institutions. Starting with Pérez's government, confrontational and violent mobilizations became more and more visible. "Confrontational" describes protests that, without causing harm to property or persons, generate tensions and threats to their targets and to nonparticipants. Such protests often involved illegal actions, such as street closings, takeovers of public buildings, or gatherings without permits (see tables 6 and 7). These types of protest proliferated during the Pérez and Caldera administrations and continue up until the present. In addition, the violent protests called "disturbances"—those that involve or result in damage to property and/or physical harm to persons—comprised about a third of all protests reported by the major national daily newspaper, El Nacional, during these years. During the Herrera Campíns and Lusinchi years, in contrast, they did not even account for a tenth of all protests.

Although comparative statistics with those previous ten years are not available, the number of protests steadily grew since 1980, and many of them were confrontational and violent.[51] Between October 1989 and September 1994—the Pérez years and the first Caldera months—the organization Provea documented a total of 958 street closings and 67 sackings and disturbances, falling to 796 street closings and 29 sackings and disturbances in the following five years. The significant change in the number, forms, and nature of popular protest, along with the appearance of the kinds of protesters rarely seen before, such as retirees and street vendors, promoted a turbulent atmosphere and showed how violent opposition to macroeconomic policies led to change in the political order.[52] Begun in the Lusinchi years, this cycle was turned into a part of daily life in the country's urban centers by the Caracazo. Since Chávez's resounding 1998 presidential election victory, popular mobilization and protest has continued, but decreased in violence. This is mainly due to a change in the police force's behavior—they have refrained from using violence in repressing. Despite a new constitution and the collapse of the traditional parties, combined with the absence until now of both new political organizations and strong institutions such as the trade unions and the judiciary,

TABLE 6. DIFFERENT FORMS OF PROTEST IN VENEZUELA (AS REPORTED BY *EL NACIONAL*) 1985–1999

YEAR	MARCHES	STREET CLOSINGS	TAKEOVERS AND INVASIONS	DISTURBANCES	FIRES	SACKINGS
1985	12	1	16	6	3	0
1986	10	2	8	4	1	0
1987	21	3	2	27	16	6
1988	13	5	6	16	4	3
1989	24	13	18	39	11	26
1990	22	4	4	29	7	7
1991	11	3	3	29	16	4
1992	10	12	10	44	18	10
1993	21	13	10	50	26	16
1994	25	30	21	61	29	13
1995	27	15	14	42	18	9
1996	28	29	17	69	25	16
1997	21	18	7	21	12	1
1998	23	20	1	18	0	0
1999	38	56	26	49	8	5
Total	305	224	163	504	194	116

Source: Base de Datos El Bravo Pueblo, 2000.

TABLE 7. TYPES OF POPULAR PROTEST (AS REPORTED BY *EL NACIONAL*) 1985–1999

YEAR	CONVENTIONAL	CONFRONTATIONAL	VIOLENT	TOTAL
1985	206	41	15	262
1986	51	16	3	70
1987	36	15	32	83
1988	70	17	16	103
1989	75	85	53	213
1990	39	54	30	123
1991	8	36	31	75
1992	13	56	64	133
1993	52	64	58	174
1994	49	65	73	187
1995	64	62	63	189
1996	53	122	98	273
1997	81	44	50	175
1998	77	67	22	166
1999	43	239	72	354

Source: Base de Datos El Bravo Pueblo, 2000.

violent protest remains as a possible form of expression of the claims and aspirations of the popular sectors within the current process of constructing a new sociopolitical project. Even though violent protest has diminished, daily violence continues at same high levels that it reached after the *Caracazo.*

The database *El Bravo Pueblo* (the brave or angry people) registered for the last three governments more than thirty motivations of protests, which can be divided into three types. First, there is a group of protests motivated by *the lack or the deterioration of public services.* This group includes protests generated by users of those services as well as those organized by workers in those services. Second is the group of protests whose objective is *to halt or at least slow down the fall in income of wage earners,* mainly in the public sector. The third group, which is smaller but no less important, is of protests motivated by *civil and human rights.*

The first group includes protests motivated by the lack of water supply, by the deterioration of the hospital, health, and education infrastructures, by the lack of material in health and school facilities, as well as increases in the costs of electricity, public transportation, gasoline, food, and medicine. Also included in this category are protests against insecurity in the streets and workplace. These protests expressed the public's reaction to the shrinking of public services caused by the fiscal crisis and by policies of reducing state activity and spending (see table 4). In fact, protests against fare increases—by users in general and by students in particular—constituted the single biggest motive recorded in the database. During the Lusinchi government, students attained a "preferential student fare," a reduced fare for students in public transport regarded at the time by the student movement as a victory against the neoliberal policies then getting under way.[53] For the lowest-income sectors, in addition, the cost of transport to get to work constituted a big part of the family budget. Amid the deterioration in spending power, fares became a highly sensitive issue for them, rapidly provoking rejection of each increase. The *Caracazo,* catalyzed by a fare increase, showed how serious this issue truly was.

The second kind of protests includes those advocating wage increases for workers, principally in the public sector. Among those were mobilizations against a lack of or reductions in the payment of wages, demanding salary increases, renewing collective labor agreements (*contratos colectivos de trabajo*), and complaining about violations of existing contractual arrangements. They also included demands for a larger budget for a state sector or institution, which generally included demands for civil servant salary increases, or to avoid a budget cut, as well as protests against delays in the payment of pensions and social security or for the increase of such payments to match the minimum wage. These protests highlighted the efforts by unions and worker organizations to resist the consequences of the fiscal crisis on remuneration, deepened by the neoliberal macroeconomic policies of the time.

Mobilization to demand an increase in wages was not a new phenomenon. It has characterized Venezuelan protest for the entire democratic period.[54] However, what was now changing was an increase in its sheer numbers, its concentration in the public sector, and its wide social involvement, including retirees, pensioners, and petroleum workers. The other two groups lacked press coverage before 1989, while the latter began to mobilize during the Lusinchi government, with a strike in 1988, after a long period without belligerent activity. The unprecedented violence characterizing these protests stemmed in part from a shift in focus from demands for wage improvements to a desperate struggle to slow down deterioration in real income and spending power amid high inflation (see table 1). While the protests did not achieve a return of income to levels prior to the era's double-digit inflation, they nevertheless did contribute, at least in some sectors, to a slowdown in the fall.

The third kind of interests expressed through popular protest during these years were about civil and human rights, often geared toward the reconstruction of "citizenship." Standing out in this kind of protest were those against police repression and violence, especially when it led to civilian and student deaths. Along with protests generated by the increase in transportation fares, this kind was the most reported by *El Nacional.* Demand for respect for human rights had been a growing part of collective action in Venezuela for many years, prompted by a gradual weakening of protections and by egregious cases of abuse, such as the killing of fourteen fishermen in the 1988 Massacre of El Amparo and the extreme levels of prison overcrowding and violence. The hundreds of popular manifestations against such abuses often targeted particular police agencies. Other protests in this category were those for a right to a "dignified life," which became a slogan popular among prisoners, street vendors, and other socially marginalized people. Attention to the administration of justice spurred protests to demand judicial reforms, to reject judicial decisions regarded as arbitrary, and to prosecute corrupt judges. There were also protests for the democratization of the electoral system, against electoral frauds, for the democratization of trade unions, and against the suspension of constitutional guarantees.

Through these protests, the country's popular sectors expressed their rejection of adjustment policies amid a crisis for the parties and institutions. The largest of the protests were without a doubt those during the Pérez government, when student, union, business, and even municipal and regional authorities came to organize and support civil stoppages against adjustment policies. Key characteristics of the protests of this period were their direct confrontation with the state, their predominance in the public sector, and their success in helping to bring an end to orthodox adjustments in the country. More significantly, the protests in this period also provide insight into "the agenda of the poor." They expressed not only hopes frustrated and cut short from the previous phase of modernization, but put the elite on notice to take them into consideration when designing and implementing public policy.

NOTES

1. Karl, "The Venezuelan Petro-State."
2. Naím, *Paper Tigers and Minotaurs.*
3. Baptista, "El desarrollo de Venezuela visto desde la economía política," p. 143.
4. Ibid., p. 92.
5. Lusinchi, "Un nuevo programa económico," pp. 141–55.
6. López Maya and Lander, "La transformación de una sociedad petrolera-rentista."
7. López Maya, "Carlos Andrés Pérez, 1989–1993," p. 289.
8. Valecillos, *El Readjuste Neoliberal en Venezuela,* p. 124.
9. Arrom and Ortoll, *Riots in the Cities.*
10. Rudé, *The Crowd in History;* Thompson, *Customs in Common.*
11. Hobsbawm, *Primitive Rebels.*
12. Walton and Seddon, *Free Markets and Food Riots.*
13. Eckstein, "Popular Power and Protest in Latin America," pp. 1–60.
14. Cloward and Piven, *Poor People's Movements,* p. 26–27.
15. *El Nacional,* February 28, 1989, p. C2.
16. *El Universal,* February 28, 1989, pp. 1–26.
17. *El Nacional,* February 28, 1989, p. C2.
18. Ojeda, "Saqueos y Barricadas," pp. 25–27
19. *El Universal,* February 28, 1989, pp. 1–26
20. Ojeda, "Saqueos y Barricadas," pp. 25–27; *El Nacional,* February 21, 1999.
21. Reinoso, "Destino: La Morgue," p. 74.
22. Testimonies given at the 1999 forum *A Diez Años de los Sucesos del 27 de Febrero de 1989* (hereafter Forum 1999) confirm that the student demonstrations in the city began early, particularly in high schools, technical schools, and university institutes (Bohórquez, informal conversation at Forum 1999). These demonstrations brought on to the streets a social group that was fully experienced in such street action.
23. Reports from Gauarenas by a reporter from *El Diario de Caracas.* What follows consists of information taken from Escobar, "Reporteros de Guerra," pp. 15–17, and the testimony of a Guarenas resident, Pedro Parés, at Forum 1999.
24. Galué García, "A merced de los Insurrectos," pp. 23–25.
25. *El Nacional,* March 2, 1989, pp. 4–14.
26. See Ojeda, "Beirut en Caracas," pp. 33–35; Galué García, "A merced de los Insurrectos," pp. 23–25; Araujo, "Un Río de Balas Cruzó Petare," p. 81.
27. Galué García, "A merced de los Insurrectos," pp. 23–25.
28. Coronil and Skurski, "Dismembering and Remembering the Nation," p. 315.
29. Ojeda, "Beirut en Caracas," pp. 33–35; Giusti, "El día que bajaron los cerros," pp. 36–38.
30. *El Universal,* March 1, 1989, pp. 4–20.
31. *El Universal,* February 2, 1989; Kiko, account given to Forum 1999.
32. *El Nacional,* March 2, 1989.
33. Araujo, "Un Río de Balas Cruzó Petare," pp. 81–83.
34. Ojeda, "Entre lluvia y basura," pp. 81–84.
35. *El Nacional,* March 3, 1989; *El Universal,* March 4, 1989.
36. Giusti, "La Muerte de la Quietud."
37. Briceño-León, "Contabilidad de la Muerte," p. 103.
38. See Ochoa Antich, *Los Golpes de Febrero,* pp. 154–389.
39. Blanco, statement at Forum 1999.
40. Briceño-León, "Contabilidad de la Muerte," p. 103.
41. *El Nacional,* March 3, 1989.

42. *El Nacional,* March 16, 1989, p. C6.
43. *El Universal,* March 2, 1989, pp. 2–12; *El Nacional,* March 2 and March 3, 1989.
44. *El Nacional,* July 3, 1989, p. D17.
45. *El Nacional,* March 11, 1989.
46. López Maya and Luis E. Lander, "Triunfos en tiempos de transición."
47. This assertion can be verified by consulting the database *El Bravo Pueblo* for the years 1984–1989, using the search terms "forms of action" and "nature of action."
48. Salamanca, "Protestas venezolanas en el segundo gobierno de Rafael Caldera."
49. Giusti, "Fue una explosión social," pp. 36–48. Blanco, statement at Forum 1999.
50. Carvallo and López Maya, "Crisis del sistema político venezolano," pp. 47–54.
51. Hillman, *Crisis and Transition in Venezuela.*
52. López Maya, "La protesta popular venezolana entre 1989 y 1993."
53. Stephany, "La Lucha contra el PLES."
54. Salamanca, "Protestas venezolanas en el segundo gobierno de Rafael Caldera," pp. 237–262.

BIBLIOGRAPHY

Araujo, Elizabeth. "Un Río de Balas Cruzó Petare." In AA.VV., *Cuando la Muerte Tomó las Calles,* 81ff. Caracas: Editora Ateneo de Caracas-El Nacional.

Arrom, Silvia, and Servando Ortoll. *Riots in the Cities: Popular Politics and the Urban Poor in Latin America, 1765–1910.* Wilmington, Del.: SR Books, 1996.

Baptista, Asdrubal. "El desarrollo de Venezuela visto desde la economía política." In A.A.V.V., *Apreciación del Proceso Histórico Venezolano.* Caracas: Fundación Metropolitana-Fondo Editorial Interfundaciones, 1986.

———. *Bases Cuantitativas de la Economía Venezolana 1830–1995.* Caracas: Fundación Polar, 1997.

BDEBP. Database *El Bravo Pueblo.* Caracas: Research Project Cendes-CDCH (UCV) No. 26-50-4047-97, 2000.

Briceño-León, Roberto. "Contabilidad de la Muerte." In AA.VV., *Cuando la Muerte Tomó las Calles,* 103. Caracas: Editora Ateneo de Caracas-El Nacional, 1990.

Carvallo, Gastón, and Margarita López Maya. "Crisis del sistema político venezolano." *Cuadernos del CENDES,* no. 10 (1989): 47–54.

Centro de Estudios Para La Paz. "Caracterización de las muertes violentas en Caracas 1986–1988." Caracas: Base de Datos, Universidad Central de Venezuela, 1999.

Cloward, Richard, and Francis Fox Piven. *Poor People's Movements: Why They Succeed, How They Fail.* New York: Vintage, 1977.

Cordiplan. *VII Plan de la Nación 1984–1988, Lineamientos Generales.* Caracas: state report, 1984.

Coronil, Fernando, and Julie Skurski. "Dismembering and Remembering the Nation: The Semantics of Political Violence in Venezuela." *Comparative Studies in Society and History,* 33, no. 2 (1991).

Eckstein, Susan. "Popular Power and Protest in Latin America." In *Power and Popular Protest: Latin American Social Movements,* edited by Susan Eckstein, 1–60. London: University of California Press, 1989.

Escobar, Ray. "Reporteros de Guerra." In Ediciones Centauro, *El Estallido de Febrero: Secuencia Escrita y Gráfica de Sucesos que Cambiaron la Historia de Venezuela,* 15–17. Caracas: Ediciones Centauro, 1989.

Galué García, Rafael. "Entrevista hecha por Roberto Giusti titulada 'A merced de los Insurrectos.'" In AA.VV., *Cuando la Muerte Tomó las Calles,* 23–25. Caracas: Editora Ateneo de Caracas-El Nacional, 1990.

Giusti, Roberto. "El día que bajaron los cerros." In AA.VV., *El Día que Bajaron los Cerros*, 36–38. Caracas: Editora El Nacional-Ateneo de Caracas, 1989.

———. "La Muerte de la Quietud." In AA.VV., *Cuando la Muerte Tomó las Calles*, 54–59. Caracas: Editora Ateneo de Caracas-El Nacional, 1990.

———. "Fue una explosión social." In AA.VV., *Cuando la Muerte Tomó las Calles*, 37–45. Caracas: Editora Ateneo de Caracas-El Nacional, 1990.

Hillman, Richard S. *Crisis and Transition in Venezuela*. Boulder: Lynne Rienner, 1994.

Hobsbawm, Eric J. *Primitive Rebels: Studies in Archaic Forms of Social Movements*. Manchester: Manchester University Press, 1959.

IESA. November 1999. Eonomic and social indicators from www.iesa.edu.ve/scripts/macroeconomia and www.iesa.edu.ve/macroeconomia/soc.

Karl, Terry. "The Venezuelan Petro-State and the Crisis of its Democracy." In *Venezuelan Democracy under Stress*, edited by Jennifer McCoy and Andrés Stambuli. New Brunswick, N.J.: Transaction Publishers, 1995.

Kornblith, Miriam. *Venezuela en los 90: La Crisis de la Democracia*. Caracas: Ediciones UCV- IESA, 1998.

Lander, Luis E. "La apertura petrolera en Venezuela: De la nacionalización a la privatización." In *Revista Venezolana de Economía y Ciencias Sociales*, 4, no. 1 (1998).

López Maya, Margarita. "Carlos Andrés Pérez: 1989–1993." In *Gran Enciclopedia de Venezuela*. Caracas: Editorial Globe, 1998.

———. "Formas de la protesta popular entre 1989 y 1994." *Revista Venezolana de Economía y Ciencias Sociales* 4 (October–December 1999): 11–42.

———. "La protesta popular venezolana entre 1989 y 1993 (en el umbral del neoliberalismo)." In *Lucha Popular, Democracia, Neoliberalismo: Protesta Popular en América Latina en los Años de Ajuste*, edited by Margarita López Maya. Caracas: Nueva Sociedad, 1999.

López Maya, Margarita, and Edgardo Lander. "La transformación de una sociedad petrolera-rentista: desarrollo económico y viabilidad democrática en Venezuela." In *Democracia y Reestructuración Económica en América Latina*, edited by Pilar Gaitán, et al. Bogota: IEPRI-CEREC, 1996.

López Maya, Margarita, and Luis E. Lander. "Triunfos en tiempos de transición. Actores de vocación popular en las elecciones venezolanas de 1998." *América Latina Hoy* 21 (April 1999).

López Maya, Margarita, et al. *De Punto Fijo al Pacto Social: Desarrollo y Hegemonía en Venezuela 1958–1985*. Caracas: Fondo Editorial Acta Científica Venezolana, 1989.

Lusinchi, Jaime. "Un nuevo programa económico. Segundo mensaje del presidente Lusinchi a los venezolanos." In *Jaime Lusinchi en 100 Días de Gobierno*. Caracas: Ediciones Centauro, 1984.

Mandato, Eleonora. *El Gasto Social en Venezuela durante el Siglo XX*. Caracas: Impregraf, 1998.

Naím, Moisés. *Paper Tigers and Minotaurs: The Politics of Venezuela's Economics Reforms*. Washington, D.C.: Carnegie Endowment, 1993.

Ochoa Antich, Enrique. *Los Golpes de Febrero*. Caracas: Fuentes Editores, 1992.

Ojeda, Fabricio. "Saqueos y Barricadas." In AA.VV., *El Día que Bajaron los Cerros*, 25–27. Caracas: Editora El Nacional-Ateneo de Caracas, 1989.

———. "Beirut en Caracas." In AA.VV., *El Día que Bajaron los Cerros*, 33–35. Caracas: Editora El Nacional-Ateneo de Caracas, 1989.

———. "Entre lluvia y basura." In AA.VV., *El Día que Bajaron los Cerros*, 81–84. Caracas: Editora El Nacional-Ateneo de Caracas, 1989.

Párraga, Régulo. "Noche de Terror." In AA.VV., *El Día que Bajaron los Cerros*, 61–63. Caracas: Editora El Nacional-Ateneo de Caracas, 1989.

Provea. *Situación de los derechos humanos en Venezuela, Informe* anual. Caracas: Edisil Impresos, 1989–1999.

Reinoso, Víctor Manuel. "Destino: La Morgue." In AA.VV., *Cuando la Muerte Tomó las Calles*, 74. Caracas: Editora Ateneo de Caracas-El Nacional, 1990.

Rudé, George. *The Crowd in History: A Study of Popular Disturbances in France and England*. London: Wiley, 1964.

Salamanca, Luis "Protestas venezolanas en el segundo gobierno de Rafael Caldera:1994–1997." In *Lucha Popular, Democracia, Neoliberalismo: Protesta Popular en América Latina en los Años de Ajuste*, edited by Margarita López Maya. Caracas: Nueva Sociedad, 1999.

———. "Rómulo Betancourt y la protesta de 1936." Paper delivered at the XXI LASA International Congress, Miami, March 2000.

Scott, James C. *The Moral Economy of the Peasant*. New Haven: Yale University Press, 1976.

Smith, William C., and Roberto Patricio Korzeniewicz. *Politics, Social Change and Economic Restructuring in Latin America*. Boulder: North-South Center Press, 1997.

Stallings, Barbara, and Robert Kaufman, ed. *Debt and Democracy in Latin America*. Boulder: Westview Press, 1989.

Stephany, Keta. "La Lucha contra el PLES" paper presented at the seminar La Protesta Popular Venezolana en la Era Neoliberal, Programa de Doctorado de FACES, Caracas, 1999.

Tarrow, Sidney. *Power in Movement: Social Movements, Collective Action and Politics*. New York: Cambridge University Press, 1996.

Thompson, E. P. *Customs in Common*. London: Penguin Books, 1993.

Tilly, Charles. *From Mobilization to Revolution*. Reading, Mass.: Addisson-Wesley, 1978.

Valecillos, Héctor. *El Readjuste Neoliberal en Venezuela*. Caracas: Monte Avila Editores, 1992.

Walton, John, and David Seddon. *Free Markets and Food Riots: The Politics of Global Adjustments*. Cambridge: Blackwell, 1994.

AUDIOVISUAL AND ORAL SOURCES

Blanco, Carlos (former minister of planning). Statement at forum *A Diez Años de los Sucesos del 27 de Febrero de 1989* (author notes). Caracas, March 8, 1999.

Blaser, Liliane, director. *Los Sucesos del 28 de Febrero*. Caracas: Contrain, 1990.

Camuñas, Matías, statement at forum *A Diez Años de los Sucesos del 27 de Febrero de 1989* (author notes). Caracas, March 8, 1999.

Celli, Humberto (former president of Acción Democrática). Statement at forum *A Diez Años de los Sucesos del 27 de Febrero de 1989* (author notes). Caracas, March 8, 1999.

Frasso (Francisco Solórzano) (reporter). Statement at forum *A Diez Años de los Sucesos del 27 de Febrero de 1989* (author notes). Caracas, March 10, 1999.

Parés, Pedro (journalist). Statement at forum *A Diez Años de los Sucesos del 27 de Febrero de 1989* (author notes). Caracas, March 10, 1999.

Rodríguez, Jorge (former student leader). Statement at forum *A Diez Años de los Sucesos del 27 de Febrero de 1989* (author notes). Caracas, March 9, 1999.

UCV-Kico, director. *Prohibido Olvidar*. Caracas: Universidad Central de Venezuela, 1999.

CHAPTER ELEVEN

The Clash Within

*Intrapsychically Created Enemies
and Their Roles in Ethnonationalist Conflict*

Jeffrey Murer

Introduction

This chapter will focus on the role of similarity, as opposed to the often cited role of "objective difference," in determining the level of intensity and violence in ethnic conflict. Many such conflicts are the result of severe social dislocations, triggering a psychological defense mechanism that requires the creation of an "enemy-other," which becomes the repository of collective self-loathing, rage, and anxiety. My analysis of this process is based upon Julia Kristeva's work on abjection, and Vamik Volkan's work on Chosen Traumas. The synthesis of the two approaches creates a model that suggests that when a society experiences dramatic social upheaval, it will select some part of its former collective self, cast it off, and transform this previous part of the self into an enemy-other. It is the previous intimate relationship with the newly created other that contributes to the intensity of conflict. The more intimate the relationship, the greater the level of violence will be.

This phenomenon is central to many of the conflicts in southeastern Europe and in the former Soviet Union as the end of state socialism was in fact a large-scale upheaval. That is, the transitions from the Communist regimes toward the neoliberal models as encouraged by the West wrought such social dislocation and ruptures in collective self-identity narratives as to induce a collective social trauma: a collective identity crisis. In contrast to the "Communism-as-refrigerator" argument, which suggests that the political forces of the Communist state suppressed ethnic identities and their accompanying "centuries-old" conflicts, this approach helps to demystify ethnic conflict by calling attention to the complex psychosocial dynamics that can transform ethnic identity into a collective political identity. This chapter will begin by examining the argument that conflict is based upon intractable difference. The chapter will then examine alternate theories on the creation of collective ethnic identities, positing that such identities are constantly in a state of flux and restructured under the perception of threats and in times of dramatic social dislocation. It will further argue that the end of state socialism and the associated economic and political transformation comprise as such a period. Understanding ethnic conflict as a part of a psychosocial collective defense dynamic opens the possibility for conflict amelioration that the primordialist argument closes. The final section of the chapter will explore the process of collective mourning and its potential to serve as a form of conflict amelioration.

The Clash of Civilizations

From numerous mentions on CNN, ITN, and the BBC, one could easily imagine that the wars in Croatia, Bosnia, and Kosovo were inevitable. Often depicting these conflicts as a continuation of the wars against the Ottoman invasion dating back to the fourteenth century, these broadcasts accepted the myth that the factions involved in the fighting represented primordial groups, constantly at war in the Balkans. Rather than evaluating mixed marriages between Croats and Serbs, or decades of peaceful coexistence, the narrative transmitted by various media saw such comingling of groups as the exception rather than the norm. Yet, what is at stake with such a depiction? The most dangerous repercussion of this essentialist perspective is the manner by which it obfuscates the politics of the moment. Put simply, what could possibly motivate mediation if the conflict is intractable? Similarly, the acceptance of the centuries-old hatred narrative absolves factions and their representatives from engaging in any act of conflict amelioration. Two recent works illustrate this point, Dodge Billingsley's film *Immortal Fortress* and Samuel Huntington's *The Clash of Civilizations*. Each stresses the role of objective difference in the cases they present.

Although Dodge Billingsley's *Immortal Fortress: A Look Inside Chechnya's Warrior Culture* offers excellent interviews with many of the participants of this conflict in Russia, as well as providing powerful footage from the battlefields, the narration of the film assures the viewer that the present conflict is yet another installment in a centuries-old conflict, originating in colonial wars of the eighteenth century.[1] By suggesting that the Chechens are "warriors," that they always have been and always will be, the producer of the film absolves not only the Chechens from the current situation, but also—and perhaps more importantly—the Russians. If the Chechens will always fight the Russians, and the world should expect this conflict because it is an essential one, why should anyone question the motives and actions of the Russians? Simply, this explanation suggests that the Russians are acting as we should expect them to act. Surely, this leaves everyone in a trap of ever present violence.

The most egregious proposition regarding the essentialist approach is presented in Samuel Huntington's *The Clash of Civilizations*. His central claim equates culture with civilization, and when different civilizations encounter one another the inevitable result is conflict. He states that "people divide themselves in terms of ancestry, religion, language, history, values, and customs," and that, in turn, the "most important distinctions among peoples are not ideological, political or economic, but cultural."[2] For Huntington these cultural differences represent the cleavages between civilizations, and conflict is born from the depths of these fault lines. He makes grand claims that contemporary conflicts are the result of the inability of civilizations to reconcile themselves and live in peaceful coexistence. Huntington goes on to construct six archetypical civilizations: the Western, the Orthodox Christian, the Islamic, the Indian, the Sinic/Chinese/Japanese, and the African. Yet, there are many problems with Huntington's construction. First, he mixes his definitions of culture. In his archetypes, he has two religious definitions, two ethnic distinctions in their own right, and two geographic constructions. That Africa appears as a residual category, and that Huntington obviously ignores Islam's significance in sub-Saharan Africa and within India itself, is surely not the least of the problems with this typology.

Huntington explains conflict in Nigeria as a tripartite split between Christianity, Islam, and traditional religions; in the Sudan it is Islam and Christianity, and in India Islam and Hinduism.[3] Simply, these examples all point to religious differences. Huntington claims that "religion is the central defining characteristic of civilization."[4] He states that "races" may be divided by civilization, while religion can unite races into a single civilization. However, the war in the Sudan, for example, has been explained at various times as an ideological struggle between Marxists and non-Marxists, between modernization forces and advocates of traditionalism, and between the geographic distinctions of the arid lowlands in the north and the savannas and rainforests of the south. To miss the larger complexities of these conflicts is to deny the potential for any type of multiethnic/multireligious society. This is akin to suggesting that the troubles in Northern Ireland are only about Catholicism versus Protestantism.

Huntington also points to the breakup of the former Soviet Union as providing numerous examples of these "fault-line" conflicts. Yet, many of these conflicts pose problems for Huntington's archetypes. Should the conflict between Azerbaijan and Armenia be framed as Islam versus Orthodoxy? How should we understand the civil conflict in South Ossetia—as internal struggle within Orthodoxy? Further, Huntington characterizes the civil strife in the Ukraine as a clash between the Orthodox and the Western civilizations.[5] Yet, this would appear to cast the Western civilization as a religious construction of Catholicism. Similarly he suggests that the conflicts in the former Yugoslavia are a direct result of the intersection of the "Western," the "Orthodox," and the "Islamic" civilizations, again casting the Western as Catholicism. While this may be the understanding that many violent participants to conflict would like the world to believe, it would be dangerous to accept this proposition without questioning it.

If the conflicts in Yugoslavia are related to an "intersection" of civilizations, as Huntington would have us believe, then never could there have been a "Yugoslav" identity. On the other hand, many Yugoslav émigrés to the United States said that they felt uncomfortable during the various wars, because they could not relate to the sectarianism that structured the fighting. Although they expressed a regional identity of Croat, or Serb, and so on, they claimed that they had a Yugoslav identity.[6] Moreover, a powerful argument can be made that the "centuries-old" enemies of the Croats were the Hungarians and Austrians (simply called Germans at the time).[7] This was not due to ethnic strife, but to the political environment of occupation and colonial domination.[8] Conflicts between Serbs and Croats do not appear until these groups, which saw one another as "brother southern Slavs," were joined in the United Kingdom of Serbs, Croats, and Slovenes.[9] The events in early-twentieth-century Yugoslavia were not dissimilar to those that shaped Serbian-Bulgarian relations in the late nineteenth century. The two groups, which had no "memories of primordial confrontation," suddenly became embroiled in the bitter Balkan War.[10] It would appear that these two groups did not have conflict when they encountered one another, but after they had been joined. Rather than accepting the Huntington principle that groups of different religions or civilization will inevitably fight, let us take up the proposition that Serbs and Croats, Azers and Armenians, Georgians and Russians, and Hutus and Tutsis for that matter, do not engage in conflict because they are primordially different, but because they are very similar and have enjoyed at one time a unified collective narrative.

Although cultural distinctions can mark difference, culture is fluid. Like other social phenomena of collective identity, such as class and gender, ethnicity and culture exhibit both constancy and flux. Thus, as some aspects of culture are stressed, others are attenuated. Traditions and customs can be assimilated just as they can become extinct. In light of the patterns of assimilation, growth, and extinction, it is difficult to argue that any given culture is exactly the same as it was centuries ago. Just as cultures change, so do conflicts. This is the most difficult problem for the essentialists-primordialists. The argument that cultural difference functions as a source of conflict appears to be a reactionary reading of the symptoms only after conflict has broken out. Collective identity can be radically altered if the face of dramatic social dislocation, and in the process of restructuring the boundaries of ethnic identity, conflicts can develop. To understand this possibility, it is necessary to explore the processes by which collective ethnic identities are formed.

Building Collective Identities

Identity itself is a dynamic process that responds to crisis; in other words, endangerment itself is often a source of identity formation. In this way, individuals form their identity, as do collectives, through a series of threats, responses, and the narrative structures that chronicle those responses. Events provide information that either reinforces or alters individual or collective identity. Thus, the disruption of fundamental patterns of myths, symbols, and collective memory affects this necessary notion of continuity of collective narrative. As Anthony Smith writes, "Changes in cultural identity refer to the degree to which traumatic developments disturb the basic patterning of cultural elements that make up the sense of continuity."[11] In turn, personal identity alters the perceptions of these events, allowing both individuals and collectivities to weave events into a narrative structure of selective forgetting and memory. This process of managing the past, or altering the perception of current events, is akin to rewriting personal autobiographies in which traumatic events become manageable and part of new identities.[12] Moreover, group memories, like individual memories, are elastic and ever changing. This memory, that guarantees our identity, is "an ongoing metamorphosis, a polymorphy."[13] In this way, collectivities draw mental representations of a traumatic event into their very identity. Vamik Volkan writes: "The ensuing mental representations serve as a marker of ethnic and national identity and thus define the original event. For each new generation the account is modified; what remains is the role it [the event] assumes in the overall psychology of the group's identity."[14] However, the memories may be reworked to serve present circumstances: what in the past may have been a humiliating incident may now serve to bond the group, paradoxically raising self-esteem. If events are perceived by the self as so disturbing that they undermine the foundations of a previously solid conception of self, an individual or collectivity may be inspired to reject those qualities or traits that are most directly vulnerable. The need to establish a contrast agent against whom the self may create a more stable self-portrait—one free of wounded or vulnerable aspects—accentuates and makes more acute the politics of ethnicity or identity. The manner in which a collectivity creates, or designates, an "enemy" other is a valuable key to understanding ethnopolitics. Group identity provides emotional borders that protect the individual self from injury, *even when there is no clearly defined enemy.*[15] By creating an enemy, a given collectivity reassures itself of its cohesion and its very existence.

However, if creating emotional borders is to provide emotional stability, this process should be seen as an intrapsychic enterprise. Through my application of Julia Kristeva's concept of abjection to a collective level, we can find that conflict arises not from the engagement of "objective" difference. Rather, under anxious conditions the importance of Freud's notion of the narcissism of minor difference heightens. Such minor differences can mark social distinctions in the mind of the collective self, but should not be treated as "objective" differences between self and other. Simple examples are regional variations in speech, or minor variations in the practice of social customs (like wearing the same clothing items but perhaps set slightly differently: right to left as opposed to members of the group in another region wearing such an item left to right). The practices are similar and can establish unity, yet they vary slightly and can establish distinction. A collectivity in a state of crisis may become obsessed with a minor difference, and use it to mark what Julia Kristeva calls the "familiar foreigner," casting that segment aside, and identifying it as the Other. Kristeva notes that the creation of the other is related both to the occurrence of a traumatic event that disrupts the continuity of the sense of self, and to the associative processes of splitting, projection, and identification. The important point is that the enemy-other is not only created by the self, but previously had been part of the self. She writes that the abject "is that which, though intimately part of an earlier experience, must be rejected so that the self can establish the borders of its unified subjectivity."[16] Abjection becomes a major component of collective identity formation when the familiar "foreign(er)" is suddenly recognized as a threat. Thus, when faced with a threat to collective identity, the group-self will cast off that familiar yet somehow subjectively foreign segment in order to reestablish the boundaries of that self. By creating an opposition, by creating an other, the self can seek solace and comfort within some protective boundaries. For Kristeva, the creation of the other in this fashion, the creation of the abject, "marks the boundary of the self and therefore constitutes the limits of *subject*."[17] The abject lies within a space marked off by the subject, a space that can only be "arrived at *a posteriori*"; in this way, the other created through abjection only exists as a mental representation of the subject.[18] The differences that will become the subject of narcissism are the unwanted traits that are projected. Thus, the differences are *perceived* by the self, and are as intrapsychically created as the group-other.

These minor differences facilitate splitting, but the other does not become other as such until it is attributed with the rejected qualities of the traumatized self. The fixation with the enemy-other, with the abject, is narcissism, but this is predicated on the existence of the ego, not an external object. A fixation with the other is actually a fixation with the self. Kristeva writes, "The ego of narcissism is … uncertain, fragile, threatened, subjected just as much as its non-object to spatial ambivalence (inside/outside uncertainty) and to ambiguity of perception (pleasure/pain)."[19] Moreover, because the struggle between the group-self and other is internally generated, the self can adjust the other as needed in order to cope with new traumatic events. The introduction of a traumatic event and the disruption of a collective sense of self are paramount in determining the creation of the enemy-other. Further, there is a resounding resemblance between self and other, precisely because the other has been invested with the unwanted traits of the self. Vamik Volkan states this simply: "Because the enemy is a reservoir of unwanted self and object representations within which elements of our projections are condensed, there should be some unconscious perception of a likeness, a reverse correspondence that binds us together while alienating us."[20]

Freud noted that the "archaic, narcissistic self, not yet demarcated by the outside world, projects *out* of itself what it experiences as dangerous or unpleasant *in* itself."[21] Kristeva takes this notion and suggests that even with mature self-representations, traumatic events will cause a similar process of demarcation, altering the boundaries of the self. This defense mechanism then protects the self by "substituting for the image of a benevolent double that used to be enough to shelter it, the image of a malevolent double into which it expels the share of destruction it cannot contain."[22] In the process of splitting, some aspects are valued, as they are associated with pleasure, and become integral to the newly constructed self. Others become dystonic and externalized. Thus, that which is perceived as strange and alien within the newly constructed other is simultaneously uncomfortably familiar because it is the *self* repressed. The resemblance is precisely the attributed qualities.

However, the self cannot acknowledge this relationship with the other; it cannot recognize the other as previously a component part of itself. By redefining what constitutes the group-self, a previous component is now seen as foreign, and must subsequently be made out to have always been foreign. The abject is a prohibition, a rigid boundary, and explicitly precludes any possibility of engaging the "other." There is, then, a constant fear of the abject returning to reclaim its previous place within the self. It is a fear of the return of the repressed. If the repressed were to return, it would destroy the new subjective sense of self; it would undermine this newly reestablished collective identity, plunging the group-self back into its chaotic and ambiguous previous position. Norma Moruzzi writes, "For the subjective identity of the nation-state, this threatened return, that would dissolve the national self into undifferentiatable physical parts, is posed by the stranger both feared and desired."[23] In this sense the abject is neither subject nor object, but a crisis for the subject: an obsessive fear of collapsing into the self-created other. This fear, or as Bataille put it, this "inability to assume with sufficient strength [that the self is capable] of the imperative act of excluding abject things" leads to a further debasement of the other.[24] The abject is created through the self-deception that the other was never part of the self. The consequence of not engaging the defensive mechanism of debasement would be the collapse of the self into abject: the return of the repressed, and the destruction of the newly constituted self. Kristeva writes: "[The subject] would be constantly menaced by the possible collapse into the object. It would lose definition. It is a question, then, of a precarious state in which the subject is menaced by the possibility of collapsing into chaos of indifference."[25] Through debasement, the self is reassured of essential difference. The fear of a lack of differentiation causes an obsessive repudiation of the other. Once the other has been so thoroughly reduced that his humanity is no longer visible, any act required to maintain the boundaries between self and other can be justified. During these encounters it is necessary, then, for the self to depersonalize the other as it cannot be engaged intersubjectively, lest the self loses its own boundaries, its own demarcations. Kristeva writes that without systematic debasement when confronting the other "whom I reject and with whom I iden-tify, I lose my boundaries. I no longer have a container, the memory of experiences when I have been abandoned overwhelm me, I lose my composure I feel 'lost,' 'indistinct,' 'hazy.' This strangeness allows for many variations: they all repeat the difficulty I have in situating myself with respect to the other and keep going over the course of identification-projection that lies at the foundation of my reaching [a perceived] autonomy."[26]

Excessive debasement allows the self to defend against its desire for reconstitu-tion. As the group-self's stress and regression continue, depersonalization and dehumanization of the enemy-other similarly increase. As the self continues to degrade and defile the other, it reassures itself with reliable prejudices of differ-ence, which serves as the defense against the disagreeable insight that the other had been the self. Alexander and Margerita Mitscherlich write that "A central psy-cho-dynamic in the creation and establishment of prejudices is the degradation of the [other] making self idealization possible."[27] A high level of anxiety that the repressed may return or reoccur accompanies the repression necessary to keep the other separate, to maintain distance. As anxiety increases, the symbol ceases to be a symbol and "takes over the full function of the thing that it symbolizes."[28] A material object replaces the imagined alien other; the representations are no longer signs of the rejected aspects of the self, but assume real importance.

The signs and symbols of the other become conflated with the fantasies of fear and desire and the material reality of the other as object. This, in turn, becomes an obsessional neurosis allowing the return of the repressed to become inscribed in the reification of the other. By reifying the other, the self moves from internal per-ception to the realm of material reality—the other *is* a walking, breathing, living embodiment of everything the self wishes to cast off. As the self "experiences" the other as the sum total of both his fantasies of desire and fear, the newly developed sense of identity is reinforced. Just as identity alters the perception of physical events, which themselves help to form identity, the perception of self is reinforced and altered by interaction with the other. However, the "material realities" experi-enced by the self when confronting the other remain the product of intrapsychi-cally created fantasies and desires.

For this reason, the abject cannot be destroyed, nor can it be discarded or ignored. The fantasy of reconciliation, the desire for the return of the repressed, prohibits such destruction. It is this prohibition that gives rise to the appearance of an obsession with the other, and by extension with politicized ethnicity. Kris-teva states that "The abject does not radically cut off the subject from what threat-ens it—on the contrary, abjection acknowledges the self to be in perpetual dan-ger."[29] The abject "represents not the object of a merely sadistic domination," but rather the object of a desire for the return to that state of undifferentiated passiv-ity where the subject, " fluctuating between inside and outside, pleasure and pain, would find death, along with nirvana."[30] A social order based on defilement and debasement of the abject serves as resistance to this terrifying desire. The self does not wish to be rid of the abject; rather, the abject serves as a reminder of the threats and trauma which the self has survived. To have no relationship with the abject would deny the self access to the previous state in which the abject was part of the self. Debasement as a defense against this desire can be seen as a parallel to phobia. Fear is hidden in aggression, desire is hidden in rejection, and both can be masked and obscured from view through an inflation of the powers of the other. The object of fear, the source of insecurity is presented as exceedingly powerful, so that the subject may not appear weak. Thus, while an individual may desire reconciliation with the other, the fear of social displacement requires the other to be excessively powerful and threatening.

Transition as Social Trauma

The end of state socialism can be seen as social trauma as it caused widespread social disorientation, particularly for those most adversely effected by the Changes.[31] Claus Offe has described these Changes as a triple transformation for the states of Central and Eastern Europe: an economic transformation to capitalism, a political transformation to democracy, and a constitutional transformation to the "rule of law" and civil society.[32] Offe then points out the difficulties and contradictions associated with this triple transformation. The transformation to democracy requires the erection of constitutional structures. However, many involved in the process of forging a new constitution had vested political interests. Thus, these politicians set the rules for the very game in which they are engaged. Similarly, the erection of constitutional structures has little to do with the implementation of market-based economic systems, unless it has been determined that the constitution should provide protection for the markets. In many ways, such a presumption undermines the concept of democracy. To have a secure and responsive government that reflects the interests of the electorate, it may be necessary to curtail those economic reforms that cause the greatest pain. In a democracy, voter preferences may directly challenge the implementation of economic reforms.

Similarly, Offe notes the contradiction between political democracy and the transformation to capitalism. Democracy solicits the people's participation and opinions; the transformation to capitalism requires great sacrifice that many may be unwilling to voluntarily accept. Thus, there is tension between market implementation and the transition to political democracy. Moreover, the types of market structures Central and Eastern Europe are encouraged to adopt by the West are not the structures of the 1950s under the Marshall Plan. Rather, the structures represent advances of late capitalism. Many of these structures induce a form of social atomization that flies in the face of the values connected to democratic forms of government. Rather than encouraging the growth of "civil society," many of these structures actually retard the development of civic and social bonds required by democratization.

Many workers find themselves isolated and devalued, as new technologies "de-skill" workers. Former employees in newly marginalized sectors may suddenly find themselves "unemployable," as their skills are no longer matched to the opportunities available. Yet under these new terms, unemployment is not seen as a structural failing of the economy; rather, the double imposition of liberalism and capitalism furthers the sense of personal failure for those workers who are displaced. Founded on Adam Smith's notion of personal responsibility and individual agency, liberal capitalism deflects responsibility away from economic institutions. Richard Sennett comments: "The rhetoric of modern management attempts to disguise power in the new economy by making the worker believe he or she is a self-directing agent."[33] Yet those displaced by capitalism are likely to see liberalism not as liberating but as oppressive and defeating. As these same individuals feel socially isolated due to the structural disintegration of social relationships, the structure of the new economy informs them that their employment dislocations are the result of their own lack of direction. If an individual's skill set is of little value, his personal worth is not only diminished because he cannot contribute to society through work, but also because he finds himself outside of the global economic "society" altogether. The social dislocation associated with the transformation of the workplace further discourages individuals from supporting the transitions to markets. As Offe anticipates, the sense of isolation and alienation created by advanced markets undermines enthusiasm for the transitions to democratization, for there is feeling that individuals' opinions or desires pale in comparison to the desires of corporations. Further, the complex relationships between international lending institutions (like the International Monetary Fund and the World Bank), Western governments, transnational corporations, and the local economy dumbfound many. Structural adjustment programs, forced currency devaluations, and the resulting decreased buying power of the local currencies are seen as dictated from outside the local economy. Money, which now shapes social interaction to a much higher degree than before, is also part of the larger global capitalist system. This has a profoundly alienating effect.

A great deal of distrust was associated with economic reforms following the Changes. Jon Elster, like Claus Offe, correctly points out that there is "an irreconcilable antagonism between democracy and price and property reform."[34] Market economies produce inequalities that must be legitimized as "reforms." As social and political liberalization increased after 1989, a growing number of people became suspicious of the promises of capitalism, seeing it as an "alien" force. Many were wary of "becoming a dependent periphery," a dumping ground for Western surplus production.[35] Foreign capital could dominate all economic activity, denying Eastern and Central Europe the economic autonomy and freedom it was seeking. Further, no inherent benefit is associated with capitalism; private ownership, the existence of markets, free competition, and free economic activity are perceived instrumentally. The market is viewed as a device "for reaching prosperity and abundance, acceptable only conditionally as long as it provides such benefits."[36] Those that do not fare well, however, might engage in a collective defense against the perceived economic threats, not to themselves, but to the "nation." The continued adherence to a collective definition of agency follows decades of socialist socialization, giving rise to the belief that any socioeconomic system should satisfy at least the minimum need of all citizens. This is not necessarily an endorsement of a return to Communism, but it is also not an expressed enthusiasm for global, transnational capitalism. Thus, there appears to be both a great desire for the material benefits of capitalism and a revulsion against capitalism because of the potential for failure. No longer secure in their own position, these adversely affected elements sought a new identity in which they could assure themselves of membership, and project their rage and frustration created by the anxiety of uncertainty.

Linking Cycles

One of the ways ethnic conflicts can appear as centuries-old is the invocation of previous conflicts, strife, or traumatic events that appear to connect the present with the past. Often the invoked crisis represents a significant unmourned loss in the historical narrative of the collectivity. These unmourned losses around which collective narratives are woven can be called, as Vamik Volkan does, Chosen Traumas. Chosen Traumas shape the form of interpretation for subsequent conflicts and traumatic events. It is necessary to see how group selves stranded in suspended mourning link unrelated conflicts to the original trauma. This is done through what I call the linking cycle. When a collectivity, unable to mourn the losses associated with a Chosen Trauma, experiences a *secondary trauma*—that is a loss unassociated with the Chosen Trauma—the self may defend against the loss by perceiving it as continued oppression by the original "victimizing" enemy-other. Losses accumulating without being adaptively worked through can cause the group-self to conflate all subsequent losses with the Chosen Trauma. The linking cycle is seen in this subsequent invocation of the abject-other created during the Chosen Trauma. The unwanted traits and qualities of the group-self exposed by the secondary trauma are easily projected into the abject, thereby reinforcing the separation of the self and the familiar foreigner. Again, the self is sure to find these unwanted traits within the abject, as it was part of the self. This process may make coping with secondary trauma easier, as the defense is so readily available; however, it perpetuates the psychopathology associated with the original Chosen Trauma.

This process also reinforces the bonds between generations, as secondary trauma generally affects second and subsequent generations. By invoking the abject created by previous generations, the collectivity is unified, allowing younger generations to experience the pain and sense of loss of their elders. Moreover, just as a Chosen Trauma threatens the continuity of the collective sense of self, so too secondary traumas require an alteration in collective narrative in order to defend the group-self. By expanding the Chosen Trauma to include losses associated with secondary trauma, the group-self "reinvents" the previously ascribed abject with the traits necessary to be applicable in the new case. The "old" enemy-other is, therefore, responsible for "new" losses. Successive generations may increase their union with earlier ones by invoking the narrative structures utilized first to create the abject. The renewed application of iconographic mechanisms, rhetorical structures, narrative imagery, and shared ego representations provides both the links to the past as well as appropriate structures for the present. Like traditions, however, previous imagery and rhetoric will be modified to reflect the secondary trauma. Hatred is particularly useful, as previously experienced rage and humiliation associated with victimization in the case of the Chosen Trauma is now validated in the new context. Further, as the abject is renewed with extended qualities and traits, a period of renewed debasement will follow. Loathing, which may have subsided in the past, is reemphasized to ensure that the self does not collapse. Both the fear of and desire for the abject, of the "return of the repressed," likewise will be reinvigorated. In fact, depending upon the magnitude and social circumstances of the secondary trauma, the process of abjection may be marked with an increased intensity and violence that was not originally connected to reactions to the Chosen Trauma. It is this process that often leads casual observers to conclude that ethnic conflicts may be "timeless." As the self experiences a new threat, it defends itself most expediently by reviving the abject. In fact, the self may bestow upon the abject a completely new set of traits, which match the circumstances of the secondary trauma. Moreover, as the self turns to previously activated defense mechanisms, the self may reexperience the sense of loss associated with the Chosen Trauma. Secondary traumas, therefore, further obstruct the mourning process of both the original and the new losses. By reexperiencing the primary loss, the self is completely ill-prepared to deal with the secondary loss.

The sudden and unanticipated social dislocations that accompanied the economic transitions after 1989 function as a secondary trauma. Heralded as liberation from Communist oppression, the capitalist system wrought unemployment, financial hardship, and a downgrading of social status for many in Central and Eastern Europe, causing a collective identity crisis. Unprepared for these social losses, those adversely affected by the Changes defended themselves by reviving the previous abject, which manifested itself as ethnocentrism, or anti-Semitism and irredentism. These forms of collective identification renew the process of abjection, erecting barriers for self-definition in the face of social dislocation and widespread social anxiety caused by the economic transition. By seeing the Changes as secondary trauma, it is possible to understand why these antimodern nationalist forms of expression invoke previous political discourse and forms of nationalism. Each manifestation will be different depending on the previous Chosen Trauma. The violence and social divisions in the former Yugoslavia revive cultural forms of abjection from the 1941–1945 Civil War.[37] In Hungary the abject has appeared as resurgent anti-Semitism. In Slovakia Meciar's form of nationalism appears as a repetition of the national identity crisis initiated during World War II. The resurgence of neo-Nazism in the new state of Germany perhaps best demonstrates this phenomenon of secondary trauma. As the traumas and losses from World War II have never been mourned in East Germany, the collective defense mechanisms invoked in the face of the Changes appear as a repetition of abject forms from fifty years ago. Those who have experienced new losses resulting from the economic transformation of the Changes invoke the readily available defense mechanisms created by previous Chosen Trauma. However, this is merely a form of purging the collective self of its anxiety. The revival of previous abjects should not be understood as a continuation of a previous conflict. Rather, the connection is an intrapsychic one.

On the other hand, the application of the linking cycle to secondary trauma may demonstrate the inapplicability or unsuitability of Chosen Trauma mechanisms. Such a realization offers collectivities the opportunity to reevaluate narrative structures, possibly initiating the mourning process. That is, as the group-self attempts to expand the Chosen Trauma through the linking cycle in order to apply it to a secondary trauma, it may become clear that these structures are simply inapt. Thus, renewed psychopathologies associated with abjection may be short-lived. After an initial period of attempted repetition, the group-self may seek to reevaluate its identity formation after the immediate threat has subsided. The necessary restructuring of the group-self boundaries to cope with the secondary trauma may then initiate adaptive mourning.

Adaptive Mourning and Conflict Amelioration

Once a collectivity no longer perceives itself as immediately threatened, it is then possible for it to engage in analysis of the narratives that comprise its traditions and sense of self. By undergoing such self-reflection, it may be possible for a collectivity to recognize the absence or nonthreatening nature of the other it has created. Similarly, it may recognize that the previous dependence upon the images of a lost object is debilitating. As these two processes are inextricably linked, so too is their resolution. That is, as they are simultaneous psychopathologies, which reinforce one another, their resolution is similarly reinforcing. As obsessive debasement of the abject decreases so too will the need to cling to hostile representations of the other, and vice versa. At its conclusion, the Chosen Trauma will be reduced to merely another event in the collective narrative, rather than being the event upon which the narrative is based. The collectivity may find a richer historical narrative available to its process of ongoing identity formation, once that narrative is no longer dominated by the singular traumatic event. Further, it will be freed from the obsessional nature of the past, providing an unencumbered vision of the future, where new possibilities can be realized. Describing this process at the individual level, Peter Homans suggests how a historical narrative can be enriched by being freed from its pathological nature: "Whenever the mourning process is allowed to deepen, one becomes more and more aware of how profoundly attached [the mourner] has been to the objects of the past. As a result of this, the ego's capacity to become separate from the past—its independence—is enhanced."[38]

In this way, the mourning process can be seen as a revaluation of the collective narrative, instilling renewed vigor and new meaning. Mourning at the collective level can be seen as a cultural activity—a collective "working through" of traumatic events. This process is the parallel to the construction of the pathological narrative. Just as film, folktales, songs, stories, literature, and oral representations are utilized to transmit the narrative of abjection, so too are these the vehicles for collective mourning. For example, just as the myth of the Battle of Kosovo was transformed from a tale of martyrdom and the downfall of Serbian feudal society into a nationalist myth in the nineteenth century and again in the late 1980s,[39] the narratives of separateness can be transformed. That is, just as nationalist narratives are constructed over time and through various media, the processes of mourning require open cultural spaces and collective engagement. For a time this "cultural activity" may even dominate the sites of the collective narrative, in literature, film, painting, sculpture, dance, the arts in general, and even television. The collectivity can, through these media, "work through" feelings of rage, hatred, guilt, humiliation, and other emotions which led to abjection, but which now can openly be discussed as part of the mourning process. The reevaluation of the collective narrative through "cultural activity" engages the immediate conscious experience of the group-self by re-presenting and mediating the lost cultural experiences of the past. For adaptive mourning to be complete it is necessary that the abjectly split self engage the other and achieve reconciliation. The introspection required by adaptive mourning allows the intrapsychically created other to be reincorporated in the image of the collective self. This is enhanced by the internalization of images of the lost object. The self will no longer feel obligated to externalize rage upon the abject-other. The internalization of ambivalent emotions concerning both the lost object and the self, previously expressed through the debasement of the other, creates a new identity, and restructures the collective self narrative. The dependence on the past would be acknowledged, but would no longer be fetishized, thus enabling the society creatively to engage the future. This can only occur if the abject is reconciled to the self, allowing a new narrative to be constructed that includes the return of the familiar foreigner.

This process, which begins once it is apparent that the collective narrative based upon the Chosen Trauma is no longer sufficient or necessary to provide a protective boundary, represents the abatement of conflict. For example it appears that the narratives of damaging "Jewish" capitalism in Hungary is no longer appropriate to defend against the damaging effects of the economic transition. While anti-Semitism continues, its widespead, venomous forms of the early 1990s appear to be in retreat. This is particularly apparent in Budapest where many efforts have been made to intitate a reconciliation with the Jewish population there.[40] Such initiatives make a *rapprochement* with the enemy-other possible. A new collective narrative, which recognizes the Serbian and Croat union in a Communist Yugoslavia, or the integral role of Jewry in Hungarian culture, can be written, ending the cycle of animosity and hostility. This is neither an easy nor short process, but it is one that contradicts the notions that these conflicts are intractable. By recognizing the very similarity that became an obsessive fixation in the process of abjection, groups can end the cycle of debasement. However, this requires a recognition of the importance of cultural activities. The shift to market capitalism must not be so brutal as to destroy the sponsorship of the arts, theater, film, and literature which can assist in the abatement of conflict. Further, by recognizing the psychodynamics of conflict, international organizations can avoid exacerbating conflict by not accepting the myths of "objective difference." By encouraging cultural engagement, as opposed to continued separation, third parties can facilitate this type of mourning process.

To quell the violence connected with ethnic conflict, and to end the string of human rights abuses connected with those conflicts, it is not of importance to emphasize similarity among groups. Rather, time should be taken to assist all groups with coping through their major social traumas and dislocations—those that preceded the outbreak of violent conflict. By helping groups to learn to cope, they might come to see a more adaptive view of the other, recognizing the traits inherent in the other, not merely those projected upon them. Groups may be capable of possessing a welded view, which recognizes both the "good" and "bad" traits of the other as a complete representation, not merely the intrapsychic fantasy that the other embodies the "bad" traits of the self. Finally, by addressing the underlying tensions and social disruptions which created social trauma in the first place, conflicts may actually be resolved rather than simply de-escalated. Most importantly, we should not accept claims of difference as objective facts. Rather, with compassion and patience, we may indeed assist all parties in overcoming their anxieties, providing a more adaptive environment for cooperation and understanding.

NOTES

1. Dodge Billingsley (director/producer), *Immortal Fortress: A Look Inside Chechnya's Warrior Culture* (USA, 1999). Presented at the 5th Association for the Study of Nationalities World Congress, New York, April 2000.

2. Samuel Huntington, *The Clash of Civilizations: Remaking World Order* (New York: Touchstone, 1996), p. 21.

3. Ibid., pp. 45–47.

4. Ibid., p. 47.

5. Ibid., p. 37.

6. Derek Reveron, "Yugoslavians in Chicago: An Identity Crisis" (typescript, University of Illinois at Chicago, n.d.).

7. Djurdja Knezevic, "The Enemy Sides of National Ideologies: Croatia at the End of the 19th Century and in the First Half of the 20th Century," in *Pride and Prejudice: Central European University History Department Working Papers* (Budapest: CEU Press, 1995), p. 109.

8. A union of the crowns of Croatia and the Kingdom of Hungary was formed in 1102. Thus began an eight-hundred-year connection to Hungary and, subsequently, in 1699 the Habsburg Empire.

9. Knezevic, "The Enemy Sides of National Ideologies," p. 110.

10. Diana Mishkova, "Friends Turned Foes: Bulgarian National Attitudes to Neighbors," in *Pride and Prejudice: Central European University History Department Working Papers*, p. 169.

11. Anthony Smith, *The Ethnic Origins of Nationalism* (London: Basil Blackwell, 1986), p. 31.

12. For further discussions on the process of forgetting and memory in personal identity, see the works of Ferenc Eros of the Cognitive Psychology Institute in Budapest, Hungary.

13. Julia Kristeva, *Strangers to Ourselves* (New York: Columbia University Press, 1991), p. 37.

14. Vamik Volkan, *The Need to Have Enemies and Allies* (London: Jason Aronson, 1988), p. xxvi.

15. Ibid., p. 93.

16. Julia Kristeva, *Powers of Horror: An Essay on Abjection* (New York: Columbia University Press, 1982), p. 9.

17. Kristeva quoted in David Spurr, *The Rhetoric of the Empire: Colonial Discourse in Journalism, Travel Writing, and Imperial Administration* (Durham, N.C.: Duke University Press, 1993), p. 78.

18. Julia Kristeva, interview in *All Area 2* (spring 1981): p. 11.

19. Kristeva, *Powers of Horror*, p. 62.

20. Volkan, *The Need to Have Enemies and Allies*, p. 99.

21. Cf. Sigmund Freud, *Das Unheimliche* (The Uncanny) Standard Edition, vol. XVII (1919), (London: Hogarth Press, 1955) p. 225; Kristeva, *Strangers to Ourselves*, p. 183.

22. Kristeva, *Strangers to Ourselves*, p. 184.

23. Norma Clair Moruzzi, "National Abjects: Julia Kristeva on the Process of Political Self-Identification," in *Ethics, Politics, and Difference in Julia Kristeva's Writing*, ed. Oliver Kelly (New York: Routledge, 1993).

24. Kristeva, *Powers of Horror*, p. 56.

25. Julia Kristeva, *Black Sun: Depression and Melancholia* (New York: Columbia University Press, 1983), p. 39.

26. Kristeva, *Strangers to Ourselves*, p. 187.
27. Alexander Mitscherlich and Margerita Mitscherlich, *The Inability to Mourn: Principles of Collective Behavior* (New York: Grove Press, 1975), p. 124.
28. Cf. Freud, *Das Unheimliche*, p. 244; Kristeva, *Strangers to Ourselves*, p. 184.
29. Kristeva, *Black Sun*, p. 9.
30. Kristeva, *Powers of Horror*, p. 64, and Spurr, *The Rhetoric of the Empire*, p. 79.
31. This term marks the various political and economic transformations in Central and Eastern Europe at the end of the 1980s and the beginning of the 1990s. While the events were revolutionary, it would be incorrect to call them revolutions, with the exceptions of Romania and perhaps the "Velvet Revolution" in Czechoslovakia. The Hungarian word *rendszerváltás*, meaning "system change," may best describe these events.
32. Cf. Claus Offe, "Capitalism by Democratic Design? Facing the Triple Transformation in East Central Europe," in *Social Research* 58, no. 4 (winter 1991).
33. Richard Sennett, "The New Capitalism," in *Social Research* 64, no. 2 (summer 1997).
34. Jon Elster, "When Communism Dissolves," in *London Review of Books*, January 24, 1990.
35. Piotr Sztompka, "Dilemmas of the Great Transition," in *Sisyphus* 8, no. 2 (1992).
36. Ibid.
37. While it is obvious that the Changes occurred in most Central European states in 1989, the tremendous rupture in the collective narrative after Tito's death functions as a dramatic social trauma in Yugoslavia in the mid-1970s. The loss of Tito, coupled with the economic crises at the end of that decade appear as secondary traumas initiating a linking cycle, prior to the conditions that will trigger similar processes elsewhere in the region.
38. Peter Homans, *The Ability to Mourn* (New York: Columbia University Press, 1989), p. 334.
39. Ger Duijzings, *Religion and the Politics of Identity in Kosovo* (New York: Columbia University Press, 2000), pp. 184–87.
40. Jeffrey Murer, "Pursuing the Familiar Foreigner: The Resurgence of Antisemitism and Nationalism in Hungary Since 1989" (Ph.D. diss., University of Illinois at Chicago, 1999).

CHAPTER TWELVE

Fear and Democracy

John Keane

> *It is not power that corrupts but fear. Fear of losing power corrupts those who wield it and fear of the scourge of power corrupts those who are subject to it.*
> —Aung San Suu Kyi (1991)

Despotism

Questions about fear today rarely feature in discussions within the fields of political philosophy and political science. When they arise, they usually appear as a matter of antiquarian interest, most often in connection with the classic work of Montesquieu, *De l'esprit des lois* (1748).[1] That work captured the imaginations of several generations of political thinkers and writers who found themselves caught up in one of the crucial political developments of the eighteenth century: the rising fear of state despotism and the hope, spawned by the military defeat of the British monarchy in the American colonies and by the first moments of the French Revolution, of escaping its clutches.[2] Montesquieu was freely read and liberally quoted during this period, especially because his work contained an entirely new understanding of the concept of despotism. Montesquieu transformed the classical Greek understanding of despotism (*despótos*) as a form of kingship exercised legitimately by a master over slaves. Rejecting as well Bodin's and Hobbes's subsequent positive rendering of despotism as a form of political rule justified by victory in war or civil war, Montesquieu entered the eighteenth-century controversies prompted by the Physiocratic defense of despotisme légal. In a highly original move against all previous reflections on the subject, he viewed despotism, with trepidation, as a type of political regime that was founded originally among Orientals, but that now threatened Europe from within. Despotism, he thought, is a type of arbitrary rule structured by fear. It ruthlessly crushes intermediate groups and classes within the state and forces its subjects to lead lives that are divided, ignorant, and timorous. Within despotic regimes, Montesquieu remarked, fear and mutual suspicion are rampant. The lives, liberties, and properties of individual subjects are scattered to the winds of arbitrary power. Everyone is forced to live at the mercy of the frightening maxim "that a single person should rule according to his own will and caprice."[3]

Montesquieu's analysis of despotism no doubt contained strongly imaginative or "fictional" elements, especially in its reliance upon a prejudiced or Orientalist view of Muslim societies.[4] Yet by linking together the subjects of fear and despotism Montesquieu powerfully gave wings to the intellectual flight from the status quo of absolute monarchy within the Atlantic region. He helped to convince many of his readers that despotism was a new and dangerous form of unlimited—concentrated and unaccountable—secular power. Guided by no ideals other than the blind pursuit of power for power's sake, and feeding upon the blind obedience of its subjects, despotism, Montesquieu implied, is a half-crazed, violent, and self-contradictory form of governance. It crashes blindly through the world, leaving behind a trail of confusion, waste, and lawlessness, to the point where it tends to destroy its own omnipotence. It consequently undoes the fear upon which it otherwise thrives. Despotism becomes the scourge of decency. It shocks and repels those who are afraid, and it encourages those who yearn to live without fear. It inspires its opponents to seek alternatives, for instance republican government, representative parliamentary power-sharing arrangements, the cultivation of free public opinion within the rule of law, and the education of citizens into the ways of civic virtue.

Democracy

Through this line of reasoning, the critics of despotism after Montesquieu helped prepare the way for the more recent view that democracies, in which the exercise of power is shared and subject to permanent public scrutiny, reduce fear to the point where it becomes of minor importance in politics. The presumption that democracies are fear-less or fear-resolving systems is sometimes stated explicitly, as in one of the very few recent serious studies of contemporary politics and fear, by Juan Corradi and his colleagues.[5] There it is argued that while democracies do not altogether do away with fear—a political order without fear is an unattainable utopia—they are historically unique in their capacity to sublimate, reduce, and control human fears creatively. Established democracies tend to "privatize" fear, which becomes at most a personal matter to be handled by individuals in their daily lives—as an intimate problem to be analyzed and treated in the company of either the psychoanalyst or the priest. Little wonder that political philosophy and political science lost interest in the subject, which is handed over to the subfield of political psychology, leaving a few isolated thinkers to ask: How do democracies actually manage to marginalize fear, to push it into the domains of intimate and transcendent experience? Corradi and his colleagues are understandably concerned with contemporary forms of state despotism in Latin America, so the thesis that democracies solve the age-old problem of fear functions mainly as a counterfactual presumption. They simply present a list of the various means used by American-style democracies to discharge fear, including the decentralization of power, the exercise of self-governance through local associations, the encouragement of state-protected religious freedoms, the possibility of rapid geographic and social mobility, and, above all, representative government.[6]

The thesis that democracies privatize fear is stimulating. But it is unconvincing, in no small measure because it only hints at the dynamic processes through which actually existing democracies do indeed tend—but not altogether successfully—to reduce the role played by fear in the overall structures of power. What then are these processes, peculiar to democracy, that perform the positive role of reducing and "privatizing" fear? And could it be that there are counterprocesses that ensure that fear is a problem that democracies do not entirely resolve? The possible answers to these questions are not immediately obvious, but commonsense reflection—let us call it the conventional view of democracy and fear—typically identifies three overlapping processes that seem to guarantee that democracies trivialize fear. In preparation for a more nuanced—less naïve—account of democracy and fear, these processes are sketched below:

Nonviolent Power-Sharing

According to the conventional view, democracies tend to reduce the fears of governors and governed alike because they institute the practice of nonviolent power-sharing at the level of governmental institutions. Just how unique that innovation is can be seen by considering that all previous modern territorial states and military empires typically sought to exercise monopoly control of the means of violence, and to rule by making others afraid of the threatened use of that violence. The armed power of these states and empires, often wielded in the name of reducing their subjects' fears, had the effect of *inspiring* fear among their subjects and rivals at home and their enemies abroad. As Guglielmo Ferrero emphasized, state and imperial rulers, equipped with the awesome capacity to take life away—the sword of the ruler should always be reddened with blood, noted Luther—developed a taste and a reputation for harsh action. All rulers armed with the sword were capable of inspiring fear, even of the extreme kind that Montesquieu called despotic. The violent persecution and attempted destruction of religious minorities, such as the Huguenots, was only an extreme instance of this rule: the use of spies and informants, the militarization of the civilian population, brutal punishments, forced conversions, and the torture and massacre of men, women, and children helped produce fear on a scale far exceeding anything described or recommended in the early modern textbooks on government written by figures like Bodin and Hobbes. Rulers' capacity for making others afraid of course applied as well to their (potential) rivals. Those who plotted the seizure or paralysis of armed power, for instance through a coup d'état or regicide, usually risked their lives, and lived in fear of doing so. That was a good and necessary thing, recommended Machiavelli. Musing on the reputation for cruelty of Cesare Borgia, he openly criticized Cicero's advice that love compared with fear is a much more effective resource in government: "it is much safer to be feared than loved."[7]

Democracies minimize such fear, initially by effecting a pact of nonviolence among rulers and their potential rivals and opponents. What might be called the Law of Damocles helps to explain the basis of this pact. In the court of Dionysius, the much-feared tyrant of Syracuse, there was a sycophantic courtier named Damocles. He yearned to wield power like his master, so Dionysius decided to teach him a lesson by inviting Damocles to preside over a splendid royal banquet. Wrapped in frippery, Damocles was flattered and acted the part remarkably well—until he discovered, dangling above his lavish golden throne, a huge sword on the end of a single strand of hair. The foolish courtier-turned-ruler cried out in horror. He had begun to learn the lesson that those who rule by fear can potentially die by fear, and that they are therefore best advised to seek means other than fear through which to govern. Democracies constitutionalize this rule: they respect the Law of Damocles by developing a consensus, among governors and governed alike, that threats of violence and government by fear are not easily containable, that nobody is safe, and that therefore such threats should not be used as techniques of government, or of opposition.

Civil Society

The conventional view of democracy and fear supposes that democracies also diminish the use of fear as a weapon wielded by those who govern by institutionalizing arms-length limits upon the scope of political power, in the form of civil society. The historical invention in early modern Europe of spaces of nonviolence called civil societies has proved to be a self-contradictory and therefore highly unstable—but nonetheless precious—process.[8] The birth of these societies was made possible by the extrusion or "clearing" of the principal means of violence from daily life and their concentration in depersonalized form in the hands of the repressive apparatuses of imperial or territorial-based governing institutions. As ownership of the means of violence shifted from the nonstate to the state realm— it was always, and still remains, a heavily contested process[9]—these civil societies became permanently vulnerable to standing armies and police forces, which could harass them from within, or periodically call on the citizens of these societies to kill external enemies in wars between heavily armed states.

The civil societies that survived, and today flourish, nevertheless served to protect an important liberty: the freedom of individuals to live without the everyday fear of violent death at the hands of others. Modern civil societies tend to transform potential enemies into "strangers" whose strangeness, Simmel pointed out, derives from their simultaneous remoteness and closeness to others around them.[10] Especially in contemporary civil societies, strangers abound and savage pleasure and unfettered hatred in destroying anything considered hostile becomes rare. The members of civil society become capable of suppressing or sublimating their aggressive impulses, whether they are directed at governments or at fellow civilians themselves. They display remarkable self-restraint, even in the face of hostility. It is as if they are guided by an inner voice warning them not to inflict violence upon others who annoy or threaten them. The social spaces connecting individuals tend to become nonviolent and "civility" itself becomes a cherished norm. There are plenty of countertrends, of course, but the capacity of civil societies to live nonviolently means that "otherness," the figure of the stranger or foreigner, for instance, can in principle be accepted, even welcomed, without fear.

Publicity

Actually existing democracies today operate within a framework of communications media. These media, the conventional theory supposes, have the effect of transforming the nature of the fear experienced by the members of civil societies by publicizing it—thereby reducing the quantity of genuine fears they experience. Beginning with the early modern printing press, so the argument runs, these communications media helped to publicize the despotic potential of governmental institutions, so encouraging the publics that sprang up with media help to believe that fear should not rule, indeed that government by fear was illegitimate. The cultivation of public opinion within nonviolent public spheres came to be seen as a weapon against the paralyzing effects of fear.[11] Much the same process encouraged the formation of civil societies by establishing spaces within which things could be said and done without fear of the consequences, and by helping to publicize their members' diffuse anxieties and their explicit fears—and so to suggest that there might be remedies for fear other than private suffering. The drying up of rumors, which once operated as the great waterway of fear,[12] was one of the long-term consequences of modern communications media. Rumors circulate fear by depending upon formulations like "people are saying," or "I heard," or "there's a rumor going around." Such hearsay has no individual subject and is therefore hard to refute; it is a hot potato that is quickly juggled and passed on to the next listener. A rumor is a quotation with a loophole— it is never clear who is being quoted or who originally set it in motion.[13] By contrast, the nonviolent conjecture and refutation, controversy and disputation that routinely take place within a public sphere have the effect of checking the veracity and tracing the source—"denaturalizing" or "desacralizing"—everyday fears.

The Triangle of Fear

The familiar proposition that democracies tend to reduce and trivialize the fears of their citizens seems so far to be plausible, but another moment's reflection easily uncovers a basic problem in the analysis of democracy and fear: the problem of how to define fear itself. Few keywords in the field of politics have been so neglected as "fear." By comparison with the huge controversies generated by other keywords like "the state," "democracy," "power," fear as a concept tends to be used as a "face-value" term—as a concept that does not merit even a definition because it is presumed that everyone who has experienced fear in their lives, or has learned about it from others, knows what it is.[14]

That presumption, that fear is fear, is manifestly misleading, as controversies within other scholarly fields, like psychology, physiological psychology, and philosophy, reveal.[15] Much could be said about these controversies, and their importance for democratic theory, but for the moment it is only necessary to draw upon them selectively for the purpose of sketching a new account of fear, understood here as an "ideal-typical" concept that can bring greater clarity to our understanding of a political subject that has suffered much neglect and is now in urgent need of attention.

Fear is the name that should be given to a particular type of psychic and bodily abreaction of an individual or group that is produced within a triangle of interrelated experiences. This triangle of experiences within which fear arises in certain times and places among human beings—and among vertebrate animals as well[16]—is historically variable. Through time, humans and animals evidently develop, phylogenetically, different fear thresholds; so too, through the process of ontogenesis, beginning in the earliest moments of infancy, individuals can and do develop their capacities for conquering fears of various kinds; and, as Montesquieu well understood, different political systems have displayed radically different forms and concentrations of fear. In every case, however, the phenomenon of fear develops within a triangle of socially and politically mediated experience. The corners of this triangle are marked by a) objective circumstances that are perceived by a subject or group of subjects to be threatening, b) bodily and mental symptoms that are induced by that object and experienced as such by the individual subject or group, and c) the individual's or group's abreactions against the object that has induced those symptoms in the first place (see figure 1).

FIGURE 1: THE TRIANGLE OF FEAR

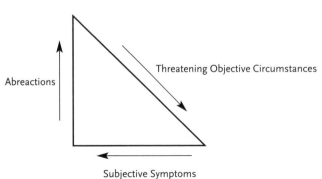

Subjective Symptoms

When seen in this way, it becomes clear that fear is not a naturally occurring substance, that it is rather the product of a dynamic relationship between individuals, their fellows, and their sociopolitical circumstances. When fear is analyzed as a particular experience that arises within the "boundaries" of these triangular coordinates, its relationship to similar but different experiences becomes clear. Outside and beyond the boundaries of the triangle the concept of fear simply doesn't apply. Consider the case of a subject who neither experiences symptoms nor reacts against dangerous circumstances—the soldier who goes numbly into battle under the influence of drugs or duty—or the case of an individual who reacts against dangerous circumstances but experiences no symptoms of fear, as when a person chooses, on the spur of the moment and almost without thinking, to avoid moving toward an army checkpoint which is felt or known to be hostile. In both cases, the concept of fear is inapplicable. This understanding of the concept of fear as a particular set of experiences codefined by the interaction of subject and object certainly helps us to see the difference between fear and anxiety. Anxiety is not a species of fear: it is rather a type of reaction to events that have occurred in the past or to possible future events—a forthcoming examination that could result in failure, or a nuclear explosion caused by a "normal accident," or concern about growing old—that are somewhere in the distance or that might in fact not happen at all. Anxiety can of course be transformed into fear, but the difference remains. Compared with anxiety, fear is immediate. It is a subjective reaction to actually existing objective circumstances. Guided by this sharpened concept of fear, let us then probe in more detail what actually goes on within the triangle of experience called fear.

Subjective Symptoms

Fear normally is experienced as subjectively felt symptoms, in the form of physiological, mental, and emotional changes. Groups in the abstract cannot experience these changes; of course, groups become afraid, but they only do so insofar as fear grips each one (or most) of their individual members. Fear is always an intensely personal experience.[17] Its physiological, mental, and emotional components come in more or less concentrated form, both in terms of the depth with which they are experienced by the individual, and the speed with which they come and go. Fear can be experienced on the surface—as when it is experienced "second hand," at a distance, in empathy with others—or it can penetrate deep down, even hiding itself in the nightly dreams of the afraid, whose sleep it disturbs. The experience of fear can be more or less sudden. It can creep up on the individual, take its time, and trap its victim by stealth. Or it can suddenly pounce upon the individual, like a prowler lurking in the dark, in which case its effects are felt immediately and frontally.

Fear is a dictator of time, for in all cases, shallow or deep, slow or fast, time seems to slow down or even stop when the individual is afraid. This is because the body is plunged into a different world. It suddenly shrinks, grows weaker, and feels vulnerable, heavier some say, as if it is filled with cold, viscous liquid. Fear is forcible submersion in a fathomless ocean. The body stiffens, then shivers. Outside voices and sounds become muffled, directionless, then jangle in the head. Tics start up in the neck, the temples, the eyelids, jumping, thumping, like an insect under the skin. Shoulders knot. The mouth grows dry. Fear rises in the throat, like bile, then turns into a tumourous lump that sticks in the throat, like a stone. Speech stammers. The heart races. Fingers become shaky, inept. Hands tremble. Concentration on anything other than fear, and being afraid, becomes impossible. Fear closes the mind and fills it with thoughts that whir like radarless bats. The pulse by this time seems to be everywhere—in the legs, arms, face, chest. Breathing naturally is difficult. It comes in short, ragged gasps. Or it seems to stop completely, so that there is no more in and out, in and out, only a gaping hole in the chest.

Objective Circumstances

These subjective symptoms of fear are always experienced within certain surroundings. Fear is a reaction by a subject to an object or objects that are perceived to be hostile or outright dangerous. It is true that fear-like symptoms can occur despite the fact that there are no signs of circumstances that are fear-producing. When a person acknowledges that there are no (immediate) signs of danger, but says, "I'm not afraid of anything in particular. I just feel like this most of the time," all the while feeling incapable of doing anything about that feeling, they may be said either to not know the meaning of the word fear or to be suffering from a phobia or some other pathological fear. In all other cases, the fear experienced by individuals or groups is typically induced by threatening circumstances within their immediate or more distant milieu. Fear can be triggered by a very large variety of objective circumstances—a critically ill child, a sudden explosion, getting the sack, cornered by a thief, the cracking roar of jets overhead. In every case, these circumstances are sensed by the individual or the group to be ill-boding, sinister, menacing, perhaps even life-threatening.

Intended Reactions

Experienced as felt symptoms induced by objective circumstances, fear usually results in some kind of intentional reaction or abreaction against the perceived object of fear. In the extreme case, fear prompts the subject to off-load its fears nastily onto others, as in xenophobia, or violently to eliminate or paralyze—kill or injure—what makes it afraid. This and other reactions are typically unpredictable, for fear is a form of radical uncertainty. With the body in such an unfamiliar and agitated state, it is never clear what will happen next. For the individual who is afraid, fear resembles peering coldly down from some shadowy height, without being able to see the ground below and without knowing how to act. The stomach churns. The afraid may suddenly feel wet and warm between their legs. Scared shitless can pass from phrase to fact. The self that is afraid is under siege. It is a desperate self. Transfixed on its object, it may freeze, or shake uncontrollably. Or the self may scream while taking a step back from the shadowy height on which it is perched, or stand firm, or run away, or jump blindly toward the ground below.

Miraculously, the afraid may also grow wings—*Timor addidit alas*, runs the original Latin expression—and fly defiantly over the head of its object, determined to make it flee. Scores of self-help manuals advise readers how to turn their fears and indecision into confident actions.[18] There it is called "fearbusting," but those influenced by classical Greek and Roman writings harbor the same point: fear can breed courage, "grace under pressure,"[19] and courage, in the circumstances, can nourish creative or daring acts that are quite literally out-of-the-ordinary. Exactly how this happens is strongly context-dependent, although when large numbers of people lose their fear the triangle of fear is typically broken by catalysis. Individuals or groups boldly wade out of the mire of fear, thereby inspiring others to follow. The October 2000 revolution in Serbia is a case in point.[20] The unexpected overthrow of the ancien régime arguably would have been impossible without fearless catalysts like the youth group *Odpor* (Resistance), which in the face of harsh repression struggled to resist the "sociocide" or implosion of civil society and to stand up to the Milosevic regime through nonviolent acts of open defiance, including doorstepping citizens in towns large and small, hosting music concerts and publicly circulating banners and leaflets that contained what seemed at the time to be make-believe slogans, like "He is finished!"

Fear that gives wings to courage and freedom is however only one type of abreaction to fear. The capacity to shake it off by confronting the perceived sources of fear can indeed be enlivening. The personal effort to draw on inner and outer resources to nurture the habit of refusing to let fear dictate one's actions can fortify the individual. And the ability to join with others in dignity and solidarity to resist the enervating miasma is a form of empowerment. The surmounting of fear can certainly add to people's self-confidence, as it does normally in the process of ontogenesis, and at a certain magical moment during the outbreak of every revolution (as Ryszard Kapuciski's fine study of the overthrow of the Pahlavi establishment emphasizes[21]). Yet fear should not be glorified universally, as if it was something like the necessary condition of courageous action, itself the precondition of democratic freedom. This is so for two main reasons. In the first place, the abreactions produced by fear can be destructive of the freedom and dignity—and sometimes the lives—of others. Fear can produce antidemocratic outcomes. The covenants extorted by fear outlined and justified in Thomas Hobbes's *De Corpore Politico* and other works can be understood as a simile of a type of fearful reaction by individuals and groups that results in their own subjugation.[22] The huddling together of the afraid and their combined efforts to project their fears nastily onto others, for instance in the form of hatred of foreigners or nationalist pride, is another instance of the possible antidemocratic effects of fear.

There is a second reason why fear should not be glorified as the mother of courageous freedom. During the experience of fear, there are always moments that feel interminably long, when the person who is afraid fails to react, or takes no appropriate action to protect himself, as when a person turns pale, breaks into a sweat, screams, and later says that he was "scared stiff" or "glued to the ground." The details of such nonaction could of course be counted—plausibly—as a type of reaction, even though it is minimal and involuntary, which serves to highlight the key point that fear is no friend of freedom. All fear is bondage, goes an old Italian and English proverb.[23] Fear is indeed a thief. It robs subjects of their capacity to act with or against others. It leaves them shaken, sometimes permanently traumatized. And when large numbers fall under the dark clouds of fear, no sun shines on civil society. Fear saps its energies and tears and twists at the institutions of political representation. Fear eats the soul of democracy.

Fear as a Public Problem

And so the question returns: Is it the case that democracies, considered as dynamic systems of publicly accountable power, contain within them mechanisms for "privatizing" and therefore trivializing, or even eradicating outright the fears that otherwise threaten the social and political freedoms that are the lifeblood of democracy? Fresh thinking is certainly required when responding to this question, if only because the conventional argument that democracies "privatize" fear is vulnerable. Deeper reflection on the subject of fear and democracy suggests that it is far too simple and even a bit smug. Much more needs to be said in particular about the several countertrends within the realms of state institutions, civil societies, and communications media introduced above. These countertrends arguably ensure not only that fears are not washed away by democracy. These countertrends also guarantee that fear is a permanent *public* problem within both potential and actually existing democracies.

War

Consider the problem of war: Within the field of governmental institutions, citizens' fears generated by war and rumors of war by no means disappear. Democracies have an excellent record in not going to war against one another,[24] but this does not mean that war is somehow forgotten or that it disappears over the horizon of experience. In our times there is undoubtedly public support for minimizing the loss of life—the number of body bags—and the casualties that result from war. The reliance upon computerized, "risk-free" aerial bombardment as the preferred means of military intervention, and the growth of a "postheroic" view of war, even an unwillingness among men and women to wave the flag, slip into military uniform, and go off to fight wars, are the main consequences. Some scholars have drawn from this the conclusion that the world has subdivided into two parts:

a zone of violent anarchy that is troubled by war, warlords, lawlessness, repression, and famine; and a "security community" of peaceful and prosperous democracies in which fear generated by war disappears.[25]

The conclusion may be comforting, but it is misleading. The so-called democratic zone of peace cannot shake off the problem of fear generated by war, and not only because the violence-ridden drugs trade and globalized arms production binds it to the fate of war-torn zones. Public calls for military intervention wherever human rights are violated—into areas suffering plagues of private violence and uncivil war stoked by gunrunners, warlords, gangsters, armed sects, rebel armies—keep fear of war in the headlines. So too does the growth of a global system of communications media, whose editors often feature war and cruelty in accordance with the rule "If it bleeds, let it lead."[26] Then there is the unresolved problem of the role to be played by nuclear-tipped states in the post–Cold War world system. This system is dominated by the United States, the world's single superpower, which can and does act as a "swing power" backed by nuclear force. As a swing power, it is engaged in several regions although not tied permanently to any of them, but its maneuvers are complicated by the fact that it is presently forced to coexist and interact peacefully with four great powers, three of whom are nuclear powers: Europe, China, Russia, and Japan. The geometry of this arrangement clearly differs from the extended freeze imposed by the Cold War, when (according to Raymond Aron's formula) the democracies lived in accordance with the rule "peace impossible, war unlikely." With the collapse of bipolar confrontation, this rule has changed. There is no evidence of the dawn of a postnuclear age, and the freedom from the fear of nuclear accident or attack that that would bring. Nowadays, as Pierre Hassner has put it so well, peace has become a little less impossible and war is a little less unlikely, principally because a form of unpredictable anarchy has settled on the whole world.[27] The probability of a nuclear apocalypse, in which the earth and its peoples are blown sky-high, may have been reduced, but major wars remain a possibility, including even the use of nuclear-tipped weapons in conflicts that originate in local wars. Depleted uranium shells are now routinely dropped on the victims of war. Nuclear weapons abound—the arsenals of the United States and the Russian federation each contain somewhere around seven thousand nuclear warheads.[28] And despite the 1972 Anti-Ballistic Missile Treaty, nuclear capacity, as can be seen in the nuclear arms races between Pakistan and India, and between Israel and the Arab states, is spreading, despite any prior agreements about the rules of nuclear confrontation and despite the fact (revealed in the so-called National Missile Defense system planned by the Bush administration) that the issue of nuclear weapons is now deeply implicated in the proliferation of so-called conventional weaponry.

Civil Society Failures

Toughly realist accounts of the fear-reducing qualities of contemporary civil societies need to be sensitive to their self-paralyzing tendencies, as well as to the measures required to ameliorate or overcome them. Civil societies undoubtedly contain fear-producing dynamics. Their restlessness (an apt word used by Hegel to describe a feature of modern civil societies) frustrates any natural tendency toward social equilibrium; and the social bonds nurtured by the conflicts they produce do not guarantee citizens' freedom from fear. Civil societies are structured by a dynamic complex of organizing principles and institutional forms that disorientate actors, generate risks, and enforce hard choices. The anxieties that result—Franz Neumann pointed out—function as the soil in which fears of various kinds spring up.[29] The disorganizing effects of the processes of commodity production and exchange associated with market economies are one example. The freedom of capital to invest and disinvest produces well-known symptoms: for instance, periods of creative destruction associated with technical innovations, surges of capital investment and hyperspeculation followed by downturns, and the periodic disemployment and wholesale redundancy of labor power. The resulting stresses and strains can and do generate genuine fears—of losing one's material livelihood (as a worker) or one's shirt (as an owner or manager of capital). To the extent that market economies intertwine and form themselves into a global economy, these fears come to be felt globally. They are compounded by the perpetual ecological disturbances caused by market-driven fossil fuel–based economies. Led by the United States, whose inhabitants currently consume between fifty and one hundred times more energy than those of Bangladesh, these economies have consumed ten times more energy during the past century than did their predecessors during the thousand years before 1900.[30]

Fears also result from the tendency of civil society to generate moral turbulence and collisions among its constituent individuals and groups. So-called communitarian critics of civil society feed upon this point. Mourning the loss of imagined stable communities of the past—and suffering from a condition that might be called *Gesellschaftsangst*—they dream fancifully of stitching together the torn shreds of morality with the blue thread of Political Community. That could not be done without destroying civil society itself, but their emphasis on its disorganizing effects, and the trepidations they generate, although exaggerated, puts a finger on the point that civil societies produce fear in considerable quantities. True, they cultivate resources—the arts of kindness and civility, the ability to duck conflicts, to bargain, and to effect give-and-take compromises—that help them weather storms of controversy and the fears they induce. A good case can be made as well for the view that conflict is an essential factor of socialization, and that civil societies benefit from the cumulative experience of tending and muddling through their own social conflicts, particularly the kind that are nonthreatening or "divisible."[31] In practice, of course, the distinction between threatening and nonthreatening conflicts is itself controversial to their protagonists, and that is the rub: civil societies conjure up fears of what others have done, or are doing, or might be planning to do, sometimes to the point where the participants themselves become mildly or acutely afraid. A disturbing example is the unease today within the European Union about national identity and the xenophobic outbursts driven by wild fantasies of "takeovers" by "foreigners," or what the Germans call *Überfremdungsangst.*

Communications Media and the Fascination with Fear

No account of the subject of fear and democracy would be plausible without considering the ways in which modern communications media fascinate their audiences with stories that not only report and circulate fears but also *induce* fears. Why is it, beginning with the Graveyard poets and the first gruesome tabloid newspaper stories, through Dracula, the films of Alfred Hitchcock, and Stephen King, that millions of people have spent so much time willfully scaring themselves, to the point where they experience mysterious pleasures associated with sudden intakes of breath and momentary prickles of the skin? Why do the communications media of contemporary democracies enjoy the power to fascinate people with matters that they should run screaming from?

Providing plausible answers to these questions is not easy, although one way of doing so is to examine the ways in which fear is rooted in the experience of death. The whole Western history of reflections on the subject of fear and politics, beginning with Thucydides, may be thought of in existential terms, as a subset of the more general, deeply visceral reactions to the irremediable fact that each and all of us is fated to die. Death always preoccupies and intrigues individuals, whether they know or accept it, or not. The preoccupation begins at an early age, when death is the object of intrigue and curiosity, but death is most often subject to taboos imposed by adults. In functional terms, adult individuals, and small and large groups, cope with death through a great variety of strategies with often unpredictable reactions. They may lapse into melancholy; with a sigh of resignation and a touch of despair, they turn in seriousness toward the great questions of life, thereby earning themselves the reputation of being a wet blanket in the company of others. Others who are preoccupied with the idea and certainty of death seek out a religion, which has the consoling effect of putting death in its place, sometimes even (in the case of Christian Science, for instance) by denying it outright. There are of course more common methods of forgetting death. Exalting the dead through fond memories and making "a supreme effort to deny death"[32] by declaring it a taboo subject are just two examples of the many ways in which the living cope temporarily with the necessity of their death. They live content, convinced of their own immortality.

It is well known that putting death on the shelf has its costs. Individuals normally pay for their denials. Sometimes the cost is high, in the form of severe symptoms like bouts of depression and psychosomatic illness. More common are those moments when individuals experience, sometimes intensely, what Freud called the uncanny (*das Unheimliche*), that diffuse feeling of fascination with the eerie, the shadowy, the strange. During these moments when they are drawn into the lairs of the uncanny, seemingly against their will, they resemble children who are both afraid of the dark and yet riveted by it. Comfortable in the conscious, if strained, recognition that there is no immediate or actual danger to their lives, they indulge their deeper concerns about death.

Whether or not "the aim of all life is death," and whether individuals chronically suffer the secret wish to die,[33] need not detain us here. The key point is this: Since the conscious fear of death would make individuals unable to function normally in everyday life, they repress that fear. In turn, that repression generates tension which, from time to time, is released through a safety valve, in order to avoid accumulating too much of it.[34] The old joke about the individual who was so afraid of death that he killed himself captures something of this equation. Under democratic conditions, there are times, in other words, when individuals are drawn fearfully toward death in order better to escape its clutches. Under democratic conditions, such fears are no longer projected onto the imagined "spirits" of nature; and religious institutions lose their monopoly powers of handling the uncanny through sacred imagery that rivets believers to images of the living God, who is represented as a terrible power capable of divine wrath. The modern experience of the uncanny consequently tends to become "homeless." Enter modern communications media: their success in creating and retaining audiences partly stems from their power of creating sites that enable individuals to fixate on symbolic representations of dying and death. Communications media enable individuals to indulge their fears of death, as if they were obsessed with a disturbing painting, like that of Dürer depicting Death as an intruder hell-bent on strangling his victim.

The Democratization of Fear

Within contemporary democracies, the fear industry—the widespread promulgation of images and stories of fear through communications media—is widely criticized for its exaggeration of the scope and intensity of violent crime and other personal and group disasters.[35] It is accused of *inciting* fears in others, sometimes to the point of so blurring their judgments about reality that they begin unnecessarily to be panicked into believing that they are living in some late modern version of the lawless state of nature described by Thomas Hobbes. Driven by ratings, the media turns fear into a commodity. It bombards its audiences with stories of homicidal au pairs, preteen mass murderers, pedophile preschool teachers, road ragers, and merciless killer viruses. The corresponding—antidemocratic—belief in Hobbesian solutions logically follows, or so it is claimed. The afraid take refuge in talk of worsening crime and getting tough on the causes of crime; they huddle under the protection of insurance policies, burglar alarms, tougher policing, and gated communities dotted with "armed response" signs.

Repressive forms of law and order may well be the offspring of citizens who are afraid, although the politics of fear is a wild horse capable of surprising twists and turns. A good countercase can be made for paying greater attention to the dialectics of the commercialization of fear through media such as film, television, and music. These media arguably have the long-term effect of relocating fears that are experienced privately into the public domain. They publicly identify those who are afraid, give them a voice, partly by giving their fears a name. The fears once experienced privately by individual victims at the hands of bullies, stalkers, child molesters, or rapists are comparatively recent examples of this trend. By identifying these fears and enabling the afraid to speak out publicly, communications media enable all citizens to understand these fears as a *public* problem for which *public* remedies can and should in principle be found.

This long-term transformation of fear into a public problem is of course subject to many and various exceptions, but its vital significance can be gauged by placing it within a wider historical context. Until the eighteenth century—until Montesquieu's pathbreaking reflections—fear had been regarded by those who studied it as a sad necessity in human affairs. Although there had been a string of laments for the undue power and folly induced by fear, discourses on its nature usually treated it as human fate. Fear was considered to be a sticky web spun by the gods, as natural as thunder and lightning, an inevitable part of the human condition—as Thucydides himself thought when analyzing fear as rooted in the human drive for security, glory, and material wealth.

During the eighteenth century this presumption of the inevitability of fear began to crumble. A long revolution in the understanding of fear broke out. So fear began to be studied by writers who distinguished between the causes and pretexts of fear. Its roots in the fabric of psychic, social, and political life were investigated, and the possibility emerged, or so these writers thought, that fear and its paralyzing effects could be overcome, not just comforted and consoled, for instance through religious faith. Fear came to be regarded as a thoroughly human problem for which there are thoroughly human remedies. Some writers thought more radically still, suggesting that a certain type of political system—a democratic republic—would prove to be something of a "school of courage" (Ferrero) and, hence, the best antidote to fears that destroy citizens' capacities for self-chosen action.

To the extent that fears once suffered in private have come to be perceived and dealt with as public problems, the ground is prepared for the understanding of fear as contingent, as a *political* problem. This long-term transformation may be described as the "democratization" of fear, not in the ridiculous sense that everyone comes to exercise their right to be afraid, or is duty-bound to be so, but rather that fear, especially its debilitating and antidemocratic forms, ceases to be seen as "natural" and comes instead to be understood as a contingent human experience, as a publicly treatable phenomenon, as a political problem for which tried and tested political remedies may be found. It is hard to know where today's democracies are positioned on the scale of fearlessness, but one thing is certain: despite the flight of contemporary political science and political philosophy away from the land of fear, its inhabitants will not remain silent. Fear is a topic that cannot be ignored, or made to wither away, simply because democracies themselves stimulate the public awareness that those who ignore fear do so at their own peril.

NOTES

1. Charles Montesquieu, *De l'esprit des lois* [1748], ed. Victor Goldschmidt (Paris: G. F. Flammaroin, 1979).

2. See my "Despotism and Democracy: The Origins and Development of the Distinction Between Civil Society and the State, 1750–1850," in *Civil Society and the State: New European Perspectives*, ed. John Keane (London and New York: Verso, 1988 [1998]), pp. 35–71.

3. Montesquieu, *De l'esprit des lois*, book 3, chap. 2, pp. 143–44.

4. See Alain Grosrichard, *Structure du sérail: la fiction du despotisme asiatique dans l'Occident classique* (Paris: ed. Du Sevil, 1979), and Chris Sparks, *Montesquieu's Vision of Uncertainty and Modernity in Political Philosophy* (London: E. Mellen Press, 1999).

5. Juan E. Corradi, Patricia Weiss Fagen, and Manuel Antonio Garretón, eds., *Fear at the Edge: State Terror and Resistance in Latin America* (Berkeley and Oxford: University of California Press, 1992).

6. Ibid., pp. 1–10, 267–92. The thesis is well summarized by Norberto Lechner, "Some People Die of Fear: Fear as a Political Problem," in ibid., pp. 33–34: "Democracy involves more than just tolerance; it involves recognizing the other as a coparticipant in the creation of a common future. A democratic process, in contrast to an authoritarian regime, allows us to learn that the future is an intersubjective undertaking. The otherness of the other is then that of the alter ego. Seen thus, the freedom of the other, its unpredictability, ceases to be a threat to self-identity; it is the condition for self-development."

7. Niccolò Machiavelli, *The Prince*, chap. xvii, in *The Prince and The Discourses*, ed. Max Lerner (New York: The Modern Library, 1950), p. 61.

8. The classic work in this field is that of Norbert Elias, *Über den Prozess der Zivilisation*, two vols. (Basel: Haus zum Falken, 1939).

9. Janice E. Thomson, *Mercenaries, Pirates, and Sovereigns: State-Building and Extraterritorial Violence in Early Modern Europe* (Princeton: Princeton University Press, 1994).

10. Georg Simmel, "Der Fremde," in *Soziologie* (Munich and Leipzig: Taschenbuch, 1908), pp. 685–91.

11. See John Keane, "Liberty of the Press," in *The Media and Democracy* (Oxford and Cambridge, Mass.: Polity Press, 1991), pp. 2–50.

12. In his study of fear during the early modern era, *La peur en Occident, XIVe-XVIIIe siècles* (Paris: Fayard, 1978), Jean Delumeau writes that the rumor is "equally acknowledgement and elucidation of a general fear and, further, the first stage in the process of abreaction, which will temporarily free the mob of its fear. It is the identification of a threat and the clarification of a situation that has become unbearable" (p. 247).

13. See Hans-Joachim Neubauer, *Fama: Eine Geschichte des Gerüchts* (Berlin: Verlag, 1998).

14. An example of this face-value usage of the concept of fear is Barry Buzan, *People, States and Fear: An Agenda for International Security Studies in the Post-Cold War Era* (Boulder: Westview Press, 1991).

15. Anthony Kenny, *Action, Emotion and Will* (London: Routledge and Kegan Paul, 1963), chap. 3.

16. Eric A. Salzen, "The Ontogeny of Fear in Animals," in *Fear in Animals and Man*, ed. Wladyslaw Sluckin (New York: Van Nostrand Reinhold, 1979), pp. 125–63. Compare p. 9: "provided we have evidence of some capacity for receiving and decoding information from the environment concerning dangers or threats, and some capacity for learning what are dangerous circumstances (or being provided with innate capacities for registering these), the concept of fear may be applied to animals other than human beings."

17. To illustrate the point: among my earliest childhood memories is the moment of fear that came upon me each day when traveling to school, past a huge white sign painted on a gray concrete bridge. It read simply, "BAN THE BOMB." As a five-year-old, I didn't understand what those hurriedly painted, dripping words meant. Nor did my older sister, who helped me carry my school bag. We simply regarded them with trepidation. Time did not dissolve that feeling. It actually intensified the memory, especially when my otherwise physically fit father suffered a series of cancers that resulted in his premature death, at age 63. Cancers grow according to a complex logic, of course. The bodily causes of cancer are the same as the causes of evolution itself: mutations. Cancer is above all a matter of statistical bad luck. (Among the best recent summaries of the current research are Mel Greaves, *Cancer: The Evolutionary Legacy* [Oxford and New York: Oxford University Press, 2000], and Robert Weinberg, *One Renegade Cell: How Cancer Begins* [New York: Basic Books, 1999].) So it could be an unfortunate coincidence, a stroke of malevolent luck, but toward the end of the 1950s, immediately after the conclusion of open-air British nuclear testing at Woomera and Maralinga, in the state of South Australia, my father was sent on a stock-check assignment by the federal government department for which he worked as a storeman. The son of a poor unemployed Irish carpenter, he was quietly proud to be offered the assignment. It was his most secure job ever and he lived on-site for six months, in the desert town of Woomera, 450 kilometers from our home. He never mentioned protective clothing, and a picture from this period shows him dressed merely in shorts and boots. I suppose that that was typical, especially given the daytime heat and the authorities' willful ignorance of the possible effects of touching, tasting, and breathing radiant dust. His first cancer developed not long after returning from Woomera. After his death, there was no official inquiry. No journalist or politician visited our home, and he was buried in a pauper's grave, without so much as the comfort of knowing that he might become a statistic—or that one day he might even be linked with the campaigners who painted those frightful words on the bridge that I crossed each day on my way to school.

18. See, for example, Susan Jeffers, *Feel the Fear and Do It Anyway* (London: Fawcett Books, 1991), and Gavin de Becker, *The Gift of Fear* (London: Dell, 2000).

19. Aung San Suu Kyi, "Freedom from Fear [1991]," in *Freedom from Fear and Other Writings* (London and New York: Penguin, 1995), p. 184.

20. Dragica Vujadinovi-Milinkovi, "Degradation of Everyday Life, Destruction of Society and Civil Society Suppression" (paper presented at the University of Bradford, March 25–26, 2000).

21. Ryszard Kapucinski, *Shah of Shahs* (London: Vintage, 1986), pp. 109–11.

22. Thomas Hobbes, *De Corpore Politico: Or the Elements of Law, Moral and Politic*, in *The English Works of Thomas Hobbes of Malmesbury*, ed. William Molesworth, vol. 4 (London: J. Bohn, 1840), part 1, chap. 2, section 13, pp. 92–93.

23. James Sanford, *The Garden of Pleasure: Contayinge most pleasante Tales..Done out of Italian into English* (London, privately published, 1573), p. 52.

24. R. J. Rummel, *Understanding Conflict and War* (Beverly Hills, Calif.: Sage Press, 1975–81), vols. 1–5.

25. Max Singer and Aaron Wildavsky, *The Real World Order: Zones of Peace/Zones of Turmoil* (Chatham, N.J.: Chatham House, 1993).

26. These points are analyzed in more detail in my "The Long Century of Violence," in *Reflections on Violence* (London and New York: Verso, 1996).

27. See the concluding interview in Pierre Hassner, *La violence et la paix: De la bombe atomique au nettoyage ethnique* (Paris: Editions Esprit, 1995): "In the past, the doctrine of deterrence matched the civil character of our societies: an invisible hand, or abstract mechanism, took charge of our security, and we did not have to bother our heads with it. But today the nuclear issue can no longer be considered in isolation, it is inextricably mixed up with everything else."

28. *The Times* (London), February 10, 2001, p. 16.

29. Franz Neumann, "Anxiety and Politics," in *The Democratic and the Authoritarian State: Essays in Political and Legal Theory* (New York: Free Press, 1957), pp. 270–300.

30. J. R. McNeill, *Something New Under the Sun: An Environmental History of the Twentieth-Century World* (London and New York: W. W. Norton, 2000), pp. 14–17.

31. See Albert Hirschman, "Social Conflicts as Pillars of Democratic Market Society," *Political Theory* 22, no. 2 (1994): 56. The socialising effects of conflict are analyzed in Georg Simmel's pathbreaking essay "Der Streit," in *Soziologie*.

32. Hattie Rosenthal, "The Fear of Death as an Indispensable Factor in Psychotherapy," in *Death: Interpretations*, ed. Hendrik M. Ruitenbeek (New York: Dell, 1969), pp. 169–70.

33. Sigmund Freud, "Beyond the Pleasure Principle," in *The Standard Edition of the Complete Psychological Works of Sigmund Freud*, ed. J. Strachey (London: Hogarth Press, 1955), vol. 18.

34. G. Zilboorg, "Fear of Death," *Psychoanalytic Quarterly* 12 (1943): 465; see also Rosenthal, "The Fear of Death as an Indispensable Factor in Psychotherapy."

35. See, for example, Barry Glassner, *The Culture of Fear: Why Americans Are Afraid of the Wrong Things* (New York: Basic Books, 1999).

Contributors

Sally Avery Bermanzohn is Associate Professor of Political Science at Brooklyn College where she teaches courses on American and urban politics. She received a BA in history from Duke University, a master's in urban planning from Hunter College, and a doctorate in political science from the City University of New York. She is currently completing *The Greensboro Massacre Through Survivors' Eyes* for Temple University Press, and *The Ku Klux Klan and Domestic Terrorism* for Lynne Rienner Publishers.

Najib Ghadbian is Assistant Professor of Political Science and Middle East Studies at the University of Arkansas. He is the author of *Democratization and the Islamist Challenge in the Arab World* (1997). Dr. Ghadbian has published numerous articles on the politics of the Middle East in English and Arabic.

John Keane is Professor of Politics at the Centre for the Study of Democracy at the University of Westminster. He is the author of *Civil Society: Old Images, New Visions* (1998), *Reflections on Violence* (1996), *The Media and Democracy* (1991), *Democracy and Civil Society* (1988), *Public Life and Late Capitalism* (1984), and the prize-winning *Tom Paine: A Political Life* (1995).

Luis E. Lander is an Engineer and Professor at the Faculty of Economy of the Universidad Central de Venezuela, and is a doctorate candidate in Social Science at the same university. His most recent publication is "Venezuela's Balancing Act: Big Oil, OPEC and National Development" (NACLA Report on the Americas, January 2001).

Margarita López Maya is Professor-Researcher at the Centro de Estudios del Desarrollo (Cendes) of the Universidad Central Venezuela, and is a historian with a doctorate in social science from the same university. She is editor of the *Revista Venezolana de Economía y Ciencias Sociales*, and her most recent publication is *Lucha social democracia y neoliberalismo: la portesta popular en América Latina en los años del neoliberalismo* (Nueva Sociedad, 1999).

Roger MacGinty is a lecturer in postwar recovery studies at the Department of Politics, University of York. He has published extensively on ethnic conflict in general and Northern Ireland in particular. *The Management of Peace Processes*, edited by John Darby and Roger MacGinty, was published by Macmillan in 2000.

Carol Mason is Assistant Professor of English and American Studies at Hobart and William Smith Colleges. Her essay is part of a book-length project on the politics of pro-life violence.

Jeffrey Murer is Assistant Professor of Political Science at Swarthmore College. His research focuses on the outbreak of ethnic conflicts and the rise of extremist politics in East Central Europe. In 2000 he was awarded the Annual Graduate Dissertation Prize at the University of Illinois at Chicago for his study of the resurgence of anti-Semitism in Hungary since 1989.

Ulric Shannon works in the Regional Security and Peacekeeping Division of the Canadian Department of Foreign Affairs and International Trade. He holds degrees in international relations and security studies from McGill University in Montreal and York University in Toronto. He specializes in peacekeeping and security in Africa, and has worked in Nairobi, Kenya, with a disarmament organization. The views expressed in his chapter are personal and do not necessarily reflect those of the Canadian government.

Lisa Sharlach is Assistant Professor of Political Science at Samford University, in Birmingham, Alabama. Her dissertation is a comparative study of rape and social inequality in Pakistan, Peru, Eritrea, South Africa, the former Yugoslavia, and Rwanda. Sharlach's interest in this topic emerged from field research experience in Zagreb in 1994 with children and teenagers displaced by the war in Croatia and Bosnia-Herzegovina.

Charles Tilly is the Joseph L. Buttenwieser Professor of Social Science at Columbia University. He has held research and teaching appointments at Delaware, Harvard, MIT, Toronto, Michigan, and the New School. His recent books include *European Revolutions* (1993), *Popular Contention in Great Britain* (1995), *Roads from Past to Future* (1997), *Work Under Capitalism* (1998), *Durable Inequality* (1998), and *Dynamics of Contention* (2001).

Mark Ungar is Assistant Professor of Political Science at Brooklyn College. He is the author of the forthcoming book *Democracy and the Rule of Law in Latin America* and of several articles on policing, constitutional law, and the judiciary in democratizing countries. He has worked for human rights organizations abroad and more recently served on a policy steering committee of Amnesty International.

Bridget Welsh is a lecturer in the Department of Political Science at Hofstra University. Her current research focuses on democratization, state policy, and political economy in Southeast Asia and the Anglophone Caribbean. She is currently working on a manuscript on state formation in Malaysia.

Kenton Worcester is Assistant Professor of Political Science and International Studies at Marymount Manhattan College. He is the author of *The Social Science Research Council, 1923–1998* (2001), and *C.L.R. James: A Political Biography* (1996), and is coeditor of *Trade Union Politics: American Unions and Economic Change, 1960s–1990s* (1995).

Index